'Tis

Angela's Ashes was a publishing phenomenon. Frank McCourt's critically acclaimed, lyrical memoir of his Irish-American childhood won the Pulitzer Prize, the National Book Critics' Circle Award, the Royal Society of Literature Award and the *Los Angeles Times* Award amongst others, and rapidly became a word-of-mouth bestseller, topping all charts worldwide for over three years. It left readers and critics alike eager to hear more about Frank McCourt's incredible, poignant life.

'Tis is the story of Frank's American journey from impoverished immigrant with rotten teeth, infected eyes and no formal education to brilliant raconteur and schoolteacher. Saved first by a straying priest, then by the Democratic party, then by the United States Army, then by New York University – which admitted him on a trial basis though he had no high school diploma – Frank had the same vulnerable but invincible spirit at nineteen that he had at eight and still has today. And *'Tis* is a tale of survival as vivid, harrowing and often hilarious as *Angela's Ashes*. Yet again, it is through the power of storytelling that Frank finds a life for himself.

'It is only the best storyteller who can so beguile his readers that he leaves them wanting more when he's done . . . McCourt proves himself one of the very best' (*Newsweek*).

FRANK MCCOURT taught for thirty years in various New York City high schools and in city colleges. His play, *The Irish and How They Got That Way*, has been produced in New York, Boston, Chicago and Melbourne, Australia. He lives in New York.

' *'Tis* is written at a tremendous pace, which makes it exhilarating to read, and is full of wry, self-deprecating humour. Bursting with gusto, unflinchingly direct and with subject matter so rich it would have done for three volumes.'   *Literary Review*

'With its joys and sorrows, its melancholy and its laughter, *'Tis* is a dignified and moving successor to *Angela's Ashes*.'   *Sunday Independent* (Ireland)

'McCourt has set himself a daunting task: to chronicle the life of a young man in the second half of the century. Unique and moving . . . we may toast McCourt's accomplishments.'   *Financial Times*

'Frank McCourt's many fans will want to catch up with his family story, and it is all here, too, funny-sad and bittersweet.'   *Express*

Also by Frank McCourt

Angela's Ashes

Frank McCourt

'Tis

A MEMOIR

Flamingo
An Imprint of HarperCollins*Publishers*

Flamingo
An imprint of HarperCollins*Publishers*
77–85 Fulham Palace Road,
Hammersmith, London w6 8jb

www.**fire**and**water**.com

Flamingo is a registered trademark of HarperCollins*Publishers* Limited.

First published in Great Britain by Flamingo 1999

This special Australian edition published by Flamingo 2000

1 3 5 7 9 8 6 4 2

Some of the names in '*Tis* have been changed.

A catalogue record for this book
is available from the British Library

ISBN 0 00 257081 5

Set in Postscript Bembo

Printed and bound in Australia by
Griffin Press Pty Ltd, Netley, South Australia

ACKNOWLEDGEMENTS

Friends and family members have smiled and bestowed on me various graces: Nan Graham, Susan Moldow and Pat Eisemann at Scribner; Sarah Mosher, formerly at Scribner; Molly Friedrich, Aaron Priest, Paul Cirone and Lucy Childs of the Aaron Priest Literary Agency; the late Tommy Butler, Mike Reardon and Nick Browne, high priests of the long bar at the Lion's Head; Paul Schiffman, poet and mariner, who served at that same bar but rocked with the sea; Sheila McKenna, Dennis Duggan, Dennis Smith, Mary Breasted Smyth and Ted Smyth, Jack Deacy, Pete Hamill, Bill Flanagan, Marcia Rock, Peter Quinn, Brian Brown, Terry Moran, Isaiah Sheffer, Pat Mulligan, Brian Kelly, Mary Tierney, Gene Secunda, the late Paddy Clancy, the late Kevin Sullivan, friends all from the Lion's Head and the First Friday Club; my brothers, of course, Alphonsus, Michael, Malachy, and their wives Lynn, Joan, Diana; Robert and Cathy Frey, parents of Ellen.

My thanks, my love.

This book is dedicated to
My daughter, Maggie, for her warm, searching heart
and to
My wife, Ellen, for joining her side to mine

'TIS

PROLOGUE

That's your dream out now.

That's what my mother would say when we were children in Ireland and a dream we had came true. The one I had over and over was where I sailed into New York Harbor awed by the skyscrapers before me. I'd tell my brothers and they'd envy me for having spent a night in America till they began to claim they'd had that dream, too. They knew it was a sure way to get attention even though I'd argue with them, tell them I was the oldest, that it was my dream and they'd better stay out of it or there would be trouble. They told me I had no right to that dream for myself, that anyone could dream about America in the far reaches of the night and there was nothing I could do about it. I told them I could stop them. I'd keep them awake all night and they'd have no dreams at all. Michael was only six and here he was laughing at the picture of me going from one of them to the other trying to stop their dreams of the New York skyscrapers. Malachy said I could do nothing about his dreams because he was born in Brooklyn and could dream about America all night and well into the day if he liked. I appealed to my mother. I told her it wasn't fair the way the whole family was invading my dreams and she said, Arrah, for the love o' God, drink your tea and go to school and stop tormenting us with your dreams. My brother, Alphie, was only two and learning words and he banged a spoon on the table and chanted, Tomentin' dreams, tomentin' dreams, till everyone laughed and I knew I could share my dreams with him anytime, so why not with Michael, why not Malachy?

★

1

When the MS *Irish Oak* sailed from Cork in October, 1949, we expected to be in New York City in a week. Instead, after two days at sea, we were told we were going to Montreal in Canada. I told the First Officer all I had was forty dollars and would Irish Shipping pay my train fare from Montreal to New York. He said, No, the company wasn't responsible. He said freighters are the whores of the high seas, they'll do anything for anyone. You could say a freighter is like Murphy's oul' dog, he'll go part of the road with any wanderer.

Two days later Irish Shipping changed its mind and gave us the happy news, Sail for New York City, but two days after that the Captain was told, Sail for Albany.

The First Officer told me Albany was a city far up the Hudson River, capital of New York State. He said Albany had all the charm of Limerick, ha ha ha, a great place to die but not a place where you'd want to get married or rear children. He was from Dublin and knew I was from Limerick and when he sneered at Limerick I didn't know what to do. I'd like to destroy him with a smart remark but then I'd look at myself in the mirror, pimply face, sore eyes, and bad teeth and know I could never stand up to anyone, especially a First Officer with a uniform and a promising future as master of his own ship. Then I'd say to myself, Why should I care what anyone says about Limerick anyway? All I had there was misery.

Then the peculiar thing would happen. I'd sit on a deck chair in the lovely October sun with the gorgeous blue Atlantic all around me and try to imagine what New York would be like. I'd try to see Fifth Avenue or Central Park or Greenwich Village where everyone looked like movie stars, powerful tans, gleaming white teeth. But Limerick would push me into the past. Instead of me sauntering up Fifth Avenue with the tan, the teeth, I'd be back in the lanes of Limerick, women standing at doors chatting away and pulling their shawls around their shoulders, children with faces dirty from bread and jam, playing and laughing and crying to their mothers. I'd see people at Mass on Sunday morning where a whisper would run through the church when some- one with a hunger weakness would collapse in the pew and have to be carried outside by men from the back of the church who'd tell everyone, Stand back, stand back, for the lovea Jaysus, can't you see she's gasping for the air, and I wanted to be a man like that telling people stand back because that gave you the right to stay outside till the Mass was over and you could go off to the pub which is why you were standing in the back with all the other men in the first place. Men who didn't drink always knelt right up there by the altar to show how good they were and how they didn't care if the pubs stayed closed till Doomsday. They knew the responses to the Mass better than anyone and they'd be blessing themselves and standing and kneel- ing and sighing over their prayers as if they felt the pain of Our Lord more than the rest of the congregation. Some had given up the pint entirely and they were the worst, always preaching the evil of the pint and looking down on the ones still in the grip as if they were on the right track to heaven. They acted as if God Himself would turn His back on a man drinking the pint when everyone knew you'd rarely hear a priest up in the pulpit denounce the pint or the men who drank it. Men with the thirst stayed in the back ready to streak out the door the minute the priest said, Ite, missa est, Go, you are dis- missed. They stayed in the back because their mouths were dry and they felt too humble to be up there with the sober ones. I stayed near the door so that I could hear the men whispering about the slow Mass. They went to Mass because it's a mortal sin if you don't though you'd wonder if it wasn't a worse sin to be joking to the man next to you that if this priest didn't hurry up you'd expire of the thirst on the spot. If Father White came out to give the sermon they'd shuffle and groan over his sermons, the slowest in the world, with him rolling

4

his eyes to heaven and declaring we were all doomed unless we mended our ways and devoted ourselves to the Virgin Mary entirely. My Uncle Pa Keating would have the men laughing behind their hands with his, I would devote myself to the Virgin Mary if she handed me a lovely creamy black pint of porter. I wanted to be there with my Uncle Pa Keating all grown up with long trousers and stand with the men in the back with the great thirst and laugh behind my hand.

I'd sit on that deck chair and look into my head to see myself cycling around Limerick City and out into the country delivering telegrams. I'd see myself early in the morning riding along country roads with the mist rising in the fields and cows giving me the odd moo and dogs coming at me till I drove them away with rocks. I'd hear babies in farmhouses crying for their mothers and farmers whacking cows back to the fields after the milking.

And I'd start crying to myself on that deck chair with the gorgeous Atlantic all around me, New York ahead, city of my dreams where I'd have the golden tan, the dazzling white teeth. I'd wonder what in God's name was wrong with me that I should be missing Limerick already, city of grey miseries, the place where I dreamed of escape to New York. I'd hear my mother's warning, The devil you know is better than the devil you don't know.

There were to be fourteen passengers on the ship but one cancelled and we had to sail with an unlucky number. The first night out the Captain stood up at dinner and welcomed us. He laughed and said he wasn't superstitious over the number of passengers but since there was a priest among us wouldn't it be lovely if His Reverence would say a prayer to come between us and all harm. The priest was a plump little man, born in Ireland, but so long in his Los Angeles parish he had no trace of an Irish accent. When he got up to say a prayer and blessed himself four passengers kept their hands in their laps and that told me they were Protestants. My mother used to say you could spot Protestants a mile away by their reserved manner. The priest asked Our Lord to look down on us with pity and love, that whatever happened on these stormy seas we were ready to be enfolded forever in His Divine Bosom. An old Protestant reached for his wife's hand. She smiled and shook her head back at him and he smiled, too, as if to say, Don't worry.

The priest sat next to me at the dinner table. He whispered that those two old Protestants were very rich from raising thoroughbred racehorses in Kentucky and if I had any sense I'd be nice to them, you never know.

I wanted to ask what was the proper way to be nice to rich Protestants who raise racehorses but I couldn't for fear the priest might think I was a fool. I heard the Protestants say the Irish people were so charming and their children so adorable you hardly noticed how poor they were. I knew that if I ever talked to the rich Protestants I'd have to smile and show my destroyed teeth and that would be the end of it. The minute I made some money in America I'd have to rush to a dentist to have my smile mended. You could see from the magazines and the films how the smile opened doors and brought girls running and if I didn't have the smile I might as well go back to Limerick and get a job sorting letters in a dark back room at the post office where they wouldn't care if you hadn't a tooth in your head.

Before bedtime the steward served tea and biscuits in the lounge. The priest said, I'll have a double Scotch, forget the tea, Michael, the whiskey helps me sleep. He drank his whiskey and whispered to me again, Did you talk to the rich people from Kentucky?

I didn't.

Dammit. What's the matter with you? Don't you want to get ahead in the world?

I do.

Well, why don't you talk to the rich people from Kentucky? They might take a fancy to you and give you a job as stable boy or something and you could rise in the ranks instead of going to New York which is one big occasion of sin, a sink of depravity where a Catholic has to fight day and night to keep the faith. So, why can't you talk to the nice people from Kentucky and make something of yourself?

Whenever he brought up the rich people from Kentucky he whispered and I didn't know what to say. If my brother Malachy were here he'd march right up to the rich people and charm them and they'd probably adopt him and leave him their millions along with stables, racehorses, a big house, and maids to clean it. I never talked to rich people in my life except to say, Telegram, ma'am, and then I'd be told go round to the servants' entrance, this is the front door and don't you know any better.

That is what I wanted to tell the priest but I didn't know how to talk to him either. All I knew about priests was that they said Mass and everything else in Latin, that they heard my sins in English and forgave me in Latin on behalf of Our Lord Himself who is God anyway. It must be a strange thing to be a priest and wake up in the morning lying there in the bed knowing you have the power to forgive people or not forgive them depending on your mood. When you know Latin and forgive sins it makes you powerful and hard to talk to because you know the dark secrets of the world. Talking to a priest is like talking to God Himself and if you say the wrong thing you're doomed.

There wasn't a soul on that ship who could tell me how to talk to rich Protestants and demanding priests. My uncle by marriage, Pa Keating, could have told me but he was back in Limerick where he didn't give a fiddler's fart about anything. I knew if he were here he'd refuse to talk to the rich people entirely and then he'd tell the priest to kiss his royal Irish arse. That's how I'd like to be myself but when your teeth and eyes are destroyed you never know what to say or what to do with yourself.

There was a book in the ship's library, *Crime and Punishment*, and I thought it might be a good murder mystery even if it was filled with confusing Russian names. I tried to read it in a deck chair but the story made me feel strange, a story about a Russian student, Raskolnikov, who kills an old woman, a moneylender, and then tries to convince himself he's entitled to the money because she's useless to the world and her money would pay for his university expenses so that he could become a lawyer and go round defending people like himself who kill old women for their money. It made me feel strange because of the time in Limerick when I had a job writing threatening letters for an old woman moneylender, Mrs Finucane, and when she died in a chair I took some of her money to help me pay my fare to America. I knew I didn't kill Mrs Finucane but I took her money and that made me almost as bad as Raskolnikov and if I died this minute he'd be the first one I'd run into in hell. I could save my soul by confessing to the priest and even though he's supposed to forget your sins the minute he gives you absolution he'd have power over me and he'd give me strange looks and tell me go charm the rich Protestants from Kentucky.

I fell asleep reading the book and a sailor, a deckhand, woke me to tell me, Your book is getting wet in the rain, sir.

Sir. Here I was from a lane in Limerick and there's a man with grey hair calling me sir even though he's not supposed to say a word to me in the first place because of the rules. The First Officer told me an ordinary sailor was never allowed to speak to passengers except for a Good Day or Good Night. He told me this particular sailor with the grey hair was once an officer on the *Queen Elizabeth* but he was fired because he was caught with a first-class passenger in her cabin and what they were doing was a cause of confession. This man's name was Owen and he was peculiar the way he spent all his time reading below and when the ship docked he'd go ashore with a book and read in a cafe while the rest of the crew got roaring drunk and had to be hauled back to the ship in taxis. Our own captain had such respect for him he'd have him up to his cabin and they'd have tea and talk of the days they served together on an English destroyer that was torpedoed, the two of them hanging on to a raft in the Atlantic drifting and freezing and chatting about the time they'd get back to Ireland and have a nice pint and a mountain of bacon and cabbage.

Owen spoke to me next day. He said he knew he was breaking the rules but he couldn't help talking to anyone on this ship who was reading *Crime and Punishment*. There were great readers in the crew right enough but they wouldn't move beyond Edgar Wallace or Zane Grey and he'd give anything to be able to chat about Dostoyevsky. He wanted to know if I'd read *The Possessed* or *The Brothers Karamazov* and he looked sad when I said I'd never heard of them. He told me the minute I got to New York I should rush to a bookshop and get Dostoyevsky books and I'd never be lonely again. He said no matter what Dostoyevsky book you read he always gave you something to chew on and you can't beat that for a bargain. That's what Owen said though I had no notion of what he was talking about.

Then the priest came along the deck and Owen moved away. The priest said, Were you talking to that man? I could see you were. Well, I'm telling you he's not good company. You can see that, can't you? I heard all about him. Him with his grey hair swabbing decks at his age. It's a strange thing you can talk to deckhands with no morals but if I ask you to talk to the rich Protestants from Kentucky you can't find a minute.

We were only talking about Dostoyevsky.

Dostoyevsky, indeed. Lotta good that'll do you in New York. You won't see many Help Wanted signs requiring a knowledge of

Dostoyevsky. Can't get you to talk to the rich people from Kentucky but you sit here for hours yacking with sailors. Stay away from old sailors. You know what they are. Talk to people who'll do you some good. Read the *Lives of the Saints*.

Along the New Jersey side of the Hudson River there were hundreds of ships docked tightly together. Owen the sailor said they were the Liberty ships that brought supplies to Europe during the war and after and it's sad to think they'll be hauled away any day to be broken up in shipyards. But that's the way the world is, he said, and a ship lasts no longer than a whore's moan.

2

The priest asks if I have anyone meeting me and when I tell him there's no one he says I can travel with him on the train to New York City. He'll keep an eye on me. When the ship docks we take a taxi to the big Union Station in Albany and while we wait for the train we have coffee in great thick cups and pie on thick plates. It's the first time I ever had lemon meringue pie and I'm thinking if this is the way they eat all the time in America I won't be a bit hungry and I'll be fine and fat, as they say in Limerick. I'll have Dostoyevsky for the loneliness and pie for the hunger.

The train isn't like the one in Ireland where you share a carriage with five other people. This train has long cars where there are dozens of people and is so crowded some have to stand. The minute we get on people give up their seats to the priest. He says, Thank you, and points to the seat beside him and I feel the people who offered up their seats are not happy when I take one because it's easy to see I'm nobody.

Farther up the car people are singing and laughing and calling for the church key. The priest says they're college kids going home for the weekend and the church key is the can opener for the beer. He says they're probably nice kids but they shouldn't drink so much and he hopes I won't turn out like that when I live in New York. He says I should put myself under the protection of the Virgin Mary and ask her to intercede with her Son to keep me pure and sober and out of harm's way. He'll pray for me all the way out there in L Angeles and he'll say a special Mass for me on the eighth of Dece ber, the Feast of the Immaculate Conception. I want to ask him v hy he'd choose that feast day but I keep silent because he might start bothering me again about the rich Protestants from Kentucky.

He's telling me this but I'm dreaming of what it would be like to be a student somewhere in America, in a college like the ones in the films where there's always a white church spire with no cross to show it's Protestant and there are boys and girls strolling the campus carrying great books and smiling at each other with teeth like snow drops.

When we arrive at Grand Central Station I don't know where to go. My mother said I could try to see an old friend, Dan MacAdorey. The priest shows me how to use the telephone but there's no answer from Dan. Well, says the priest, I can't leave you on your own in Grand Central Station. He tells the taxi driver we're going to the Hotel New Yorker.

We take our bags to a room where there's one bed. The priest says, Leave the bags. We'll get something to eat in the coffee shop downstairs. Do you like hamburgers?

I don't know. I never had one in my life.

He rolls his eyes and tells the waitress bring me a hamburger with french fries and make sure the burger is well done because I'm Irish and we overcook everything. What the Irish do to vegetables is a crying shame. He says if you can guess what the vegetable is in an Irish restaurant you get the door prize. The waitress laughs and says she understands. She's half-Irish on her mother's side and her mother is the worst cook in the world. Her husband was Italian and he really knew how to cook but she lost him in the war.

Waw. That's what she says. She really means war but she's like all Americans who don't like to say 'r' at the end of a word. They say caw instead of car and you wonder why they can't pronounce words the way God made them.

I like the lemon meringue pie but I don't like the way Americans leave out the 'r' at the end of a word.

While we're eating our hamburgers the priest says I'll have to stay the night with him and tomorrow we'll see. It's strange taking off my clothes in front of a priest and I wonder if I should get down on my two knees and pretend to say my prayers. He tells me I can take a shower if I like and it's the first time in my life I ever had a shower with plenty of hot water and no shortage of soap, a bar for your body and a bottle for your head.

When I'm finished I dry myself with the thick towel draped on the bathtub and I put on my underwear before going back into the room. The priest is sitting in the bed with a towel wrapped around his fat belly, talking to someone on the phone. He puts down the phone and stares at me. My God, where did you get those drawers?

In Roche's Stores in Limerick.

If you hung those drawers out the window of this hotel people would surrender. Piece of advice, don't ever let Americans see you in those drawers. They'll think you just got off Ellis Island. Get briefs. You know what briefs are?

I don't.

Get 'em anyway. Kid like you should be wearing briefs. You're in the USA now. OK, hop in the bed, and that puzzles me because there's no sign of a prayer and that's the first thing you'd expect of a priest. He goes off to the bathroom but he's no sooner in there than he sticks his head out and asks me if I dried myself.

I did.

Well, your towel isn't touched so what did you dry yourself with?

The towel that's on the side of the bathtub.

What? That's not a towel. That's the bathmat. That's what you stand on when you get out of the shower.

I can see myself in a mirror over the desk and I'm turning red and wondering if I should tell the priest I'm sorry for what I did or if I should stay quiet. It's hard to know what to do when you make a mistake your first night in America but I'm sure in no time I'll be a regular Yank doing everything right. I'll order my own hamburger, learn to call chips french fries, joke with waitresses, and never again dry myself with the bathmat. Some day I'll say war and car with no 'r' at the end but not if I ever go back to Limerick. If I ever went back to Limerick with an American accent they'd say I was putting on airs and tell me I had a fat arse like all the Yanks.

The priest comes out of the bathroom, wrapped in a towel, patting his face with his hands, and there's a lovely smell of perfume in the air. He says there's nothing as refreshing as after-shave lotion and I can put on some if I like. It's right there in the bathroom. I don't know what to say or do. Should I say, No, thanks, or should I get out of the bed and go all the way to the bathroom and slather myself with after-shave lotion? I never heard of anyone in Limerick putting stuff on their faces after they shaved but I suppose it's different in America. I'm sorry I didn't look for a book that tells you what to do on your first night in New York in a hotel with a priest where you're liable to make a fool of yourself right and left. He says, Well? and I tell him, Ah, no, thanks. He says, Suit yourself, and I can tell he's a bit impatient the way he was when I didn't talk to the rich Protestants from Kentucky. He could easily tell me leave and there I'd be out on the street with my brown suitcase and nowhere to go in New York. I don't want to chance that so I tell him I'd like to put on the after-shave lotion after all. He shakes his head and tells me go ahead.

I can see myself in the bathroom mirror putting on the after-shave lotion and I'm shaking my head at myself feeling if this is the way it's going to be in America I'm sorry I ever left Ireland. It's hard enough coming here in the first place without priests criticizing you over your failure to hit it off with rich Kentucky Protestants, your ignorance of bathmats, the state of your underwear and your doubts about after-shave lotion.

The priest is in the bed and when I come out of the bathroom he tells me, OK, into the bed. We've got a long day tomorrow.

He lifts the bedclothes to let me in and it's a shock to see he's wearing nothing. He says, Good night, turns off the light and starts snoring without even saying a Hail Mary or a prayer before sleep. I always thought priests spent hours on their knees before sleeping but this man must be in a great state of grace and not a bit afraid of dying. I wonder if all priests are like that, naked in the bed. It's hard to fall asleep in a bed with a naked priest snoring beside you. Then I wonder if the Pope himself goes to bed in that condition or if he has a nun bring in pajamas with the Papal colors and the Papal coat of arms. I wonder how he gets out of that long white robe he wears, if he pulls it over his head or lets it drop to the floor and steps out of it. An old Pope would never be able to pull it over his head and he'd probably have to call a passing cardinal to give him a hand unless the cardinal himself was too old and he might have to call a nun unless the Pope was wearing nothing under the white robe which the cardinal would know about anyway because there isn't a cardinal in the world that doesn't know what the Pope wears since they all want to be Pope themselves and can't wait for this one to die. If a nun is called in she has to take the white robe to be washed down in the steaming depths of the Vatican laundry room by other nuns and novices who sing hymns and praise the Lord for the privilege of washing all the clothes of the Pope and the College of Cardinals except for the underwear which is washed in another room by old nuns who are blind and not liable to think sinful thoughts because of what they have in their hands and what I have in my own hand is what I shouldn't have in the presence of a priest in the bed and for once in my life I resist the sin and turn on my side and go to sleep.

Next day the priest finds a furnished room in the paper for six dollars a week and he wants to know if I can afford it till I get a job. We go to East Sixty-Eighth Street and the landlady, Mrs Austin, takes me upstairs to see the room. It's the end of a hallway blocked off with a partition and a door with a window looking out on the street. There's barely space for the bed and a small chest of drawers with a mirror and a table and if I stretch my arms I can touch the walls on both sides. Mrs Austin says this is a very nice room and I'm lucky it wasn't snapped up. She's Swedish and she can tell I'm Irish. She hopes I don't drink and if I do I'm not to bring girls into this room under any circumstances, drunk or sober. No girls, no food, no drink. Cockroaches smell food a mile away and once they're in you have them forever. She says, Of course you never saw a cockroach in Ireland. There's no food there. All you people do is drink. Cockroaches would starve to death or turn into drunks. Don't tell me, I know. My sister is married to an Irishman, worst thing she ever did. Irishmen great to go out with but don't marry them.

She takes the six dollars and tells me she needs another six for security, gives me a receipt and tells me I can move in anytime that day and she trusts me because I came with that nice priest even if she's not Catholic herself, that it's enough her sister married one, an Irishman, God help her, and she's suffering for it.

The priest calls another taxi to take us to the Biltmore Hotel across the street from where we came out at Grand Central Station. He says it's a famous hotel and we're going to the headquarters of the

Democratic Party and if they can't find a job for an Irish kid no one can.

A man passes us in the hallway and the priest whispers, Do you know who that is?

I don't.

Of course you don't. If you don't know the difference between a towel and a bathmat how could you know that's the great Boss Flynn from the Bronx, the most powerful man in America next to President Truman.

The great Boss presses the button for the elevator and while he's waiting he shoves a finger up his nose, looks at what he has on his fingertip and flicks it away on the carpet. My mother would call that digging for gold. This is the way it is in America. I'd like to tell the priest I'm sure De Valera would never pick his nose like that and you'd never find the Bishop of Limerick going to bed in a naked state. I'd like to tell the priest what I think of the world in general where God torments you with bad eyes and bad teeth but I can't for fear he might go on about the rich Protestants from Kentucky and how I missed the opportunity of a lifetime.

The priest talks to a woman at a desk in the Democratic Party and she picks up the telephone. She says to the telephone, Got a kid here . . . just off the boat . . . you got a high school diploma? . . . na, no diploma . . . well, whaddya expect . . . Old Country still a poor country . . . yeah, I'll send him up.

I'm to report on Monday morning to Mr Carey on the twenty-second floor and he'll put me to work right here in the Biltmore Hotel and aren't I a lucky kid walking into a job right off the boat. That's what she says and the priest tells her, This is a great country and the Irish owe everything to the Democratic Party, Maureen, and you just clinched another vote for the party if the kid here ever votes, ha ha ha.

The priest tells me go back to the hotel and he'll come for me later to go to dinner. He says I can walk, that the streets run east and west, the avenues north and south, and I'll have no trouble. Just walk across Forty-Second to Eighth Avenue and south till I come to the New Yorker Hotel. I can read a paper or a book or take a shower if I promise to stay away from the bathmat, ha ha. He says, If we're lucky we might meet the great Jack Dempsey himself. I tell him I'd rather meet Joe Louis if that's possible and he snaps at me, You better learn to stick with your own kind.

At night the waiter at Dempsey's smiles at the priest. Jack's not here, Fawdah. He's over to the Gawden checkin' out a middleweight from New Joisey.

Gawden. Joisey. My first day in New York and already people are talking like gangsters from the films I saw in Limerick.

The priest says, My young friend here is from the Old Country and he'd prefer to meet Joe Louis. He laughs and the waiter laughs and says, Well, that's a greenhorn talkin', Fawdah. He'll loin. Give him six months in this country and he'll run like hell when he sees a darky. An' what would you like to order, Fawdah? Little something before dinner?

I'll have a double martini dry and I mean dry straight up with a twist.

And the greenhorn?

He'll have a . . . well, what'll you have?

A beer, please.

You eighteen, kid?

Nineteen.

You don't look it though it don't matter nohow long as you with the fawdah. Right, Fawdah?

Right. I'll keep an eye on him. He doesn't know a soul in New York and I'm going to settle him in before I leave.

The priest drinks his double martini and orders another with his steak. He tells me I should think of becoming a priest. He could get me a job in Los Angeles and I'd live the life of Riley with widows dying and leaving me everything including their daughters, ha ha, this is one hell of a martini excuse the language. He eats most of his steak and tells the waiter bring two apple pies with ice cream and he'll have a double Hennessy to wash it down. He eats only the ice cream, drinks half the Hennessy and falls asleep with his chin on his chest moving up and down.

The waiter loses his smile. Goddam, he's gotta pay his check. Where's his goddam wallet? Back pocket, kid. Hand it to me.

I can't rob a priest.

You're not robbing. He's paying his goddam check and you're gonna need a taxi to take him home.

Two waiters help him to a taxi and two bellhops at the New Yorker Hotel haul him through the lobby, up the elevator, and dump him on the bed. The bellhops tell me, A buck tip would be nice, a buck each, kid.

They leave and I wonder what I'm supposed to do with a drunken priest. I remove his shoes the way they do when someone passes out in the films but he sits up and runs to the bathroom where he's sick a long time and when he comes out he's pulling at his clothes, throwing them on the floor, collar, shirt, trousers, underwear. He collapses on the bed on his back and I can see he's in a state of excitement with his hand on himself. Come here to me, he says, and I back away. Ah, no, Father, and he rolls out of the bed, slobbering and stinking of drink and puke and tries to grab my hand to put it on him but I back away even faster till I'm out the door to the hallway with him standing in the door, a little fat priest crying to me, Ah, come back, son, come back, it was the drink. Mother o' God, I'm sorry.

But the elevator is open and I can't tell the respectable people already in it and looking at me that I changed my mind, that I'm running back to this priest who, in the first place, wanted me to be polite to rich Kentucky Protestants so that I could get a job cleaning stables and now waggles his thing at me in a way that's surely a mortal sin. Not that I'm in a state of grace myself, no, I'm not, but you'd expect a priest to set a good example and not make a holy show of himself my second night in America. I have to step into the elevator and pretend I don't hear the priest slobbering and crying, naked at the door of his room.

There's a man at the front door of the hotel dressed up like an admiral and he says, Taxi, sir. I tell him, No, thanks, and he says, Where you from? Oh, Limerick. I'm from Roscommon myself, over here four years.

I have to ask the man from Roscommon how to get to East Sixty-Eighth Street and he tells me walk east on Thirty-Fourth Street which is wide and well lit till I come to Third Avenue and I can get the El or if I'm anyway lively I can walk straight up till I come to my street. He tells me, Good luck, stick with your own kind and watch out for the Puerto Ricans, they all carry knives and that's a known fact, they got that hot blood. Walk in the light along the edge of the sidewalk or they'll be leppin' at you from dark doorways.

★　　★　　★

Next morning the priest calls Mrs Austin and tells ʌ ᵇould come get my suitcase. He tells me, Come in, the door is opᵉ ᵗ's in his black suit sitting on the far side of the bed with his bac. me and my suitcase is just inside the door. Take it, he says. I'm ₒoing to a retreat house in Virginia for a few months. I don't want to look at you and I don't want to see you ever again because what happened was terrible and it wouldn't have happened if you'd used your head and gone off with the rich Protestants from Kentucky. Goodbye.

It's hard to know what to say to a priest in a bad mood with his back to you who's blaming you for everything so all I can do is go down in the elevator with my suitcase wondering how a man like that who forgives sins can sin himself and then blame me. I know if I did something like that, getting drunk and bothering people to put their hands on me, I'd say I did it. That's all, I did it. And how can he blame me just because I refused to talk to rich Protestants from Kentucky? Maybe that's the way priests are trained. Maybe it's hard listening to people's sins day in day out when there's a few you'd like to commit yourself and then when you have a drink all the sins you've heard explode inside you and you're like everyone else. I know I could never be a priest listening to those sins all the time. I'd be in a constant state of excitement and the Bishop would be worn out shipping me off to the retreat house in Virginia.

3

When you're Irish and you don't know a soul in New York and you're walking along Third Avenue with trains rattling along on the El above there's great comfort in discovering there's hardly a block without an Irish bar: Costello's, the Blarney Stone, the Blarney Rose, P. J. Clarke's, the Breffni, the Leitrim House, the Sligo House, Shannon's, Ireland's Thirty-Two, the All Ireland. I had my first pint in Limerick the day before I turned sixteen and it made me sick and my father nearly destroyed the family and himself with the drink but I'm lonely in New York and I'm lured in by Bing Crosby on jukeboxes singing "Galway Bay" and blinking green shamrocks the likes of which you'd never see in Ireland.

There's an angry-looking man behind the end of the bar in Costello's and he's saying to a customer, I don't give a tinker's damn if you have ten pee haitch dees. I know more about Samuel Johnson than you know about your hand and if you don't comport yourself properly you'll be out on the sidewalk. I'll say no more.

The customer says, But.

Out, says the angry man. Out. You'll get no more drink in this house.

The customer claps on his hat and stalks out and the angry man turns to me. And you, he says, are you eighteen?

I am, sir. I'm nineteen.

How do I know?

I have my passport, sir.

And what is an Irishman doing with an American passport?

I was born here, sir.

He allows me to have two fifteen-cent beers and tells me I'd be better off spending my time in the library than in bars like the rest of our miserable race. He tells me Dr Johnson drank forty cups of tea a day and his mind was clear to the end. I ask him who Dr Johnson was and he glares at me, takes my glass away, and tells me, Leave this bar. Walk west on Forty-Second till you come to Fifth. You'll see two great stone lions. Walk up the steps between those two lions, get yourself a library card and don't be an idiot like the rest of the bogtrotters getting off the boat and stupefying themselves with drink. Read your Johnson, read your Pope and avoid the dreamy micks. I want to ask him where he stands on Dostoyevsky till he points at the door, Don't come back here till you've read *The Lives of the Poets*. Go on. Get out.

It's a warm October day and I have nothing else to do but what I'm told and what harm is there in wandering up to Fifth Avenue where the lions are. The librarians are friendly. Of course I can have a library card and it's so nice to see young immigrants using the library. I can borrow four books if I like as long as they're back on the due date. I ask if they have a book called *The Lives of the Poets* by Samuel Johnson and they say, My, my, my, you're reading Johnson. I want to tell them I never read Johnson before but I don't want them to stop admiring me. They tell me feel free to walk around, take a look at the Main Reading Room on the third floor. They're not a bit like the librarians in Ireland who stood guard and protected the books against the likes of me.

The sight of the Main Reading Room, North and South, makes me go weak at the knees. I don't know if it's the two beers I had or the excitement of my second day in New York but I'm near tears when I look at the miles of shelves and know I'll never be able to read all those books if I live till the end of the century. There are acres of shiny tables where all sorts of people sit and read as long as they like seven days a week and no one bothers them unless they fall asleep and snore. There are sections with English, Irish, American books, literature, history, religion, and it makes me shiver to think I can come here anytime I like and read anything as long as I like if I don't snore.

I stroll back to Costello's with four books under my arm. I want to show the angry man I have *The Lives of the Poets* but he's not there. The barman says that would be Mr Tim Costello himself that was going on about Johnson and as he's talking the angry man comes out of the kitchen. He says, Are you back already?

I have *The Lives of the Poets*, Mr Costello.

You may have *The Lives of the Poets* under your oxter, young fellow, but you don't have them in your head so go home and read.

It's Thursday and I have nothing to do till the job starts on Monday. For lack of a chair I sit up in the bed in my furnished room and read till Mrs Austin knocks on my door at eleven and tells me she's not a millionaire and it's house policy that lights be turned off at eleven to keep down her electricity bill. I turn off the light and lie on the bed listening to New York, people talking and laughing, and I wonder if I'll ever be part of the city, out there talking and laughing.

There's another knock at the door and this young man with red hair and an Irish accent tells me his name is Tom Clifford and would I like a fast beer because he works in an East Side building and he has to be there in an hour. No, he won't go to an Irish bar. He wants nothing to do with the Irish so we walk to the Rhinelander on Eighty-Sixth Street where Tom tells me how he was born in America but was taken to Cork and got out as fast as he could by joining the American Army for three good years in Germany when you could get laid ten times over for a carton of cigarettes or a pound of coffee. There's a dance floor and a band in the back of the Rhinelander and Tom asks a girl from one of the tables to dance. He tells me, Come on. Ask her friend to dance.

But I don't know how to dance and I don't know how to ask a girl to dance. I know nothing about girls. How could I after growing up in Limerick? Tom asks the other girl to dance with me and she leads me out on the floor. I don't know what to do. Tom is stepping and twirling and I don't know whether to go backwards or forwards with this girl in my arms. She tells me I'm stepping on her shoes and when I tell her I'm sorry she says, Oh, forget it. I don't feel like clumping around. She goes back to her table and I follow her with my face on fire. I don't know whether to sit at her table or go back to the bar till she says, You left your beer on the bar. I'm glad I have an excuse to leave her because I wouldn't know what to say if I sat. I'm sure she wouldn't be interested if I told her I spent hours reading Johnson's *The Lives of the Poets* or if I told her how excited I was at the Forty-Second Street Library. I might have to find a book in the library on how to talk to girls or I might have to ask Tom who dances and laughs and has no trouble with the talk. He comes back to the bar and says he's going to call in sick which means he's not going to work. The girl likes him and says she'll let him take her home. He whispers to me he might get laid which means he might go to bed with her. The only problem is the other girl. He calls her my girl. Go ahead, he says. Ask her if you can take her home. Let's sit at their table and you can ask her.

The beer is working on me and I'm feeling braver and I don't feel shy about sitting at the girls' table and telling them about Tim Costello and Dr Samuel Johnson. Tom nudges me and whispers, For Christ's sake, stop the Samuel Johnson stuff, ask her home. When I look at her I see two and I wonder which I should ask home but if I look between the two I see one and that's the one I ask.

Home? she says. You kiddin' me. That's a laugh. I'm a secretary, a private secretary, and you don't even have a high school diploma. I mean, did you look in the mirror lately? She laughs and my face is on fire again. Tom takes a long drink of beer and I know I'm useless with these girls so I leave and walk down Third Avenue taking the odd look at my reflection in shop windows and giving up hope.

4

Monday morning my boss, Mr Carey, tells me I'll be a houseman, a very important job where I'll be out front in the lobby dusting, sweeping, emptying ashtrays and it's important because a hotel is judged by its lobby. He says we have the best lobby in the country. It's the Palm Court and known the world over. Anyone who's anyone knows about the Palm Court and the Biltmore clock. Chrissakes, it's right there in books and short stories, Scott Fitzgerald, people like that. Important people say, Let's meet under the clock at the Biltmore, and what happens if they come in and the place is covered with dust and buried in garbage. That's my job, to keep the Biltmore famous. I'm to clean and I'm not to talk to guests, not even look at them. If they talk to me I'm to say, Yes, sir or ma'am, or No, sir or ma'am, and keep working. He says I'm to be invisible, and that makes him laugh. Imagine that, eh, you're the invisible man cleaning the lobby. He says this is a big job and I'd never have it if I hadn't been sent by the Democratic Party at the request of the priest from California. Mr Carey says the last guy on this job was fired for talking to college girls under the clock but he was Italian so whaddya expect. He tells me keep my eye on the ball, don't forget to take a shower every day, this is America, stay sober, stick with your own kind of people, you can't go wrong with the Irish, go easy with the drink, and in a year I might rise to the rank of porter or busboy and make tips and, who knows, rise up to be a waiter and wouldn't that be the end of all my worries. He says anything is possible in America, Look at me, I have four suits.

The head waiter in the lobby is called maitre d'. He tells me I'm to sweep up only what falls to the floor and I'm not to touch anything on the tables. If money falls to the floor or jewelry or anything like that I'm to hand it to him, the maitre d' himself, and he'll decide what to do with it. If an ashtray is full I'm to wait for a busboy or a waiter to tell me empty it. Sometimes there are things in ashtrays that need to be taken care of. A woman might remove an earring because of the soreness and forget she left it in the ashtray and there are earrings worth thousands of dollars, not that I'd know anything about that just off the boat. It's the job of the maitre d' to hold on to all earrings and return them to the women with the sore ears.

There are two waiters working in the lobby and they rush back and forth, running into each other and barking in Greek. They tell me, You, Irish, come 'ere, clean up, clean up, empty goddam ashtray, take garbage, come on, come on, less go, you drunk or sompin'? They yell at me in front of the college students who swarm in on Thursdays and Fridays. I wouldn't mind Greeks yelling at me if they'd didn't do it in front of the college girls who are golden. They toss their hair and smile with teeth you see only in America, white, perfect, and everyone has tanned movie star legs. The boys sport crewcuts, the teeth, football shoulders, and they're easy with the girls. They talk and laugh and the girls lift their glasses and smile at the boys with shining eyes. They might be my age but I move among them ashamed of my uniform and my dustpan and broom. I wish I could be invisible but I can't when the waiters yell at me in Greek and English and something in between or a busboy might accuse me of interfering with an ashtray that had something on it.

There are times when I don't know what to do or say. A college boy with a crewcut says, Do you mind not cleaning around here just now? I'm talking to the lady. If the girl looks at me and then looks away I feel my face getting hot and I don't know why. Sometimes a college girl will smile at me and say, Hi, and I don't know what to say. I'm told by the hotel people above me I'm not to say a word to the guests though I wouldn't know how to say Hi anyway because we never said it in Limerick and if I said it I might be fired from my new job and be out on the street with no priest to get me another one. I'd like to say Hi and be part of that lovely world for a minute except that a crewcut boy might think I was gawking at his girl and report me to the maitre d'. I could go home tonight and sit up in the bed and practice smiling and saying Hi. If I kept at it I'd surely be able to handle the Hi but I'd have to say it without the smile for if I drew my lips back at all I'd frighten the wits out of the golden girls under the Biltmore clock.

There are days when the girls take off their coats and the way they look in sweaters and blouses is such an occasion of sin I have to lock myself in a toilet cubicle and interfere with myself and I have to be quiet for fear of being discovered by someone, a Puerto Rican busboy or a Greek waiter, who will run to the maitre d' and report that the lobby houseman is wankin' away in the bathroom.

5

There's a poster outside the Sixty-Eighth Street Playhouse that says *Hamlet* with Laurence Olivier: Coming Next Week. I'm already planning to treat myself to a night out with a bottle of ginger ale and a lemon meringue pie from the bakery like the one I had with the priest in Albany, the loveliest taste I ever had in my life. There I'll be watching Hamlet on the screen tormenting himself and everybody else, and I'll have tartness of ginger ale and sweetness of pie clashing away in my mouth. Before I go to the cinema I can sit in my room and read *Hamlet* to make sure I know what they're all saying in that Old English. The only book I brought from Ireland is the *Complete Works of Shakespeare* which I bought in O'Mahony's Bookshop for thirteen shillings and sixpence, half my wages when I worked at the post office delivering telegrams. The play I like best is *Hamlet* because of what he had to put up with when his mother carried on with her husband's brother, Claudius, and the way my own mother in Limerick carried on with her cousin, Laman Griffin. I could understand Hamlet raging at his mother the way I did with my mother the night I had my first pint and went home drunk and slapped her face. I'll be sorry for that till the day I die though I'd still like to go back to Limerick some day and find Laman Griffin in a pub and tell him step outside and I'd wipe the floor with him till he begged for mercy. I know it's useless talking like that because Laman Griffin will surely be dead of the drink and the consumption by the time I return to Limerick and he'll be a long time in hell before I ever say a prayer or light a candle for him even if Our Lord says we should forgive our enemies and turn the other cheek. No, even if Our Lord came back on earth and ordered me to forgive Laman Griffin on pain of being cast into the sea with a millstone around my neck, the thing I fear most in the world, I'd have to say, Sorry, Our Lord, I can never forgive that man for what he did to my mother and my family. Hamlet didn't wander around Elsinore forgiving people in a made-up story, so why should I in real life.

The last time I went to the Sixty-Eighth Street Playhouse the usher wouldn't let me in with a bar of Hershey's chocolate in my hand. He said I couldn't bring in food or drink and I'd have to consume it outside. Consume. He couldn't say eat, and that's one of the things that bothers me in the world the way ushers and people in uniforms in general always like to use big words. The Sixty-Eighth Street Playhouse isn't a bit like the Lyric Cinema in Limerick where you could bring in fish and chips or a good feed of pig's feet and a bottle of stout if the humor was on you. The night they wouldn't let me in with the chocolate bar I had to stand outside and gobble it with the usher glaring at me and he didn't care that I was missing funny parts of the Marx Brothers. Now I have to carry my black raincoat from Ireland over my arm so that the usher won't spot the bag with the lemon meringue pie or the ginger ale bottle stuck in a pocket.

The minute the film starts I try to go at my pie but the box crackles and people say, Shush, we're trying to watch this film. I know they're not the ordinary type of people who go to gangster films or musicals. These are people who probably graduated from college and live on Park Avenue and know every line of *Hamlet*. They'll never say they go to movies, only films. I'll never be able to open the box silently and my mouth is watering with the hunger and I don't know what to do till a man sitting next to me says, Hi, slips part of his raincoat over my lap and lets his hand wander under it. He says, Am I disturbing you? and I don't know what to say though something tells me take my pie and move away. I tell him, Excuse me, and go by him up the aisle and out to the men's lavatory where I'm able to open my pie box in comfort without Park Avenue shushing me. I feel sorry over missing part of *Hamlet* but all they were doing up there on the screen was jumping around and shouting about a ghost.

Even though the men's lavatory is empty I don't want to be seen opening my box and eating my pie, so I sit on the toilet in the cubicle eating quickly so that I can get back to *Hamlet* as long as I don't have to sit beside the man with the coat on his lap and the wandering hand. The pie makes my mouth dry and I think I'll have a nice drink of ginger ale till I realize you have to have some class of a church key to lift off the cap. There's no use going to an usher because they're always barking and telling people they're not supposed to be bringing in food or drink from the outside even if they're from Park Avenue. I lay the pie box on the floor and decide the only way to knock the cap off the ginger ale bottle is to place it against the sink and give it a good rap with the back of my hand and when I do the neck of the bottle breaks and the ginger ale gushes up in my face and there's blood on the sink where I cut my hand on the bottle and I feel sad with all the things happening to me that my pie is being drowned on the floor with blood and ginger ale and wondering at the same time will I ever be able to see *Hamlet* with all the troubles I'm having when a desperate-looking grey-haired man rushes in nearly knocking me over and steps on my pie box destroying it entirely. He stands at the urinal firing away, trying to shake the box off his shoe, and barking at me, Goddam, goddam, what the hell, what the hell. He stands away and swings his leg so that the pie box flies off his shoe and hits the wall all squashed and beyond eating. The man says, What the hell is going on here? and I don't know what to tell him because it seems like a long story going all the way back to how excited I was weeks ago about coming to see *Hamlet* and how I didn't eat all day because I had a delicious feeling about doing everything at the same time, eating my pie, drinking ginger ale, seeing *Hamlet* and hearing all the glorious speeches. I don't think the man is in the mood from the way he dances from one foot to the other telling me the toilet is not a goddam restaurant, that I have no goddam business hanging around public bathrooms eating and drinking and I'd better get my ass outa there. I tell him I had an accident trying to open the ginger ale bottle and he says, Didn't you ever hear of an opener or are you just off the goddam boat? He leaves the lavatory and just as I'm wrapping toilet paper around my cut the usher comes in and says there's a customer complaint about my behavior in here. He's like the grey-haired man with his goddam and what the hell and when I try to explain what happened he says, Get your ass outa here. I tell him I paid to see

Hamlet and I came in here so that I wouldn't be disturbing all the Park Avenue people around me who know *Hamlet* backwards and forwards but he says, I don't give a shit, get out before I call the manager or the cops who will surely be interested in the blood all over the place.

Then he points to my black raincoat draped on the sink. Take that goddam raincoat outa here. Whaddya doin' with a raincoat on a day there ain't a cloud in the sky? We know the raincoat trick and we're watching. We know the whole raincoat brigade. We're on to your little queer games. You sit there lookin' innocent and the next thing the hand is wandering over to innocent kids. So get your raincoat outa here, buddy, before I call the cops, you goddam pervert.

I take the broken ginger ale bottle with the drop left and walk down Sixty-Eighth Street and sit on the steps of my rooming house till Mrs Austin calls through the basement window there is to be no eating or drinking on the steps, cockroaches will come running from all over and people will say we're a bunch of Puerto Ricans who don't care where they eat or drink or sleep.

There is no place to sit anywhere along the street with landladies peering and watching and there's nothing to do but to wander over to a park by the East River and wonder why America is so hard and complicated that I have trouble going to see *Hamlet* with a lemon meringue pie and a bottle of ginger ale.

6

The worst part of getting up and going to work in New York is the way my eyes are so infected I have to pull the lids apart with thumb and forefinger. I'm tempted to pick at the hard yellow crust but if I do the eyelashes will come away with it and leave my eyelids red and sore, worse than they were before. I can stand in the shower and let hot water run on my eyes till they feel warm and clean even if they're still blazing red in my head. I try to freeze the red away with icy cold water but it never works. It just makes my eyeballs ache and things are bad enough without me going to the Biltmore lobby with an ache in the eyeball.

I could put up with the aching eyeballs if I didn't have the soreness and the redness and the yellow ooze. At least people wouldn't be staring at me as if I were some class of a leper.

It's shameful enough going around the Palm Court in the black houseman's uniform which means I'm just above the Puerto Rican dishwashers in the eyes of the world. Even the porters have a touch of gold on their uniforms and the doormen themselves look like admirals of the fleet. Eddie Gilligan, the union shop steward, says it's a good thing I'm Irish or it's down in the kitchen I'd be with the spics. That's a new word, spics, and I know from the way he says it that he doesn't like Puerto Ricans. He tells me Mr Carey takes good care of his own people and that's why I'm a houseman with a uniform instead of an apron down there with the PRs singing and yelling Mira mira all day. I'd like to ask him what's wrong with singing when you're washing dishes and yelling Mira mira when the humor is on you but I'm wary of asking questions for fear of being foolish. At least the Puerto Ricans are together down there singing and banging away on pots and pans, carried away with their own music and dancing around the kitchen till the bosses tell them cut it out. Sometimes I go down to the kitchen and they give me bits of leftover food and call me Frankie, Frankie, Irish boy, we teach you Sponish. Eddie Gilligan says I'm paid two dollars and fifty cents a week more than the dishwashers and I have opportunities for advancement they'll never have because all they want to do is not learn English and make enough money to go back to Puerto Rico and sit under trees drinking beer and having big families because that's all they're good for, drinking and screwing till their wives are worn out and die before their time and their kids run the streets ready to come to New York and wash dishes and start the whole goddam thing over again and if they can't get jobs we have to support them, you an' me, so they can sit on their stoops up in East Harlem playing their goddam guitars and drinking beer outa paper bags. That's the spics, kid, and don't you forget it. Stay away from that kitchen because they wouldn't think twice about pissing in your coffee. He says he saw them pissing in the coffee urn that was being sent to a big lunch for the Daughters of the British Empire and the Daughters never guessed for one second they were drinking Puerto Rican piss.

Then Eddie smiles and laughs and chokes on his cigarette because he's Irish-American and he thinks the PRs are great for what they did to the Daughters of the British Empire. He calls them PRs now instead of spics because they did something patriotic the Irish should have thought of in the first place. Next year he'll piss in the coffee urns himself and laugh himself to death watching the Daughters drink coffee that's Puerto Rican and Irish piss. He says it's a great pity the Daughters will never know. He'd like to get up there on the balcony of the nineteenth-floor ballroom and make a general announcement, Daughters of the British Empire, you have just drunk coffee filled with spick-mick piss and how does that feel after what you did to the Irish for eight hundred years? Oh, that'd be a sight, the Daughters clutching each other and throwing up all over the ballroom and Irish patriots dancing jigs in their graves. That'd be something, says Eddie, that'd be really something.

Now Eddie says maybe the PRs aren't that bad at all. He wouldn't want them marrying his daughter or moving into his neighborhood but you have to admit they're musical and they send up some pretty good baseball players, you have to admit that. You go down to that kitchen and they're always happy like kids. He says, They're like the Negroes, they don't take nothin' serious. Not like the Irish. We take everything serious.

The bad days in the lobby are Thursday and Friday when the boys and girls meet and sit and drink and laugh, nothing on their minds but college and romance, sailing around in the summer, skiing in the winter, and marrying each other so that they'll have children who will come to the Biltmore and do the same. I know they don't even see me in my houseman's uniform with my dustpan and broom and I'm glad because there are days my eyes are so red they look bloody and I dread it when a girl might say, Excuse me where is the rest room? It's hard to point with your dustpan and say, Over there beyond the elevators, and keep your face turned away at the same time. I tried that with one girl but she went to the maitre d' and complained I was rude and now I have to look at everyone who asks a question and when they stare at me I blush so hard I'm sure my skin matches my eyes in the redness department. Sometimes I blush out of pure anger and I want to snarl at the people who stare but if I did I'd be fired on the spot.

They shouldn't stare. They should know better the way their mothers and fathers are spending fortunes to make them educated and what's the use of all that education if you're so ignorant you stare at people just off the boat with red eyes? You'd think the professors would be standing in front of their classes telling them that if you go to the Biltmore Hotel lobby or any lobby you're not to be staring at people with red eyes or one leg or any class of a disfigurement.

The girls stare anyway and the boys are worse the way they look at me and smile and nudge and pass remarks that make everyone laugh and I'd like to break my dustpan and broom over their heads till blood spurted and they begged me to stop and promise they'll never again pass remarks on anyone's sore eyes.

One day there's a yelp from a college girl and the maitre d' rushes over. She's crying and he's moving things around on the table before her and looking under it, shaking his head. He calls across the lobby, McCourt, get over here right now. Did you clean up around this table?

I think I did.

You think you did? Godammit, excuse me, miss, don't you know?

I did, sir.

Did you remove a paper napkin?

I cleaned up. I emptied the ash trays.

Paper napkin that was here. Did you take it?

I don't know.

Well, lemme tell you something, McCourt. This young lady here is the daughter of the President of the Traffic Club that rents a huge space in this hotel and she had a paper napkin with a phone number from a Princeton boy and if you don't find that piece of paper your ass is in hot water, excuse me, miss. Now what did you do with the trash you took away?

It's gone down to the big garbage bins near the kitchen.

All right. Go down there and search for that paper napkin and don't come back without it.

The girl who lost the napkin sobs and tells me her father has a lotta influence here and she wouldn't want to be me if I don't find that piece of paper. Her friends are looking at me and I feel my face is on fire with my eyes.

The maitre d' snaps at me again. Go get it, McCourt, and report back here.

The garbage bins by the kitchen are overflowing and I don't know how I'm going to find a small piece of paper lost in all that waste, coffee grounds, bits of toast, fishbones, eggshells, grapefruit skins. I'm on my knees poking and separating with a fork from the kitchen where the Puerto Ricans are singing and laughing and banging on pots and that makes me wonder what I'm doing on my knees.

So I get up and go into the kitchen saying nothing to the Puerto Ricans calling to me, Frankie, Frankie, Irish boy, we teach you Sponish. I find a clean paper napkin, write a made-up phone number on it, stain it with coffee, hand it to the maitre d' who hands it to the girl with her friends cheering on all sides. She thanks the maitre d' and passes him a tip, a whole dollar, and my only sorrow is that I won't be there when she calls that number.

33

7

There's a letter from my mother to say times are hard at home. She knows my wages aren't great and she's grateful for the ten dollars every week but could I spare an extra few dollars for shoes for Michael and Alphie? She had a job taking care of an old man but he was a great disappointment the way he died unexpected when she thought he'd hang on till the New Year so that she'd have a few shillings for shoes and a Christmas dinner, ham or something with a bit of dignity in it. She says sick people shouldn't hire people to take care of them and give them false hope of a job when they know very well they're in the throes. There's nothing coming in now but the money I'm sending and it looks as if poor Michael will have to leave school and get a job the minute he turns fourteen next year and that's a shame and she'd like to know, Is this what we fought the English for that half the children of Ireland should be wandering street, field and boreen with nothing between them and their feet but the skin?

I'm already sending her the ten dollars out of the thirty-two I get at the Biltmore Hotel though it's more like twenty-six when they deduct the Social Security and the income tax. After the rent I have twenty dollars and my mother gets ten of that and I have ten for food and the subway when it rains. The rest of the time I walk to save the nickel. Now and then I go mad with myself and go to a film at the Sixty-Eighth Street Playhouse and I know enough to sneak in a Hershey bar

34

or two bananas which is the cheapest food on earth. Sometimes when I peel my banana people from Park Avenue with sensitive noses will sniff and whisper to each other, Is that a banana I'm smelling? and the next thing is they're threatening to complain to the management.

But I don't care anymore. If they go to the usher to complain I'm not going to skulk in the men's room eating my banana. I'll go to the Democratic Party in the Biltmore Hotel and tell them I'm an American citizen with an Irish accent and why am I being tormented over eating a banana during a Gary Cooper film?

The winter might be coming in Ireland but it's colder here and the clothes I brought from Ireland are useless for a New York winter. Eddie Gilligan says if that's all I'm going to wear on the streets I'll be dead before I'm twenty. He says if I'm not too proud I can go to that big Salvation Army place on the West Side and get all the winter clothes I need for a few dollars. He says make sure I get clothes that make me look like an American and not the Paddy-from-the-bog stuff that makes me look like a turnip farmer.

But I can't go to the Salvation Army now because of the fifteen-dollar international money order for my mother and I can't get left-overs from the Puerto Ricans in the Biltmore kitchen anymore for fear they might catch my eye disease.

Eddie Gilligan says there's talk about my eyes. He was called in by personnel because he's the shop steward and they told him I'm never to go near the kitchen again in case I might touch a towel or something and leave all the Puerto Rican dishwashers and Italian cooks half blind with conjunctivitis or whatever I have. The only reason I'm kept on the job at all is that I was sent by the Democratic Party and they pay plenty for the big offices they rent in the hotel. Eddie says Mr Carey might be a tough boss but he stands up for his own kind and tells personnel where to get off, tells them the minute they try to lay off a kid with bad eyes the Democratic Party will know about it and that will be the end of the Biltmore Hotel. They'll see a strike that'll bring out the whole goddam Hotel Workers' Union. No more room service. No elevators. Eddie says, Fat bastards will have to walk and the chambermaids won't be putting toilet paper in the bathrooms. Imagine that: fat old bastards stuck with nothing to wipe their asses and all because of your bad eyes, kid.

We'll walk, says Eddie, the whole goddam union. We'll close down every hotel in the city. But I gotta tell you they gave me the name of this eye doctor on Lexington Avenue. You gotta see him and report back in a week.

The doctor's office is in an old building, up four flights of stairs. Babies are crying and a radio is playing

> *Boys and girls together*
> *Me and Mamie O'Rourke*
> *We'll trip the light fantastic*
> *On the sidewalks of New York.*

The doctor tells me, Come in, sit in this chair, whassa matter with your eyes? You here for glasses?

I have some kind of infection, doctor.

Jesus, yeah. That's some infection all right. How long you had this?

Nine years, doctor. I was in the eye hospital in Ireland when I was eleven.

He pokes at my eyes with a little piece of wood and pats them with cotton swabs which stick to the lids and make me blink. He tells me stop blinking, how the hell do I expect him to examine my eyes if I sit there blinking like a maniac? But I can't help it. The more he pokes and swabs the more I blink till he's so irritated he throws the stick with the swab stuck to it out the window. He pulls out drawers in his desk and curses and slams them in again till he finds a small bottle of whiskey and a cigar and that puts him in such a good humor he sits at his desk and laughs.

Still blinking, eh? Well, kid, I've been looking at eyes for thirty-seven years and I never saw anything like that. What are you, Mexican or something?

No, I'm Irish, doctor.

What you have there they don't have that in Ireland. And that's not conjunctivitis. I know conjunctivitis. That's something else and I can tell you you're lucky you have eyes at all. What you have I saw in guys coming back from the Pacific, New Guinea and places like that. You ever in New Guinea?

No, doctor.

Now what you have to do is shave that head completely. You've got some kind of infectious dandruff like the guys from New Guinea and it's falling into your eyes. That hair will have to come off and you'll have to scrub that scalp every day with a prescription soap. Scrub that scalp till it tingles. Scrub that scalp till it shines and come back to see me. That'll be ten dollars, kid.

The prescription soap is two dollars and the Italian barber on Third Avenue charges me another two dollars plus tip for cutting my hair and shaving my scalp. He tells me it's a crying shame shaving off a nice head of hair, if he had a head of hair like that they'd have to cut off his head to get it, that most of these doctors don't know shit from Shinola anyway but if that's what I want who is he to object.

He holds up a mirror to show how bald I look in the back and I feel weak with the shame of it, the bald head, the red eyes, the pimples, the bad teeth, and if anyone looks at me on Lexington Avenue I'll push him into traffic because I'm sorry I ever came to America which threatens to fire me over my eyes and makes me go bald through the streets of New York.

Of course they stare at me on the streets and I want to stare back in a threatening way but I can't with the yellow ooze in my eyes mixing with strands of cotton and blinding me entirely. I look up and down side streets for the ones least crowded and I zigzag across town and up. The best street is Third Avenue with the El rattling overhead and shadows everywhere and people in bars with their own troubles minding their own business and not staring at every pair of sore eyes that passes by. People coming out of banks and dress shops always stare but people in bars brood over their drinks and wouldn't care if you went eyeless on the avenue.

Of course Mrs Austin is gawking out the basement window. No sooner am I in the front door than she's up the stairs asking what happened to my head, did I have an accident, was I in a fire or something, and I want to snap at her and say, Does this look like a damn fire? But I tell her my hair was only singed in the hotel kitchen and the barber said it would be better to cut it off at the roots and start all over again. I have to be polite to Mrs Austin for fear she might tell me pack up and leave and there I'd be out on the street on a Saturday with a brown suitcase and a bald head and three dollars to my name. She says, Well, you're young, and goes back downstairs and all I can do is lie on my bed listening to people on the street talking and laughing, wondering how I can go to work on Monday morning in my baldy condition even if I am obeying the hotel and the doctor's orders.

I keep going to the mirror in my room, shocking myself with the whiteness of my scalp, and wishing I could stay here till the hair comes back but I'm hungry. Mrs Austin forbids food and drink in the room but once the darkness falls I go up the street for the big *Sunday Times* that will shield the bag with a sweet bun and a pint of milk from Mrs Austin's gawk. Now I have less than two dollars to last me till Friday and here it is only Saturday. If she stops me I'll say, Why shouldn't I have a sweet bun and a pint of milk after the way the doctor told me I had a New Guinea disease and a barber shaved my head to the bone? I wonder about all those films where they're waving the Stars and Stripes and placing their hands on their chests and declaring to the world this is the land of the free and the home of the brave and you know yourself you can't even go to see *Hamlet* with your lemon meringue pie and your ginger ale or a banana and you can't go into Mrs Austin's with any food or drink.

But Mrs Austin doesn't appear. Landladies never appear when you don't care.

I can't read the *Times* unless I wash out my eyes in the bathroom with warm water and toilet paper and it's lovely to lie in the bed with the paper and the bun and milk till Mrs Austin calls up the stairs complaining her electric bills are sky high and would I kindly put out the light, she's not a millionaire.

Once I switch off the light I remember it's time to smear my scalp with ointment but then I realize if I lie down the ointment will be all over the pillow and Mrs Austin will be at me again. The only thing to do is sit up with my head resting against the iron bedstead where I can wipe off any stray ointment. The iron is made up of little scrolls and flowers with petals that stick out and make it impossible to get a decent sleep and the only thing I can do is get out and sleep on the floor where Mrs Austin will have nothing to complain about.

Monday morning there's a note on my time card telling me report to the nineteenth floor. Eddie Gilligan says it's nothing personal but they don't want me in the lobby anymore with the bad eyes and now the bald head. It's a well-known fact that people who lose their hair suddenly are not long for this world even if you were to stand up in the middle of the lobby and announce it was the barber who did it. People want to believe the worst and they're in the personnel office saying, Bad eyes, bald head, put the two together and you have big problems with the guests in the lobby. When the hair grows back and the eyes clear up I might be returned to the lobby, maybe as busboy some day, and I'd be making tips so big I'd be able to support my family in Limerick in high style but not now, not with with this head, these eyes.

8

Eddie Gilligan works on the nineteenth floor with his brother, Joe. Our job is to set up for functions, meetings in rooms and banquets and weddings in the ballroom, and Joe isn't much use the way his hands and fingers are like roots. He walks around with a long-handled broom in one hand and a cigarette in the other pretending to look busy but he spends most of his time in the lavatory or smoking with Digger Moon the carpetman who claims he's a Blackfoot Indian and can lay carpet faster and tighter than anyone in the US of A unless he's had a few and then watch out because he remembers the sufferings of his people. When Digger remembers the sufferings of his people the only man he can talk to is Joe Gilligan because Joe himself is suffering with arthritis and Digger says Joe understands. When you have arthritis so bad you can barely wipe your ass you understand all kinds of suffering. That's what Digger says and when Digger isn't going from floor to floor laying carpet or pulling up carpet he sits cross-legged on the floor of the carpet room suffering with Joe, one with the past, the other with the arthritis. No one is going to bother Digger or Joe because everyone in the Biltmore Hotel knows of their suffering and they can spend days in the carpet room or stepping across the street to McAnn's Bar for relief. Mr Carey himself suffers with a bad stomach. He makes his inspection rounds in the morning suffering from the breakfast his wife cooks and on the afternoon inspection he's suffering from the lunch his wife packs. He tells Eddie his wife is a beautiful woman, the only one he ever loved, but she's killing him slowly and she's not in such good shape herself with her legs all swollen with rheumatism. Eddie tells Mr Carey his wife is in bad shape, too, after four miscarriages and now some kind of blood infection that has the doctor worried. The morning we set up for the annual banquet of the American-Irish Historical Society, Eddie and Mr Carey stand at the entrance to the nineteenth-floor ballroom, Eddie smoking a cigarette and Mr Carey in his double-breasted suit draped nicely to make you think he doesn't have that much of a belly, stroking it to ease the pain. Eddie tells Mr Carey he never smoked till he was hit on Omaha Beach and some asshole, excuse the language, Mr Carey, shoved a cigarette in his mouth while he was lying there waiting for the medics. He took a drag on that cigarette and it gave him such relief lying there with his gut hanging out on Omaha Beach he's been smoking ever since, can't give 'em up, tried, Christ knows, but can't. Now Digger Moon strolls up with a huge carpet on his shoulder and tells Eddie something has to be done about his brother, Joe, that that poor son-of-a-bitch is suffering more than seven Indian tribes and Digger knows something about suffering after his stint with the infantry all over the goddam Pacific when he was hit with everything the Japs could throw at him, malaria, everything. Eddie says, Yeah, yeah, he knows about Joe and he's sorry, after all it's his brother, but he has his own troubles with his wife and her miscarriages and blood infection and his own gut messed up from not being put back right and he worries about Joe the way he mixes alcohol and all kinds of pain-killers. Mr Carey belches and groans and Digger says, You still eating shit? because Digger isn't afraid of Mr Carey or anyone else. That's how it is when you're a great carpetman, you can say what you like to anyone and if they fire you there's always a job in the Hotel Commodore or the Hotel Roosevelt or even, Jesus, yeah, the Waldorf-Astoria, where they're always trying to steal Digger away. Some days Digger is so overcome by the sufferings of his people he refuses to lay any carpet and when Mr Carey won't fire him Digger says, That's right. White man can't get along without us Indians. White man gotta have Iroquois sixty floors up the skyscrapers to dance along steel beams. White man gotta have Blackfoot to lay good carpet. Every time Digger hears Mr Carey belch he tells him stop eating shit and have a nice beer because beer never bothered nobody and it's Mrs

41

Carey's sandwiches that are killing Mr Carey. Digger tells Mr Carey he has a theory about women, that they're like black widow spiders who kill the males after they screw, bite their goddam heads off, that women don't care about men, once they're past the age of having kids men are really useless unless they're up on the horse attacking another tribe. Eddie Gilligan says you'd look pretty fuckin' silly riding your horse up Madison Avenue to attack another tribe and Digger says that's exactly what he means. He says a man is put on this earth to paint his face, ride the horse, throw the spear, kill the other tribe and when Eddie says, Aw, bullshit, Digger says, Aw, bullshit, my ass, what are you doin', Eddie? spending your life here setting up for dinners and weddings? Is that a way for a man to live? Eddie shrugs and puffs on his cigarette and when Digger suddenly swings around to walk away he catches Mr Carey and Eddie with the end of the carpet and knocks them five feet into the ballroom.

It's an accident and no one says anything but still I admire the way Digger goes through the world not giving a fiddler's fart like my Uncle Pa in Limerick just because no one can lay carpet like him. I wish I could be like Digger but not with carpets. I hate carpets.

If I had the money I could buy a torch and read till dawn. In America a torch is called a flashlight. A biscuit is called a cookie, a bun is a roll. Confectionery is pastry and minced meat is ground. Men wear pants instead of trousers and they'll even say this pant leg is shorter than the other which is silly. When I hear them saying pant leg I feel like breathing faster. The lift is an elevator and if you want a WC or a lavatory you have to say bathroom even if there isn't a sign of a bath there. And no one dies in America, they pass away or they're deceased and when they die the body, which is called the remains, is taken to a funeral home where people just stand around and look at it and no one sings or tells a story or takes a drink and then it's taken away in a casket to be interred. They don't like saying coffin and they don't like saying buried. They never say graveyard. Cemetery sounds nicer.

If I had the money I could buy a hat and go out but I can't wander the streets of Manhattan in my bald state for fear people might think they were looking at a snowball on a pair of scrawny shoulders. In a week when the hair darkens my scalp I'll be able to go out again and there's nothing Mrs Austin can do about that. That's what gives me such pleasure, lying on the bed and thinking of the things you can do that nobody else can interfere with. That's what Mr O'Halloran, the headmaster, used to tell us in school in Limerick, Your mind is a treasure house that you should stock well and it's the one part of you the world can't interfere with.

New York was the city of my dreams but now I'm here the dreams are gone and it's not what I expected at all. I never thought I'd be going around a hotel lobby cleaning up after people and scouring toilet bowls in the lavatories. How could I ever write my mother or anyone in Limerick and tell them the way I'm living in this rich land with two dollars to last me for a week, a bald head and sore eyes, and a landlady who won't let me turn on the light? How could I ever tell them I have to eat bananas every day, the cheapest food in the world, because the hotel won't let me near the kitchen for leftovers for fear the Puerto Ricans might catch my New Guinea infection? They'd never believe me. They'd say, Go away ower that, and they'd laugh because all you have to do is look at the films to see how well off Americans are, the way they fiddle with their food and leave something on their plate and then push the plate away. It's hard even to feel sorry for Americans who are supposed to be poor in a film like *The Grapes of Wrath* when everything dries up and they have to move to California. At least they're dry and warm. My Uncle Pa Keating used to say if we had a California in Ireland the whole country would flock there, eat oranges galore and spend the whole day swimming. When you're in Ireland it's hard to believe there are poor people in America because you see the Irish coming back, Returned Yanks they're called, and you can spot them a mile away with their fat arses waggling along O'Connell Street in trousers too tight and colors you'd never see in Ireland, blues, pinks, light greens, and even flashes of puce. They always act rich and talk through their noses about their refrigerators and automobiles and if they go into a pub they want American drinks no one ever heard of, cocktails if you don't mind, though if you act like that in a Limerick pub the barman will put you in your place and remind you how you went to America with your arse hanging out of your trousers and don't be putting on airs here, Mick, I knew you when the snot hung from your nose to your kneecaps. You can always spot the Real Yanks, too, with their light colors and fat arses and the way they look around and smile and give pennies to raggedy children. Real Yanks don't put on airs. They don't have to after coming from a country where everyone has everything.

If Mrs Austin won't let me have a light I can still sit up in the bed or lie down or I can decide to stay in or go out. I won't go out tonight because of my bald head and I don't mind because I can stay here and turn my mind into a film about Limerick. This is the greatest discovery I've made from lying in the room, that if I can't read because of my eyes or Mrs Austin complaining about the light I can start any kind of a film in my head. If it's midnight here it's five in the morning in Limerick and I can picture my mother and brothers asleep with the dog, Lucky, growling at the world and my uncle, Ab Sheehan, snorting away in his bed from all the pints he had the night before and farting from his great feed of fish and chips.

I can float through Limerick and see people shuffling through the streets for the first Sunday Mass. I can go in and out of churches, shops, pubs, graveyards and see people asleep or groaning with pain in the hospital at the City Home. It's magic to go back to Limerick in my mind even when it brings the tears. It's hard to pass through the lanes of the poor and look into their houses and hear babies crying and women trying to start fires to boil water in kettles for the breakfast of tea and bread. It's hard to see children shivering when they have to leave their beds for school or Mass and there's no heat in the house like the heat we have here in New York with radiators singing away at six in the morning. I'd like to empty out the lanes of Limerick and bring all the poor people to America and put them in houses with heat and give them warm clothes and shoes and let them stuff themselves with porridge and sausages. Some day I'll make millions and I'll bring the poor people to America and send them back to Limerick fat arsed and waddling up and down O'Connell Street in light colors.

I can do anything I like in this bed, anything. I can dream about Limerick or I can interfere with myself even if it's a sin, and Mrs Austin will never know. No one will ever know unless I go to confession and I'm too doomed for that.

Other nights when I have hair on my head and no money I can walk around Manhattan. I don't mind that one bit because the streets are as lively as any film at the Sixty-Eighth Street Playhouse. There's always a fire engine screaming around a corner or an ambulance or a police car and sometimes they come screaming together and you know there's a fire. People always watch for the fire engine to slow down and that tells you what block to go to and where to look for smoke and flames. If someone is at a window ready to jump that makes it more exciting. The ambulance will wait with flashing lights and cops will tell everyone move back. That's the main job of cops in New York, telling everyone move back. They're powerful with their guns and sticks but the real hero is the fireman especially if he climbs a ladder and plucks a child from a window. He could save an old man with crutches and nothing on but a nightshirt but it's different when it's a child sucking her thumb and resting her curly head on the fireman's broad shoulder. That's when we all cheer and look at each other and know we're all happy about the same thing.

And that's what makes us look in the *Daily News* the next day to see if there's any chance we might be in the picture with the brave fireman and the curly-haired child.

9

Mrs Austin tells me her sister, Hannah, that's married to the Irishman, is coming for a little visit on Christmas before they go out to her house in Brooklyn and she'd like to meet me. We'll have a sandwich and a Christmas drink and that will get Hannah's mind off her troubles with that crazy Irishman. Mrs Austin doesn't understand herself why Hannah would want to spend Christmas Eve with the likes of me, another Irishman, but she was always a bit strange and maybe she likes the Irish after all. Their mother warned them a long time ago back in Sweden, over twenty years, would you believe it, to stay away from Irishmen and Jews, to marry their own kind and Mrs Austin doesn't mind telling me her husband, Eugene, was half Swedish, half Hungarian, that never drank a drop in his life though he loved to eat and that's what killed him in the end. She doesn't mind telling me he was big as a house when he died, that when she wasn't cooking he was raiding the refrigerator and when they got a TV set that was really the end of him. He'd sit there eating and drinking and worrying about the state of the world so much his heart just stopped, just like that. She misses him and it's hard after twenty-three years especially when they had no kids. Her sister, Hannah, has five kids and that's because the Irishman won't ever leave her alone, a couple of drinks and he's jumping on her, just like a typical Irish Catholic. Eugene wasn't like that, he had respect.

In any case she'll expect to see me after work on Christmas Eve.

On the day itself Mr Carey invites the housemen of the hotel and four chambermaid supervisors to his office for a little Christmas drink. There's a bottle of Paddy's Irish whiskey and a bottle of Four Roses which Digger Moon won't touch. He wants to know why anyone would drink piss like Four Roses when they can have the best thing that ever came out of Ireland, the whiskey. Mr Carey strokes his belly along the double-breasted suit and says it's all the same to him, he can't drink anything. It would kill him. But drink anyway, here's to a Merry Christmas and who knows what the next year will bring.

Joe Gilligan is already smiling from whatever he's been swigging all day from the flask in his back pocket and between that and the arthritis there's the odd stumble. Mr Carey tells him, Here, Joe, sit in my chair, and when Joe tries to sit he lets out a great groan and there are tears on his cheeks. Mrs Hynes, the head of all the chambermaids, goes over to him and holds his head against her chest and pats him and rocks him. She says, Ah, poor Joe, poor Joe, I don't know how the good Lord could twist your bones after what you did for America in the war. Digger Moon says that's where Joe got the arthritis, in the goddam Pacific, where they have every goddam disease known to man. Remember this, Joe, it was the goddam Japs gave you that arthritis the way they gave me malaria. We haven't been the same since, Joe, you an' me.

Mr Carey tells him take it easy, take it easy with the language, there are ladies present, and Digger says, okay, Mr Carey, I respect you for that and it's Christmas so what the hell. Mrs Hynes says, That's right, it's Christmas and we must love each other and forgive our enemies. Digger says, Forgive my ass. I don't forgive the white man and I don't forgive the Japs. But I forgive you, Joe. You suffered more than ten Indian tribes with that goddam arthritis. When he grabs Joe's hand to shake it Joe howls with pain and Mr Carey says, Digger, Digger. Mrs Hynes says, Will you, for the love o' Jesus, have respect for Joe's arthritis. Digger says, Sorry, ma'am, I have the greatest respect for Joe's arthritis, and to prove it he holds a large glass of Paddy's to Joe's lips.

Eddie Gilligan stands over in a corner with his glass and I wonder why he looks and says nothing when the world is worried about his brother. I know he has his own troubles with his wife's blood infection but I can't understand why he won't at least stand closer to his brother.

Jerry Kerrisk whispers we should get away from this crazy crowd and have a beer. I don't like spending money in bars with the trouble my mother is in but it's Christmas and the whiskey I had already makes me feel better about myself and the world in general and why shouldn't I be good to myself. It's the first time in my life I ever drank whiskey like a man and now that I'm in a bar with Jerry I can talk and not worry about my eyes or anything. Now I can ask Jerry why Eddie Gilligan is so cold to his brother.

Women, says Jerry. Eddie was engaged to this girl when he was drafted but when he went away she and Joe fell in love and when she sent Eddie back the engagement ring he went crazy and said he'd kill Joe the minute he saw him. But Eddie was sent to Europe and Joe to the Pacific and they were busy killing other people and while they were away Joe's wife, the one Eddie was supposed to marry, got the drinking habit and now makes Joe's life hell. Eddie said that was punishment for the son of a bitch for stealing his girl. He met a nice Italian girl himself in the army, a W A C, but she has the blood infection and you'd think there's a curse on the whole Gilligan family.

Jerry says he thinks the Irish mothers are right after all. You should marry your own kind, Irish Catholics, and make sure they're not alcoholics or Italians with blood infections.

He laughs when he says that but there's something serious in his eyes and I don't say anything because I know I don't want to marry an Irish Catholic myself and spend the rest of my life dragging the kids to confession and communion and saying, Yes, Father, oh, indeed, Father, every time I see a priest.

Jerry wants to stay in the bar and drink more beer and he turns peevish when I tell him I have to visit Mrs Austin and her sister, Hannah. Why would I want to spend Christmas Eve with two old Swedish women, forty years old at least, when I could be having a grand time for myself with girls from Mayo and Kerry up at Ireland's Thirty-Two? Why?

I can't answer him because I don't know where I want to be or what I'm supposed to do. That's what you're faced with when you come to America, one decision after another. I knew what to do in Limerick and I had answers for questions but this is my first Christmas Eve in New York and here I am pulled one way by Jerry Kerrisk, Ireland's Thirty-Two, the promise of girls from Mayo and Kerry, and the other way by two old Swedish women, one always gawking out the window in case I might smuggle in food or drink, the other unhappy with her Irish husband and who knows what way she'll jump. I'm afraid if I don't go to Mrs Austin she might turn savage on me and tell me leave and there I'll be out on the street on Christmas Eve with my brown suitcase and only a few dollars left after sending money home, paying my rent, and now buying beer right and left in this bar. After all this I can't afford to spend the night doling out beer money for the women of Ireland and that's the part Jerry understands, the part that takes away his peevishness. He knows money has to be sent home. He says, Happy Christmas, and laughs, I know you'll have a wild night with the old Swedish girls. The barman has his ear cocked and he says, Mind yourself at them Swedish parties. They'll be giving you their native drink, the glug, and if you drink that stuff you won't know Christmas Eve from the Feast of the Immaculate Conception. It's black and thick and you'd need a strong constitution for it, and then they make you eat all kinds of fish with it, raw fish, salty fish, smoked fish, all kinds of fish you wouldn't give a cat. The Swedes drink that glug and it makes them so crazy they think they're Vikings all over again.

Jerry says he didn't know the Swedes were Vikings. He thought you had to be a Dane.

Nodatall, says the barman. All them people in northern places were Vikings. Whenever you saw ice you were sure to see a Viking.

Jerry says it's remarkable the things people know and the barman says, I could tell you a story or two.

Jerry orders one more beer for the road and I drink it though I don't know what's going to become of me after my two large whiskeys in Mr Carey's office and four beers here with Jerry. I don't know how I'm going to face a night of glug and all kinds of fish if the barman is right in his prophecy.

We walk up Third Avenue singing "Don't Fence Me In" with people rushing past us frantic over Christmas, giving us nothing but hard stares. There are dancing Christmas lights everywhere, but up around Bloomingdale's the lights dance too much and I have to hold on to a Third Avenue El pillar and throw up. Jerry pushes in my stomach with his fist. Get it all up, he says, and you'll have plenty of room for the glug and you'll be a new man tomorrow. Then he says glug glug glug and laughs so hard over the sound of the word he's nearly hit by a car and a cop tells us move on, that we should be ashamed of ourselves, Irish kids that should respect the birthday of the Savior, goddamit.

There's a diner at Sixty-Seventh Street and Jerry says I should have coffee to straighten me out before I see the Swedes, he'll pay for it. We sit at the counter and he tells me he's not going to spend the rest of his life working like a slave at the Biltmore Hotel. He's not going to wind up like the Gilligans who fought for the USA and what the hell did they get for it? Arthritis and wives with blood infections and drinking problems, that's what they got. Oh, no, Jerry is heading for the Catskill Mountains on Memorial Day, the end of May, the Irish Alps. Plenty of work up there waiting on tables, cleaning up, anything, and the tips are good. There are Jewish places up there, too, but they're not too active in the tipping department because they pay for everything in advance and don't have to carry cash. The Irish drink and leave money on tables or the floor and when you clean up it's all yours. Sometimes they come back squawking but you didn't see a thing. You don't know nothing. You just sweep up the way you're paid to. Of course they don't believe you and they call you a liar and say things about your mother but there's nothing they can do except take their business elsewhere. There are plenty of girls up in the Catskills. Some places have outdoor dances and all you have to do is waltz your Mary into the woods and before you know it you're in a state of mortal sin. The Irish girls are mad for it once they get to the Catskills. They're hopeless in the city they way they all work in fancy places like Schrafft's with their little black dresses and little white aprons, Ah, yes, ma'am, ah, indeed, ma'am, are the mashed potatoes a little too lumpy, ma'am? but get them up in the mountains and they're like cats, up the pole, getting pregnant, and before they know what hit them, dozens of Seans and Kevins are dragging their arses up the aisle with the priests glaring at them and the girls' big brothers threatening them.

I want to sit in the diner all night listening to Jerry talking about Irish girls in the Catskills but the man says it's Christmas Eve and he's closing out of respect to his Christian customers even though he's Greek and it's not really his Christmas. Jerry wants to know how it could not be his Christmas since all you have to do is look out the window for proof but the Greek says, We're different.

That's enough for Jerry who doesn't argue about such things and that's what I like about him, the way he goes through life having another beer and dreaming of grand times in the Catskills and not arguing with Greeks about Christmas. I wish I could be like him but there's always some dark cloud at the back of my head, Swedish women waiting for me with glug, or a letter from my mother saying thanks for the few dollars, Michael and Alphie will have shoes and we'll have a nice goose for Christmas with the help of God and His Blessed Mother. She never mentions she needs shoes for herself and once I think of that I know I'll have another dark cloud at the back of my head. I wish there was a little panel I could slide back to release the clouds but there isn't and I'll have to find another way or stop collecting dark clouds.

The Greek says, Goodnight, gen'men, and would we like to take some day-old doughnuts. Take 'em, he says, or I trow out. Jerry says he'll have one to keep him going to Ireland's Thirty-Two where he'll have a feed of corned beef and cabbage and floury white potatoes. The Greek fills a bag with doughnuts and confectionery and tells me I look like I could use a decent meal, so take the bag.

Jerry says goodnight at Sixty-Eighth Street and I wish I could go with him. The whole day has me dizzy and it's still not over with the Swedes there waiting, stirring the glug, slicing the raw fish. The thought of it makes me puke all over again there on the street and people passing by, frantic with Christmas, make sounds of disgust and step away from me, telling their little children, Don't look at that disgusting man. He's drunk. I want to tell them, please don't turn the little children against me. I want to tell them this is not a habit I have. There are clouds at the back of my head, my mother has a goose, at least, but she needs shoes.

But there's no use trying to talk to people with parcels and children by the hand and their heads ringing with Christmas carols because they're going home to bright apartments and they know God's in His heaven, all's right with the world, as the poet said.

Mrs Austin opens the door. Oh, look, Hannah, Mr McCourt brought us a whole bag of doughnuts and pastries. Hannah gives a little wave from the couch and says, That's nice, you never know when you might need a bag of doughnuts. I always thought the Irish brought a bottle but you're different. Give the boy a drink, Stephanie.

Hannah is drinking red wine but Mrs Austin goes to a bowl on the table and ladles out the black stuff into a glass, the glug. My stomach turns again and I have to control it.

Siddown, says Hannah. Lemme tell you something, Irish boy. I don't give a shit about your people. You may be nice, my sister says you're nice, you bring nice doughnuts, but right under your skin you're nothing but shit.

Please, Hannah, says Mrs Austin.

Please Hannah, my ass. What did you people ever do for the world besides drink? Stephanie, give him some fish, decent Swedish food. Moon-faced mick. You make me sick, you little mick. Ah, ha, didja hear the poetry in that?

She cackles away over her poetry and I don't know what to do with my glug in one hand and Mrs Austin pushing fish at me with the other. Mrs Austin is drinking the glug, too, and she staggers from me to the bowl to the couch where Hannah is holding out her glass for more wine. She slurps her wine and glares at me. She says, A kid I was when I married that mick. Nineteen. How many years ago? Jesus, twenty-one. Whadda you, Stephanie? Forty-something? Wasted my life on that mick. And what are you doin' here? Who sent you?

Mrs Austin.

Mrs Austin. Mrs Austin. Speak up, you little spud-shitter. Drink your glug and speak up.

Mrs Austin sways before me with her glug glass. Come on, Eugene, less go to bed.

Oh, I'm not Eugene, Mrs Austin.

Oh.

She turns and wobbles away into another room and Hannah cackles again, See that. She still doesn't know she's a widow. Wish I was a goddam widow.

The glug I drank is making my stomach turn and I try to rush to the street but the door has three locks and I'm throwing up in the basement vestibule before I can get out. Hannah lurches from the couch and tells me get into the kitchen, get a mop and soap and clean up this goddam mess, don't you know it's Christmas Eve for Chrissakes and is this how you treat your gracious host.

From kitchen to door I go with dripping mop, swabbing, squeezing, rinsing in the kitchen sink and back again. Hannah pats my shoulder and kisses my ear and tells me I'm not such a bad mick after all, that I must have been well brought up the way I clean my mess. She tells me help myself to anything, glug, fish, even one of my own doughnuts, but I place the mop back where I found it and walk past

Hannah, with the idea in my head that once I cleaned up I don't have to listen to her anymore or anyone like her. She calls to me, Where you going? Where the hell do you think you're going? but I'm up the stairs to my room, my bed, so that I can lie there listening to Christmas carols on the radio with the world spinning around me and a great wonder in my head about the rest of my life in America. If I wrote to anyone in Limerick and told them about my Christmas Eve in New York they'd say I was making it up. They'd say New York must be a lunatic asylum.

In the morning there's a knock at my door and it's Mrs Austin in dark glasses. Hannah is farther down the stairs and she's in dark glasses, too. Mrs Austin says she heard I had an accident in her apartment but no one can blame her or her sister since they were prepared to offer the finest of Swedish hospitality and if I chose to arrive at their little party in a certain state they couldn't be blamed and it's too bad because they wanted nothing but a truly Christian Christmas Eve and I just wanted to tell you, Mr McCourt, we don't appreciate your behavior one bit, isn't that right, Hannah?

There's a croak from Hannah as she coughs and puffs on a cigarette.

They go back down the stairs and I want to call after Mrs Austin to see if there's any chance she could spare me a doughnut from the Greek's bag since I'm so empty from all the throwing up last night but they're out the door and from my window I can see them loading Christmas parcels into a car and driving off.

I can stand at the window all day looking at the happy people with children by the hand going off to church, as they say in America, or I can sit up in the bed with *Crime and Punishment* and see what Raskolnikov is up to but that will stir up all kinds of guilt and I don't have the strength for it and it's not the right kind of reading for a Christmas Day anyway. I'd like to go up the street for Communion at St Vincent Ferrer's but it's years since I went to confession and my soul is as black as Mrs Austin's glug. The happy Catholic people with children by the hand are surely going to St Vincent's and if I follow them I'm bound to have a Christmas feeling.

It's lovely to go into a church like St Vincent's where you know the Mass will be just like the Mass in Limerick or anywhere in the world. You could go to Samoa or Kabul and they'd have the same Mass and even if they wouldn't let me be an altar boy in Limerick I still have the Latin my father taught me and no matter where I go I can respond to the priest. No one can scoop out the contents of my head, all the saints' feast days I know by heart, the Mass Latin, the chief towns and products of the thirty-two counties of Ireland, songs galore of Ireland's sufferings, and Oliver Goldsmith's lovely poem, "The Deserted Village". They could put me in jail and throw away the key but they could never stop me from dreaming my way around Limerick and out along the banks of the Shannon or thinking about Raskolnikov and his troubles.

The people who go to St Vincent's are like the ones who go to the Sixty-Eighth Street Playhouse for *Hamlet* and they know the Latin responses the way they know the play. They share prayer books and sing hymns together and smile at each other because they know Brigid the maid is back there in the Park Avenue kitchen keeping an eye on the turkey. Their sons and daughters have the look of coming home from school and college and they smile at other people in the pews also home from school and college. They can afford to smile because they all have teeth so dazzling if they dropped them in snow they'd be lost forever.

The church is so crowded there are people standing in the back but I'm so weak with the hunger and the long Christmas Eve of whiskey, glug and throwing up I want to find a seat. There's an empty spot at the end of a pew far up the center aisle but as soon as I slip into it a man comes running at me. He's all dressed up in striped trousers, a coat with tails, and a frown over his face and he whispers to me, You must leave this pew at once. This is for regular pew holders, come on, come on. I feel my face turning red and that means my eyes are worse and when I go down the aisle I know the whole world is looking at me, the one who sneaked into the pew of a happy family with children home from school and college.

There's no use even standing at the back of the church. They all know and they'll be giving me looks, so I might as well leave and add another sin to the hundreds already on my soul, the mortal sin of not going to Mass on Christmas Day. At least God will know I tried and it's not my fault if I wandered into a happy family from Park Avenue pew.

I'm so empty now and hungry I want to go mad with myself and have a feast at the Horn and Hardart Automat but I don't want to be seen there for fear people might think I'm like the ones who sit there half the day with a cup of coffee, an old newspaper and nowhere to go. There's a Chock Full o'Nuts a few blocks away and that's where I have a bowl of pea soup, a nutted cheese on raisin bread, a cup of coffee, a doughnut with white sugar and a read of the *Journal-American* that someone left behind.

It's only two in the afternoon and I don't know what to do with myself when all the libraries are closed. People walking by with children by the hand might think I have nowhere to go so I keep my head up and walk up one street and down the other as if I were rushing for a turkey dinner. I wish I could open a door somewhere and have people say, Oh, hi, Frank, you're just in time. The people walking here and there on the streets of New York take it all for granted. They bring presents and get presents and have their big Christmas dinners and they never know there are people walking up one street and down the other on the holiest day of the year. I wish I could be an ordinary New Yorker stuffed after my dinner, talking to my family with Christmas carols on the radio in the background. Or I wouldn't mind being back in Limerick with my mother and brothers and the nice goose but here I am in the place I always dreamed about, New York, and I'm worn out with all these streets where there isn't even a bird to be seen.

There's nothing to do but go back to my room, listen to the radio, read *Crime and Punishment* and fall asleep wondering why Russians have to drag things out. You'd never find a New York detective wandering around with the likes of Raskolnikov talking about everything but the murder of the old woman. The New York detective would nab him, book him and the next thing is the electric chair in Sing Sing, and that's because Americans are busy people with no time for detectives to be chatting with people they already know committed the murder.

There's a knock on the door and it's Mrs Austin. Mr McCourt, she says, would you come downstairs a minute?

I don't know what to say. I'd like to tell her kiss my arse after the way her sister talked to me and the way she talked to me herself this morning but I follow her down and there she has all kinds of food laid out on the table. She says she brought it from her sister's, that they were worried I might have no place to go or nothing to eat on this beautiful day. She's sorry about the way she talked to me this morning and hopes I'm in a forgiving mood.

There's turkey and stuffing and all kinds of potatoes, white and yellow, with cranberry sauce to make everything sweet and all this puts me in a forgiving mood. She'd give me some glug but her sister threw it out and it's just as well. It made everyone sick.

When I'm finished she invites me to sit and watch her new television set where there's a program about Jesus that's so holy I fall asleep in the armchair. When I awake the clock on her mantelpiece says twenty past four in the morning and Mrs Austin is in the other room letting out little cries, Eugene, Eugene, and that proves you can have a sister and go to her house for Christmas dinner but if you don't have your Eugene you're as lonely as anyone sitting in the Automat and it's a great comfort to know my mother and brothers in Limerick have a goose and next year when I'm promoted to busboy at the Biltmore I'll send them the money that will let them stroll around Limerick dazzling the world with their new shoes.

10

Eddie Gilligan tells me go to the lockers and get into my street clothes because there's a priest in Mr Carey's office who met me coming over on the ship and now wants to take me to lunch. Then he says, What are you blushing for? It's only a priest and you're getting the free lunch.

I wish I could say I don't want to meet the priest for lunch but Eddie and Mr Carey might ask questions. If a priest says come to lunch you have to go and it doesn't matter what happened in the hotel room even if it wasn't my fault. I could never tell Eddie or Mr Gilligan how the priest came at me. They'd never believe me. People sometimes say things about priests, that they're fat or pompous or mean, but no one would ever believe a priest would interfere with you in a hotel room especially people like Eddie or Mr Carey with sick wives always running to confession in case they die in their sleep. People like that wouldn't be surprised if priests walked on water.

Why can't this priest go back to Los Angeles and leave me alone? Why is he taking me to lunch when he should be out there visiting the sick and the dying? That's what priests are for. It's four months since he went off to that retreat house in Virginia to beg forgiveness and here he is still on this side of the continent with nothing on his mind but lunch.

Now Eddie comes to me in the locker room and tells me the

priest had another idea, meet him across the street in McAnn's.

It's hard to walk into a restaurant and sit down opposite a priest who came at you in a hotel room four months ago. It's hard to know what to do when he looks at you directly, shakes your hand, holds your elbow, eases you into your seat. He tells me I'm looking good, that I filled out a bit in the face and I must be eating right. He says America is a great country if you give it a chance but I could tell him how they won't let the Puerto Ricans give me leftovers anymore and how I'm weary of bananas but I don't want to say much in case he might think I've forgotten the New Yorker Hotel. I don't have any grudge against him. He didn't hit anyone or starve anyone and what he did came from the drink. What he did was not as bad as running off to England and leaving your wife and children to starve the way my father did but what he did was bad because he's a priest and they're not supposed to murder people or interfere with them in any way.

And what he did makes me wonder if there are any other priests wandering the world going at people in hotel rooms.

There he is gazing at me with his big grey eyes, his face all scrubbed and shiny, with his black suit and his gleaming white collar, telling me he wanted to make this one stop before returning to Los Angeles forever. It's easy to see how pleased he is to be in a state of grace after his four months in the retreat house and I know now it's hard for me to eat a hamburger with someone in such a state of grace. It's hard to know what to do with my own eyes when he gazes at me as if I were the one who went at someone in a hotel room. I'd like to be able to look right back at him but all I know of priests is what I've seen of them on altars, pulpits, and in the darkness of confessionals. He's probably thinking I've been up to all kinds of sin and he's right but at least I'm not a priest and I never bothered anyone else.

He tells the waiter, Yes, a hamburger is fine and no, no, Lord no, he won't have a beer, water is fine, nothing alcoholic will ever cross his lips again, and he smiles at me as if I should understand what he's talking about and the waiter smiles, too, as if to say isn't this a saintly priest.

He tells me he went to confession to a bishop in Virginia and even though he received absolution and spent four months in work and prayer he feels it wasn't enough. He has given up his parish and he'll spend the rest of his days with the poor Mexicans and Negroes in Los Angeles. He calls for the bill, tells me he never wants to see me again, it's too painful, but he'll remember me in his Masses. He says I should be careful of the Irish curse, the drink, and whenever I'm tempted to sin I should meditate like him on the purity of the Virgin Mary, good luck, God bless, go to night school, and he's into a taxi to Idlewild Airport.

There are days the rain is so heavy I have to spend a dime on the subway and I see people my own age with books and bags that say Columbia, Fordham, NYU, City College, and I know I want to be one of them, a student.

I know I don't want to spend years in the Biltmore Hotel setting up banquets and meetings and I don't want to be the houseman cleaning up in the Palm Court. I don't even want to be a busboy getting a share of the waiters' tips which they get from the rich students who drink their gin and tonic, talk about Hemingway and where should they have dinner and should they go to Vanessa's party on Sutton Place, it was such a bore last year.

I don't want to be houseman where people look at me as if I were part of a wall.

I see the college students in the subway and I dream that some day I'll be like them, carrying my books, listening to professors, graduating with a cap and gown, going on to a job where I'll wear a suit and tie and carry a briefcase, go home on the train every night, kiss the wife, eat my dinner, play with the kids, read a book, have the excitement with the wife, go to sleep so that I'll be rested and fresh the next day.

I'd like to be a college student in the subway because you can see from the books they're carrying their heads must be stuffed with all kinds of knowledge, that they could sit down with you and chat forever about Shakespeare and Samuel Johnson and Dostoyevsky. If I could go to college I'd make sure to ride the subways and let people see my books so that they could admire me and wish they could go to college, too. I'd hold up the books to let people see I was reading *Crime and Punishment* by Fyodor Dostoyevsky. It must be grand to be a student with nothing to do but listen to professors, read in libraries, sit under campus trees and discuss what you're learning. It must be grand to know you'll be getting a degree that puts you ahead of the rest of the world, that you'll marry a girl with a degree and you'll be sitting up in bed the rest of your life having great chats about the important matters.

But I don't know how I'll ever get a college degree and rise in the world with no high school diploma and two eyes like piss holes in the snow, as everyone tells me. Some old Irishmen tell me there's nothing wrong with hard work. Many a man made his way in America by the sweat of his brow and his strong back and it's a good thing to learn your station in life and not be getting above yourself. They tell me that's why God put pride at the top of the Seven Deadly Sins so that young fellas like me won't be getting off the boat with big notions. There's plenty of work in this country for anyone who wants to earn an honest dollar with his two hands and the sweat of his brow and no getting above himself.

The Greek in the diner on Third Avenue tells me his cleaning-up Puerto Rican quit on him and would I like to work an hour every morning, come in at six, sweep out the place, mop it, clean out the toilets. I could have an egg, a roll, a cup of coffee and two dollars and, who knows, it might lead to something permanent. He says he likes the Irish, they're like the Greeks, and that's because they came from Greece a long time ago. That's what a professor at Hunter College told him though when I said this to Eddie Gilligan at the hotel he said the Greek and the professor were full of shit, that the Irish were always there on their little island since the beginning of time and what the hell do Greeks know anyway? If they knew anything they wouldn't be slinging hash in restaurants and babbling in their own language that no one understands.

I don't care where the Irish came from with the Greek feeding me every morning and paying me two dollars adding up to ten for the week, five for my mother and her shoes and five for me so that I can get proper clothes for myself and not look like Paddy-off-the-boat.

I'm lucky to have an extra few dollars a week especially after Tom Clifford knocked on my door at Mrs Austin's and said, Let's get the hell outa here. He says there's a huge room the size of an apartment for rent up on Third Avenue and Eighty-Sixth Street over a shop called Harry's Hats and if we shared the rent we'd still be paying six dollars a week and we wouldn't have Mrs Austin watching every move. We could bring in anything we liked, food, drink, girls.

Yeah, says Tom, girls.

The new room has a front and a back and looks out on Third Avenue where we can watch the El pass right before us. We wave at the passengers and discover they don't mind waving back in the evening on the way home from work though very few wave in the morning because of the bad mood they're in going to work.

Tom works on the night shift at an apartment building and that leaves me on my own in the room. It's the first time in my life I ever had the feeling of freedom, no bosses, no Mrs Austin telling me put out the light. I can walk around the neighborhood and look at the German shops, bars, cafes and all the Irish bars on Third Avenue. There are Irish dances at the Caravan, the Tuxedo, the Leitrim House, the Sligo House. Tom won't go to the Irish dances. He wants to meet German girls because of his three happy years in Germany and because he's able to speak German. He says the Irish can kiss his ass and I don't understand that because every time I hear Irish music I feel tears coming and I want to be standing on the banks of the Shannon looking at swans. It's easy for Tom to talk to German girls or Irish girls when he's in the mood but it's never easy for me to talk to anyone because I know they're looking at my eyes.

Tom had a better education in Ireland than I did and he could go to college if he liked. He says he'd rather make money, that's what America is there for. He tells me I'm a fool for breaking my ass working at the Biltmore Hotel when I could look around and find a job with a decent wage.

He's right. I hate working at the Biltmore Hotel and cleaning up for the Greek every morning. When I clean the toilet bowls I feel angry with myself because it reminds me of the time I had to empty the chamber pot of my mother's cousin, Laman Griffin, for a few pennies and the loan of his bike. And I wonder why I'm so particular about the toilet bowls, why I want them to be spotless when I could give them a swish of the mop and let them be. No, I have to use plenty of detergent and make them sparkle as if people were going to have their dinners out of them. The Greek is pleased though he gives me strange looks that say, Very nice but why? I could tell him this extra ten dollars a week and the morning food is a gift and I don't want to lose it. Then he wants to know what I'm doing here in the first place. I'm a nice Irish boy, I know English, I'm intelligent, and why am I cleaning toilet bowls and working in hotels when I could be getting an education. If he knew English he'd be in a university studying the wonderful history of Greece and Plato and Socrates and all the great Greek writers. He wouldn't be cleaning toilet bowls. Anyone who knows English should not be cleaning toilet bowls.

11

Tom dances with Emer, a girl at the Tuxedo Ballroom, who is there with her brother, Liam, and when Tom and Liam go for a drink she dances with me even though I don't know how. I like her because she's kind even when I step on her feet and when she presses my arm or my back to go in the right direction for fear of colliding with the men and women of Kerry, Cork, Mayo and other counties. I like her because she laughs easily even though I feel sometimes she's laughing at my awkward ways. I'm twenty years of age and I never in my life took a girl to a dance or a film or even a cup of tea and now I have to learn how to do it. I don't even know how to talk to girls because we never had one in the house except my mother. I don't know anything after growing up in Limerick and listening to priests on Sundays thundering against dancing and walking out the road with girls.

The music ends and Tom and Liam are over there at the bar laughing over something and I don't know what to say or do with Emer. Should I stand in the middle of the ballroom and wait for the next dance or should I lead her over to Liam and Tom? If I stand here I'll have to talk to her and I don't know what to talk about and if I start walking her towards Tom and Liam she'll think I don't want to be with her and that would be the worst thing in the world because I do want to be with her and I'm so nervous over the state I'm in my heart is going like a machine gun and I can barely breathe and I wish Tom would come and cut in so that I could laugh with Liam though I don't want Tom to cut in since I want to be with Emer but he doesn't anyway and there I am with the music starting again, a jitterbug or something, where men throw girls around the room and up in the air, the kind of dancing I could never dream of doing when I'm so ignorant I can barely put one foot before the other and now I have to put my hands somewhere on Emer for the jitterbug and I don't know where till she takes my hand and leads me to where Tom and Liam are laughing with Liam telling me a few more nights in the Tuxedo and I'll be a regular Fred Astaire and they all laugh because they know that could never be true and when they laugh I blush because Emer is looking at me in a way that shows she knows more than what Liam is talking about or that she even knows about my heart beating and making me short of breath.

I don't know what to do without the high school diploma. I drag on from day to day not knowing how to escape till a small war breaks out in Korea and I'm told if it gets any bigger I'll be drafted into the US Army. Eddie Gilligan says, Not a chance. Army's gonna take a look at your scabby eyes and send you home to your momma.

But the Chinese jump into the war and there's a letter from the government that says, Greetings. I'm to report to Whitehall Street to see if I'm fit to fight the Chinese and the Koreans. Tom Clifford says if I don't want to go I should rub salt on my eyes to make them raw and I should moan when the doctor examines them. Eddie Gilligan says I should complain of headaches and pain and if they have me read from a chart to give them all the wrong letters. He says I shouldn't be a fool. Why should I get my ass shot off by a bunch of gooks when I could stay here at the Biltmore and rise in the ranks. I could go to night school, get my eyes and teeth fixed, put on a little weight and in a few years I'd be like Mr Carey, all togged out in double-breasted suits.

I can't tell Eddie or Tom or anyone else how I'd like to get down on my two knees and thank Mao Tse-tung for sending his troops into Korea and liberating me from the Biltmore Hotel.

The army doctors at Whitehall Street don't look at my eyes at all. They tell me read that chart on the wall. They say OK. They look in my ears. Beep. Can you hear that? Fine. They look in my mouth. Jesus, they say. First thing you do is see the dentist. No one was ever rejected from this man's army for teeth and a good thing because most of the men who come in here have teeth like garbage dumps.

We're told to line up in a room and a sergeant comes in with a doctor and tells us, Awright, you guys, drop your socks and grab your cocks. Now milk 'em. And the doctor looks at us one by one to see if there's any discharge from our dongs. The sergeant barks at one man, You, what's your name?

Maldonado, sergeant.

Is that a hard-on I see there, Maldonado?

Ah, no, sergeant. I . . . a . . . I . . . a . . .

You gettin' excited, Maldonado?

I want to look at Maldonado but if you look anywhere but straight ahead the sergeant barks at you and wants to know what the hell you're looking at, who told you to look, buncha goddam fairies. Then he tells us turn around, bend over, spread 'em, I mean spread your cheeks. And the doctor sits on a chair and we have to back up with our arses open for inspection.

We're lined up outside the cubicle of a psychiatrist. He asks me if I like girls and I blush because that's a silly question and I say, I do, sir.

Then why are you blushing?

I don't know, sir.

But you prefer girls to boys?

Yes, sir.

OK, move on.

We're sent to Camp Kilmer, New Jersey, for orientation and indoctrination, uniforms and equipment, and haircuts that leave us bald. We're told we're no-good sorry pieces of shit, the worst set of recruits and draftees ever to come into this camp, a disgrace to Uncle Sam, lumps of meat for Chinese bayonets, nothing but cannon fodder and don't you forget it for one minute you lazy ass-dragging gang of dropouts. We're told straighten up and fly right, chin in, chest out, shoulders back, suck in that belly, goddamit, boy, this is the army not a goddam beauty parlor, oh girls, you step so pretty, whaddya doin' Sattaday night?

I'm sent to Fort Dix, New Jersey, for sixteen weeks of basic infantry training and we're told once again and every day we're no good hup ho hup ho hup hup hup ho, get in line there, soldier, goddamit, kills me to call you soldier, goddam pimple on the ass of the army, get in line or you'll get a corporal's boot up your fat ass, hup ho, hup ho, come on come on sing it sound off.

I got a gal in Jersey City
She got gumboils on her titty.
Sound off, cadence count,
Sound off, cadence count,
One two three four
One two three four.

This is your rifle, ya listenin' to me, your rifle, not your goddam gun, call this a gun and I'll ram it up your ass, your rifle, soldier, your piece, got that? This is your rifle, your M1, your piece, your girlfriend the rest of your army life. This is what you sleep with. This is what comes between you and the goddam gooks and goddam Chinks. Got that? You hold this goddam piece the way you hold a woman, no, tighter'n a woman. Drop this and your ass is in a sling. Drop this piece and you're in the goddam stockade. A dropped rifle is a rifle that can go off, blow off somebody's ass. That happens, girls, and you're dead, you're fuckin' dead.

The men who drill and train us are draftees and recruits themselves, a few months ahead of us. They're known as training cadre and we have to call them corporals even if they're privates like us. They yell at us as if they hate us and if you ever talk back you're in trouble. They tell us, Your ass is in a sling, soldier. We got your balls and we're ready to squeeze.

There are men in my platoon who had fathers and brothers in World War Two and know everything about the army. They say you can't be a good soldier till the army breaks you down and builds you up again. You come into this man's army with all kinds of smartass ideas, think you're big shit, but the army's been around a long time, all the way back to Julius fuckin' Caesar and knows how to deal with shitass recruits with attitude. Even if you come in all gung-ho the army will knock that outa you. Gung-ho or negative all means shit to the army because the army will tell you what to think, army will tell you what to feel, army will tell you what to do, army will tell you when to shit, piss, fart, squeeze your fuckin' pimples and if you don't like it write to your Congressman, go ahead, and when we hear about that we will kick your little white ass from one end of Fort Dix to the fuckin' other so that you'll be cryin' for your momma, your sister, your girlfriend and the whore on the next street.

Before lights out I lie on my bunk and listen to the talk about girls, families, Mom's home cooking, what Dad did in the war, high school proms where everyone got laid, what we're gonna do when we get out of the goddam army, how we can't wait till we get to Debbie or Sue or Cathy and how we're gonna screw ourselves blue, shit, man, I won't wear my goddam clothes for a month, get into that goddam bed with my girl, my brother's girl, any girl, and I won't come up for air, and when I get discharged, get me a job, start a business, live out on Long Island, come home every night an' tell the wife, drop them panties, babe, I'm ready for action, have kids, yeah.

Awright, you guys, shut your miserable asses, lights out, not a goddam sound or I'll have you on KP quicker'n a whore's fart.

And when the corporal leaves it starts again, the talk, oh, that first weekend pass after five weeks of basic training, into the city, into Debbie, Sue, Cathy, anyone.

I wish I could say something like I'm going into New York on my first weekend pass to get laid. I wish I could say something that would make everyone smile, even nod their heads to show I'm one of them. But I know if I open my mouth they'll say, Yeah, get a load of the Irishman talking about girls, or one of them, Thompson, will start singing, "When Irish Eyes are Smiling", and they'll all laugh because they know my eyes.

In a way I don't mind because I can lie here on the bunk all clean and comfortable after the evening shower, tired from the day of marching and running with my sixty-pound backpack the corporals say is heavier than the packs carried in the French Foreign Legion, a day of training in weapons, taking them apart, reassembling, firing on ranges, crawling under barbed wire with machine guns clattering over my head, climbing ropes, trees, walls, charging at bags with fixed bayonets and screaming, fuckin' gook, the way the corporals tell me, wrestling in woods with men from other companies wearing blue helmets to show they're the enemy, running up hills with fifty-caliber machine gun barrels over my shoulder, scrambling through mud, swimming with my sixty-pound backpack, sleeping all night in the woods with backpack for pillow and mosquitoes feasting on my face.

When we're not out in the field we're in large rooms listening to lectures on how dangerous and sneaky the Koreans are, the North Koreans, and the Chinese who are even worse. The whole world knows what sneaky bastards the Chinks are and if there's anyone in this outfit who's Chinese tough shit but that's the way it is, my father was German, men, and he had to put up with a lotta shit during World War Two when sauerkraut was liberty cabbage, that's the way it was. This is war, men, and when I look at you specimens my heart sinks thinking of the future of America.

There are films about what a glorious army this is, the US Army, that fought the English, the French, the Indians, the Mexicans, the Spanish, the Germans, the Japs, and now the goddam gooks and Chinks, and never lost a war, never. Remember that, men, never lost a goddam war.

There are films about weapons and tactics and syphilis. The one about syphilis is called *The Silver Bullet* and shows men losing their voices and dying and telling the world how sorry they are, how foolish they were to go with diseased women in foreign places and now their penises are falling off and there's nothing they can do about it but ask God's forgiveness and the forgiveness of their families back home, Mom and Dad sipping lemonade on the porch, Sis laughing on a backyard swing pushed by Chuck the quarterback home from college.

The men in my platoon lie on their bunks and talk about *The Silver Bullet*. Thompson says that was a stupid fuckin' movie, you'd have to be a real horse's ass to get syphed up like that and what the hell do we have rubbers for, right, Di Angelo, you went to college?

Di Angelo says you have to be careful.

Thompson says, What the hell do you know, goddam spaghetti-eating guinea?

Di Angelo says, Say that again, Thompson, and I'll have to ask you to step outside.

Thompson laughs, Yeah, yeah.

Go ahead, Thompson, say it again.

Nah, you probably got a knife there. All you guineas got knives.

No knife, Thompson, just me.

Don't trust you, Di Angelo.

No knife, Thompson.

Yeah.

The whole platoon is quiet and I wonder why people like

Thompson have to talk to other people like that. It shows you're always something else in this country. You can't just be an American.

There's an old regular army corporal, Dunphy, who works in weapons, issuing and repairing, and smelling always of whiskey. Everyone knows he should have been kicked out of the army long ago but Master Sergeant Tole takes care of him. Tole is a huge black man with a belly so great it takes two cartridge belts to go around him. He's so fat he can't go anywhere without a jeep and he roars at us all the time that he can't stand the sight of us, we're the laziest lumps it has ever been his misfortune to see. He tells us and the whole regiment that if anyone bothers Corporal Dunphy he'll break their backs with his bare hands, that the corporal was killing Krauts at Monte Cassino when we were just starting to beat our meat.

The corporal sees me one night pushing a cleaning rod up and down in my rifle barrel. He snatches the rifle from me and tells me follow him to the latrine. He breaks down the rifle and plunges the barrel into hot soapy water and I want to tell him how we were warned by all the cadre corporals never never use water on your piece, use linseed oil, because water causes rust and the next thing is your piece is rotting and jamming in your hands and how the hell are you gonna defend yourself against a million Chinks swarming over a mountain.

The corporal says, Bullshit, dries the barrel with a rag on the end of the cleaning rod and peers down the barrel to the reflection of his thumbnail. He hands the barrel to me and I'm dazzled by the shine inside and I don't know what to say to him. I don't know why he's helping me and all I can say is, Thanks, corporal. He tells me I'm a nice kid and not only that he's going to let me read his favorite book.

It's *The Young Manhood of Studs Lonigan* by James T. Farrell, a paperback, falling apart. The corporal tells me I'm to guard this book with my life, that he reads it all the time, that James T. Farrell is the greatest writer that ever lived in the USA, a writer that understands you an' me, kid, not like those blue-ass bullshit artists they have in New England. He says I can have this book till I finish basic training and then I have to get my own copy.

Next day is colonel's inspection and we're confined to barracks after chow time to clean and scrub and shine. Before lights out we have to stand by our bunks for closer inspection by Master Sergeant Tole and two regular army sergeants who stick their noses into everything. If they find anything wrong we have to do fifty push-ups with Tole resting his foot on our backs and humming "Swing Low, Sweet Chariot, comin' for to carry me home".

The colonel doesn't check every rifle but when he looks down my barrel he steps back, stares at me, and says to Sergeant Tole, This is a hell of a clean rifle, sergeant and asks me, Who's the Vice-President of the United States, soldier?

Alben Barkley, sir.

Good. Name the city where the second atomic bomb was dropped.

Nagasaki, sir.

OK, sergeant, this is our man. And that's a hell of a clean rifle, soldier.

After formation a corporal tells me I'm to be colonel's orderly next day, all day, riding in his car with the driver, opening his door, saluting, closing the door, waiting, saluting, opening the door again, saluting, closing the door.

And if I'm a good colonel's orderly and don't fuck up I'll get a three-day pass next week, Friday night to Monday night, and I can go to New York and get laid. The corporal says there's isn't a man in Fort Dix who wouldn't pay fifty dollars to be colonel's orderly and they don't know why the hell I got it just for having a clean rifle barrel. Where the hell did I learn to clean a rifle like that?

In the morning the colonel has two long meetings and I have nothing to do but sit with and listen to his driver, Corporal Wade Hansen, complaining about the way the Vatican is taking over the world and if there's ever a Catholic President in this country he'll emigrate to Finland where they keep Catholics in their place. He's from Maine and he's a Congregationalist and proud of it and doesn't hold with foreign religions. His second cousin married a Catholic and she had to move out of the state to Boston which is crawling with Catholics all leaving their money to the Pope and those cardinals who like little boys.

It's a short day with the colonel because he gets drunk at lunch and dismisses us. Hansen drives him to his quarters and then tells me get out of the car, he wants no fish heads in his car. He's a corporal and I don't know what to say to him but even if he were a private I wouldn't know what to say because it's hard to understand people when they talk like that.

It's only two o'clock and I'm free till chow time at five so I can go to the PX and read magazines, listen to Tony Bennett on the juke box singing "Because of you there's a song in my heart", and I can dream about my three-day pass and seeing Emer, the girl in New York, and how we'll go out to dinner and a movie and maybe an Irish dance where she'll have to teach me the steps and it's a lovely dream because the weekend of my three-day pass is my birthday and I'll be twenty-one.

12

The Friday of my three-day pass I have to stand on line outside the orderly room with men waiting for ordinary weekend passes. A cadre corporal, Sneed, whose real name is a Polish name no one can pronounce, tells me, Hey, soldier, pick up that butt.

Oh, I don't smoke, Corporal.

I didn't ask you if you fuckin' smoked. Pick up that butt.

Howie Abramowitz nudges me and whispers, Don't be an asshole. Pick up the fuckin' butt.

Sneed has his hands on his hips. Well?

I didn't drop the butt, Corporal. I don't smoke.

OK, soldier, come with me.

I follow him into the orderly room and he picks up my pass. Now, he says, we're going to your barracks and you're changing into fatigues.

But, Corporal, I have a three-day pass. I was colonel's orderly.

I don't give a shit if you wiped the colonel's ass. Get into your fatigues and on the double and get your entrenching tool.

It's my birthday, Corporal.

On the double, soldier, or I'll have you in the fuckin' stockade.

He marches me past the men waiting on line. He waves my pass at them and tells them say bye bye to my pass and they laugh and wave because there's nothing else to do and they don't want to get into trouble. Only Howie Abramowitz shakes his head as if to say he's sorry over what's happening.

Sneed marches me across the parade ground and into a clearing in the woods beyond. OK, asshole, dig.

Dig?

Yeah, dig me a nice hole three feet deep, two feet wide, and the faster you do it the better for you.

That must mean the sooner I finish this the sooner I can take my pass and go. Or is it something else? Everyone in the company knows Sneed is bitter because he was a big football star at Bucknell University and wanted to play for the Philadelphia Eagles only the Eagles wouldn't have him and now he goes around making people dig holes. It's unfair. I know men have been forced to dig holes and bury their passes and dig them up again and I don't know why I should have to do that. I keep telling myself I wouldn't mind if this were an ordinary weekend pass but this is a three-day pass and it's my birthday and why do I have to do this? But there's nothing I can do about it. I might as well dig as fast as I can and bury the pass and dig it up again.

And while I'm digging I'm dreaming that what I'd really like to do is wrap my little shovel around Sneed's head and smash him till his head is raw and bloody and I wouldn't mind one bit digging a hole for his big fat football body. That's what I'd like to do.

He hands me the pass to bury and when I finish shoveling in the earth he tells me pat it with my entrenching tool. Make it nice, he says.

I don't know why he wants me to make it nice when I'll be digging it up in a minute but now he tells me, 'Bout face, forrard harch, and he marches me back the way we came, past the orderly room where the line of men waiting for passes is gone, and I'm wondering if he's had enough satisfaction for the day so that he might march inside for a replacement pass but, no, he keeps me going right to the mess hall and tells the sergeant there I'm a candidate for KP, that I need a little lesson in obeying orders. They have a good laugh over that and the sergeant says they must have a drink together sometime and talk about the Philadelphia Eagles, isn't that some goddam team. The sergeant calls over another man, Henderson, to show me my job, the worst job you can get in any mess hall, pots and pans.

Henderson tells me scrub those mothers till they shine because there's constant inspection and one spot of grease on any utensil will get me another hour of KP and at that rate I could be here till the gooks and Chinese are long gone home to their families.

It's dinner time and the pots and pans are piled high around the sinks. Garbage cans lined up against the wall behind me are alive with the feasting flies of New Jersey. Mosquitoes buzz in through open windows and feast on me. Everywhere there is steam and smoke from gas burners and ovens and running hot water and I'm sodden with sweat and grease in no time. Corporals and sergeants pass through and run their fingers around the pots and pans and tell me do them over and I know that's because Sneed is out in the mess hall telling football stories and telling them how they can have a little fun with the draftee on pots and pans.

When it grows quieter in the mess hall and the work slows the sergeant tells me I'm free for the night but I'm to report back here tomorrow morning, Saturday, 0600 hours and he means 0600. I want to tell him I'm supposed to have a three-day pass for being colonel's orderly, that tomorrow is my birthday, that there's a girl waiting for me in New York, but I know now it's better to say nothing because every time I open my mouth things get worse. I know what the army means: Tell 'em nothing but your name, rank and serial number.

Emer cries on the phone, Oh, Frank, where are you now?

I'm in the PX.

What is the PX?

Post Exchange. It's where we buy things and make phone calls.

And why aren't you here? We have a little cake and everything.

I'm on KP, pots, pans, tonight, tomorrow, maybe Sunday.

What is that? What are you talking about? Are you all right?

I'm worn out from digging holes and washing pots and pans.

Why?

I didn't pick up a butt.

Why didn't you pick up a butt?

Because I don't smoke. You know I don't smoke.

But why would you have to pick up a butt?

Because a fucking corporal, excuse me, a cadre corporal who was rejected by the Philadelphia Eagles told me pick up the butt and I told him I didn't smoke and that's why I'm here when I should be with you on my fucking, excuse me, birthday.

Frank, I know it's your birthday. Are you drinking?

No, I'm not drinking. How could I be drinking and digging holes and doing KP all at the same time?

But why were you digging holes?

Because they made me bury my damn pass.

Oh, Frank. When will I see you?

I don't know. You may never see me. They say every grease spot I leave on a pot gets me another hour of KP and I could be here till I'm discharged washing pots and pans.

My mother is saying couldn't you see a priest or something, a chaplain?

I don't want to see a priest. They're worse than corporals the way they . . .

The way they what?

Oh, nothing.

Oh, Frank.

Oh, Emer.

Saturday dinner is cold cuts and potato salad and the cooks are easy on the pots and pans. At six the sergeant tells me I'm finished and I don't have to report on Sunday morning. He shouldn't be saying this, he says, but that Sneed is a goddam Polack prick that no one likes and you can see why the Philadelphia Eagles didn't want him. The sergeant says he's sorry but there was nothing he could do about putting me on KP when I disobeyed a direct order. Yeah, he knew I was colonel's orderly and all but this is the army and the best policy for a draftee like me is a shut mouth. Tell them nothing but your name, rank and serial number. Do what you're told, keep your mouth shut especially when you have a brogue that stands out, and if you do that you'll see your girlfriend again with your balls intact.

Thank you, sergeant.

OK, kid.

The company area is deserted except for men in the orderly room and men confined to barracks.

Di Angelo is lying on his bunk confined to barracks because of the way he spoke up after they showed a film on how poor everyone is in China. He said Mao Tse-tung and the Communists would save China and the lieutenant showing the film said communism is evil, godless, unAmerican, and Di Angelo said capitalism was evil, godless

75

and unAmerican and he wouldn't give two cents for isms anyway because people with isms cause all the troubles in the world and you may have noticed there is no ism in democracy. The lieutenant told him he was out of order and Di Angelo said this is a free country and that got him confined to barracks and no weekend pass for three weeks.

He's on his bunk reading the copy of *The Young Manhood of Studs Lonigan* Corporal Dunphy loaned me and when he sees me he says he borrowed it from top of my locker and who, for God's sakes, dipped me in a grease pit. He says he did KP like that one weekend and Dunphy told him how to get the grease off the fatigues. What I should do now is stand in a hot shower in my fatigues, hot as I can bear it, and scrub off the grease with a scrubbing brush and a bar of the carbolic soap they use for cleaning lavatories.

While I'm in the shower scrubbing Dunphy sticks his head in and wants to know what I'm doing and when I tell him he says he used to do that, too, only he'd bring in his rifle and do everything at one time. When he was a kid first time in the army he had the cleanest fatigues and rifle in his outfit and if it wasn't for the goddam booze he'd be Top Sergeant by now and ready to retire. Speaking of booze, he's heading to the PX for a beer and would I like to come along after getting out of my soapy fatigues, of course.

I'd like to ask Di Angelo along but he's confined to barracks for praising the Chinese Communists. While I'm changing into khakis I tell him how much I owe Mao Tse-tung for attacking Korea and liberating me from the Palm Court at the Biltmore Hotel and he says I'd better be careful what I say or I'll wind up like him, confined to barracks.

Dunphy calls from the end of the barracks, Come on, kid, come on, I'm gasping for a beer. In a way I'd rather stay and talk to Di Angelo, he has such a gentle way about him, but Dunphy helped me become colonel's orderly, for all the good it did me, and he might need the company. If I were a regular army corporal I wouldn't be hanging around the base on a Saturday night but I know there are people like Dunphy who drink and have no one, no home to go to. Now he drinks beer so fast I could never keep up with him. I'd be sick if I tried. He drinks and smokes and points at the sky all the time with the middle finger of his right hand. He tells me the army is a great life especially in peacetime. You're never lonely unless you're some kind of asshole like Sneed, the goddam football player, and if you get married and have kids the army will take care of everything. All you have to do is keep yourself fit to fight. Yeah, yeah, he knows he's not keeping himself fit but he carries so much Kraut shrapnel in his body he could be sold for scrap metal and the drink is the only pleasure he has. He had a wife, two kids, all gone. Indiana, that's where they went, back to his wife's daddy and mom, and who the hell wants to go to Indiana. He takes pictures from his wallet, the wife, the two girls, and holds them up for me to see. I'm ready to tell him how lovely they are but he starts to cry so hard it brings on a cough and I have to clap him on the back to save him from choking. OK, he says, OK. Goddam, it gets to me every time I look at them. Look what I lost, kid. I could have them waiting for me in a little house near Fort Dix. I could be home with Monica making dinner, me with my feet up, taking a little nap in my Top Sergeant's uniform. OK, kid, let's go. Let's get outa here and see if I can straighten out my shit and go to Indiana.

Halfway to the barracks he changes his mind and goes back for more beer and I know from this he'll never get to Indiana. He's like my father and when I'm in my bunk I wonder if my father remembered the twenty-first birthday of his oldest son, if he raised his glass to me in a pub in Coventry.

I doubt it. My father is like Dunphy who will never see Indiana.

13

It's a surprise on Sunday morning when Di Angelo asks me if I'd like to go to Mass with him, a surprise because you'd think that people who sing the praises of Chinese Communists would never step into church, chapel, nor synagogue. On the way to the base chapel he explains the way he feels, that the Church belongs to him, he doesn't belong to the Church, and he doesn't agree with the way the Church acts like a big corporation declaring they own God and it's their right to dole Him out in little bits and pieces as long as people do what they're told by Rome. He sins every week himself by receiving Communion without first confessing his sins to a priest. He says his sins are nobody's business but his and God's and that's who he confesses to every Saturday night before he falls asleep.

He talks about God as if He were in the next room having a pint and smoking a cigarette. I know if I went back to Limerick and talked like that I'd be hit on the head and thrown on the next train to Dublin.

We might be on an army base with barracks all around us but inside the chapel it's pure America. There are officers with their wives and children and they have the clean scrubbed look that comes from shower and shampoo and a constant state of grace. They have the look of people from Maine or California, small towns, church on Sundays, leg of lamb afterwards, peas, mashed potatoes, apple pie, iced tea, Dad snoozing with the big Sunday paper dropped to the floor, kids reading comics, Mom in the kitchen washing dishes and humming "Oh, what a beautiful morning". They have the look of people who brush their teeth after every meal and fly the flag on the Fourth. They might be Catholics but I don't think they'd feel comfortable in Irish or Italian churches where there might be old men and women mumbling and snuffling, a suspicion of whiskey or wine in the air, a whiff of bodies untouched for weeks by soap and water.

I'd like to be part of an American family, to sidle up to a blonde blue-eyed teenage daughter of an officer and whisper I'm not what I seem. I might have pimples and bad teeth and fire alarm eyes but, underneath, I'm just like them, a well-scrubbed soul dreaming of a house in a suburb with a tidy lawn where our child, little Frank, pushes his tricycle and all I want is a read of the Sunday paper like a real American dad and maybe I'd wash and clean our spanking new Buick before we drive over to visit Mom's grandpa and grandma and rock on their porch with glasses of iced tea.

The priest is mumbling away on the altar and when I whisper the Latin responses Di Angelo nudges me and wants to know if I'm all right, if I'm hung over from my beer night with Dunphy. I wish I could be like Di Angelo, making up my own mind about everything, not giving a fiddler's fart like my Uncle Pa Keating back in Limerick. I know Di Angelo would laugh if I told him I'm so steeped in sin I'm afraid to go to confession for fear of being told I'm so far gone that only a bishop or a cardinal could give me absolution. He'd laugh if I told him that some nights I'm afraid to fall asleep in case I die and go to hell. How could hell be invented by a God who's in the next room with a beer and a cigarette?

This is when the dark clouds flutter like bats in my head and I wish I could open a window and release them.

Now the priest is asking for volunteers to pick up baskets from the back of the chapel and make the collection. Di Angelo gives me a little push and we're out in the aisle genuflecting and sending the baskets along the pews. Officers and non-coms with families always hand their contributions to their children to drop in the basket and that makes everyone smile, the little one is so proud and the parents are so proud of the little one. Officers' wives and non-coms' wives smile at each other as if to say, We're all one under the roof of the Catholic Church, though you know once they're outside they know they're different.

The basket goes from pew to pew till it's taken by a sergeant who will count the money and pass it on to the chaplain. Di Angelo whispers he knows this sergeant and when the money is counted it's two for you and one for me.

I tell Di Angelo I'm not going to Mass anymore. What's the use when I'm in such a state of sin for impurity and everything else? I can't be in the chapel with all those clean American families and their state of grace. I'll wait till I get the courage to go to confession and Communion and if I keep committing mortal sins by not going to Mass it won't matter since I'm doomed anyway. One mortal sin will get you into hell just as easily as ten mortal sins.

Di Angelo tells me I'm full of shit. He says I should go to Mass if I want to, that the priests don't own the Church.

I can't think like Di Angelo, not yet. I'm afraid of the priests and the nuns and the bishops and the cardinals and the Pope. I'm afraid of God.

Monday morning I'm told report to Master Sergeant Tole in his room at Company B. He's sitting in an armchair and sweating so much his khaki uniform is dark. I want to ask him about the book on the table next to him, *Notes from the Underground* by Dostoyevsky, and I'd like to tell him about Raskolnikov but you have to be careful what you say to master sergeants and the army in general. Say the wrong thing and you're back with the pots and pans.

He tells me stand easy and wants to know why I disobeyed a direct order and who the hell do I think I am defying a superior non-com even if he is training cadre, eh?

I don't know what to say because he knows everything and I'm afraid if I open my mouth I might be shipped to Korea tomorrow. He says Corporal Sneed or whatever the hell his Polish name is had every right to discipline me but he went too far especially when it was a three-day pass for the colonel's orderly. I'm entitled to that pass and if I still want it he'll arrange it for the coming weekend.

Thanks, sergeant.

OK. Dismissed.

Sergeant?

Yeah?

I read *Crime and Punishment*.

Oh, yeah? Well, I could have guessed you're not as dumb as you look. Dismissed.

In our fourteenth week of basic training there are rumors we're being shipped to Europe. In the fifteenth week the rumors say we're going to Korea. In the sixteenth week we're told we're definitely going to Europe.

14

We're shipped to Hamburg and from there to Sonthofen, a replacement depot in Bavaria. My outfit from Fort Dix is broken up and sent all over the European Command. I'm hoping they'll send me to England so that I can travel easily to Ireland. Instead they send me to a caserne in Lenggries, a small Bavarian village, where I'm assigned to dog training, the canine corps. I tell the captain I don't like dogs, they chewed my ankles to bits when I delivered telegrams in Limerick, but the captain says, Who asked you? He turns me over to a corporal chopping up great slabs of bloody red meat who tells me, Stop whining, fill that goddam tin plate with meat, get in that cage and feed your animal. Put the plate down and get your hand outa the way case your animal thinks it's his dinner.

I have to stay in the cage and watch my dog eating. The corporal calls this familiarization. He says, This animal will be your wife while you're on this base, well, not your wife exactly, because it's not a bitch, you know what I mean. Your M1 rifle and your animal will be all you'll have for a family.

My dog is a black German shepherd and I don't like him. His name is Ivan and he's not like the other dogs, the shepherds and Dobermans, who howl at anything that moves. When he's finished eating he looks at me, licks his lips and backs away, baring his teeth. The corporal is outside the cage telling me that's a hell of a goddam dog I have there, doesn't howl and make a lotta bullshit noise, the kinda dog you want in combat when one bark will get you killed. He tells me bend slowly, pick up the plate, tell my dog he's a good dog, good Ivan, nice Ivan, see you in the morning, honey, back out nice and easy, close the gate, drop that lock, get your hand outa the way. He tells me I did OK. He can see Ivan and I are already asshole buddies.

Every morning at eight I turn out with a platoon of dog handlers from all over Europe. We march in a circle with the corporal in the middle calling hup ho hup ho hup hup hup ho heel, and when we yank on the dogs' leashes we're glad they're growling behind muzzles.

For six weeks we march and run with the dogs. We climb the mountains behind Lenggries and race along the banks of rivers. We feed and groom them till we're ready to remove their muzzles. We're told this is the big day, like graduation or marriage.

And then the company commander sends for me. His company clerk, Corporal George Shemanski, is going stateside on furlough in three months and they're sending me to company clerk school for six weeks so that I can replace him. Dismissed.

I don't want to go to company clerk school. I want to stay with Ivan. Six weeks together and we're pals. I know when he growls at me he's just telling me he loves me though he still has a head of teeth in case I displease him. I love Ivan and I'm ready to remove his muzzle. No one else can remove his muzzle without losing a hand. I want to take him on maneuvers with the Seventh Army in Stuttgart where I'll dig a hole in the snow and we'll be warm and comfortable. I want to see what it would be like to turn him loose on a soldier pretending to be Russian and watch Ivan tear his protective clothing to bits before I bring him to heel. Or watch him lunge for the crotch and not the throat when I swing a dummy Russian at him. They can't send me to company clerk school for six weeks and let someone else handle Ivan. Everyone knows it's one man, one dog, and it takes months to break in another handler.

I don't know why they have to pick me for company clerk school when I never even went to high school and the base is filled with high school graduates. It makes me wonder if company clerk school is punishment for never going to high school.

My head is filled with dark clouds and I wish I could bang it against the wall. The only word in my head is fuck and that's a word

I hate because it means hate. I'd like to kill the company commander, and now here's this second lieutenant barking at me because I passed him without saluting.

Soldier, get over here. What do you do when you see an officer?

Salute him, sir.

And?

I'm sorry, sir. I didn't see you.

Didn't see me? Didn't see me? You'd go to Korea and claim you didn't see the gooks coming over the hill? Right, soldier?

I don't know what to say to this lieutenant who's my age and trying to grow a moustache with sad ginger hair. I want to tell him they're sending me to company clerk school and isn't that enough punishment for not saluting a thousand second lieutenants? I want to tell him about my six weeks with Ivan and my troubles back in Fort Dix when I had to bury my pass but there are dark clouds and I know I should be quiet, tell 'em nothing but your name, rank, serial number. I know I should be quiet but I'd like to tell this second lieutenant fuck off, kiss my ass with your miserable ginger mustache.

He tells me report to him in fatigues at twenty-one hundred hours sharp and he makes me pull weeds on the parade ground while other dog handlers pass by on their way to a beer in Lenggries.

When I'm finished I go to Ivan's cage and remove his muzzle. I sit on the ground and talk to him and if he chews me to pieces I won't have to go to company clerk school. But he growls a bit and licks my face and I'm glad there's no one here to see how I feel.

Company clerk school is in the Lenggries caserne. We sit at desks while instructors come and go. We're told the company clerk is the single most important soldier in an outfit. Officers get killed or move on, non-coms too, but an outfit without a clerk is doomed. The company clerk is the one in combat who knows when the outfit is under strength, who's dead, who's wounded, who's missing, the one who takes over when the supply clerk gets his fuckin' head blown off. The company clerk, men, is the one who delivers your mail when the mail clerk gets a bullet up his ass, the one who keeps you in touch with the folks back home.

After we've learned how important we are we learn to type. We have to type up a model of a daily attendance report with five carbon copies and if one mistake is made, one little stroke too much, an error in addition, a strikeover, the whole thing is to be retyped.

No erasures, goddamit. This is the United States Army and we don't allow erasures. Allow erasures on a report and you invite sloppiness all along the front. We're holding the line against the goddam Reds here, men. Can't have sloppiness. Perfection, men, perfection. Now type, goddamit.

The clatter and rattle of thirty typewriters makes the room sound like a combat zone with howls from soldier/typists hitting wrong keys and having to tear reports from machines and start all over. We punch our heads and shake our fists at heaven and tell the instructors we were almost finished, couldn't we please, please erase this one little goddam mark.

No erasures, soldier, and watch your language. I have my mother's picture in my pocket.

At the end of the course they give me a certificate with a rating of Excellent. The captain handing out the certificates says he's proud of us and they're proud of us all the way up to the Supreme Commander in Europe, Dwight D. Eisenhower himself. The Captain is proud to say that only nine men washed out in the course and the twenty-one of us who passed are a credit to the folks back home. He hands us our certificates and chocolate chip cookies baked by his wife and two small daughters and we have permission to eat our cookies right here and now this being a special occasion. Behind me men are cursing and mumbling these cookies taste like cat shit and the Captain smiles and gets ready to make another speech till a major whispers to him and what I hear later is that the major told him, Shaddap, you been drinking, and that's true because the Captain has the kind of face that never turned away from a whiskey bottle.

If Shemanski hadn't been granted a furlough I'd still be up in the kennels with Ivan or down in a *bierstube* in Lenggries with the other dog handlers. Now I have to spend a week watching him by his desk in the orderly room typing reports and letters and telling me I should be thanking him for getting me away from dogs and into a good job that might be useful in civilian life. He says I should be happy I learned to type, I might write another *Gone With the Wind* some day, ha ha ha.

The night before his furlough there's a party in a Lenggries beer hall. It's Friday night and I have a weekend pass. Shemanski has to return to the caserne because his furlough doesn't start till tomorrow and when he leaves his girlfriend, Ruth, asks me where I'm staying on my weekend pass. She tells me come to her place for a beer, Shemanski won't be there, but the minute we're in the door we're in the bed going wild with ourselves. Oh, Mac, she says, oh, Mac, you're so young. She's old herself, thirty-one, but you'd never know it the way she carries on depriving me of any sleep and if this is the way she is with Shemanski all the time it's no wonder he needs a long furlough in the USA. Then it's dawn and there's a knock on the door downstairs and when she peeks out the window she lets out a little squeal, Oh, *mein Gott*, it's Shemanski, go, go, go. I jump up and dress as fast as I can but there's a problem when I put on my boots and then try to pull my pants over them and the legs are stuck and entangled and Ruth is hissing and squealing, Out ze window, oh, pliss, oh, pliss. I can't leave by the front door with Shemanski standing there banging away, he'd surely kill me, so it's out the window into three feet of snow which saves my life and I know Ruth is up there shutting the window and pulling the curtain so that Shemanski won't see me trying to get my boots off so that I can slip on my pants, then boots again, so cold my dong is the size of a button, with snow everywhere, halfway up my belly, in my pants, filling my boots.

Now I have to sneak away from Ruth's house and into Lenggries looking for hot coffee in a cafe where I can dry out but nothing is open yet and I wander back up to the caserne wondering, Did God put Shemanski on this earth to destroy me entirely?

Now that I'm company clerk I sit at Shemanski's desk and the worst part of the day is typing up the attendance report every morning. Master Sergeant Burdick sits at the other desk drinking coffee and telling me how important this report is, that they're waiting for it over at HQ so that they can add it to the other company reports that go to Stuttgart to Frankfurt to Eisenhower to Washington so that President Truman himself will know the strength of the United States Army in Europe in case of sudden attack by those goddam Russians who wouldn't hesitate if we were short a man, one man, McCourt. They're waiting, McCourt, so get that report done.

The thought of the world waiting for my report makes me so nervous I hit wrong keys and have to start all over. Every time I say, Shit, and pull the report from the typewriter. Sergeant Burdick's eyebrows shoot to his hairline. He drinks his coffee, looks at his watch, loses control of his eyebrows, and I feel so desperate I'm afraid I'll break down and weep. Burdick takes phone calls from HQ to say the colonel is waiting, the general, the Chief of Staff, the President. A messenger is sent to pick up the report. He waits by my desk and that makes it even worse and I wish I could be back in the Biltmore Hotel scouring toilets. When the report is finished without error he takes it away and Sergeant Burdick wipes his forehead with a green handkerchief. He tells me forget the other work, that I'm to stay at this desk all day and practice practice practice till I get these goddam reports down right. They're gonna be talking up at HQ and wondering what kind of asshole he is for taking on a clerk that can't even type a report. All the other clerks knock off that report in ten minutes and he doesn't want Company C to be the laughing stock of the caserne.

So, McCourt, you go nowheres till you type perfect reports. Start typing.

All day and night he drills me, handing me different numbers, telling me, You'll thank me for this.

And I do. In a few days I can type the reports so fast they send a lieutenant from HQ to see if these are made-up numbers done the night before. Sergeant Burdick says, No, no, I'm right on his case, and the lieutenant looks at me and tells him, We got corporal material here, sergeant.

The sergeant says, Yes, sir, and when he smiles his eyebrows are lively.

When Shemanski returns I expect to be re-assigned to Ivan but the captain tells me I'm staying on as clerk in charge of supplies. I'll be responsible for sheets, blankets, pillows and condoms which I'll distribute to dog handler trainees from all over the European Command making sure everything is returned when they're leaving, everything but the condoms, ha ha ha.

How can I tell the captain I don't want to be a clerk down in the basement where I have to requisition everything in language that is backwards, cases, pillow, white, or balls, Pong Ping, counting things and making lists when all I want to do is get back to Ivan and the dog handlers and drink beer and look for girls in Lenggries, Bad Tolz, Munich?

Sir, is there any chance I could be reassigned to the dogs?

No, McCourt. You're a damn fine clerk. Dismissed.

But, sir . . .

Dismissed, soldier.

There are so many dark clouds fluttering in my head I can barely make my way out of his office and when Shemanski laughs and says, He gave you the shaft, eh? Won't let you back to your bow wow? I tell him fuck off and I'm hauled back into the captain's office for a reprimand and told if this ever happens again I'll face a court martial that will make my army record look like Al Capone's arrest record. The captain barks that I'm a private first class now and if I behave myself and keep accurate accounts and control the condoms I could rise to corporal within six months and now get outa here, soldier.

In a week I'm in trouble again and it's because of my mother. When I came to Lenggries I went to the HQ offices to fill out an application for an allotment for my mother. The army would retain half my pay, match it, and send her a check every month.

Now I'm having a beer in Bad Tolz and Davis, the allotment clerk, is in the same room drunk on schnapps and when he calls to me, Hey, McCourt, too bad your mother is up shit creek, the dark clouds in my head are so blinding I throw my beer stein and lunge at him with every wish to strangle him till I'm pulled away by two sergeants and held for the MPs.

I'm locked up for the night in Bad Tolz and taken before a captain in the morning. He wants to know why I'm assaulting corporals who are drinking a beer and minding their own business and when I tell him about the insult to my mother he asks, Who's the allotment clerk?

Corporal Davis, sir.

And you, McCourt, where you from?

New York, sir.

No, no. I mean, where you really from?

Ireland, sir.

Goddam it. I know that. You've got the map on your face. What part?

Limerick, sir.

Oh, yeah? My parents are from Kerry and Sligo. It's a pretty country but it's poor, right?

Yes, sir.

OK, send in Davis.

Davis comes in and the captain turns to the man beside him who is taking notes. Jackson, this is off the record. Now, Davis, you said something about this man's mother in public?

I . . . only . . .

You said something of a confidential nature about the lady's financial problems?

Well . . . sir . . .

Davis, you're a prick and I could send you for a company court martial but I'll just say you had a few beers and your jaw flapped.

Thank you, sir.

And if I ever hear of you making comments like that again I'll ram a cactus up your ass. Dismissed.

When Davis leaves the captain says, The Irish, McCourt. We gotta stick together. Right?

Yes, sir.

In the hallway Davis puts out his hand. Sorry about that, McCourt. I should know better. My mother gets the allotment, too, and she's Irish. I mean, her parents were Irish so that makes me half Irish.

This is the first time in my life anyone ever apologized to me and all I can do is mumble and turn red and shake Davis' hand because I don't know what to say. And I don't know what to say to people who smile and tell me their mothers and fathers and grandparents are Irish. One day they're insulting your mother, the next day they're bragging their own mothers are Irish. Why is it the minute I open my mouth the whole world is telling me they're Irish and we should all have a drink? It's not enough to be American. You always have to be something else, Irish-American, German-American, and you'd wonder how they'd get along if someone hadn't invented the hyphen.

15

When they made me supply clerk the captain didn't tell me that twice a month on Tuesdays I'd have to bundle company bedding and take it by truck to the military laundry outside Munich. I don't mind because it's a day away from the caserne and I can lie on the bundles with two other supply clerks, Rappaport and Weber, and talk about civilian life. Before we leave the caserne we stop at the PX to get our monthly ration of a pound of coffee and a carton of cigarettes to sell to the Germans. Rappaport has to pick up a supply of Kotex to save his bony shoulders from the weight of the rifle when he's on sentry duty. Weber thinks that's funny and tells us he has three sisters but he'd be goddamned if he'd ever step up to a sales clerk and ask for Kotex. Rappaport gives a little smile and says, If you have sisters, Weber, they're still in the rag stage.

No one knows why we're allowed a pound of coffee but the other supply clerks tell me I'm a lucky bastard I don't smoke. They wish they didn't smoke so they could sell the cigarettes to German girls for sex. Weber from Company B says a carton will get you a whole load of poontang and that makes him so excited he burns a hole with his cigarette in a bundle of Company A sheets and Rappaport, the Company A clerk on his first trip like me, tells him watch it or he'll beat the shit out of him. Weber says, Oh, yeah? but the truck stops and Buck the driver says, Everybody out, because we're at a secret little beer place and if we're lucky there might be a few girls in the back room ready to do anything for a few packs from our cartons. The other men are offering me low prices for my cigarettes but Buck tells me, Don't be a goddam fool, Mac, you're a kid, you need to get laid too or you'll get strange in the head.

Buck has grey hair and medals from World War Two. Everyone knows he had a battlefield commission but time and time again he drank and went wild and was busted all the way down to buck private. That's what they say about Buck though I'm learning that no matter what anyone in the army says about anything you have to take it with a grain of salt thrown over your left shoulder. Buck reminds me of Corporal Dunphy back in Fort Dix. They were wild men, they did their bit in the war, they don't know what to do with themselves in peacetime, they can't be sent to Korea with their drinking, and the army is the only home they'll have till they die.

Buck speaks German and seems to know everyone and all kinds of secret little beer places on the road from Lenggries to Munich. There are no girls in the back room anyway and when Weber complains Buck tells him, Aw, fuck off, Weber. Why don't you go out behind that tree and jerk off. Weber says he doesn't have to go behind a tree. It's a free country and he can jerk off anywhere he likes. Buck tells him, All right, Weber, all right, I don't give a shit. Take out your pecker and wave it in the middle of the road for all I care.

Buck tells us get back in the truck and we continue to Munich with no more stops at secret little beer places.

Sergeants shouldn't tell you take the laundry to a place like this without telling you what the place is. They shouldn't tell Rappaport, especially, because he's Jewish, and they shouldn't wait till he looks up from the truck and screams, Oh, Christ, when he sees the name of this place on the gate, Dachau.

What can he do but jump off the truck when Buck slows for the MP at the gate, jump from the truck and run down the Munich road screaming like a madman? Now Buck has to move the truck over and we watch while two MPs chase Rappaport, grab him, push him into the jeep and bring him back. I feel sorry for him the way he's turned white, the way he's shivering like one left out in the cold a long time. He keeps saying, I'm sorry, I'm sorry, I can't, I can't, and the MPs are soft with him. One makes a phone call from the sentry box and when he returns he tells Rappaport, OK, soldier, you don't have to go in. You can stay with a lieutenant near here and wait till your laundry is done. Your buddies can take care of your bundles.

While we unload the trucks I wonder about the Germans who are helping us. Were they in this place in the bad days and what do they know? Soldiers unloading other trucks joke and laugh and hit each other with bundles but the Germans work and don't smile and I know there are dark memories in their heads. If they lived in Dachau or Munich they must have known about this place and I'd like to know what they think about when they come here every day.

Then Buck tells me he can't talk to them because they're not Germans at all. They're refugees, displaced persons, Hungarians, Yugoslavians, Czechs, Romanians. They live in camps all over Germany till someone decides what to do with them.

When the unloading is finished Buck says it's lunch time and he's heading for the mess hall. Weber, too. I can't go to lunch until I walk around and look at this place I've been seeing in newspapers and newsreels since I grew up in Limerick. There are tablets with inscriptions in Hebrew and German and I'm wondering if they're over mass graves.

There are ovens with the doors open and I know what went in there. I saw the pictures in magazines and books and pictures are pictures but these are the ovens and I could touch them if I wanted to. I don't know if I want to touch them but if I went away and never came back to this place with the laundry I'd say to myself, You could have touched the ovens at Dachau and you didn't and what will you say to your children and grandchildren? I could say nothing but what good would that do me when I'm alone and saying to myself, Why didn't you touch the ovens at Dachau?

So I step past the tablets and touch the ovens and wonder if it's proper to say a Catholic prayer in the presence of the Jewish dead. If I were killed by the English would I mind if the likes of Rappaport touched my tombstone and prayed in Hebrew? No, I wouldn't mind after priests telling us that all prayers that are unselfish and not for ourselves reach God's ears.

Still, I can't say the usual three Hail Marys since Jesus is mentioned and He wasn't any way helpful to the Jews in recent times. I don't know if it's proper to say the Our Father touching the door of an oven but it seems harmless enough and it's what I say hoping the Jewish dead will understand my ignorance.

Weber is calling to me from the door of the mess hall, McCourt, McCourt, they're closing down here. You want lunch you get your ass in here.

I take my tray with the bowl of Hungarian goulash and bread to the table by the window where Buck and Weber are sitting but when I look out there are the ovens and I'm not much in the mood for Hungarian goulash anymore and this is the first time in my life I ever pushed food away. If they could see me in Limerick now pushing away the food they'd say I was gone mad entirely but how can you sit there eating Hungarian goulash with open ovens staring at you and thoughts of the people burned there especially the babies. Whenever newspapers show pictures of mothers and babies dying together they show how the baby is laid on the mother's bosom in the coffin and they're together for eternity and there's comfort in that. But they never showed that in the pictures of Dachau or the other camps. The pictures would show babies thrown over to the side like dogs and you could see if they were buried at all it was far from their mothers' bosoms and into eternity alone and I know sitting here that if anyone ever offers me Hungarian goulash in civilian life I'll think of the ovens in Dachau and say, No, thanks.

I ask Buck if there are mass graves under the tablets and he says there's no need for mass graves when you burn everyone and that's what they did at Dachau, the sons-of-bitches.

Weber says, Hey, Buck, I didn't know you were Jewish.

No, asshole. Do you have to be Jewish to be human?

Buck says Rappaport must be hungry and we should bring him a sandwich but Weber says that's the most ridiculous thing he ever heard of. The lunch was goulash and how you gonna make a sandwich outa that? Buck says you can make a sandwich out of anything and if Weber wasn't so stupid he could see that. Weber gives him the finger and says, Your mother, and Buck has to be stopped from attacking him by the duty sergeant who tells us all get out, the place is closed unless we'd like to stick around and do a little mopping.

Buck gets into the cab of the truck and Weber and I take a nap in the back till the laundry is ready and we load up. Rappaport is sitting by the gate reading the *Stars and Stripes*. I want to talk to him about the ovens and the bad things in this place but he's still white and cold-looking.

We're halfway to Lenggries when Buck pulls off the main road and follows a narrow path to some kind of encampment, a place of shacks, lean-tos, old tents where small children are running barefoot in cold spring weather and grown people are sitting on the ground around fires. Buck jumps from the cab and tells us bring our coffee and cigarettes and Rappaport wants to know what for.

To get laid, kid, to get laid. They're not giving it away.

Weber says, Come on, come on, they're only DPs.

The refugees come running, men and women, but all I can look at is the girls. They smile and pull at the coffee cans and cigarette cartons and Buck yells, Hold on, don't let them take your stuff. Weber disappears into a shack with an old woman about thirty-five and I look around for Rappaport. He's still in the truck, looking over the side, pale. Buck signals to one of the girls and tells me, OK, this is your honey, Mac. Give her the cigarettes and keep the coffee and watch your wallet.

The girl has on a ragged dress with pink flowers and there's so little flesh on her it's hard to tell how old she is. She takes me by the hand into a hut and it's easy for her to be naked because there's nothing under the dress. She lies on a pile of rags on the floor and I'm so desperate to be at her I pull my pants down around my legs where they can't go any farther because of the boots. Her body is cold but she's hot inside and I'm so excited I'm finished in a minute. She rolls away and goes to a corner to squat on a bucket and that makes me think of the days in Limerick when we had a bucket in the corner. She gets off the bucket, pulls her dress on, and holds out her hand.

Cigarettes?

I don't know what I'm supposed to give her. Should I give her the whole carton for that one minute of excitement or should I give her a pack of twenty?

She says it again, Cigarettes, and when I look at the bucket in the corner I give her the whole carton.

But she's not satisfied. Coffee?

94

I tell her, No, no. No coffee, but she comes at me, opening my fly and I'm so excited we're down on the rags again and she smiles for the first time over the riches of cigarettes and coffee and when I see her teeth I know why she doesn't smile much.

Buck gets back into the truck cab without a word to Rappaport and I say nothing because I think I'm ashamed of what I did. I try to tell myself I'm not ashamed, that I paid for what I got, even gave the girl my coffee. I don't know why I should be ashamed in the presence of Rappaport. I think it's because he had respect for the refugees and refused to take advantage of them but if that's so why wouldn't he show his respect and sorrow by giving them his cigarettes and coffee?

Weber doesn't care about Rappaport. He goes on about what a great piece of ass that was and how little he paid for it. He gave the woman only five packs and has the rest of his coffee and he can get laid in Lenggries for a week.

Rappaport tells him he's a moron and they trade insults till Rappaport jumps on him and they're all over the laundry with bloody noses till Buck stops the truck and tells them cut it out and all I worry about is the blood that might be on the laundry of Company C.

16

The day after the Dachau laundry detail my neck swells up and the doctor tells me pack a bag, he's sending me back to Munich, that I've got the mumps. He wants to know if I was near children because that's where the mumps come from, children, and when a man gets them it could be the end of his line.

Know what I mean, soldier?

No, sir.

It means you might never have kids yourself.

I'm sent in a jeep with a driver, Corporal John Calhoun, who tells me the mumps is God's punishment for fornicating with German women and I should take this as a sign. He stops the jeep and when he tells me kneel with him by the side of the road to beg God's forgiveness before it's too late I have to obey because of his two stripes. There's froth at the corners of his mouth and I know from growing up in Limerick that's a sure sign of lunacy and if I don't drop to my knees with John Calhoun he might turn violent in the name of God. He raises his arms to the sky and praises God for sending me the gift of the mumps just in time to mend my ways and save my soul and he would like God to keep sending me further gentle reminders of my sinful ways, chickenpox, toothache, measles, severe headaches, and pneumonia if necessary. He knows it was no accident he was chosen to drive me to Munich with my mumps. He knows the Korean

War was started so that he could be drafted and sent to Germany to save my soul and the souls of all the other fornicators. He thanks God for the privilege and promises to watch over the soul of Private McCourt in the mumps ward of the Munich military hospital as long as the Lord desires. He tells the Lord he is happy to be saved, that he's joyous, oh, joyous, indeed, and he sings a song about gathering by the river and pounds the steering wheel and drives so fast I wonder if I'll be dead in a ditch before I'm ever cured of the mumps.

He leads me down the hospital hall, sings his hymns, tells the world I am saved, that the Lord hath sent a sign, yeah verily, the mumps, that I am ready to repent. Praise God. He tells the admissions medic, a sergeant, that I am to be given a Bible and time for prayer and the sergeant tells him get the hell outa heah. Corporal Calhoun blesses him for that, blesses him from the bottom of his heart, promises to pray for the sergeant who is clearly on the side of the devil, tells the sergeant he's lost but if he'll right now drop to his knees and accept the Lord Jesus he'll know the peace that passeth all understanding and he foams so much at the mouth his chin is snow.

The sergeant comes from behind his desk and pushes Calhoun down the hall to the front door with Calhoun telling him, Repent, sergeant, repent. Let us pause, brother, and pray for this Irishman touched by the Lord, touched with the mumps. Oh, let us gather by the river.

He is still pleading and praying when the sergeant propels him into the Munich night.

A German orderly tells me his name is Hans and takes me to a six-bed ward where I'm issued hospital pajamas and two cold bulging ice packs. When he tells me, Zis iss for your neck and zis iss for your bollez, four men in the beds chant, Zis iss for your neck and zis iss for your bollez. He smiles and places one ice pack on my neck, the other in my groin. The men lob ice packs at him for more ice and tell him, Hans, you're so good at catching you could play baseball.

One man in a corner bed whimpers and doesn't throw his ice pack. Hans goes to his bed. Dimino, would you like ice?

No, I don't want ice. What's the use?

Oh, Dimino.

Oh, Dimino, my ass. Goddam krauts. Look what you did to me. Gave me the goddam mumps. I'll never have kids.

Oh, you will haf kids, Dimino.

How would you know? My wife will think I'm a fairy.

Oh, Dimino, you're not a fairy, and Hans turns to the other men, Is Dimino a fairy?

Yeah, yeah, he's a fairy, you're a fairy, Dimino, and he turns to the wall, sobbing.

Hans touches his shoulder. They don't mean it, Dimino.

And the men chant, We mean it, we mean it. You're a fairy, Dimino. We got swollen balls and you got swollen balls but you're a crybaby fairy.

And they chant till Hans pats Dimino's shoulder again, hands him ice packs and tells him, Here, Dimino, keep your bollez cool and you will have many chiltren.

Will I, Hans? Will I?

Oh, you will, Dimino.

Thanks, Hans. You're an OK kraut.

Thanks, Dimino.

Hans, you a fairy?

Yes, Dimino.

That why you like putting ice packs on our balls?

No, Dimino. Iss my job.

I don't mind if you're a fairy, Hans.

Thanks you, Dimino.

You're welcome, Hans.

Another orderly pushes a book cart into the ward and I have a feast of reading. Now I can finish the book I started coming from Ireland on the ship, Dostoyevsky's *Crime and Punishment*. I'd rather read F. Scott Fitzgerald or P. G. Wodehouse but Dostoyevsky is hanging over me with his story of Raskolnikov and the old woman. It makes me feel guilty all over again after the way I stole money from Mrs Finucane in Limerick when she was dead in the chair and I wonder if I should ask for an army chaplain and confess my awful crime.

No. I might be able to confess in the darkness of an ordinary church confession box but I could never do it here in daylight all swollen with the mumps with a screen around the bed and the priest looking at me. I could never tell him how Mrs Finucane was planning to leave her money for priests to say Masses for her soul and how I stole some of that money. I could never tell him about the sins I committed with the girl in the refugee camp. Even while I think of her I get so excited I have to interfere with myself under the blankets and there I am with one sin on top of another. If I ever confessed to a priest now I'd be excommunicated altogether so my only hope is that I'll be hit by a truck or something falling from a great height and that will give me a second to say a perfect Act of Contrition before I die and no priest will be necessary.

Sometimes I think I'd be the best Catholic in the world if they'd only do away with priests and let me talk to God there in the bed.

17

After the hospital two good things happen. I'm promoted to corporal because of my powerful typing when I turn in supply reports and the reward is a two-week furlough to Ireland if I want it. My mother wrote to me weeks ago to say how lucky she was to get one of the new corporation houses up in Janesboro and how lovely it is to have a few pounds for new furniture. She'll have a bathroom with a tub, a sink, a toilet and hot and cold water. She'll have a kitchen with a gas range and a sink and a sitting room with a fireplace where she can sit and warm her shins and read the paper or a nice romance. She'll have a garden in the front for little flowers and plants and a garden in the back for all kinds of vegetables and she won't know herself with all the luxury.

All the way on the train to Frankfurt I'm dreaming of the new house and the comfort it's bringing my mother and my brothers, Michael and Alphie. You'd think that after all the miserable days in Limerick I wouldn't even want to go back to Ireland but when the plane approaches the coast and the shadows of clouds are moving across the fields and it's all green and mysterious I can't stop myself from crying. People look at me and it's a good thing they don't ask me why I'm crying. I wouldn't be able to tell them. I wouldn't be able to describe the feeling that came around my heart about Ireland because there are no words for it and because I never knew I'd feel this way. It's strange to think there are no words for the way I feel unless they're in Shakespeare or Samuel Johnson or Dostoyevsky and I didn't notice them.

My mother is at the railway station to meet me, smiling with her new white teeth, togged out in a bright new frock and shiny black shoes. My brother, Alphie, is with her. He's going on twelve and wearing a grey suit that must have been his confirmation suit last year. You can see he's proud of me, especially my corporal's stripes, so proud he wants to carry my duffel bag. He tries but it's too heavy and I can't let him drag it along the ground because of the cuckoo clock and the Dresden china I brought my mother.

I feel proud myself knowing that people are looking at me in my American army uniform. It isn't every day you see an American corporal getting off the train at the Limerick railway and I can't wait to walk the streets knowing the girls are going to be whispering, Who's that? Isn't he gorgeous? They'll probably think I fought the Chinese hand to hand in Korea, that I'm back for a rest from the serious wound which I'm too brave to show.

When we leave the station and walk to the street I know we're not going the right way. We should be going towards Janesboro and the new house, instead we're walking by the People's Park the way we did when we first came from America and I want to know why we're going to grandma's house in Little Barrington Street. My mother says that, well, the electricity and the gas aren't in the new house yet.

Why not?

Well, I didn't bother?

Why didn't you bother?

Wisha, I don't know.

That puts me in a rage. You'd think she'd be glad to be out of that slum in Little Barrington Street and up there in her new house planting flowers and making tea in her new kitchen that looks out on the garden. You'd think she'd be longing for the new beds with the clean sheets and no fleas and a bathroom. But no. She has to hang on to the slum and I don't know why. She says 'tis hard moving out and leaving her brother, my Uncle Pat, that he's not well in himself and barely hobbling. He still sells papers all around Limerick but, God help him, he's a bit helpless and didn't he let us stay in that house when we were in a bad way. I tell her I don't care, I'm not going back to that house in the lane. I'll stay here in the National Hotel till she gets the electricity and gas up in Janesboro. I hoist my duffel bag to my shoulder and when I walk away she whimpers after me, Oh, Frank, Frank, one night, one last night in my mother's house, sure it wouldn't kill you, one night.

I stop and turn and bark at her, I don't want one night in your mother's house. What the hell is the use of sending you the allotment if you want to live like a pig?

She cries and reaches her arms to me and Alphie's eyes are wide, but I don't care. I sign in at the National Hotel and throw my duffel bag on the bed and wonder what kind of a stupid mother I have who'll stay in a slum a minute more than she has to. I sit on the bed in my American army uniform and my new corporal's stripes and wonder if I should stay here in a fit of rage or walk the streets so that the world can admire me. I look out the window at Tait's clock, the Dominican Church, the Lyric Cinema beyond where small boys are waiting at the entrance to the gods where I used to go for tuppence. The boys are raggedy and rowdy and if I sit at this window long enough I can imagine I'm looking back at my own days in Limerick. It's only ten years since I was twelve and falling in love with Hedy Lamarr up there on the screen with Charles Boyer, the two of them in Algiers and Charles saying, Come wiz me to ze Casbah. I went around saying that for weeks till my mother begged me to stop. She loved Charles Boyer herself and she'd prefer to hear it from him. She loved James Mason, too. All the women in the lane loved James Mason, he was so handsome and dangerous. They all agreed it was the dangerous part they loved. Sure a man without danger is hardly a man at all. Melda Lyons would tell all the women in Kathleen O'Connell's shop how she was mad for James Mason and they'd laugh when she said, Bejesus, if I met him I'd have him naked as an egg in a minute. That would make my mother laugh harder than anyone in Kathleen O'Connell's shop and I wonder if she's over there now telling Melda and the women how her son, Frank, got off the train and wouldn't come home for a night and I wonder if the women will go home and say Frankie McCourt is back in his American uniform and he's too high and mighty now for his poor mother below there in the lane though we should have known for he always had the odd manner like his father.

It wouldn't kill me to walk over to my grandmother's house this one last time. I'm sure my brothers, Michael and Alphie, are bragging to the whole world that I'm coming home and they'll be sad if I don't stroll down the lane in my corporal's stripes.

The minute I go down the steps of the National Hotel the boys at the Lyric Cinema call across Pery Square, Hoi, Yankee soldier, yoo hoo, do you have any choon gum? Do you have a spare shilling in your pocket or a bar of candy in your pocket?

They pronounce candy like Americans and that makes them laugh so hard they fall against each other and the wall.

There's one boy off to the side who stands with his hands in his pockets and I can see he has two red scabby eyes in a face full of pimples and a head shaved to the bone. It's hard for me to admit that's the way I looked ten years ago and when he calls across the square, Hoi, Yankee soldier, turn around so we can all see your fat arse, I want to give him a good fong in his own scrawny arse. You'd think he'd have respect for the uniform that saved the world even if I'm only a supply clerk now with dreams of getting my dog back. You'd think Scabby Eyes would notice my corporal's stripes and have a bit of respect but no, that's the way it is when you grow up in a lane. You have to pretend you don't give a fiddler's fart even when you do.

Still, I'd like to cross the square to Scabby Eyes and shake him and tell him he's the spitting image of me when I was his age but I didn't stand outside the Lyric Cinema tormenting Yanks over their fat arses. I'm trying to convince myself that's the way I was myself, till another part of my mind tells me I wasn't a bit different from Scabby Eyes, that I was just as liable as him to torment Yanks or Englishmen or anyone with a suit or a fountain pen in his top pocket riding around on a new bike, that I was just as liable to throw a rock through the window of a respectable house and run away laughing one minute and raging the next.

All I can do now is walk away keeping myself twisted to the wall so that Scabby Eyes and the boys won't see my arse and have ammunition.

It's all confusion and dark clouds in my head till the other idea comes. Go back to the boys like a GI from the films and give them change from your pocket. It won't kill you.

They watch me coming and they look as if they're about to run though no one wants to be a coward and run first. When I dole out the change all they can say is, Ooh, God, and the different way they look at me makes me feel happy. Scabby Eyes takes his share and says nothing till I'm walking away and he calls after me, Hey, mister, sure you don't have any arse at all at all.

And that makes me feel happier than anything.

The minute I turn off Barrington Street and down the hill to the lane I hear people saying, Oh, God, here's Frankie McCourt in his American uniform. Kathleen O'Connell is at the door of her shop laughing and offering me a piece of Cleeve's toffee. Sure, didn't you always love that, Frankie, even if it destroyed the teeth of Limerick. Her niece is here, too, the one that lost an eye when the knife she was using to open a bag of potatoes slipped and went into her head. She's laughing over the Cleeve's toffee, too, and I'm wondering how you can still laugh with an eye gone.

Kathleen calls down to the little fat woman at the corner of the lane, He's here, Mrs Patterson, a regular film star he is. Mrs Patterson takes my face in her hands and tells me, I'm happy for your poor mother, Frankie, the terrible life she had.

And there's Mrs Murphy who lost her husband at sea in the war, living now in sin with Mr White, nobody in the lanes the slightest bit shocked, and smiling at me, You are a film star, indeed, Frankie, and how's your poor eyes. Sure, they look grand.

The whole lane is out standing at doors and telling me I'm looking grand. Even Mrs Purcell is telling me I'm looking grand and she's blind. But I understand that's what she'd tell me if she could see and when I come near her she holds out her arms and tells me, Come here outa that, Frankie McCourt, and give me a hug for the sake of the days we listened to Shakespeare and Sean O'Casey on the wireless together.

And when she puts her arms around me she says, Arrah, God above, there isn't a pick on you. Aren't they feeding you in the American Army? But what matter, you smell grand. They always smell grand, the Yanks.

It's hard for me to look at Mrs Purcell and the delicate eyelids that barely flutter on the eyes set back in her head and remember the nights when she let me sit in the kitchen listening to plays and stories on the wireless and the way she'd think nothing of giving me a mug of tea and a big cut of bread and jam. It's hard because the people in the lane are at their doors delighted and I'm ashamed of myself for walking away from my mother and sulking on the bed in the National Hotel. How could she explain to the neighbors that she met me at the station and I wouldn't come home? I'd like to walk the few steps to my mother at her door and tell her how sorry I am but I can't say a word for fear the tears might come and she'd say, Oh, your bladder is near your eye.

I know she'd say that to bring on a laugh and keep her own tears back so that we wouldn't all feel shy and ashamed of our tears. All she can do now is say what any mother would in Limerick, You must be famished. Would you like a nice cup of tea?

My Uncle Pat is sitting in the kitchen and when he lifts his face to me it makes me sick to see the redness of his eyes and the yellow ooze. It reminds me of little Scabby Eyes over at the Lyric Cinema. It reminds me of myself.

Uncle Pat is my mother's brother and he's known all over Limerick as Ab Sheehan. Some people call him the Abbot and no one knows why. He says, That's a grand uraform you have there, Frankie. Where's your big gun? He laughs and shows the yellow stubs of teeth in his gums. His hair is black and grey and thick on his head from not being washed and there's dirt in the creases on his face. His clothes, too, shine with the grease of not being washed and I wonder how my mother can live with him and not keep him clean till I remember how stubborn he is about not washing himself and wearing the same clothes day and night till they fall from his body. My mother couldn't find the soap once and when she asked him if he had seen it he said, Don't be blamin' me for the soap. I didn't see the soap. I didn't wash meself in a week. And he said it as if everyone should admire him. I'd like to strip him in the backyard and hose him down with hot water till the dirt left the creases on his face and the pus ran from his eyes.

Mam makes the tea and it's good to see she has decent cups and saucers now not like the old days when we drank from jam jars. The Abbot refuses the new cups. I want me own mug, he says. My mother argues with him that this mug is a disgrace with all the dirt in the cracks where all kinds of diseases might be lurking. He doesn't care. He says, That was me mother's mug that she left to me, and there's no arguing with him when you know he was dropped on his head in his infancy. He gets up to limp out to the backyard lavatory and when he's gone Mam says she did everything to move him out of this house and stay with her for a while. No, he won't go. He's not going to leave his mother's house and the mug she gave him long ago and the little statue of the Infant of Prague and the big picture of the Sacred Heart of Jesus above in the bedroom. No, he's not going to leave all that. What matter. Mam has Michael and Alphie to take care of, Alphie still in school and poor Michael washing dishes down at the Savoy Restaurant, God help him.

We finish our tea and I take a walk with Alphie down O'Connell Street so that everyone will see me and admire me. We meet Michael coming up the street from his job and there's a pain in my heart when I see him, the black hair falling down to his eyes and his body a bag of bones with clothes as greasy as the Abbot's from washing dishes all day. He smiles in his shy way and says, God, you're looking very fit, Frankie. I smile back at him and I don't know what to say because I'm ashamed of the way he looks and if my mother were here I'd yell at her and ask her why Michael has to look like this. Why can't she get him decent clothes or why can't the Savoy Restaurant at least give him an apron to save himself from the grease? Why did he have to leave school at fourteen to wash dishes? If he came from the Ennis Road or the North Circular Road he'd be in school now playing rugby and going to Kilkee on his holidays. I don't know what's the use of coming back to Limerick where children are still running around in bare feet and looking at the world through scabby eyes, where my brother, Michael, has to wash dishes and my mother takes her time moving to a decent house. This is not the way I expected it to be and it makes me so sad I wish I were back in Germany drinking beer in Lenggries.

Some day I'll get them out of here, my mother, Michael, Alphie, over to New York where Malachy is already working and ready to join the air force so that he won't be drafted and sent to Korea. I don't want Alphie to leave school at the age of fourteen like the rest of us. At least he's at the Christian Brothers and not a National school like Leamy's, the one we went to. Some day he'll be able to go to secondary school so that he'll know Latin and other important things. Now at least he has clothes and shoes and food and he needn't be ashamed of himself. You can see how sturdy he is, not like Michael, the bag of bones.

We turn and make our way back up O'Connell Street and I know people are admiring me in my GI uniform till some call out, Jesus, is that you, Frankie McCourt? and the whole world knows I'm not a real American GI, that I'm just someone from the back lanes of Limerick all togged out in the American uniform with the corporal's stripes.

My mother is coming down the street all smiles. The new house will have electricity and gas tomorrow and we can move in. Aunt Aggie sent word she heard I'd arrived and she wants us to come over for tea. She's waiting for us now.

Aunt Aggie is all smiles, too. It's not like the old days when there was nothing in her face but bitterness over not having children of her own and even if there was bitterness she was the one who made sure I had decent clothes for my first job. I think she's impressed with my uniform and my corporal's stripes the way she keeps asking if I'd like more tea, more ham, more cheese. She's not that generous with Michael and Alphie and you can see it's up to my mother to make sure they have enough. They're too shy to ask for more or they're afraid. They know she has a fierce temper from not having children of her own.

Her husband, Uncle Pa Keating, doesn't sit at the table at all. He's over by the coal range with a mug of tea and all he does is smoke cigarettes and cough till he's weak, clutching at himself and laughing, These feckin' fags will kill me in the end.

My mother says, You should give 'em up, Pa, and he says, And if I did, Angela, what would I do with myself? Would I sit here with my tea and stare at the fire?

She says, They'll kill you, Pa.

And if they do, Angela, I won't give a fiddler's fart.

That's the part of Uncle Pa I always loved, the way he doesn't give a fiddler's fart about anything. If I could be like him I'd be free though I wouldn't want his lungs the way they were destroyed by German gas in the Great War, then years working in the Limerick Gas Works and now fags by the fireplace. I'm sad he's sitting there killing himself when he's the only man who ever told the truth. He's the one that told me don't get caught taking tests for the post office when I could save my money and go to America. You could never imagine Uncle Pa telling a lie. It would kill him faster than gas or the fags.

He's still all black from shoveling coke and coal at the Gas Works and there's no flesh on his bones. When he looks up from his place by the fire the whites of his eyes are dazzling around the blue. You can see when he looks over at us he has a special fondness for my brother Michael. I wish he had that fondness for me but he doesn't and it's enough to know he bought me my first pint long ago and told me the truth. I'd like to tell him the way I feel about him. No, I'm afraid someone would laugh.

After the tea at Aunt Aggie's I'm thinking of going back to my room at the National Hotel but I'm afraid my mother will get the hurt look in her eyes again. Now I'll have to doss in my grandmother's bed with Michael and Alphie and I know the fleas will drive me mad. Ever since I left Limerick there hasn't been a flea in my life but now that I'm a GI with a bit of flesh on my bones I'll be eaten alive.

Mam says, No. There's a powder called DDT that kills everything and she has it sprinkled all over the house. I tell her it's what we were sprayed with from small planes flying over our heads in Fort Dix so that we'd be saved from the torment of mosquitoes.

Still, it's crowded in the bed with Michael and Alphie. The Abbot is in his bed across the room grunting and eating from a paper of fish and chips the way he always did. I can't sleep listening to him and thinking of the days when I licked the grease from the newspaper that held his fish and chips. Here I am in the old bed with my uniform hanging over the back of a chair with nothing changed in Limerick but the DDT that keeps the fleas away. It's a comfort to think of the children who can sleep now with the DDT and not have the torment of the fleas.

The next day my mother tries for the last time to get Uncle Pat, her brother, to move up to Janesboro with us. He says, Noah, noah. That's the way he talks from being dropped on his head. He won't go. He'll stay here and when we're all gone he'll move into the big bed, his mother's bed that all of us slept in for years. He always wanted that bed and now he'll have it and he'll have his tea from his mother's mug every morning.

My mother looks at him and the tears are there again. It makes me impatient and I want her to take her things and go. If the Abbot wants to be that stupid and stubborn let him be. She says, You don't know what it is to have a brother like this. You're lucky all your brothers are whole.

Whole? What is she talking about?

Lucky you are to have brothers that are sensible and healthy and never dropped on their heads.

She cries again and asks the Abbot if he'd like a nice cup of tea and he says, Noah.

Wouldn't he like to come up to the new house and have a nice warm bath in the new bathtub?

Noah.

Oh, Pat, oh, Pat, oh, Pat.

She's so helpless with tears she has to sit down and he does nothing but stare at her out of his oozing eyes. He stares at her without a word till he reaches for his mother's mug and says, I'll have me mother's mug and me mother's bed that ye kept me out of all these years.

Alphie goes over to Mam and asks her if we can go to our new house. He's only eleven and he's excited. Michael is already at the Savoy Restaurant washing dishes and when he's finished he can come to the new house where he'll have hot and cold running water and he can take the first bath of his life.

Mam dries her eyes and stands. Are you sure now, Pat, you won't come? You can bring the mug if you like but we can't bring the bed.

Noah.

And that's the end of it. She says, This is the house I grew up in. When I went to America I didn't even look back going up the lane. 'Tis all different now. I'm forty-four years of age and 'tis all different.

She puts on her coat and stands looking at her brother and I'm so tired of her moaning I want to pull her out of the house. I tell Alphie, Come on, and we move out the door so that she has to follow us. Whenever she's hurt her face grows whiter and her nose sharper and that's the way it is now. She won't talk to me, treats me as if I had done something wrong by sending the allotment so that she could have some kind of a decent life. I don't want to talk to her either because it's hard to feel sympathy for someone, even your mother, who wants to stay in a slum with a brother who's simple from being dropped on his head.

She's like that in the bus all the way up to Janesboro. Then, at the door of the new house, she starts foostering in her bag. Oh, God, she says, I must have left the key behind, which shows she didn't want to leave her old house in the first place. That's what Corporal

Dunphy told me once in Fort Dix. His wife had that habit of forgetting keys and when you have that habit it means you don't want to go home. It means you have a dread of your own door. Now I have to knock next door to see if they'll let me go around to the back in case there's a window open for me to climb in.

That puts me in such a bad mood I can barely enjoy the new house. It's different with her. The minute she steps into the hall the paleness goes from her face and the sharpness from her nose. The house is already furnished, at least she did that, and now she says what every mother in Limerick would say, Well, we might as well have a nice cup of tea. She's like Captain Boyle yelling at Juno in *Juno and the Paycock*, Tay, tay, tay, if a man was dyin', you'd be tryin' to make him swally a cup o' tay.

18

All the years I grew up in Limerick I watched people go to dances at Cruise's Hotel or the Stella Ballroom. Now I can go myself and I needn't be a bit shy with the girls with my American uniform and my corporal's stripes. If they ask me was I ever in Korea and was I wounded I'll give them a small smile and act as if I don't want to talk about it. I might limp a little and that might be enough of an excuse for not being able to dance properly which I never could anyway. There might be at least one nice girl who will be sensitive about my wound and take me to a table for a glass of lemonade or stout.

Bud Clancy is up on the stage with his band and recognizes me the minute I walk in. He signals for me to go up to him. How are you, Frankie? Back from the wars, ha ha ha. Would you like us to play a special request?

I tell him "American Patrol" and he talks into the microphone. Ladies and Gentlemen, here's one of our own home from the wars, Frankie McCourt. And I'm in heaven with everyone looking at me. They don't look long because once "American Patrol" starts they're twirling and swinging away on the floor. I stand by the bandstand wondering how they can go on dancing and ignoring an American corporal in their midst. I never thought I'd be ignored like this and now I have to ask a girl to dance to save face. The girls are ranged in seats along the walls, drinking lemonade, chatting, and when I ask them to dance they shake their heads, No, thanks. Only one says yes, and when she gets up I notice she has a limp and that puts me in a quandary wondering if I should postpone my own limp for fear she might think I was mocking her. I can't leave her standing there all night so I lead her out to the dance floor and now I notice everyone looking at me because her limp is so bad she nearly loses her balance every time she steps forward on the right leg that's shorter than the left. It's hard to know what to do when you have to dance with someone with such a serious limp. I know now how foolish it would be for me to put on my false war limp. The whole world would be laughing at us, me going one way, she the other way. What's worse is I don't know what to say to her. I know that if you have the right thing to say you can save any situation but I'm afraid to say anything. Should I say, Sorry for your limp, or, How did you get it? She doesn't give me a chance to say anything. She barks at me, Are you going to stand there gawking all night? and I can't do anything but lead her to the floor with Bud Clancy's band playing "Chattanooga choo choo, won't you hurry me home". I don't know why Bud has to play fast tunes when girls with limps like this are barely able to put one foot before the other. Why couldn't he play "Moonlight Serenade" or "Sentimental Journey" so that I could use the few steps I learned from Emer in New York? Now the girl is asking me if I think this is a funeral and I notice she has the flat accent that shows she's from a poor part of Limerick. Come on, Yank, start swinging, she says, and steps away and twirls on her one good leg as fast as a top. Another couple bumps against us and they tell her, Powerful, Madeline, powerful. You're out on your picky tonight, Madeline. Better than Ginger Rogers herself.

Girls along the wall are laughing. My face is on fire and I wish to God Bud Clancy would play "Three O'Clock in the Morning" so that I could lead Madeline back to her seat and give up dancing forever but, no, Bud starts a slow one, "The Sunny Side of the Street", and Madeline presses herself up against me with her nose in my chest and pushes me around the floor, clumping and limping, till she steps back from me and tells me if this is the way Yanks dance then she'll dance from this day out with the men of Limerick who know how, thank you very much, indeed.

The girls along the wall laugh even harder. Even the men who can't get anyone to dance with them and spend their time drinking pints are laughing and I know I might as well leave because no one will dance with me after the spectacle I made of myself. I have such a desperate feeling and I'm so ashamed of myself that I want them to feel ashamed and the only way to do that is to put on the limp and hope they'll think it's a war wound but when I hobble towards the door the girls shriek and turn so hysterical with laughter I run down the stairs and into the street so ashamed I want to throw myself into the River Shannon.

The next day Mam tells me she heard I went to a dance last night, that I danced with Madeline Burke from Mungret Street and everyone is saying, Wasn't that very good of Frankie McCourt to dance with Madeline the way she is, God help us, an' him in his uniform an' all.

It doesn't matter. I won't go out in my uniform anymore. I'll wear civilian clothes and no one will be looking to see if I have a fat arse. If I go to a dance I'll stand by the bar and drink pints with the men who pretend they don't care when the girls say no.

I have ten days left on my furlough and I wish it was ten minutes so that I could go back to Lenggries and get whatever I want for a pound of coffee and a carton of cigarettes. Mam says I'm acting very dour but I can't explain the strange feelings I have for Limerick after all the bad times of my childhood and now the way I disgraced myself at the dance. I don't care if I was good to Madeline Burke and her limp. That's not what I came back to Limerick for. I'll never try to dance with anyone again without looking to see if they have legs the same length. It should be easy if I watch them going to the lavatory. In the long run it's easier to be with Buck and Rappaport, even Weber, taking the laundry to Dachau.

But I can't tell my mother any of this. It's hard to tell anyone anything especially if it's about coming and going. You have to get used to a big powerful place like New York where you could be dead in your bed for days with a strange odor coming from your room before anyone would notice. Then you're put into the army and you have to get used to men from all over America, all colors and shapes. When you go to Germany you look at people on the streets and in the beer places. You have to get used to them, too. They seem ordinary though you'd like to lean across to the group at the next table and say, Did anyone here kill Jews? Of course we were told in army orientation sessions to keep our mouths shut and treat Germans as allies in the war against godless communism but you'd still like to ask out of pure curiosity or to see the looks on their faces.

The hardest part of all the coming and going is Limerick. I'd like to walk around and be admired for my uniform and corporal's stripes and I suppose I would if I hadn't grown up here but I'm known to too many people because of the time I spent delivering telegrams and working for Eason's and now all I get is, Ah, Jaysus, Frankie McCourt, is that yourself? Aren't you lookin' grand entirely. How're your poor eyes and how's your poor mother? You never looked better, Frankie.

I could be wearing the uniform of a general but all I am to them is Frankie McCourt the scabby-eyed telegram boy with the poor suffering mother.

The best part of being in Limerick is walking around with Alphie and Michael though Michael is usually busy with a girl who's mad about him. All the girls are mad about him with his black hair and blue eyes and shy smile.

Oh, Mikey John, they say, isn't he gorgeous.

If they say it to his face he blushes and that makes them love him even more. My mother says he's a grand dancer, that's what she heard, and no one is better singing "When April showers, they come your way". He was having his dinner one day and the news came on the radio that Al Jolson had died and he got up, crying, and walked away from his dinner. It's a very serious thing when a boy walks away from his dinner and it proved how much Michael loved Al Jolson.

With all his talent I know Michael should be in America and he will because I'll make sure of it.

There are days I walk the streets in civilian clothes by myself. I have a notion that when I visit all the places we lived in I'm in a tunnel through the past where I know I'll be happy to come out at the other end. I stand outside Leamy's School where I got whatever education I have, good or bad. Next door is the St Vincent de Paul Society where my mother went to keep us from starving. I wander the streets from church to church, memories everywhere. There are voices, choirs, hymns, priests preaching or murmuring during confession. I can look at the doors on every street in Limerick and know I delivered telegrams at every one.

I meet schoolmasters from Leamy's National School and they tell me I was a fine boy even if they forget how they whacked me with stick and cane when I couldn't remember the proper answers for the catechism or the dates and names in Ireland's long sad history. Mr Scanlon tells me there's no use in being in America unless I make a fortune for myself and Mr O'Halloran, the headmaster, stops his car to ask me about my life in America and to remind me of what the Greeks said, that there is no royal road to knowledge. He'll be very surprised, he says, if I turn my back on books to join the shopkeepers of the world, to fumble in the greasy till. He smiles with his President Roosevelt smile and drives away.

I meet priests from our own church, St Joseph's, and other churches where I might have gone to confession or delivered telegrams but they pass me. You have to be rich to get a nod from a priest, unless he's a Franciscan.

Still I sit in silent churches to look at altars, pulpits, confessionals. I'd like to know how many Masses I attended, how many sermons frightened the life out of me, how many priests were shocked by my sins before I gave up going to confession altogether. I know I'm doomed the way I am though I'd confess to a kindly priest if I could find one. Sometimes I wish I could be a Protestant or a Jew because they don't know any better. When you belong to the True Faith there are no excuses and you're trapped.

There's a letter from my father's sister, Aunt Emily, to say my grand-mother is hoping I'll be able to travel to the North to see them before I leave for Germany. My father is living with them, working as a farm laborer all around Toome, and he'd like to see me too after all these years.

I don't mind traveling to the North to see my grandmother but I don't know what I'll say to my father. Now that I'm twenty-two I know from walking around Munich and Limerick and looking at children in the streets I could never be the father that walked away from them. He left us when I was ten to work in England and send us money but, as my mother said, he chose the bottle over the babies. Mam says I should go to the North because my grandmother is frail and might not last till the next time I come home. She says there are some things you can do only once and you might as well do them that once.

It's surprising she should talk about my grandmother like this after the cold reception she got when she landed from America with my father and four small children but there are two things she hates in the world, holding grudges and owing money.

If I go to the North in a train I should wear my uniform for the admiration I'm sure to get though I know if I open my gob with my Limerick accent people will turn away or stick their heads in books and newspapers. I could put on an American accent but I already tried that with my mother and she went into hysterics, laughing. She said I sounded like Edward G. Robinson under water.

If anyone talks to me the only thing I can do is nod my head or shake it or put on the look of a secret sadness caused by a severe war wound.

It's all for nothing. The Irish are so used to American soldiers coming and going since the end of the war I might as well be invisible in my corner of the carriage on the train to Dublin and then Belfast. There's no curiosity, no one saying, Are you back from Korea? Aren't those Chinamen terrible? and I don't even want to put on the limp anymore. A limp is like a lie, you have to remember to keep it going.

My grandmother says, Och, don't you look grand in your uniform, and Aunt Emily says, Och, you're a man now.

My father says, Och, you're here. How's your mother?

She's grand.

And your brother Malachy and your brother Michael and your wee brother what's his name?

Alphie.

Och, aye, Alphie. How's your wee brother Alphie?

They're all grand.

He lets out a small Och and sighs, That's grand.

Then he wants to know if I take a drink and my grandmother says, Now, Malachy, enough of that talk.

Och, I only wanted to warn him of the bad company to be found in pubs.

This is my father who left us when I was ten to spend every penny he earned in the pubs of Coventry with German bombs dropping all around him, his family next to starvation in Limerick and here he is putting on the air of one in the grip of sanctifying grace and all I can think of is there must be some truth to the story he was dropped on his head or the other story that he had a disease like meningitis.

That might be an excuse for the drinking, the dropping on the head or the meningitis. German bombs couldn't be an excuse because there were other Limerickmen sending money home from Coventry, bombs or no bombs. There were even men who fell in with English-women and still sent money home though that money would slow down to nothing because Englishwomen are notorious for not wanting their Irishmen to support their families at home when they have three or four snotty-nosed English brats of their own running around demanding bangers and mash. Many an Irishman at the end of the war was so desperate trapped between his Irish and English families there was nothing for him to do but jump on a ship to Canada or Australia never to be heard from again.

That wouldn't be my father. If he had seven children with my mother it was only because she was there in the bed doing her wifely duty. Englishwomen are never that easy. They'd never suffer an Irishman who would leap on them in the bravery of a few pints and that means there are no little McCourt bastards running the streets of Coventry.

I don't know what to say to him with his little smile and his Och aye because I don't know if I'm talking to a man in his right mind or the man dropped on his head or the one with meningitis. How can I talk to him when he gets up, sticks his hands deep into his trouser pockets and marches around the house whistling "Lili Marlene"? Aunt Emily whispers he hasn't had a drink in ages and it's a great struggle for him. I want to tell her it was a greater struggle for my mother to keep us all alive but I know he has the sympathy of his whole family and anyway what use is there going over the past. Then she tells me how he suffered over my mother's disgraceful doings with her cousin, how the story drifted back to the North that they were living as man and wife, that when my father heard about it in Coventry, with the bombs dropping all around him, it drove him so mad he was in the pubs day, night and in between. Men home from Coventry would tell how my father would run into the streets during the air raids lifting his arms to the Luftwaffe and begging them to drop one on his poor tormented head.

My grandmother nods her head, agreeing with Aunt Emily, Och, aye. I want to remind them my father drank long before the bad days in Limerick, that we had to hunt him in pubs all over Brooklyn. I want to tell them that if he'd only sent money we could have stayed in our own house instead of being evicted and having to move in with Mam's cousin.

But my grandmother is frail and I have to control myself. My face feels tight and there are dark clouds in my head and all I can do is stand and tell them my father drank all through the years, drank when babies were born and babies died and drank because he drank.

She says, Och, Francis, and shakes her head as if to disagree with me, as if to defend my father, and that causes such a rage in me I hardly know what to do till I'm pulling my duffel bag down the stairs and out on the road to Toome, Aunt Emily at the hedge calling, Francis, oh, Francis, come back, your grandmother wants to talk to you, but I keep walking though I'm aching to go back, that bad as my father is I'd at least like to know him, that my grandmother was doing only what any mother would do, defending her son who was dropped on his head or had meningitis, and I might go back except that a car stops and a man offers me a lift to the bus station in Toome and once I'm in the car there's no going back.

I'm not in the mood for talk but I have to be polite to the man even when he says the McCourts of Moneyglass are a fine family even if they're Catholics.

Even if they're Catholics.

I'd like to tell the man stop the car and let me out with my duffel bag but if I do I'll be only halfway to Toome and I'd be tempted to walk back to my grandmother's house.

I can't go back. The past won't go away in this family and there would surely be talk again of my mother and her great sin and then we'd have an explosion and I'd be dragging my duffel bag along the Toome road again.

The man lets me out and when I say thanks I wonder to myself if he marches around on the Twelfth of July beating a drum with the other Protestants but he has a kind face and I can't imagine him beating a drum for anything.

All the way on the bus to Belfast and the train from Belfast to Dublin I have the ache to go back to the grandmother I might never see again and to see if I could get past my father's little smiles and the och ayes but once I'm on the train to Limerick there's no going back. My head is cluttered with images of my father, my Aunt Emily, my grandmother, and the sadness of their lives in the farmhouse with seven useless acres. Then there's my mother in Limerick, forty-four years of age with seven children, three dead, and all she wants, as she says, is a little peace, ease and comfort. There's the sadness of Corporal Dunphy's life in Fort Dix and Buck in Lenggries, the two of them who found a home in the army because they wouldn't know what to do with the outside world, and I'm afraid if I don't stop thinking this way the tears will come and I'll disgrace myself in this carriage with five people gawking at me in my uniform saying, Jaysus, who's the Yank weeping in the corner? My mother would say, Your bladder is near your eye, but the people in the carriage might say, Is this a specimen of what's fighting the Chinese hand to hand over there in Korea?

Even if there weren't another soul in the carriage I'd have to control myself because the slightest hint of a tear and the salt in it makes my eyes redder than they are and I don't want to get off the train and walk the streets of Limerick with eyes like two pissholes in the snow.

My mother opens the door and clutches at her chest. Mother o' God, I thought you were an apparition. What are you doing back so soon? Sure, didn't you leave only yesterday morning. Gone one day, back the next?

I can't tell her how I'm home because of the bad things they were saying in the North about her and her terrible sin. I can't tell her how they had my father nearly canonized for his suffering over that same sin. I can't tell her because I don't want to be tormented by the past and I don't want to be trapped between the North and the South, Toome and Limerick.

I have to lie and tell her my father is drinking and that makes her face go white again and her nose pointed. I ask her why she acts so surprised. Isn't this the way he always was?

She says she hoped he might have given up the drink so that we'd have a father we could talk to, even in the North. She'd like Michael and Alphie to see this father they barely knew and she wouldn't want them to see him in his wildness. When he was sober he was the best husband in the world, the best father. He'd always have a song or a story or a comment about the state of the world that made her laugh. Then everything was destroyed with the drink. The demons came, God help us, and children were better off without him. She's better off now by herself with the few pounds coming in and the peace, ease and comfort that's in it and the best thing now would be a nice cup of tea for I must be famished after my travels to the North.

* * *

All I can do with the days left in Limerick is walk around again knowing I'll have to make my way in America and I won't return for a long time. I kneel in St Joseph's Church by the box where I made my First Confession. I move to the altar rail to look at the place where the bishop patted my cheek at Confirmation and made me a soldier of the True Church. I wander up to Roden Lane where we lived for years and wonder how families can still live there all sharing the one lavatory. The Downes house is a shell and that's a sign there are other places to go besides the slums. Mr Downes brought his whole family over to England and that's what comes of working and not drinking the wages that should go to wife and children. I could wish I had a father like Mr Downes but I didn't and there's no use complaining.

19

With the months left in Lenggries there is nothing to do most of the day but run the supply room and read books from the base library.

There are no more laundry trips to Dachau. Rappaport told someone about our visit to the refugee camp and when the story reached the captain we were hauled in and reprimanded for unsoldierly conduct and confined to barracks for two weeks. Rappaport says he's sorry. He didn't mean for some asshole to spill the beans but he felt terrible over the women in the camp. He tells me I shouldn't go around with the likes of Weber. Buck is OK but Weber fell out of a tree. Rappaport says I should concentrate on getting an education, that if I were Jewish that's all I'd be thinking about. How would he know about the times I looked at college students in New York and dreamed I'd be like them. He tells me when I'm discharged I'll have the Korean GI Bill and I can go to college but what use is that when I don't even have the high school diploma? Rappaport says I shouldn't think about why I can't do something. I should think about why I *can* do it.

That's the way Rappaport talks and I suppose that's the way it is when you're Jewish.

I tell him I can't go back to New York and go to high school if I have to earn a living.

Nights, says Rappaport.

And how long will it take me to get a high school diploma that way?

A few years.

I can't do that. I can't spend years working by day, going to school by night. I'd be dead in a month.

So what else are you going to do?

I don't know.

So? says Rappaport.

My eyes are red and oozing and Sergeant Burdick sends me on sick call. The army doctor wants to know about my last treatment and when I tell him about the doctor in New York who said I had a disease from New Guinea he says that's it, that's what you got, soldier, go get your head shaved and report back in two weeks. It's not so bad getting your head shaved in the army with the way you have to wear a cap or helmet except that if you go to a *bierstube* the Lenggries girls might call out, Oh, Irishman's got the clap, and if you try to explain it's not the clap they only pat your cheek and tell you come to them any time clap or no clap. In two weeks there's no improvement in my eyes and the doctor says I have to go back to the military hospital in Munich for observation. He doesn't say he's sorry for making a great mistake, for making me get my head shaved, that it probably wasn't the dandruff at all or anything from New Guinea. He says these are desperate times, Russians massing on the border, our troops have to be healthy, and he's not going to take a chance on this eye disease from New Guinea spreading all over the European Command.

They send me in a jeep again but the driver now is a Cuban corporal, Vinnie Gandia, who is asthmatic and plays drums in civilian life. It was hard for him being in the army but the music business was slow and he needed some way to send money to the family in Cuba. They were going to kick him out of the army in basic training because his shoulders were so bony he couldn't carry a rifle or a fifty-millimeter machine gun barrel till he saw a picture of a Kotex on a box and a light went on in his head. Jesus. That was it. Slip the Kotex pads under his shirt as a pad on his shoulders and he was ready for anything the army could throw at him. After remembering Rappaport did the same thing I wonder if Kotex knew how they were helping the fighting men of America. All the way to Munich Vinnie guides the steering wheel with his elbows so that he can tap with his drumsticks on every hard surface. He gasps bits of songs, Mister Whatyoucallit whatcha doin' tonight, and bap bap da do bap do do de do bap to go along with the beat and then he's so excited the asthma hits him and he's gasping so hard he has to stop the jeep and pump his inhaler. He rests his forehead on the steering wheel and when he looks up there are tears on his cheeks from the strain of trying to breathe. He tells me I should be grateful all I have is sore eyes. He wishes he had sore eyes instead of asthma. He could still play the drums without stopping for his goddam inhaler. Sore eyes never stopped a drummer. He wouldn't care if he went blind long as he could play the drums. What's the use of living if you can't play your goddam drums? People don't appreciate not having asthma. They sit around moaning and bitching about life and all the time breathing breathing nice and normal and taking it for granted. Give 'em one day of asthma and they'll spend the rest of their lives thanking God with every breath they take, just one day. He's gonna have to invent some kind of gadget you hang on your head so you can breathe when you play, some kind of helmet maybe, and you're in there breathing like a baby in fresh air and you're rapping away on them drums, shit, man, that would be heaven. Gene Krupa, Buddy Rich, they don't have asthma, lucky bastards. He says if I can still see when I get out of the army he'll take me to joints on Fifty-Second Street, the greatest street in the world. If I can't see he'll still take me. Shit, you don't have to see to hear the sounds, man, and wouldn't that be something, him gasping and me with a white cane or a seeing-eye dog up and down Fifty-Second Street. I could sit with this blind guy, Ray Charles, and we could compare notes. That makes Vinnie laugh and brings on the attack again and when he gets his breath back he says asthma is a bitch because if you think of something funny you laugh and that takes your breath away. That pisses him off, too, the way people go around laughing and taking it for granted and never think what it would be like to play drums with asthma, never think what it's like when you can't laugh. People just don't think about things like that.

The army doctor in Munich says the doctors in New York and Lenggries are full of shit and pours something silvery into my eyes that feels like acid. He tells me stop whining, be a man, you're not the only unit to get this infection, goddamit. I should be thankful I'm not a unit in Korea getting my ass shot off, that half these fat-ass units in Germany should be over there fighting with their *paisans* in Korea. He tells me look up, look down, look right, look left, and that will get the drops into every corner of my eyes. And how the hell, he wants to know, how the hell did they let these two eyes into this man's army? Good thing they sent me to Germany. In Korea I'd need a seeing-eye dog to fight off the goddam Chink units. I'm to stay in the hospital a few days and if I keep my eyes open and my mouth shut I'll be an okay unit.

I don't know why he keeps calling me a unit and I'm beginning to wonder if eye doctors in general are different from other doctors.

The best part of being in the hospital is that even with the bad eyes I can read all day and into the night. The doctor says I'm supposed to rest the eyes. He tells the medic to pour the silvery liquid into the eyes of this unit every day until further notice but the medic, Apollo, tells me the doctor is full of shit and brings a tube of penicillin ointment which he smears on my eyelids. Apollo says he knows a thing or two because he went to medical school himself but had to drop out because of a broken heart.

In a day the infection disappears and now I'm afraid the doctor will send me back to Lenggries and that will be the end of my easy days reading Zane Grey, Mark Twain, Herman Melville. Apollo tells me not to worry. If the doctor comes into my ward I should rub my eyes with salt and they'll look like

Two pissholes in the snow, I say.

Right.

I tell him my mother made me rub salt on my eyes a long time ago to make them look sore so that we'd get money for food from a mean man in Limerick. Apollo says, Yeah, but this is now.

He wants to know about my coffee and cigarette ration which, obviously, I'm not using and he'll be glad to take them off my hands in return for the penicillin ointment and the salt treatment. Otherwise the doctor will come with the silvery stuff and in no time I'll be back in Lenggries counting out sheets and blankets till my discharge in three months. Apollo says Munich is crawling with women and it's easy to get laid but he wants high-class stuff not some whore in a bombed-out building.

The cause of all my misfortunes is a book by Herman Melville called *Pierre, or The Ambiguities* which isn't a bit like *Moby Dick* and so dull it puts me to sleep in the middle of the day and there's the doctor shaking me awake and waving the tube of penicillin left behind by Apollo.

Wake up goddamit. Where did you get this? Apollo, right? That unit, Apollo. That goddam drop-out from a half-ass medical school in Mississippi.

He marches to the door and roars down the hall, Apollo, get your ass in here, and there's Apollo's voice, Yes, sir, yes, sir.

You, goddamit, you. Did you supply this unit with this tube?

In a way, sir, yes, sir.

What the hell are you talking about?

He was suffering, sir, screaming with his eyes.

How the hell do you scream with your eyes?

I mean, sir, the pain. He would scream. I would apply the penicillin.

Who told you, eh? You a goddam doctor?

No, sir. It's just something I saw them doing in Mississippi.

Fuck Mississippi, Apollo.

Yes, sir.

And you, soldier, what are you reading there with those eyes?

Pierre, or The Ambiguities, sir.

Christ. What the hell is it about?

I don't know, sir. I think it's about this Pierre who's caught between a dark-haired woman and a fair-haired woman. He's trying to write a book in a room in New York and he's so cold the women have to heat up hot bricks for his feet.

Christ. You're going back to your outfit, soldier. If you can lie on your ass here reading books about units like that you can be an active unit again. And you, Apollo, you're lucky I don't have your ass before a firing squad.

Yes, sir.

Dismissed.

Next day Vinnie Gandia drives me back to Lenggries and he drives without his drumsticks. He says he can't do it anymore, that he nearly got himself killed after he brought me to Munich the last time. You can't drive, drum and handle your asthma, simple as that. You gotta choose, and the drumsticks had to go. If he got into an accident and had damaged hands and couldn't play he'd stick his head in the oven, simple as that. He can't wait to get back to New York and hang out around Fifty-Second Street, the greatest street in the world. He makes me promise we'll meet in New York and he'll take me to all the great jazz joints, no charge, no cost, because he knows everyone and they know if he didn't have this goddam asthma he'd be right up there with Krupa and Rich, right up there.

There's a law that says I can sign up for another nine months in the army and avoid the six-year army reserve requirement. If I re-up they can't call me back any time the United States decides to defend democracy in distant places. I could stay here in the supply room for the nine months doling out sheets, blankets, condoms, drinking beer in the village, going home with an occasional girl, reading books from the base library. I could journey back to Ireland to tell my grandmother my sorrow over walking out in anger. I could take dancing lessons in Munich so that all the girls in Limerick would be queueing up to get out on the floor with me in my sergeant's stripes which I'd surely get.

But I can't afford another nine months in Germany with the letters coming from Emer telling me how she's counting the days till my return. I never knew she liked me that much and now I like her for liking me because that's the first time in my life I've heard that from a girl. I'm so excited over being liked by Emer I write and tell her I love her and she tells me she loves me, too, and that puts me in heaven and makes me want to pack my duffel bag and jump on a plane to her side.

I write and tell her how I long for her and how I'm here in Lenggries inhaling the perfume from her letters. I dream of the life we'll have in New York, how I'll go to my job every morning, a warm indoor job where I'll sit at a desk and scribble important decisions. Every night we'll have dinner and go to bed early so that we'll have plenty of time for the excitement.

Of course I can't mention the excitement part in the letters because Emer is pure and if her mother ever knew I had such dreams the door would be slammed in my face forever and there I'd be, deprived of the company of the only girl ever to say she liked me.

I can't tell Emer about the way I coveted college girls at the Biltmore Hotel. I can't tell her about the excitement I've had with girls in Lenggries and Munich and the refugee camp. She'd be so shocked she might tell her whole family, especially her big brother Liam, and there would be threats on my life.

Rappaport says that before you get married it's your obligation to tell the bride about all the things you've done with other girls. Buck says, That's bullshit, the best thing in life is to keep your mouth shut especially with someone you're going to marry. It's like the army, never tell, never volunteer.

Weber says, I wouldn't tell nobody nothing, and Rappaport tells him go swing from a tree. Weber says when he gets married he'll do one thing for the girl, he'll make sure he doesn't have the clap because that can be passed on and he wouldn't want any kid of his born with the clap.

Rappaport says, Jesus, the beast has feelings.

The night before I go stateside there's a party in a Bad Tolz restaurant. Officers and non-coms bring their wives and that means ordinary soldiers cannot bring their German girlfriends. Officers' wives would disapprove knowing that certain ordinary soldiers have wives waiting back home and it's not proper to sit with German girls who might be destroying good American families.

The captain makes a speech and says I was one of the finest soldiers he ever had under his command. Sergeant Burdick makes a speech and presents me with a scroll honoring me for my tight control of sheets, blankets, and protective devices.

When he says protective devices there is snickering along the table till the officers give the warning glares that tell the men, Cut it out, our wives are here.

One officer has a wife, Belinda, who is my age. If she didn't have a husband I might have a few beers to give me the courage to talk to her but I don't have to because she leans over and whispers that all the wives think I'm handsome. That makes me blush so hard I have to go out to the lavatory and when I return Belinda is saying something to the other wives that makes them laugh and when they look at me they laugh even harder and I'm sure they're laughing over what Belinda said to me. That makes me blush again and I wonder if there's anyone you can trust in this world.

Somehow Buck seems to know what happened. He whispers, The hell with these women, Mac. They shouldn't mock you like that.

I know he's right but I'm sad that the last memory of Lenggries I'll carry away with me is Belinda and the mocking officers' wives.

20

The day of my discharge from the army at Camp Kilmer I met Tom Clifford at the Breffni Bar on Third Avenue in Manhattan. We had corned beef and cabbage slathered with mustard and beer galore to cool our mouths. Tom had found an Irish bed and breakfast place in the South Bronx, Logan's Boarding House, and once I dropped off my duffel bag there we could come back down and see Emer after work in her apartment at East Fifty-Fourth Street.

Mr Logan seemed to be an old man with a bald head and a meaty red face. He might have been old but he had a young wife, Nora from Kilkenny, and a baby a few months old. He told me he was high up in the Ancient Order of Hibernians and the Knights of Columbus and I should make no mistake about where he stood on religion and morality in general, that none of his twelve boarders could expect a Sunday morning breakfast unless they could show they had attended Mass and, if at all possible, Holy Communion. For those who attended Communion and had at least two witnesses to prove it there would be sausages with the breakfast. Of course every boarder had two other boarders to testify he went to Communion. There was testifying right and left and Mr Logan was so upset over what he had to pay out in sausages he disguised himself in Nora's hat and coat and shuffled up to the middle of the church to discover not only that the boarders hadn't gone to Communion but that Ned Guinan and Kevin Hayes were the only ones to go to Mass at all. The rest were over on Willis Avenue slipping in the back door of a bar for an illegal drink before noon opening time and when they came streeling back for the breakfast, reeking, Mr Logan wanted to smell their breath. They told him feck off, this was a free country, and if they had to get their breaths smelled for the sake of a sausage they'd stay content with the watery eggs and milk, the stale bread and watery tea.

Also, there was to be no swearing or any kind of blaguarding in Mr Logan's house or we'd be asked to desist and depart. He would not allow his wife and child, Luke, to be exposed to any kind of disgraceful behavior from the twelve young Irish boarders. Our beds might be in the basement but he would always know about disgraceful behavior. No, indeed, it takes years to build up a boarding house business and he was not going to let twelve laborers from the Old Country tear it down. Bad enough that Negroes were moving in right and left and destroying a neighborhood, people with no morality, no jobs and no fathers for their children running the streets like savages.

The weekly rate was eighteen dollars for bed and breakfast and if I wanted dinner that would be an extra dollar a day. There were eight beds for twelve boarders and that was because everyone worked different shifts on the docks and various warehouses and what was the use of having extra beds cluttering up the two rooms in the basement, the only time all the beds were filled was Saturday night and then you had to bunk in with someone else. It didn't matter because Saturday night was the night to get drunk up on St Nicholas Avenue and you wouldn't care if you slept with man, woman or sheep.

There was one bathroom for all of us, bring your own soap, and two long narrow towels that used to be white. Each towel had a black line to separate the top from the bottom and that was how you were supposed to use them. There was a handwritten sign on the wall telling you the top was for anything above your navel, the bottom for anything below, signed J. Logan, prop. The towels were changed every two weeks though there were always fights between the boarders who were careful about the rules and the ones who might have had a drink.

Chris Wayne from Lisdoonvarna was the oldest boarder, forty-two, working in construction and saving to bring over his girlfriend, twenty-three, so that they could get married and have children while he still had a tittle of power in himself. The boarders called him Duke because of his last name and because of the silliness in it. He didn't drink or smoke, went to Mass and Communion every Sunday, and avoided the rest of us. He had tufts of grey in his curly black hair and he was gaunt from piety and frugality. He had his own towel, soap, and two sheets he carried around in a bag for fear we might use them. Every night he knelt by his bed and said the entire rosary. He was the only one who had secured a bed of his own since no one, drunk or sober, would climb in with him or use the bed in his absence because of the odor of sanctity around it. He worked from eight to five every work day and ate dinner with the Logans every night. They loved him for that because it brought in an extra seven dollars a week and they loved him even more for the small amounts he put into his scrawny frame. They didn't love him later when he started coughing and spitting and there were specks of blood on his handkerchief. They told him they had a child to think of and he'd better find another place. He told Mr Logan he was a son-of-a-bitch and a pathetic bastard that he felt sorry for. If he thought he was really the father of that child Mr Logan should look around at his boarders and if he wasn't completely blind he'd detect a marked resemblance to the child on the face of one of the boarders. Mr Logan struggled out of his armchair gasping that if he didn't have the bad heart he'd kill Chris Wayne on the spot. He tried to rush at the Duke but his heart wouldn't let him and he had to listen to Nora from Kilkenny screeching at him, begging him to stop or she'd be a widow with an orphan child.

The Duke laughed till he gasped at Nora, Don't worry, that child will always have a father. Sure, isn't he in this room.

He coughed his way out of the room and down the stairs to the basement and no one ever saw him again.

It was hard to live there after that. Mr Logan was suspicious of everyone and you could hear him roaring at Nora from Kilkenny at all hours. He took away one of the towels and saved money by buying old bread at the bakery and serving powdered milk and eggs for breakfast. He wanted to make us all go to confession so that he could watch our faces and know if what the Duke said was true. We refused. There were only four boarders long enough in the house to be suspects and Peter McNamee, the longest one there, told Mr Logan to his face that fooling around with Nora from Kilkenny was the last thing he'd ever think of. She was such a bag of bones from running the house you could hear her rattle and clank coming up the stairs.

Mr Logan gasped in his armchair and told Peter, That hurt me, Peter, that you'd say my wife clanks and you the finest boarder we ever had even if we were fooled a long time by the false piety of the fella that just left, thank God.

I'm sorry to hurt you, Mr Logan, but Nora from Kilkenny is not by any means a morsel. No one here would give her a second look on a dance floor.

Mr Logan looked around the room at us. Is that right, lads? Is that right?

'Tis, Mr Logan.

Are you sure of that, Peter?

I am, Mr Logan.

Thank God for that, Peter.

The boarders earn good money on the docks and in the warehouses. Tom works at Port Warehouses loading and unloading trucks and if he works extra hours he goes on time and a half or double time so that his pay is well over a hundred dollars a week.

Peter McNamee works at Merchants Refrigerating Company unloading and storing the meat from the freezer trucks from Chicago. The Logans like him for the slabs of beef or pork he hauls home every Friday night, drunk or sober, and that meat takes the place of the eighteen dollars. We never see this meat and some boarders swear Mr Logan sells it to a butcher shop on Willis Avenue.

All the boarders drink even though they say they want to save money and go back to Ireland for the peace and quiet that's in it. Only Tom says he'll never go back, that Ireland is a miserable bog of a place, and they take that as a personal insult and offer to settle it if he'll step outside. Tom laughs. He knows what he wants and it's not a life of fighting and drinking and moaning about Ireland and sharing towels in flophouses like this. The only one who agrees with Tom is Ned Guinan and it doesn't matter with him because he has the consumption like the Duke and he's not long for this world. He's saving enough money so that he can go home to Kildare and die in the house he was born in. He has dreams of Kildare where he's leaning on a fence at the Curragh watching the horses training in the morning, trotting through the mist that clouds the track till the sun breaks through and turns the whole world green. When he talks like this his eyes glisten and there's a slight pink flush on his cheeks and he smiles in such a way you'd like to go over and hold him a minute though that's the kind of thing they might frown on in an Irish boarding house. It's remarkable that Mr Logan allows him to stay but Ned is so delicate Mr Logan treats him like a son and forgets the baby who might be threatened by coughs, spits and flecks of blood. It's remarkable the way they keep him on the payroll at the Baker and Williams warehouse where they have him in the office answering the phone because he's so weak he can't lift a feather. When he's not answering the phone he studies French so that he can talk to St Thérèse, the Little Flower, when he goes to heaven. Mr Logan tells him very gently he might be on the wrong track in this matter, that Latin is the language you need in heaven and that leads to a long discussion among the boarders as to what language Our Lord spoke, Peter McNamee declaring for a fact it was Hebrew. Mr Logan says you might be right there, Peter, because he doesn't want to contradict the man who brings the Sunday meat home on a Friday night. Tom Clifford laughs that we should all brush up on our Irish in case we run into St Patrick or St Brigid and everyone glares at him, everyone but Ned Guinan who smiles at everything because it doesn't matter one way or the other when you're dreaming of the horses in Kildare.

Peter McNamee says it's a wonder a single one of us is alive with all the things against us in this world, the weather in Ireland, the TB, the English, the De Valera government, the One Holy Roman Catholic and Apostolic Church, and now the way we have to break our arses to make a few dollars on the docks and the warehouses. Mr Logan begs him to mind his language in the presence of Nora from Kilkenny and Peter says he's sorry, he gets carried away.

Tom tells me of a job unloading trucks at Port Warehouses. Emer says no, I should work in an office where I can use my brains. Tom says warehouse jobs are better than office jobs that pay less and make you wear a suit and tie and have you sitting so much you get an arse on you the size of a cathedral door. I'd like to work in an office but the warehouse pays seventy-five dollars a week and that's more than I ever dreamed of after my thirty-five dollars a week at the Biltmore Hotel. Emer says that's fine as long as I save something and get an education. She talks like that because everyone in her family went to school and she doesn't want me lifting and hauling till I'm a broken old man at the age of thirty-five. She knows from the way Tom and I talk about the boarders that there's drinking and all kinds of blaguarding and she wouldn't like me to be spending my time in bars when I could be making something of myself.

Emer has a clear head because she doesn't drink or smoke and the only meat she eats is an occasional morsel of chicken for her blood. She goes to a business school at Rockefeller Center so that she can earn a living and make something of herself in America. I know her clear head is good for me but I want that warehouse money and I promise her and myself I'll go to school some day.

Mr Campbell Groel who owns Port Warehouses isn't too sure if he wants to hire me, that I might be too scrawny. Then he looks at Tom Clifford who is smaller and scrawnier and the best worker on the platform and if I'm half as strong and fast I have the job.

The platform boss is Eddie Lynch, a fat man from Brooklyn, and when he talks to me or Tom he laughs and puts on a Barry Fitzgerald accent which I don't think is a bit funny though I have to smile because he's the boss and I want the seventy-five dollars every Friday.

At noon we sit on the platform with our lunches from the diner on the corner, long liverwurst and onion sandwiches dripping with mustard and Rheingold beer so cold it gives me a pain in my forehead. The Irish talk about the drinking they did last night and they laugh over their great sufferings in the morning. Italians eat the food they've brought from home and don't know how we can eat that liverwurst shit. The Irish are offended and want to fight except that Eddie Lynch says anyone in a fight on this platform can go looking for a job.

There's one black man, Horace, and he sits away from the rest of us. He smiles once in a while and says nothing because that's the way it is.

When we finish at five someone will say, OK, let's go for a beer, one beer, just one, and we all laugh at the idea of one beer. We drink at bars with longshoremen from the piers who are always fighting over whether their union, the ILA, should join the AFL or the CIO and when they're not fighting about that they're fighting about unfair hiring practices. Hiring bosses and gang foremen go to different bars farther into Manhattan for fear they might have trouble along the waterfront.

There are nights when I stay out so late and I'm so confused with the drink there's no sense going back to the Bronx at all and it's just as easy to sleep on the platform where the bums keep fires going in great drums on the street till Eddie Lynch comes along with his Barry Fitzgerald accent and tells us, Off your awrse and on your feet. Even when I'm hung over I want to tell him arse is pronounced with a flat 'a' but he's from Brooklyn and he's the boss and he'll say awrse forever.

Sometimes there's night work on the piers unloading ships and if there aren't enough longshoremen with ILA cards they'll hire ware-housemen like myself with Teamster cards. You have to be careful you're not taking jobs from longshoremen because they think nothing of sinking a baling hook in your skull and pushing you down between ship and dock on the chance you'll be crushed beyond recognition. They make better money on the docks than we do in the warehouses but the work is unsteady and they have to fight for it every day. I carry my own hook from the warehouse but I've never learned to used it for anything but lifting.

After three weeks at the warehouse and all the liverwurst and beer I'm scrawnier than ever. Eddie Lynch says in his Brooklyn brogue, Faith an' begorrah, I could slip you and Clifford through the awrse of a sparrow, two o' youse.

With the nights of drinking and working on the piers my eyes are flaring up again. They're worse when I have to handle sacks of hot Cuban peppers from United Fruit ships. Sometimes the only thing that will give me relief is beer and Eddie Lynch says, Jesus Christ, the kid is so desperate for the beer he's pouring it through his eyes.

The warehouse money is good and I should be content except that there's nothing in my head but confusion and darkness. The Third Avenue El is packed every morning with people in suits and dresses, fresh and clean and happy in themselves. If they're not reading news-papers they're talking and I hear them describing their vacation plans or bragging about how well their children are doing in school or college. I know they'll work every day till they're old and silver-haired and they'll be content with their children and grandchildren and I wonder if I'll ever live like that.

In June the papers are filled with stories about university commencement exercises and pictures of happy graduates and their families. I try to look at the pictures but the train rocks and jolts and I'm thrown against passengers who give me superior looks because of my work clothes. I want to announce that this is only temporary, that one day I'll be going to school and wearing a suit like them.

21

I wish I could be stronger at the warehouse and say no when someone laughs about going for a beer, one beer, just one. I should say no especially when I'm supposed to meet Emer to go to a movie or eat a piece of chicken. Sometimes after hours of drinking I call her and tell her I had to work overtime but she knows better and the more I lie the colder her voice and there's no use calling and lying anymore.

Then, deep into the summer, Tom tells me Emer is going with someone else, she's engaged, she's wearing a big ring from her fiancé, an insurance man from the Bronx.

She won't talk to me on the phone and when I knock on her door she won't let me in. I beg her for a minute so that I can tell her how I'm a changed man, how I'm going to mend my ways and lead a decent life, no more stuffing myself with liverwurst sandwiches, no more guzzling beer till I can hardly stand.

She won't let me in. She's engaged and there's a glint of diamond on her hand that sends me into such a wildness I want to pound the wall, tear out my hair, throw myself on the floor at her feet. I don't want to stumble away from her to Logan's boarding house and the one towel and the warehouses and the docks and the drinking till all hours while the rest of the world, Emer and her insurance man included, lead clean lives with towels galore, all happy on graduation day and smiling with their perfect American teeth brushed after every meal. I want her to take me in so that we can talk about the days before us when I'll have a suit and an office job and we'll have our own apartment and I'll be safe from the world and all temptation.

She won't let me in. She has to go now. She has to see someone and I know it's the insurance man.

Is he inside?

She says no but I know he is and I yell that I want to see him, trot the bugger out and I'll deal with him, I'll lay him out.

Then she shuts the door in my face and I'm so shocked my eyes dry up and all the heat leaves my body. I'm so shocked I wonder if my life is a series of doors closed in my face, so shocked I don't even want to go to the Breffni Bar for a beer. People are passing me on the streets and cars are honking but I feel so cold and alone I could be in a prison cell. I sit on the Third Avenue El to the Bronx and think of Emer and her insurance man, how they're having a cup of tea and laughing at the way I disgraced myself, how clean and whole-some they are, the two of them, not drinking, not smoking, waving away the chicken.

I know that's the way it is around the country, people sitting in their living rooms, smiling, secure, resisting temptation, growing old together because they're able to say, No, thank you, I don't want a beer, not one.

I know Emer is acting like this because of my behavior and I know I'm the one she wants, not this man who's probably sipping tea boring her to distraction with insurance stories. Still, she might like me again and take me back if I give up the warehouse, the docks, the liverwurst, the beer, and get a decent job. There's still a chance for me since Tom told me they won't be getting married till next year and if I improve myself starting tomorrow she'll surely take me back although I don't like thinking of him sitting for months on the couch kissing her and running his paws all over her shoulder blades.

Of course he's an Irish-American Catholic, that's what Tom told me, and of course he'll respect her purity till the wedding night, this insurance man, but I know Irish-American Catholics have filthy minds. They have all the dirty dreams I have myself, especially insurance men. I know Emer's man is thinking of the things they'll be doing on their wedding night though he'll have to confess his dirty thoughts to the priest before he gets married. It's a good thing I'm not getting married myself because I'd have to confess to the things I did with women all over Bavaria and across the border to Austria itself and sometimes even Switzerland.

There's an employment agency advertisement in the paper offering office jobs, steady, secure, well-paid, six-week paid training session, suit and tie required, preference given veterans.

The application form wants to know where I graduated from high school and when and that forces me to lie, Christian Brothers Secondary School, Limerick, Ireland, June 1947.

The agency man tells me the name of the company offering employment, Blue Cross.

Sir, what kind of company is that?

Insurance.

But.

But what?

Oh, it's all right, sir.

It's all right because I realize if I'm hired by this insurance company I might move up in the world and Emer will take me back. All she has to do is choose between two insurance men even if the other one has already given her a diamond ring.

Before I can even talk to her again I have to finish my six-week training course at the Blue Cross. The offices are on Fourth Avenue in a building with an entrance like the door of a cathedral. There are seven men in the training session, all high school graduates, one so badly wounded from the Korean War his mouth has moved around to the side of his head and he dribbles on his shoulder. It takes days to understand what he's trying to say, that he wants to work for Blue Cross so that he can help veterans like himself who were wounded and have no one. Then a few days into the course he discovers he's in the wrong place, that it was the Red Cross he wanted all along and he curses the instructor for not telling him before. We're glad to see him go even after the way he suffered for America but it's hard to be sitting all day with a man whose mouth is on the side of his head.

The instructor is Mr Puglio and the first thing he tells us is that he's studying for his master's degree in business at NYU and, second, all the information we wrote on our application will be carefully checked, so if anyone claims he went to college, and didn't, correct it now or else. The one thing Blue Cross won't tolerate is a lie.

The boarders at Logan's laugh every morning when I put on my suit, shirt, tie. They laugh even harder when they hear what my pay is, forty-seven dollars a week rising to fifty when I finish the training session.

There are only eight boarders left. Ned Guinan went home to Kildare to look at horses and die and two others married waitresses from Schrafft's who are famous for saving up to go home and buy the old family farm. The towel marked Top and Bottom is still there but no one uses it after Peter McNamee caused a sensation by going out and buying a towel of his own. He says he was weary of looking at grown men dripping after their showers walking around and shaking themselves dry like old dogs, men who would squander half their wages on whiskey but couldn't see their way to buying a towel. He says it was the last straw one Saturday when five boarders sat around on their beds drinking duty-free Irish whiskey from Shannon Airport, talking and singing along with an Irish radio program, putting them-selves in the mood for a dance in Manhattan that night. After they took showers the towel was useless and instead of walking around to shake themselves dry they began to dance jigs and reels to the music on the radio and they were having a grand time except that Nora from Kilkenny came to replace toilet paper and walked in without knocking and when she saw what she saw she screamed like a banshee and ran up the stairs hysterical to Mr Logan who came down to find the dancers rolling around naked and laughing and not giving a fiddler's fart about Mr Logan and his yelling that they were a disgrace to the Irish nation and Mother Church and he had a good mind to throw the lot of them into the street in their pelts and what kind of mothers did they have at all. He went back upstairs mumbling because he'd never evict five boarders paying eighteen dollars each a week.

When Peter brought his own towel home everyone was astonished and tried to borrow it but he told them bugger off and hid it in various places though hiding it was a problem because a towel, to dry, needs to be hung up and will only grow damp and musty if folded and hidden under the mattress or the bathtub itself. It made Peter bitter that he couldn't hang his towel to dry till Nora from Kilkenny told him she'd take it upstairs and watch over it while it dried, she and Mr Logan were that grateful for the meat he never failed to deliver every Friday night. That was a nice solution till Mr Logan became agitated every time Peter went up for his dry towel and chatted a few minutes with Nora from Kilkenny. Mr Logan would stare at his baby boy, Luke, then at Peter and back again at the baby and his frown would grow so severe his eyebrows met. He could stand it no longer and called up the stairs, Does it take all day, Peter, to get your dry towel? Nora has work to do in this house. Peter would come down the stairs. Ah, sorry, Mr Logan, very sorry, but that doesn't satisfy Mr Logan who is staring at little Luke again and back at Peter. I have something to tell you, Peter. We won't be needing your meat anymore and you'll have to find a way to keep your towel dry yourself. Nora has enough to do without standing guard over your towel while it dries.

That night there is screaming and yelling in the Logan room and next morning Mr Logan pins a note to Peter's towel telling him he'll have to leave, that he's caused too much damage to the Logan family the way he took advantage of their good nature in the matter of drying the towel.

Peter doesn't mind. He's moving out to Long Island to his cousin's house. We'll all miss him, the way he opened up the world of towels to us, and now we all have them, they're hanging everywhere and everyone is honorable about not using other men's towels because they never dry anyway in the dampness of the basement bedroom.

22

It's easier traveling on the train every morning in my suit and tie and the *New York Times* held up so that the world will see I'm not the kind of yob that reads comics in the *Daily News* or the *Mirror*. People will see that this is a man in a suit that can handle big words on his way to an important job in an insurance office.

I might be wearing a suit and reading the *Times* and getting admiring looks but I still can't help committing my daily deadly sin, Envy. I see the college students with the covers on their books, Columbia, Fordham, NYU, CCNY, and I feel empty thinking I'll never be one of them. I'd like to go to one of the bookshops and buy college book covers I could flaunt on the train except I know I'd be found out and laughed at.

Mr Puglio teaches us the different health insurance policies offered by Blue Cross, family, individual, company, widows, orphans, veterans, cripples. When he teaches he becomes excited and tells us it's a wonderful thing to sleep at night knowing people have nothing to worry about if they get sick as long as they have Blue Cross. We sit in a small room where the air is thick with cigarette smoke for lack of a window and it's hard to stay awake on a summer's afternoon with Mr Puglio getting worked up over premiums. Every Friday he gives us a test and it's a misery on Monday when he praises the higher scorers and frowns at the low scorers like me. My scores are low because I don't care about insurance and I wonder if Emer is in her right mind getting engaged to an insurance man when she could be with a man who went from training German shepherds to typing the fastest morning reports in the European Command. I feel like calling her up and telling her now that I'm inside the insurance business it's driving me mad and is she happy she did this to me. I could still be working at Port Warehouses enjoying my liverwurst and beer if she hadn't broken my heart entirely. I'd like to call her but I'm afraid she'll be cold and that will drive me to the Breffni Bar for relief.

Tom is at the Breffni and he says the best thing is to let the wound heal, have a drink, and where did you get that awful suit. It's bad enough to be suffering over the Blue Cross and Emer without having your suit sneered at and when I tell Tom fuck off he laughs and tells me I'll live. He's moving out of the boarding house himself to a small apartment in Woodside, Queens, and if I'd like to share the cost is ten dollars a week, cook our own food.

Once again I feel like calling Emer and telling her about my big job at Blue Cross and the apartment I'm getting in Queens but her face is fading in my memory and there's another place in my mind that tells me I'm glad to be single in New York.

If Emer doesn't want me what's the use of being in the insurance business where I'm suffocated every day in an airless room with Mr Puglio becoming hostile whenever I doze off? It's hard to sit there when he tells us that the first duty of a married man is to train his wife to be a widow and I daydream about Mrs Puglio getting the widow lecture. Does Mr Puglio give her the lecture at the dinner table or sitting up in the bed?

On top of everything my appetite is gone from sitting all day in my suit and if I buy a liverwurst sandwich I throw most of it to the pigeons in Madison Park.

I sit in that park and listen to men in white shirts and ties talking about their jobs, the stock market, the insurance business, and I wonder if they're content knowing this is what they'll be doing till their hair turns grey. They tell each other how they told off the boss, how he didn't have a word to say, his mouth going like this, you know, him stuck to his chair. They'll be bosses themselves some day with people telling them off and how will they like that. There are days I'd give anything to be strolling along the banks of the Shannon or out the Mulcaire River or even climbing the mountains behind Lenggries.

One of the Blue Cross trainees passes me on his way back to the office.

Yo, McCourt, it's two o'clock. You coming?

He says yo because he drove a tank in a cavalry outfit in Korea and that's how they talked when the cavalry had horses. He says yo because that tells the world he wasn't an ordinary infantry soldier.

We walk to the insurance building and I know I can't go through that cathedral entrance. I know I'm not cut out for the world of insurance.

Yo, McCourt, come on, it's late. Puglio will have a shit fit.

I'm not going in.

What?

Not going in.

I walk away down Fourth Avenue.

Yo, McCourt, you crazy, man? You gonna be fired. Shit, man, I gotta go.

I keep going in the bright July sun till I reach Union Square where I sit and wonder what have I done. They say if you quit a job in any big firm or get fired all the other firms are informed and doors are closed to you forever. Blue Cross is a big firm and I might as well give up hope of ever having a big job in any big firm. But it's a good thing I quit now rather than wait to have the lies on my application form discovered. Mr Puglio told us that was such a serious offence you'd not only be fired but Blue Cross would demand repayment of the wages paid for the training session and on top of that your name is sent to all the other big firms with a little red flag waving at the top of the page to warn them. That little red flag, said Mr Puglio, means you're forever barred from the American corporate system and you might as well move to Russia.

Mr Puglio loved talking like that and I'm glad I'm away from him, leaving Union Square to stroll down Broadway with all the other New Yorkers who don't seem to have anything to do. It's easy to see that some have that little red flag on their names, men with beards and jewelry and women with long hair and sandals who would never be allowed inside the door of the American corporate system.

There are New York places I'm seeing today for the first time, City Hall, the Brooklyn Bridge in the distance, a Protestant church, St Paul's, which has the grave of Thomas Addis Emmet, brother of Robert who was hanged for Ireland, and farther down Broadway, Trinity Church, looking the length of Wall Street.

Down where the Staten Island ferries come and go there's a bar, the Bean Pot, where I have the appetite for a whole liverwurst sandwich and a stein of beer because my tie is off and my jacket is over the back of a chair and I feel relieved I escaped with the little red flag on my name. There's something about finishing the liverwurst sandwich that tells me I've lost Emer forever. If she ever hears of my troubles with the American corporate system she might shed a tear of pity for me though she'll be grateful in the long run she settled for the insurance man from the Bronx. She'll be secure knowing she's insured for everything, that she can't take a step that's not covered by insurance.

It's a nickel for the Staten Island ferry and the sight of the Statue of Liberty and Ellis Island reminds me of the morning in October, 1949, I sailed into New York on the *Irish Oak*, past the city and up the river to anchor that night in Poughkeepsie and on the next day to Albany where I took the train back down to New York.

That was nearly four years ago and here I am on the Staten Island ferry with my tie stuffed in the pocket of the jacket hanging from my shoulder. Here I am without a job in the world, my girlfriend gone, and the little red flag waving on my name. I could go back to the Biltmore Hotel and take up where I left off, cleaning the lobby, scouring toilet bowls, laying carpet, but no, a man who was a corporal can never sink that low again.

Looking at Ellis Island and an old wooden ferry rotting between two buildings makes me think of all the people who passed here before me, before my father and mother, all the people escaping the Famine in Ireland, all the people from all over Europe landing here with their hearts in their mouths for fear they might be caught with diseases and sent back and when you think of that a great moaning moves across the water from Ellis Island and you wonder if the people sent back had to return with their babies to places like Czechoslovakia and Hungary. People who were sent back like that were the saddest people in all of history, worse than people like me who might have bad eyes and the little red flag but are still secure with the American passport.

They won't let you stay on the ferry when it docks. You have to go inside, pay your nickel and wait for the next ferry and while I'm there I might as well have a beer at the terminal bar. I keep thinking about my mother and father sailing into this harbor over twenty-five years ago and as I sail back and forth on the ferry, six times, having a beer at each end, I keep thinking of the people with diseases who were sent back and that makes me so sad I leave the ferry altogether to call Tom Clifford at Port Warehouses and ask him to meet me at the Bean Pot so that I'll know how to get home to the small apartment in Queens.

He meets me at the Bean Pot and when I tell him the liverwurst sandwiches here are delicious he says he's finished with liverwurst, he's moving on. Then he laughs and tells me I must have had a few, that I'm having trouble getting my tongue around the word liverwurst and I tell him, no, it's the day I've had with Puglio and the Blue Cross and the airless room and the little red flag and the ones who were sent back, the saddest of all.

He doesn't know what I'm talking about. He tells me my eyes are crossing in my head, put on my jacket, home to Queens and into the bed.

Mr Campbell Groel takes me back at Port Warehouses and I'm glad to be getting decent wages again, seventy-five dollars a week going up to seventy-seven for operating the forklift truck two days a week. Regular platform work means you're on your feet in the truck loading pallets with boxes, crates, sacks of fruits and peppers. Working the forklift is easier. You hoist up the loaded pallets, store them inside and wait for the next load. No one minds if you read the paper while you wait but if you read the *New York Times* they laugh and say, Look at the big intellectual on the forklift.

One of my jobs is to store bags of hot peppers off United Fruit ships in the fumigation room. On a slow day it's a good place to bring in a beer, read the paper, take a nap, and no one seems to mind. Even Mr Campbell Groel on his way out of the office might look in and smile, Take it easy, men. It's a hot day.

Horace, the black man, sits on a bag of peppers and reads a paper from Jamaica or he reads a letter over and over from his son who is in university in Canada. When he reads that letter he slaps his thigh and laughs, Oh, mon, oh, mon. The first time I ever heard him talk his accent sounded so Irish I asked him if he was from County Cork and he couldn't stop laughing. He said, All people from the islands have Irish blood, mon.

Horace and I nearly died together in that fumigation room. The beer and the heat made us so drowsy we fell asleep on the floor till we heard the door slam shut and the gas hissing into the room. We tried to push the door back but it was jammed and the gas was making us sick till Horace climbed up on a mound of pepper sacks, broke a window and called for help. Eddie Lynch was closing up outside and heard us and slid the door back.

You're two lucky bastards, he said, and he wanted to take us up the street for a few beers to clear our lungs and to celebrate. Horace says, No, mon, I can't go to that bar.

What the hell you talking about? says Eddie.

Black man not welcome in that bar.

Fuck that for a story, says Eddie.

No, mon, no trouble. There's another place we have a beer, mon.

I don't know why Horace has to give in like that. He has a son in university in Canada and he can't have a beer himself in a New York bar. He tells me I don't understand, that I'm young and I can't fight the black man's fight.

Eddie says, Yeah, you're right, Horace.

In a few weeks Mr Campbell Groel says the Port of New York is not what it used to be, business is slow, he has to lay off a few men and, of course, I'm the junior man, the first to go.

A few blocks away is Merchants Refrigerating Company and they need a platform man to fill in for men on summer vacation. They tell me, We might be having a heat wave but dress warm.

My job is unloading meat from the freezer trucks that bring sides of beef from Chicago. It's August on the platform but inside where we hang the meat it's freezing. The men laugh and say we're the only workers who travel so fast from the North Pole to the Equator and back.

Peter McNamee is platform boss while the regular man is on vacation and when he sees me he says, What in the name of the crucified Jesus are you doing here? I thought you had a brain in your head.

He tells me I should be going to school, that there's no excuse for me humping sides of beef in and out in and out when I could be using the GI Bill and moving up in the world. He says this is no job for the Irish. They come here and the next thing they're hacking and coughing up blood discovering they had TB all along, the curse of the Irish race but the last generation to be afflicted. It's Peter's job to report if anyone is hacking or coughing all over the sides of beef. Board of Health inspectors would close the place down in a minute and we'd be on the street scratching our arses looking for work.

Peter tells me he's weary of the whole game himself. He couldn't get along with the cousin on Long Island and now he's back in another boarding house in the Bronx and it's the same old game, bring home the side of beef or any kind of meat on a Friday night and he gets the free lodging. His mother torments him with her letters. Why can't he find a nice girl and settle down and give her a grandson or is he waiting for her to sink into the grave? She nags him so much about finding a wife he doesn't want to read her letters anymore.

My second Friday at Merchants Refrigerating Peter wraps the side of beef in newspaper and asks me if I'd like a drink up the street. He rests the side of beef on a bar stool but the meat begins to defrost and there are blood spots and that upsets the bartender. He tells Peter he can't have that kind of thing in the bar and he'd better put it some- where. Peter says, All right, all right, and when the bartender isn't looking he takes the side of beef into the men's lavatory and leaves it there. He returns to the bar and when he starts talking about the way his mother nags him he shifts from beer to whiskey. The bartender sympathizes with him because they're both from the County Cavan and they tell me I wouldn't understand.

There's a sudden roar from the men's lavatory and a big man stumbles out yelling that there's a huge rat sitting on the toilet seat. The bartender barks at Peter, Damn it to hell, McNamee, is that where you put that goddam meat? Get it outa this bar.

Peter retrieves his meat. Come on, McCourt, that's the end of it. I'm worn out dragging the meat around on Friday nights. I'm going to a dance to get a wife.

We take a taxi to the Jaeger House but they won't let Peter in with the meat. He offers to leave it at the coat check but they won't accept it. He creates a disturbance and when the manager says, Come on, come on, get that meat outa here, Peter swings at him with the side of beef. The manager calls for help and Peter and I are pushed down the stairs by two big men from Kerry. Peter yells that he's only looking for a wife and they should be ashamed of themselves. The Kerrymen laugh and tell him he's an arsehole and if he doesn't behave himself they'll wrap that meat around his head. Peter stands still in the middle of the sidewalk and gives the Kerrymen a peculiar sober look. You're right, he says, and offers them the meat. They won't take it. He offers it to people passing by but they shake their heads and hurry past him.

I don't know what to do with this meat, he says. Half the world is starving but no one wants my meat.

We go to Wright's Restaurant on Eighty-Sixth Street and Peter asks if they'd give us two dinners in exchange for a side of beef. No, they can't do that. Board of Health regulations. He runs to the middle of the street, lays the meat on the center line, runs back and laughs at the way cars swerve to avoid the meat, laughs even more when there's the sound of sirens and a police car and an ambulance scream around the corner and stop with flashing lights and men stand around the meat scratching their heads and then laughing till they drive away with the meat in the back of the police car.

He seems to be sober now and we order eggs and bacon at Wright's. It's Friday, says Peter, but I don't give a shit. That's the last time I'll drag meat through the streets and subways of New York. I'm tired of being Irish anyway. I'd like to wake up in the morning and be nothing or some kind of American Protestant. So will you pay for my eggs because I have to save my money and go to Vermont and be nothing.

And he walks out the door.

23

On a slow day at Merchants Refrigerating we're told we can go home. Instead of taking the train back to Queens I walk up Hudson Street and stop at a bar called the White Horse Tavern. I'm nearly twenty-three but I have to prove I'm eighteen before they'll give me a beer and a knockwurst sandwich. It's quiet in the bar even though I've read in the paper it's a favorite place of poets, especially the wild man, Dylan Thomas. People sitting at tables by the windows look like poets and artists and they're probably wondering why I'm sitting at the bar with trousers caked with beef blood. I wish I could sit there by the windows with a long-haired girl and tell her how I've read Dostoyevsky and how Herman Melville got me thrown out of the hospital in Munich.

There's nothing to do but sit at the bar tormenting myself with questions. What am I doing here with this knockwurst and beer? What am I doing in the world at all? Will I spend the rest of my life hauling sides of beef from truck to freezer and vice versa? Will I end my days in a small apartment in Queens while Emer is happy raising a family in a suburb completely protected by insurance? Will I ride the subways all my life envying people carrying books from universities?

I shouldn't be eating knockwurst at a time like this. I shouldn't be drinking beer when I don't have an answer in my head. I shouldn't be in this bar with poets and artists all sitting there with their serious whispered conversations. I'm weary of knockwurst and liverwurst and the feel of frozen meat on my shoulders every day.

I push the knockwurst away and leave a half stein of beer and walk out the door, across Hudson Street, along Bleecker Street, not knowing where I'm going but knowing I have to keep walking till I know where I'm going, and here I am in Washington Square and there's New York University and I know that's where I have to go with my GI Bill, high school or no high school. A student points to the admissions office and the woman gives me an application. She says I didn't fill it in properly, that they need to know my high school graduation, where and when.

I never went.

You never went to high school?

No, but I have the GI Bill and I've been reading books all my life.

Oh, my, but we require high school graduation or the equivalency.

But I read books. I've read Dostoyevsky and I've read *Pierre, or The Ambiguities*. It's not as good as *Moby Dick* but I read it in a hospital in Munich.

You actually read *Moby Dick*?

I did and *Pierre, or The Ambiguities* got me thrown out of the hospital in Munich.

I can see she doesn't understand. She goes into another office with my application and brings out the Dean of Admissions, a woman with a kind face. The Dean tells me I'm an unusual case and wants to know about my schooling in Ireland. It's her experience that European students are better prepared for college work and she will allow me to enroll at NYU if I can maintain a B average for a year. She wants to know what kind of work I do and when I tell her about the meat she says, My, my, I learn something every day.

Since I'm not a high school graduate and work full time I'm allowed to take only two courses, Introduction to Literature and The History of Education in America. I don't know why I have to be introduced to literature but the woman in the admissions office says it's a requirement even though I've read Dostoyevsky and Melville and that's admirable for someone without a high school education. She says The History of Education in America course will provide me with the broad cultural background I need after my inadequate European education.

I'm in heaven and the first thing to do is buy the required text-books, cover them with the purple and white NYU book jackets so that people in the subway will look at me admiringly.

All I know of university classes is what I saw a long time ago in the movies in Limerick and here I am sitting in one, The History of Education in America, with Professor Maxine Green up there on the platform telling us how the Pilgrims educated their children. All around me are students scribbling away in their notebooks and I wish I knew what to scribble myself. How am I supposed to know what's important out of all the things she's saying up there? Am I supposed to remember everything? Some students raise their hands to ask questions but I could never do that. The whole class would stare at me and wonder who's the one with the accent. I could try an American accent but that never works. When I try it people always smile and say, Do I detect an Irish brogue?

The professor is saying the Pilgrims left England to escape religious persecution and that puzzles me because the Pilgrims were English themselves and the English were always the ones who persecuted everyone else, especially the Irish. I'd like to raise my hand and tell the professor how the Irish suffered for centuries under English rule but I'm sure everyone in this class has a high school diploma and if I open my mouth they'll know I'm not one of them.

Other students are easy about raising their hands and they always say, Well, I think.

Some day I'll raise my hand and say, Well, I think, but I don't know what to think about Pilgrims and their education. Then the professor tells us ideas don't drop fully formed from the skies, that the Pilgrims were, in the long run, children of the Reformation with an accompanying world-view and their attitudes to children were so informed.

There is more notebook scribbling around the room, the women busier than the men. The women scribble as if every word out of Professor Green's mouth were important.

Then I wonder why I have this fat textbook on American edu-cation which I carry in the subways so that people can admire me for being a college student. I know there will be examinations, a mid-term and a final, but where will the questions come from? If the professor talks and talks and the textbook is seven hundred pages I'll surely be lost.

There are good-looking girls in the class and I'd like to ask one if she knows what I should know before the mid-term exam in seven weeks. I'd like to go to the university cafeteria or a Greenwich Village coffee shop and chat with the girl about the Pilgrims and their Puritan ways and how they frightened the life out of their children. I could tell the girl how I read Dostoyevsky and Melville and she'd be impressed and fall in love with me and we'd study the history of education in America together. She'd make spaghetti and we'd go to bed for the excitement and then we'd sit up in the bed reading the fat textbook and wondering why people in old New England made themselves so miserable.

Men in the class look at the scribbling women and you know they're not paying the professor a scrap of attention. You know they're deciding which girls they'll talk to afterwards and when this first class ends they move towards the good-looking ones. They smile easily with their fine white teeth and they're used to chatting because that's what they did in high school where boys and girls sit together. A good-looking girl will always have someone waiting for her in the hall outside and the man in the class who started chatting with her will lose his smile.

The lecturer in the Saturday morning class is Mr Herbert. The girls in the class seem to like him and they must know him from other classes because they ask him about his honeymoon. He smiles and jingles the change in his trouser pocket and tells us about his honeymoon and I wonder what this has to do with Introduction to Literature. Then he asks us to write two hundred words on an author we'd like to meet and why. My author is Jonathan Swift and I write that I'd like to meet him because of *Gulliver's Travels*. A man with an imagination like that would be a great one to have a cup of tea or a pint with.

Mr Herbert stands on his platform, looks through the essays, and says, Hmmm, Frank McCourt. Where is Frank McCourt?

I raise my hand and feel my face turning red. Ah, says Mr Herbert, you like Jonathan Swift?

I do.

For his imagination, eh?

Yes.

His smile is gone and his voice doesn't sound friendly and I feel uncomfortable with the way everyone in the class is looking at me. He says, You do know that Swift was a satirist, don't you?

I have no notion of what he's talking about. I have to lie and say, I do.

He says, You do know he was perhaps the greatest satirist in English literature.

I thought he was Irish.

Mr Herbert looks at the class and smiles. Does that mean, Mr McCourt, that if I'm from the Virgin Islands I'm a virgin?

There is laughter around the room and I feel my face on fire. I know they're laughing at me because of the way Mr Herbert toyed with me and put me in my place. Now he tells the class that my essay is a perfect example of a simplistic approach to literature, that while *Gulliver's Travels* may be enjoyed as a children's story it is important in English literature, not Irish, ladies and gentlemen, for its satiric brilliance. He says, When we read great works of literature in college we endeavor to rise above the mundane and the childish, and when he says that he looks at me.

The class ends and the girls gather around Mr Herbert to smile and tell him how they enjoyed his honeymoon story and I feel so ashamed I walk down six flights of stairs so that I don't have to be in the elevator with students who might despise me for enjoying *Gulliver's Travels* for the wrong reasons or even students who might feel sorry for me. I put my books in a bag because I don't care anymore if people in the subway look at me admiringly. I can't hold on to a girl, I can't keep an office job, I make a fool of myself in my first literature class and I wonder why I left Limerick at all. If I'd stayed there and taken the exam I'd be a postman now strolling from street to street, handing out letters, chatting with the women, going home for my tea without a worry in the world. I could have read Jonathan Swift to my heart's content not giving a fiddler's fart whether he was a satirist or a seanachie.

24

Tom is in the apartment singing, making Irish stew, chatting with the wife of the landlord, the Greek downstairs with the dry cleaning shop. The landlord's wife is a thin blonde and I can see she doesn't want me to be there. I walk through Woodside to the library to borrow a book I looked at the last time I was there, Sean O'Casey's *I Knock at the Door*. It's a book about growing up poor in Dublin and I never knew you could write about things like that. It was all right for Charles Dickens to write about poor people in London but his books always end with characters discovering they're the long-lost sons of the Duke of Somerset and everyone lives happily ever after.

There is no happily ever after in Sean O'Casey. His eyes are worse than mine, so bad he can barely go to school. Still he manages to read, teaches himself to write, teaches himself Irish, writes plays for the Abbey Theatre, meets Lady Gregory and the poet Yeats, but has to leave Ireland when everyone turns against him. He would never sit in a class and let someone mock him over Jonathan Swift. He'd fight back and then walk out even if he walked into the wall with his bad eyes. He's the first Irish writer I ever read who writes about rags, dirt, hunger, babies dying. The other writers go on about farms and fairies and the mist that do be on the bog and it's a relief to discover one with bad eyes and a suffering mother.

What I'm discovering now is that one thing leads to another.

When Sean O'Casey writes about Lady Gregory or Yeats I have to look them up in the *Encyclopedia Britannica* and that keeps me busy till the librarian starts turning the light on and off. I don't know how I could have reached the age of nineteen in Limerick ignorant of all that went on in Dublin before my time. I have to go to the *Encyclopedia Britannica* to learn how famous the Irish writers were, Yeats, Lady Gregory, AE, and John Millington Synge who wrote plays where the people talk in a way I never heard in Limerick or anywhere else.

Here I am in a library in Queens discovering Irish literature, wondering why the schoolmaster never told us about these writers till I discover they were all Protestants, even Sean O'Casey whose father came from Limerick. No one in Limerick would want to give Protestants credit for being great Irish writers.

The second week of Introduction to Literature Mr Herbert says that from his personal point of view one of the most desirable ingredients in a work of literature is gusto and that is certainly found in the works of Jonathan Swift and his admirer, our friend Mr McCourt. If there is a certain innocence in Mr McCourt's apprehension of Swift it is leavened with enthusiasm. Mr Herbert tells the class I was the only one of thirty-three people who selected a truly great writer, that it discourages him to think there are people in this class who consider Lloyd Douglas or Henry Morton Robinson great writers. Now he wants to know how and when I first read Swift and I have to tell him how a blind man in Limerick paid me to read Swift to him when I was twelve.

I don't want to talk in class like this because of the shame last week but I have to do what I'm told or I might be kicked out of the university. The other students are looking at me and whispering to each other and I don't know whether they're sneering at me or admiring me. When the class ends I take the stairs again instead of the elevator but I can't get out the door at the bottom because of the sign that says Fire Exit and warns me if I push anything there will be alarms. I climb back to the sixth floor to take the elevator but that door and the doors on the other floors are locked and there's nothing to do but push the door on the ground floor till the alarm goes off and I'm taken to an office to fill out a form and write a statement as to what I was doing in that place causing alarms to go off.

There's no use making a statement about my troubles with the teacher who mocked me the first week and praised me the second week, so I write that even though I dread elevators I'll take them from this day out. I know this is what they want to hear and I learned from the army it's easier to tell people in offices what they want to hear because if you don't there's always someone higher up who wants you to fill out a longer form.

25

Tom says he's tired of New York, he's going to Detroit where he knows people and he can make good money working on assembly lines in car factories. He tells me I should come with him, forget college, I won't get a degree for years and even if I do I won't make much money. If you're fast on the assembly line you're promoted to foreman and supervisor and before you know it you're in an office telling people what to do, sitting there in your suit and tie with your secretary in a chair opposite tossing her hair, crossing her legs and asking if there's anything you'd like, anything.

Of course I'd like to go with Tom. I'd like to have money to drive around Detroit in a new car with a blonde beside me, a Protestant with no sense of sin. I could go back to Limerick in bright American clothes except that they'd want to know what kind of work I was doing in America and I could never tell them I stood all day sticking bits and pieces into Buicks rolling past on the assembly line. I'd prefer to tell them I'm a student at New York University even though some would say, University? How in God's name did you ever get into a university, you that left school at fourteen and never set foot inside secondary school? They might say in Limerick I always had the makings of a swelled head, that I was too big for my boots, that I had a great notion of myself, that God put some of us here to hew wood and draw water and who do I think I am anyway after my years in the lanes of Limerick?

* ★ ★ ★

Horace, the black man I nearly died with in the fumigation chamber, tells me if I leave the university I'm a fool. He works to keep his son in college in Canada and that's the only way in America, mon. His wife cleans offices on Broad Street and she's happy because they've got a good boy up there in Canada and they're saving a few dollars for his graduation day in two years. Their son, Timothy, wants to be a child doctor so that he can go back to Jamaica to heal the sick children.

Horace tells me I should thank God I'm white, a young white man with the GI Bill and good health. Maybe a little trouble there with the eyes but still, better in this country to be white with bad eyes than black with good eyes. If his son ever told him he wanted to quit school to stand on an assembly line sticking cigarette lighters into cars he'd go up to Canada and break his head.

There are men in the warehouse who laugh at me and want to know why the hell I sit there with Horace during lunch hour. What is there to talk about with a guy whose grandparents just fell out of a tree? If I sit off at the end of the platform reading a book for my classes they ask if I'm some kind of a fairy and they let their hands go limp at the wrists. I'd like to sink my baling hook into their skulls but Eddie Lynch tells them cut it out, leave the kid alone, that they're ignorant slobs whose grandparents were still in the mud and wouldn't know a tree if it was rammed up their asses.

The men won't answer Eddie but they get back at me when we're unloading trucks by suddenly dropping boxes or crates so that my arms are jerked down and there's pain. If one is operating the forklift he'll try to pin me to the wall and laugh, Whoops, didn't see you there. After lunch they might act friendly and ask how I enjoyed my sandwich and if I say fine they'll say, Shit, man, didn't you taste the pigeon shit Joey spread on your ham?

There are dark clouds in my head and I want to go after Joey with my baling hook but the ham rises in my throat and I'm throwing up off the platform with the men clutching each other and laughing, the only ones not laughing are Joey at the river end of the platform looking at the sky because everyone knows he's not right in the head and Horace at the other end watching and saying nothing.

But after all the ham comes up and the retching stops I know what Horace is thinking. He's thinking that if this were his son,

Timothy, he'd tell him walk away from this and I know that's what I have to do. I walk to Eddie Lynch and pass him my baling hook, making sure to offer him the handle to avoid the insult of the hook itself. He takes it and shakes hands with me. He says, OK, kid, good luck, and we'll send your paycheck. Eddie might be a platform boss with no education who worked his way up but he knows the situation, he knows what I'm thinking. I walk to Horace and shake hands with him. I can't say anything because I have a strange feeling of love for him that makes it hard to talk and I wish he could be my father. He doesn't say anything either because he knows there are times like this when words have no meaning. He pats my shoulder and nods and the last sound I hear at Port Warehouses is Eddie Lynch, Get back to work, you bunch of limp pricks.

On a Saturday morning Tom and I ride the train to the bus station in Manhattan. He's on his way to Detroit and I'm taking my army duffel bag to a boarding house in Washington Heights. Tom gets his ticket, stows his bags in the luggage compartment, steps up on the bus and says, Are you sure? Are you sure you don't want to come to Detroit? You could have a hell of a life.

I could easily get on that bus. Everything I own is in the duffel bag and I could throw it in there with Tom's bags, get a ticket and be on my way to a great adventure with money and blondes and secretaries offering me everything, anything, but I think of Horace telling me what a fool I'd be and I know he's right and I shake my head at Tom before the bus door closes and he makes his way to his seat, smiling and waving.

All the way up to Washington Heights on the A train I'm caught between Tom and Horace, Detroit and New York University. Why couldn't I just get a job in a factory, eight to five, an hour for lunch, two weeks' vacation every year? I could go home in the evening, take a shower, go out with a girl, read a book when I felt like it. I wouldn't have to worry about professors mocking me one week, praising me the next. I wouldn't have to worry about papers and reading assignments from fat textbooks and exams. I'd be free.

But if I traveled on trains and buses in Detroit I might see students with their books and I'd wonder what kind of a fool I was to give up New York University for the sake of making money on the assembly line. I know I'd never be content without a college degree and always wondering what I missed.

Every day I'm learning how ignorant I am especially when I go for a coffee and a grilled cheese sandwich in the cafeteria at NYU. There are always crowds of students who drop their books on the floor and seem to have nothing to do but talk about their courses. They complain about professors and curse them for giving low grades. They brag about how they used the same term paper for more than one course or they laugh over the ways you can fool a professor with papers copied directly from encyclopedias or paraphrased from books. Most of the classes are so big the professors can only skim the papers and if they have assistants they don't know from shit. That's what the students say and going to college seems to be a great game with them.

Everyone talks and no one listens and I can see why. I'd like to be an ordinary student talking and complaining but I wouldn't be able to listen to people talking about something called the grade average. They talk about the average because that's what gets you into good graduate schools and that's what the parents fret over.

When they're not talking about their averages the students argue about the meaning of everything, life, the existence of God, the terrible state of the world, and you never know when someone is going to drop in the one word that gives everyone the deep serious look, existentialism. They might talk about how they want to be doctors and lawyers till one throws up his hands and declares everything is meaningless, that the only person in the world who makes any sense is Albert Camus who says your most important act every day is deciding not to commit suicide.

If ever I'm to sit with a group like this with my books on the floor and turn gloomy over how empty everything is I'll have to look up existentialism and find out who Albert Camus is. That's what I intend to do till the students start talking about the different colleges and I discover I'm in the one everyone looks down on, the School of Education. It's good to be in business school or the Washington Square College of Arts and Sciences but if you're in the School of Ed you're at the bottom of the scale. You're going to be a teacher and who wants to be a teacher. Some of the students' mothers are teachers and they don't get paid shit, man, shit. You break your ass for a bunch of kids who don't appreciate you and what do you get? *Bubkes,* that's what you get.

I know from the way they say it that *bubkes* isn't good and that's another word I have to look up along with existentialism. It gives me a dark feeling sitting there in the cafeteria listening to all the bright talk around me knowing I'll never catch up with the other students. There they are with their high school diplomas and their parents working away to send them to NYU to be doctors and lawyers but do their parents know how much time their sons and daughters spend in the cafeteria going on about existentialism and suicide? Here I am, twenty-three with no high school diploma, bad eyes, bad teeth, bad everything and what am I doing here at all. I feel lucky I didn't try to sit with the clever suicidal students. If they ever found out I wanted to be a teacher I'd be the laughing stock of the group. I should probably sit in some other part of the cafeteria with future teachers from the School of Education though that would show the world I'm with the losers who couldn't get into the good colleges.

The only thing to do is finish my coffee and grilled cheese sandwich and go to the library to look up existentialism and find out what makes Camus so sad, just in case.

26

My new landlady is Mrs Agnes Klein and she shows me a room
for twelve dollars a week. It's a real room, not like the end of a hallway Mrs Austin rented me on Sixty-Eighth Street. There's a bed, a
desk, a chair, a small couch in the corner by the window where my
brother, Michael, can sleep when he comes from Ireland in a few
months.

I'm hardly in the door when Mrs Klein is telling me her history.
She tells me I'm not to jump to any conclusions. Her name might be
Klein but that was her husband who was Jewish. Her own name is
Canty and I should know very well you can't get more Irish than that
and if I have no place to go at Christmas I can spend it with her and
her son, Michael, what's left of him. Her husband, Eddie, was the
cause of all her troubles. Just before the war he ran off to Germany
with their four-year-old son, Michael, because his mother was dying
and he expected to inherit her fortune. Of course they were rounded
up, the whole tribe of Kleins, mother and all, and ended up in a camp.
No use telling the damn Nazis Michael was an American citizen
born in Washington Heights. The husband was never seen again, but
Michael survived and, at the end of the war, the poor kid was able
to tell the Americans who he was. She tells me what's left of him is
in a little room down the hall. She says I should come to her kitchen
Christmas Day about two in the afternoon and have a little drink

before dinner. There won't be turkey. She'd like to cook European, if I don't mind. She tells me don't say yes unless I mean it, that I don't have to come for Christmas dinner if I have some place to go, some Irish girl making mashed potatoes. Don't worry about her. It wouldn't be her first Christmas with no one but Michael at the end of the hall, what's left of him.

On Christmas Day there are strange smells from the kitchen and there's Mrs Klein pushing things around in a frying pan. Pierogis, she says, Polish. Michael loves them. Have a vodka with a little orange juice. Good for you this time of year with the flu coming on.

We sit in her living room with our drinks, and she talks about her husband. She says we wouldn't be sitting around drinking vodka and cooking up the old pierogis if he were here. For him Christmas was business as usual.

She leans over to adjust a light and her wig falls off and the vodka in me makes me laugh out loud at the sight of her skull with little tufts of brown hair. Go ahead, she says. Some day your mother's wig will fall off and we'll see if you laugh then. And she claps the wig back on her head.

I tell her my mother has a fine head of hair and she says, No wonder. Your mother never had a lunatic husband that walked into the arms of the Nazis, for Christ's sakes. If it wasn't for him Michael what's left of him would be out of that bed there, having a vodka with his poor mouth watering for his pierogis. Oh, my God, the pierogis.

She jumps from her chair and runs to the kitchen. Well, they're a little burned, but that only makes them nice and crisp. My philosophy is, do you want to know my philosophy? is whatever goes against you in the kitchen you can turn it to your advantage. We might as well have another vodka while I cook the sauerkraut and kielbasa.

She pours the drinks and barks at me when I ask her what kielbasa is. She says she can't believe the ignorance in the world. Two years in the US Army and you don't know from kielbasa? No wonder the Communists are taking over. It's Polish, for Christ's sakes, sausage, and you should watch me fry it in case you marry someone who's not Irish, a nice girl who might demand her kielbasa.

We stay in the kitchen with another vodka while the kielbasa sizzles and the sauerkraut stews with a vinegar smell. Mrs Klein puts three plates on a tray and pours a glass of Manischewitz for Michael what's left of him He loves it, she says, loves the Manischewitz with the pierogis and kielbasa.

I follow her through her bedroom into a small dark room where Michael, what's left of him, sits up in the bed, staring ahead. We bring in chairs and use his bed as a table. Mrs Klein turns on the radio and we listen to oompah oompah accordion music. That's his favorite music, she says. Anything European. He gets nostalgic, you know, nostalgic for Europe, for Christ's sakes. Don't you, Michael? Don't you? I'm talking to you. Merry Christmas, Michael, merry goddam Christmas. She tears off her wig and throws it into a corner. No more pretending, Michael. I've had it. Talk to me or next year I cook American. Next year the turkey, Michael, the stuffing, the cranberry sauce, the works, Michael.

He stares straight ahead and the kielbasa grease glistens around his plate. His mother fiddles with the radio till she finds Bing Crosby singing "White Christmas".

Better get used to it, Michael. Next year Bing and the stuffing. To hell with kielbasa.

She pushes her plate aside on the bed and falls asleep with her head by Michael's elbow. I wait awhile, take my dinner to the kitchen, dump it into the garbage, return to my room and fall into my own bed.

Timmy Coin works at Merchants Refrigerating Company and lives at Mary O'Brien's boarding house at 720 West 180 Street around the corner from where I live. He tells me drop in any time for a cup of tea, Mary is that friendly.

It's not a real boarding house, it's a big apartment, and there are four boarders each paying eighteen dollars a week. They get a decent breakfast anytime they like not like Logan's in the Bronx where we had to go to Mass or be in a state of grace. Mary herself would rather sit in her kitchen on a Sunday morning, drinking tea, smoking cigarettes and smiling over the boarders and their stories of how they got these desperate hangovers that make them swear never again. She tells me I can always move in there if one of the boys leaves to go back to Ireland. They're always going back, she says. They think they can get a few dollars together and settle down on the old farm with some girl from the village but what do you do night after night with nothing but the wife opposite you knitting by the light of the fire and you thinking of the lights of New York, the dance halls on the East Side and the lovely cozy bars on Third Avenue.

I'd like to move into Mary O'Brien's to get away from Mrs Agnes Klein who seems to stand forever on the other side of her door waiting for me to turn the key in the lock so that she can shove a vodka and orange juice into my hand. It doesn't matter to her that I have to read or write papers for my classes at NYU. It doesn't matter that I'm worn out from the midnight shift on the piers or warehouse platforms. She wants to tell me the story of her life, how Eddie charmed her ass off better than any Irishman and watch out for the Jewish girls, Frank, they can be very charming, too, and very what-do-you-call-it? very sensual and before you know it you're stepping on the glass.

Stepping on the glass?

That's right, Frank. Do you mind if I call you Frank? They won't marry you without you stepping on the wine glass, smashing it. Then they want you to convert so the kids will be Jewish and inherit everything. But I wouldn't. I was going to but my mother said if I ever turned Jewish she'd throw herself off the George Washington Bridge and between you and me I didn't give a shit if she jumped and bounced off a passing tugboat. She's not the one that stopped me from turning Jewish. I kept the faith for my dad, decent man, little problem with the drink, but what could you expect with a name like Canty that's all over the County Kerry which I expect to see some day if God grants me health. They say the County Kerry is so green and pretty and I never see green. I see nothing but this apartment and the supermarket, nothing but this apartment and Michael what's left of him at the end of the hall. My father said it would break his heart if I became Jewish, not that he had anything against them, poor suffering people, but hadn't we suffered, too, and was I going to turn my back on generations of people getting hanged and burned right and left? He came to the wedding but not my mother. She said what I was doing was putting Christ back up there suffering on the cross, wounds an' all. She said people in Ireland starved to death before they'd take the Protestant soup and what would they say about my behavior? Eddie held me in his arms and told me he had trouble with his family, too, told me when you love someone you can tell the whole world kiss your ass, and look what happened to Eddie, wound up in a goddam oven, God forgive the language.

She sits on my bed, puts her glass on the floor, covers her face with her hands. Jesus, Jesus, she says. I can't sleep thinking what they did to him and what did Michael see. What did Michael see? I saw the pictures in the papers. Jesus. And I know them, the Germans. They live here. They have delicatessens and children and I ask them, Did you kill my Eddie? and they look at me.

She cries, lies back on my bed and falls asleep and I don't know if I should wake her and tell her I'm worn out myself, that I'm paying twelve dollars a week so that she can fall asleep in my bed while I try to sleep on the hard couch in the corner which is waiting for my brother Michael coming here in a few months.

I tell this to Mary O'Brien and her boarders and they get hysterical laughing. Mary says, Ah, God love her. I know poor Agnes and all belongin' to her. There are days she loses her wits entirely and wanders the neighborhood without her wig asking everyone where's the rabbi so that she can convert for the sake of her son, poor Michael in the bed what's left of him.

Every fortnight two nuns come to help Mrs Klein. They wash Michael what's left of him and change his sheets. They clean the apartment and watch over her while she takes a bath. They brush her wig so that it doesn't have that tangled look. She doesn't know it but they weaken her vodka with water and if she gets drunk it's all in her head.

Sister Mary Thomas is curious about me. Do I practice my religion and what school do I go to because she sees books and notebooks? When I tell her NYU she frowns and wonders if I'm not worried about losing my religion in such a place. I can't tell her I stopped going to Mass years ago, she and Sister Beatrice are so good to Mrs Klein and Michael in the bed what's left of him.

Sister Mary Thomas whispers to me something I'm never to tell another soul unless it's a priest, that she took the liberty of baptizing Michael. After all, he's not really Jewish since his mother is Irish Catholic and Sister would hate to think what might happen to Michael if he died without the sacrament. Didn't he suffer enough in Germany, little boy looking at his father being led off or worse? And doesn't he deserve the purification of baptism in case he doesn't wake up some morning in there in the bed?

She wants to know now what is my situation here? Am I encouraging Agnes to drink or is it vice-versa? I tell her I don't have time for anything I'm so busy with school and work and trying to sleep a little. She wants to know if I'd do her a little favor, something to ease her soul. If I have a moment and poor Agnes is sleeping or passed out with the watery vodka would I go down the hall, kneel by Michael's bed and say a few Hail Marys, maybe a decade of the rosary. He might not understand but you never know. With God's help the Hail Marys might sink into his poor troubled brain and help him return to the realm of the living, back to the True Faith which came down to him on his mother's side.

If I do that she'll pray for me. Above all, she'll pray that I leave NYU which everyone knows is a hotbed of Communism where I'm in great danger of losing my immortal soul and what doth it profit a man if he gain the world and lose his immortal soul? God knows there must be a place for me at Fordham or St John's which are not hotbeds of atheistic Communism like NYU. I'd be better off out of NYU before Senator McCarthy goes after it, God bless him and keep him. Isn't that right, Sister Beatrice?

The other nun nods yes because she's always so busy she rarely speaks. While Sister Mary Thomas tries to save my soul from atheistic communism Sister Beatrice is giving Mrs Klein a bath or cleaning Michael what's left of him. Sometimes when Sister Beatrice opens Michael's door the smell that drifts up the hall is enough to make you sick but that doesn't stop her from going in. She still washes him and changes his bedclothes and you can hear her humming hymns. If Mrs Klein has drunk too much and gets cranky over having to take a bath Sister Beatrice holds her, hums her hymns, and strokes the little brown tufts on her skull till Mrs Klein is a child in her arms. That makes Sister Mary Thomas impatient and she tells Mrs Klein, You have no right to waste our time like this. We have other poor souls to visit, Catholics, Mrs Klein, Catholics.

Mrs Klein whimpers, I'm a Catholic. I'm a Catholic.

That's debatable, Mrs Klein.

And if Mrs Klein sobs Sister Beatrice holds her harder, presses her whole open hand on her head and hums away with a little smile towards heaven. Sister Mary Thomas waggles her finger at me and tells me, Beware of marrying outside the True Faith. This is what happens.

27

There's a letter telling me report to my faculty advisor in the English Department, Mr Max Bogart. He says my grades are unsatisfactory, B minus in The History of Education in America and C in Introduction to Literature. I'm supposed to maintain a B average on my year's probation if I want to stay in college. After all, he says, the Dean did you a favor letting you in without a high school diploma and now you let her down.

I have to work.

What do you mean you have to work? Everyone has to work.

I have to work nights, sometimes days, on piers, in warehouses.

He says I have to make a decision, work or college. He'll give me a break this time and put me on probation on top of the probation I already have. Next June he wants to see me with a straight B average or better.

I never thought college would be all numbers and letters and grades and averages and people putting me on probation. I thought this would be a place where kindly learned men and women would teach in a warm way and if I didn't understand they'd pause and explain. I didn't know I'd go from course to course with dozens of students, sometimes over a hundred, with professors lecturing and not even looking at you. Some professors look out the window or up at the ceiling and some stick their noses in notebooks and read from paper that is yellow and crumbling with age. If students ask questions they're waved away. In English novels students at Oxford and Cambridge were always meeting in professors' rooms and sipping sherry while discussing Sophocles. I'd like to discuss Sophocles, too, but I'd have to read him first and there's no time after my nights at Merchants Refrigerating.

And if I'm to discuss Sophocles and get gloomy over existentialism and the Camus suicide problem I'll have to give up Merchants Refrigerating. If I didn't have the night job I might be able to sit in the cafeteria and talk about *Pierre, or The Ambiguities* or *Crime and Punishment* or Shakespeare in general. There are girls in the cafeteria with names like Rachel and Naomi and they're the ones Mrs Klein told me about, Jewish girls who are very sensual. I wish I had the courage to talk to them because they're probably like Protestant girls, all in a state of despair over the emptiness of it all, no sense of sin and ready for all kinds of sensuality.

In the spring of 1954 I'm a full-time student at NYU working only part-time on the docks and the warehouses or when the Manpower agency sends me on a temporary job. The first one is at a hat factory on Seventh Avenue where the owner, Mr Meyer, tells me it's easy work. All I have to do is take these women's hats, neutral colors all of them, dip these feathers into different dye pots, let the feather dry, match the color against the hat, attach feather to hat. Easy, right? Yeah, that's what you'd think, says Mr Meyer, but when I let some of my Puerto Rican help try this job they came up with color combinations that would blind you. These PRs think life is an Easter Parade and it ain't. You gotta have taste when you match a feather with a hat, taste, my friend. Little Jewish ladies in Brooklyn don't want to be wearing the Easter Parade on their heads on Passover, know't I mean?

He tells me I look intelligent enough, college boy, right? Easy job like this shouldn't be a problem. If it is I shouldn't even be in college. He's going away for a few days so I'll be on my own except for the Puerto Rican ladies working on the sewing machines and the cutting tables. Yeah, he says, the PR ladies will take care of you, ha ha.

I want to ask him if there are colors that match and colors that don't but he's gone. I dip feathers into pots and when I attach them to the hats the Puerto Rican women and girls start to giggle and laugh. I finish a batch of hats and they take them to shelves along the walls and bring me another batch. All the time they try not to laugh but they can't help themselves and I can't stop blushing. I try to vary the color schemes by dipping the feathers into different pots for a rainbow effect. I use a feather as a paint brush and on the other feathers I try to make dots, stripes, sunsets, moons waxing and waning, wavy rivers with fish waggling along and birds roosting, and the women laugh so hard they can't operate the sewing machines. I wish I could talk to them and ask them what I'm doing wrong. I wish I could tell them I wasn't put into this world to stick feathers on hats, that I'm a college student who trained dogs in Germany and worked on the piers.

In three days Mr Meyer returns and when he sees the hats he stops inside the door like a man paralyzed. He looks at the women and they shake their heads as if to say there's madness in the world. He says, What did you do? and I don't know what to say back. He says, Jesus. I mean are you Puerto Rican or what?

No, sir.

Irish, right? Yeah, that's it. Maybe you're color blind. I didn't ask you about that. Did I ask you about your color blindness?

No, sir.

If you're not color blind then I don't know how you can explain these combinations. You make the Puerto Ricans look dull, y'know that? Dull. I guess it's the Irish thing, no sense of color, no art, f'Chrissakes. I mean where are the Irish painters? Name one.

I can't.

You heard of Van Gogh, right? Rembrandt? Picasso?

I did.

That's what I mean. You're nice people, the Irish, great singers, John McCormack. Great cops, politicians, priests. Lotta Irish priests but no artists. When didja ever see an Irish painting on the wall? A Murphy, a Reilly, a Rooney? Nah, kid. I think it's because your people know one color, green. Right? So my advice to you is stay away from anything to do with color. Join the cops, run for office, pick up your paycheck and have a nice life, no hard feelings.

They shake their heads in the Manpower office. They thought this would be the perfect job for me, college boy, right? What's so hard about sticking feathers on hats? Mr Meyer called them and said, Don't send me no more Irish college boys. They're color blind. Send me someone stoopid that knows colors and won't mess with my hats.

They say if I could type they'd send me out on all kinds of jobs. I tell them I can type, that I learned in the army and I'm powerful.

They send me to offices all over Manhattan. From nine to five I sit at desks and type lists, invoices, addresses on envelopes, bills of lading. Supervisors tell me what to do and talk to me only when I make mistakes. The other office workers ignore me because I'm only temporary, a temp they say, and I might not even be here tomorrow. They don't even see me. I could die at my desk and they'd talk past me about what they saw on TV last night and how they're getting outa here fast Friday afternoon and heading for the Jersey shore. They send out for coffee and pastries and don't ask me if I have a mouth in my head. Whenever anything unusual happens it's an excuse for a party. There are presents for people being promoted, getting pregnant, people getting engaged or married, and they'll all stand around the other end of the office drinking wine, eating crackers and cheese for the hour before they go home. Women will bring in their new babies and all the other women will rush over to tickle them and say, Isn't she just beautiful? Got your eyes, Miranda, definitely got your eyes. Men will say, Hi, Miranda. Looking good. Nice kid. That's all they can say because men are not supposed to be enthusiastic or excited over babies. I'm not invited to the parties and I feel strange with my typewriter clacking away and everyone having a good time. If a supervisor is giving a small speech and I'm at the typewriter they'll call across the office, Excuse me, you over there, quit the racket a minute, will ya? Can't hear ourselves think here.

I don't know how they can work in these offices day after day, year in, year out. I can't stop looking at the clock and there are times I think I'll just get up and walk away the way I did at the Blue Cross insurance company. The people in their offices don't seem to mind. They go to the water cooler, they go to the toilet, they walk from desk to desk and chat, they call from desk to desk on the telephone, they admire each other's clothes, hair, makeup, and anytime someone loses a few pounds on a diet. If a woman is told she lost weight she smiles for an hour and keeps running her hands over her hips. Office people brag about their children, their wives, their husbands and they dream about the two-week vacation.

I'm sent to an import-export firm on Fourth Avenue. I'm given a pile of papers that have to do with importing Japanese dolls. I'm supposed to copy this paper to that paper. It's nine thirty a.m. by the office clock. I look out the window. The sun is shining. A man and woman are kissing outside a coffee shop across the avenue. It's nine thirty-three a.m. by the office clock. The man and woman separate and walk in opposite directions. They turn. They run towards each other to kiss again. It's nine thirty-six a.m. by the office clock. I take my jacket from the back of the chair and slip it on. The office manager stands at his cubicle door and says, Hey, what's up? I don't answer. People are waiting for the elevator but I head for the stairs and run as fast as I can down seven flights. The kissing people have disappeared and I'm sorry. I wanted to see them once more. I hope they're not going to offices where they'll be typing lists of Japanese dolls or telling everyone they're engaged so that the officer manager will allow them an hour of wine and cheese and crackers.

With my brother Malachy in the air force sending a monthly allotment my mother is comfortable in Limerick. She has the house with gardens front and back where she can grow flowers and onions if she likes. She has enough money for clothes and bingo and excursions to the seaside at Kilkee. Alphie is in school at the Christian Brothers where he'll get a secondary school education and all kinds of opportunities. With the comfort of the new house, beds, sheets, blankets, pillows, he doesn't have to worry about battling fleas all night, there's DDT, and he doesn't have to struggle to light a fire in the grate every morning, there's the gas stove. He can have an egg every day if he likes and not even think about it the way we did. He has decent clothes and shoes and he's warm no matter how bad it is outside.

It's time for me to send for Michael so that he can come to New York and get on in the world. When he arrives he's so thin I want to take him out and fill him with hamburgers and apple pie. He stays with me awhile at Mrs Klein's and works at different jobs but there's the threat of being drafted into the army and he thinks it's better to join the air force because the uniform is a nice shade of blue, more glamorous than the shitty brown of the army uniform and more likely to attract girls. Once Malachy is out of the air force Michael can continue the monthly allotment that will keep my mother going for another three years and I will have only myself to worry about till I finish at NYU.

28

_____

When she saunters into the psychology class the professor himself
lets his jaw drop and he grips a piece of chalk so hard it cracks and
breaks. He says, Excuse me, miss, and she gives him such a smile all
he can do is smile back. Excuse me, miss, he says, but we're seated
alphabetically and I'd need to know your name.

Alberta Small, she says, and he points to a row behind me and
we don't mind one bit if she takes all day getting to her seat because
we're feasting on her blonde hair, blue eyes, luscious lips, a bosom
that is an occasion of sin, a figure that makes you throb in the middle
of your body. A few rows back she whispers, Excuse me, and there's
a shuffle and a flutter where students have to stand to let her get to
her seat.

I'd like to be one of the students standing to let her by, to have
her brush against me and touch me.

When the class ends I want to make sure I let her pass up the
aisle so that I can watch her coming and see her going with that figure
you see only in films. She passes and gives me a little smile and I
wonder why God is so kind to me that He lets me have a smile from
the loveliest girl in all of NYU, so blonde and blue-eyed she must
hail from a tribe of Scandinavian beauties. I wish I could say to her,
Hi, would you like to go for a cup of coffee and a grilled cheese
sandwich and discuss existentialism? but I know that will never happen

especially when I see who's meeting her in the hallway, a student the size of a mountain wearing a jacket that says New York University Football.

At the next meeting of the psychology class the professor asks me a question about Jung and the collective unconscious and the moment I open my mouth I know everyone is staring at me as if to say, Who's the one with the Irish brogue? The professor himself says, Oh, do I detect an Irish accent? and I have to admit he does. He tells the class that, of course, the Catholic Church has been traditionally hostile to psychoanalysis. Isn't that right, Mr McCourt? and I feel he's accusing me. Why is he talking about the Catholic Church just because I tried to answer his question on the collective unconscious and am I supposed to defend the Church?

I don't know, Professor.

There's no use telling him that one Redemptorist priest in Limerick ranted from the pulpit on Sunday mornings denouncing Freud and Jung and promising they'd wind up in the deepest hole in hell, the two of them. If I talk in class I know no one is listening to what I'm saying. They're listening only to my accent and there are times when I wish I could reach into my mouth and tear my accent out by the roots. Even when I try to sound American people look puzzled and say, Do I detect an Irish brogue?

At the end of the class I wait for the blonde to pass by but she stops, the blue eyes smile at me, and she says, Hi, and my heart bangs in my chest. She says, My name is Mike.

Mike?

Well, actually, my name is Alberta but they call me Mike.

There is no football player outside and she says she has two hours till her next class and would I like to have a drink at Rocky's?

I have a class in ten minutes but I'm not going to miss this chance to be with this girl everyone is staring at, this girl who picked me out of all the people in the world to say hello to. We have to walk quickly to Rocky's so that we won't run into Bob the football player. He might be upset if he knew she was having a drink with another boy.

I wonder why she calls all males boy. I'm twenty-three.

She says she's kinda engaged to Bob, that they're pinned, and I don't know what she's talking about. She says a girl who's pinned is engaged to be engaged and you can tell if a girl is pinned when she wears her boyfriend's high school graduation ring on a necklace. It makes me wonder why she's not wearing Bob's ring. She says he gave her a gold bracelet with her name on it to wear around her ankle that would show she's taken but she doesn't wear it because it's what Puerto Rican girls do and they're too flashy. The bracelet is what you get just before the engagement ring and she'll wait for that, thank you very much.

She tells me she's from Rhode Island. She was reared there from the age of seven by her father's mother. Her own mother was only sixteen when she was born and her father twenty so you can guess what happened there. Shotgun. When the war came and he was drafted and sent to Seattle it was the end of the marriage. Even though Mike was a Protestant she graduated from a Catholic convent school in Fall River, Massachusetts, and she smiles at the memory of that graduation summer when she had a different date nearly every night. She might be smiling but I feel a great surge of rage and envy and I'd like to kill the boys who ate popcorn with her and probably kissed her in drive-in movies. Now she's living with her father and stepmother up on Riverside Drive and her grandmother is here for a while till she settles in and gets used to the city. She's not a bit shy about telling me she likes my Irish accent and she even liked looking at the back of my head in class the way my hair is black and wavy. This makes me blush and even though it's dark in Rocky's she can see the blush and she thinks it's cute.

I have to get used to the way they say cute in New York. If you say someone is cute in Ireland you're saying he's cunning and sneaky.

I'm in Rocky's and I'm in heaven drinking beer with this girl who could have stepped down from a movie screen, another Virginia Mayo. I know I'm the envy of every man and boy in Rocky's, that it'll be the same on the streets, heads turning and wondering who I am that I'm with the loveliest girl in NYU and Manhattan itself.

After two hours she has to go to her next class. I'm ready to carry her books they way they do in the movies but she says, No, better that I stay here awhile in case we run into Bob who wouldn't be a bit pleased to see her with the likes of me. She laughs and reminds me he's big, thanks for the beer, see you next week in class, and she's gone.

Her glass is still on the table and it's marked with pink lipstick. I put it to my lips for the taste of her and dream that some day I'll kiss the lips themselves. I press her glass against my cheek and think of her kissing the football player and there are dark clouds in my head. Why would she sit with me in Rocky's if she's kinda engaged to him? Is that the way it is in America? If you love a woman you're supposed to be loyal to her at all times. If you don't love her then it's all right to drink beer in Rocky's with someone else. If she goes to Rocky's with me then she doesn't love him and that makes me feel better.

Is it that she feels sorry for me with my Irish accent and my red eyes? Is she able to guess that it's hard for me to talk to girls unless they talk to me first?

All over America there are men who walk up to girls and say, Hi. I could never do that. I'd feel foolish saying Hi in the first place because I didn't grow up with it. I'd have to say Hello or something grown-up. Even when they talk to me I never know what to say. I don't want them to know I never went to high school and I don't want them to know I grew up in an Irish slum. I'm so ashamed of the past that all I can do is lie about it.

The lecturer in English Composition, Mr Calitri, would like us to write an essay on a single object from our childhood, an object that had significance for us, something domestic, if possible.

There isn't an object in my childhood I'd want anyone to know about. I wouldn't want Mr Calitri or anyone in the class to know about the slum lavatory we shared with all those families in Roden Lane. I could make up something but I can't think of anything like the things other students talk about, the family car, Dad's old baseball mitt, the sled they had so much fun with, the old ice box, the kitchen table where they did their homework. All I can think of is the bed I shared with my three brothers and even though I'm ashamed of it I have to write about it. If I make up something that's nice and respectable and don't write about the bed I'll be tormented. Besides, Mr Calitri will be the only one reading it and I'll be safe.

THE BED

When I was growing up in Limerick my mother had to go to the St Vincent de Paul Society to see if she could get a bed for me and my brothers, Malachy, Michael, and Alphie who was barely walking. The man at the St Vincent de Paul said he could give her a docket to go down to the Irishtown to a place that sold secondhand beds. My mother asked him couldn't we get a new bed because you never know what you're getting with an old one. There could be all kinds of diseases.

The man said beggars can't be choosers and my mother shouldn't be so particular.

But she wouldn't give up. She asked if it was possible at least to find out if anyone had died in the bed. Surely that wasn't asking too much. She wouldn't want to be lying in her own bed at night thinking about her four small sons sleeping on a mattress that someone had died on, maybe someone that had a fever or consumption.

The St Vincent de Paul man said, Missus, if you don't want this bed give me back the docket and I'll give it to someone that's not so particular.

Mam said, Ah, no, and she came home to get Alphie's pram so that we could carry the mattress, the spring and the bedstead. The man in the shop in the Irishtown wanted her to take a mattress with hair sticking out and spots and stains all over but my mother said she wouldn't let a cow sleep on a bed like that, didn't the man have another mattress over there in the corner? The man grumbled and said, All right, all right. Bejesus, the charity cases is gettin' very particular these days, and he stayed behind his counter watching us drag the mattress outside.

We had to push the pram up and down the streets of Limerick three times for the mattress and the different parts of the iron bedstead, the head, the end, the supports, and the spring. My mother said she was ashamed of her life and wished she could do this at night. The man said he was sorry for her troubles but he closed at six sharp and wouldn't stay open if the Holy Family came for a bed.

It was hard pushing the pram because it had one bockety wheel that wanted to go its own way and it was harder still with Alphie buried under the mattress screaming for his mother.

My father was there to drag the mattress upstairs and he helped us put the spring and the bedstead together. Of course he wouldn't help us push the pram two miles from the Irishtown because he'd be ashamed of the spectacle. He was from the North of Ireland and they must have a different way of bringing home the bed.

We had old overcoats to put on the bed because the St Vincent de Paul Society wouldn't give us a docket for sheets and blankets. My mother lit the fire and when we sat around it drinking tea she said at least we're all off the floor and isn't God good.

The next week Mr Calitri sits on the edge of his desk on the platform. He pulls our essays from his bag and tells the class, Not a bad set of essays, some a little too sentimental. But there's one I'd like to read you if the author doesn't mind, "The Bed".

He looks towards me and lets his eyebrows go up as if to say, Do you mind? I don't know what to say though I'd like to tell him, No, no, please don't tell the world what I came from, but the heat is in my face already and I can only shrug to him as if I don't care.

He reads "The Bed". I can feel the whole class looking at me and I'm ashamed. I'm glad Mike Small isn't in this class. She'd never look at me again. There are girls in the class and they're probably thinking they should move away from me. I want to tell them this is a made-up story but Mr Calitri is up there talking about it now, telling the class why he gave it an A, that my style is direct, my subject matter rich. He laughs when he says rich. You know what I mean, he says. He tells me I should continue to explore my rich past, and he smiles again. I don't know what he's talking about. I'm sorry I ever wrote about that bed and I'm afraid everyone will pity me and treat me like a charity case. The next time I have to take a class in English Composition I'll put my family in a comfortable house in the suburbs and I'll make my father a postman with a pension.

At the end of the class students nod to me and smile and I wonder if they're already feeling sorry for me.

Mike Small came from another world, she and her football player. They might be from different parts of America but they were teenagers and it was the same all over. They went on dates on Saturday nights where the boy would have to meet the girl at her house and of course she would never be at the door waiting for him because that would show she was too eager and word would get around and she'd be alone every Saturday night the rest of her life. The boy would have to wait in the living room with a silent dad who always looked disapproving behind his newspaper knowing what he did on dates in the old days himself and wondering what was going to be done to his little daughter. The mother would fuss and want to know what movie they were going to and what time they'd be home because her daughter was a nice girl who needed a good night's sleep to keep that glow in her complexion for church tomorrow morning. At the movies they held hands and if the boy was lucky he might get a kiss and accidentally touch her breast. If that happened she'd give him a sharp look and that meant the body was being reserved for the honeymoon. After the movie they'd have hamburgers and milkshakes at the soda fountain with all the other high school kids, the boys in crewcuts and the girls in skirts and bobbysox. They'd sing along with the jukebox and the girls would squeal over Frankie. If the girl liked the boy she might let him have a long kiss at her door, maybe one dart of a tongue in the mouth, but if he tried to keep the tongue in there she'd back away and tell him goodnight, she had a nice time, thank you, and that was another reminder the body was being reserved for the honeymoon.

Some girls would let you touch and feel and kiss but they wouldn't let you go all the way and they were known as ninety percenters. There was some hope for ninety percenters but the all-the-way girls had such a reputation no one in town would want to marry them and they were the ones who would pack up one day and go to New York where everyone does everything.

That is what I saw in the movies or what I heard in the army from GIs who came from all over the country. If you had a car and a girl said yes she'd go with you to a drive-in movie you knew she was expecting more than popcorn and the doings up there on the screen. There was no sense in just going for a kiss. You could get that in a regular movie house. The drive-in was where you got the tongue into the mouth and the hand on the breast and if she let you get to the nipple, man, she was yours. The nipple was like a key that opened the legs and if you weren't with another couple it was into the back seat and who cared about the goddam movie?

The GIs said there were funny nights when you might be making out but your friend was having trouble in the back seat with his girl who was sitting up and watching the movie or it might be vice versa

179

where your buddy is making out and you're so frustrated you want to explode in your pants. Sometimes your buddy might be finished with his girl and she's ready to take you on and that's pure heaven, man, because not only are you getting laid the one who rejected you is sitting there stonefaced pretending to watch the movie but really listening to you back there and sometimes she can't stand it anymore and climbs on you and you're caught between two broads in the back seat. Goddam.

Men in the army said you'd have no respect later for the girl who let you go all the way and you'd have only a little respect for the ninety percenter. Of course you'd have complete respect for the girl who said no and sat up watching the movie. That's the girl that was pure, not damaged goods, and the girl you'd want to be the mother of your children. If you married a girl who fooled around how would you ever know you were the real father of your kids?

I know that if Mike Small ever went to a drive-in she was the one who sat up and watched the movie. Anything else would be too much of a pain to think about especially when it's hard to think of her even kissing the football player at her own door with her father inside waiting.

The nuns tell me Mrs Klein is losing her wits with the drink and neglecting poor Michael what's left of him. They're moving them to places where they can be cared for, Catholic homes, though it's better not to tell anyone about Michael for fear some Jewish organization would claim him. Sister Mary Thomas is not against Jews but she doesn't want to lose a precious soul like Michael's.

One of Mary O'Brien's boarders is gone back to Ireland to settle on his father's five acres and marry a girl from down the road. I can have his bed for eighteen dollars a week and help myself in the morning to whatever is in the fridge. The other Irish boarders work on the piers and warehouses and they bring home canned fruits or bottles of rum and whiskey from cases that accidentally fell when ships were being unloaded. Mary says isn't it wonderful that when you say there's something you'd like a whole case of it is accidentally dropped the next day on the docks. There are Sunday mornings we don't bother cooking breakfast we're that happy in the kitchen with slices of pine-apple in heavy syrup and glasses of rum to wash it down. Mary reminds us about Mass but we're content enough with our pineapple and rum and soon Timmy Coin is calling for a song even if it's a Sunday morning. He works in Merchants Refrigerating and often brings home a great side of beef on Friday nights. He's the only one who cares about going to Mass though he makes sure he's back in no time for the pineapple and rum which can't last forever.

Frankie and Danny Lennon are twins, Irish-Americans. Frankie lives in another apartment and Danny is a boarder with Mary. Their father, John, lives on the streets, wanders around with a pint of wine in a brown paper bag, and cleans Mary's apartment in exchange for a shower, a sandwich and a few drinks. His sons laugh and sing, "Oh, my papa, to me he was so wonderful".

Frankie and Danny take classes at City College, one of the best colleges in the country and free. Even though they're studying accounting they're always excited over their courses in literature. Frankie talks about seeing a girl on the subway reading James Joyce's *A Portrait of the Artist as a Young Man* and how anxious he was to sit beside her and discuss Joyce. All the way from Thirty-Fourth Street to 181st Street he would leave his seat and move towards her, never having the courage to talk to her, and losing his seat each time to another passenger. At last when the train pulled in to 181st Street he bent to her and said, Great book, isn't it? and she jerked back from him and let out a cry. He wanted to tell her, Sorry, sorry, but the doors were closing and he was out on the platform with people in the train glaring at him.

They love jazz and they're like two mad professors in the living room, putting records on the phonograph, clicking their fingers to the beat, telling me all about the great musicians on this Benny Goodman record, Gene Krupa, Harry James, Lionel Hampton, Benny himself. They tell me this was the greatest jazz concert of all time and the first time a black man was allowed on the Carnegie Hall stage. And listen to him, listen to Lionel Hampton, all velvet and glide, listen to him and Benny coming in, listen, and here comes Harry sending in a few notes to tell you watch out, I'm flying, I'm flying, and Krupa going bap-bap-bap-do-bap-de-bap, hands, feet going, sing sing sing, and the whole damn band wild, man, wild, and the audience, listen to that audience, outa their mind, man, outa their ever-lovin' mind.

They play Count Basie, point their fingers and laugh when the Count hits those single notes, and when they play Duke Ellington they're all over the living room clicking fingers and stopping to tell me, listen, listen to this and I listen because I never listened like this before and now I hear what I never heard before and I have to laugh with the Lennons when the musicians take passages from tunes and turn them upside down and inside out and put them back again as if to say, look, we borrowed your little tune awhile to play our own way but don't worry, here it's back again and you go hum it, honey, you sing that mother, man.

The Irish boarders complain this is just a lot of noise. Paddy Arthur McGovern says, Shure, yeer not Irish at all with that stuff. What about some Irish songs on that machine? What about a few Irish dance tunes?

The Lennons laugh and tell us their father left the bogs a long time ago. Danny says, This is America, men. This is the music. But Paddy Arthur pulls Duke Ellington off the phonograph and puts on Frank Lee's Tara Ceilidhe Band and we sit around the living room, listening, tapping slightly, and not moving our faces. The Lennons laugh, and leave.

29

Sister Mary Thomas somehow found my new address and sent me a note to say it would be very nice if I came over and said goodbye to Mrs Klein and Michael what's left of him and to pick up two books I'd left under my bed. There's an ambulance waiting outside the apartment house and upstairs Sister Mary Thomas is telling Mrs Klein she has to put on her wig and, no, she can't have a rabbi, they don't have rabbis where she's going and she'd be better off on her knees saying a decade of the rosary and praying for forgiveness, and down the hall Sister Beatrice is crooning to Michael what's left of him and telling him a brighter day is dawning, that where he's going there will be birds and flowers and trees and a risen Lord. Sister Mary Thomas calls down the hall, Sister, you're wasting your time. He doesn't understand a word you're saying. But Sister Beatrice answers back, It doesn't matter, Sister. He's a child of the Lord, a Jewish child of the Lord, Sister.

He's not Jewish, Sister.

Does it matter, Sister? Does it matter?

It matters, Sister, and I'd advise you to consult your confessor.

Yes, Sister, I will. And Sister Beatrice goes on with her cheerful words and hymns to Michael what's left of him who may or may not be Jewish.

Sister Mary Thomas says, Oh, I nearly forgot your books. They're under the bed.

She hands me the books and rubs her hands together as if to clean them. Don't you know, she says, that Anatole France is on the Index of the Catholic Church and D. H. Lawrence was a completely depraved Englishman who is now howling in the depths of hell, the Lord save us all? If that's what you're reading at New York University I fear for your soul and I'll light a candle for you.

No, Sister, I'm reading *Penguin Island* for myself and *Women in Love* for one of my classes.

She rolls her eyes to heaven. Oh, the arrogance of youth. I feel sorry for your poor mother.

There are two men in white coats at the door with a stretcher and they go down the hall for Michael what's left of him. Mrs Klein sees them and calls, Rabbi, Rabbi, help me in my hour, and Sister Mary Thomas pushes her back into her chair. They shuffle back down the hall, the men in white with Michael what's left of him on the stretcher and Sister Beatrice stroking the top of his head that looks like a skull. Alannah, alannah, she says in her Irish accent, sure there's nothing left of you. But you'll see the sky now and the clouds in it. She goes down with him in the elevator and I'd like to go myself to get away from Sister Mary Thomas and her remarks on the state of my soul and the terrible things I'm reading but I have to say goodbye to Mrs Klein all dressed up in her wig and hat. She takes my hand, Take care of Michael what's left of him, won't you, Eddie?

Eddie. I feel a fierce pain in my heart because of this and a terrible memory of Rappaport and the laundry at Dachau and I wonder if I'll ever know anything in the world but darkness. Will I ever know what Sister Beatrice promised Michael what's left of him, birds, flowers, trees, and a risen Lord?

What I learned in the army comes in useful at NYU. Never raise your hand, never let them know your name, never volunteer. Students just graduated from high school, eighteen years of age, raise their hands regularly to tell the class and the professor what they think. If professors look directly at me and ask questions I can never finish the answers with the way they always say, Oh, do I detect a brogue? After that I have no peace. Whenever an Irish writer is mentioned, or anything Irish, everyone turns to me as if I'm the authority. Even the professors seem to think I know all about Irish literature and history. If they say anything about Joyce or Yeats they look at me as if I am the expert, as if I should nod and confirm what they say. I nod all the time because I don't know what else to do. If ever I shook my head in doubt or disagreement the professors would dig deeper with their questions and expose my ignorance for all to see, especially the girls.

It's the same with Catholicism. If I answer a question they hear my accent and that means I'm a Catholic and ready to defend Mother Church to the last drop of my blood. Some professors like to taunt me by sneering at the Virgin Birth, the Holy Trinity, the celibacy of St Joseph, the Inquisition, the priest-ridden people of Ireland. When they talk like that I don't know what to say because they have the power to lower my grade and damage my average so that I won't be able to follow the American dream and that might drive me to Albert Camus and the daily decision not to commit suicide. I fear professors with their high degrees and the way they might make me look foolish before the other students, especially the girls.

I'd like to stand up in those classes and announce to the world that I'm too busy to be Irish or Catholic or anything else, that I'm working day and night to make a living, trying to read books for my courses and falling asleep in the library, trying to write term papers with footnotes and bibliographies on a typewriter that betrays me with the letters "a" and "j" so that I have to go back and retype whole pages since it's impossible to avoid "a" and "j", falling asleep on subway trains all the way to the last stop so that I'm embarrassed I have to ask people where I am when I don't even know what borough I'm in.

If I didn't have red eyes and an Irish accent I could be purely American and I wouldn't have to put up with professors tormenting me with Yeats and Joyce and the Irish Literary Renaissance and how clever and witty the Irish are and what a beautiful green country it is though priest-ridden and poor with a population ready to vanish from the face of the earth due to Puritanical sexual repression and what do you have to say to that, Mr McCourt?

I think you're right, Professor.

Oh, he thinks I'm right. And, Mr Katz, what do you say to that?

I guess I agree, Professor. I don't know too many Irish.

Ladies and gentlemen, you must consider what has just been said by Mr McCourt and Mr Katz. Here we have the intersection of the

Celtic and the Hebraic, both ready to accommodate and compromise. Isn't that right, Mr McCourt, Mr Katz?

We nod and I remember what my mother used to say, A nod is as good as a wink to a blind horse. I'd like to say this to the professor but I can't take the risk of offending him with all the power he has to keep me from the American dream and make me look foolish before the class, especially the girls.

Monday and Wednesday mornings in the fall term Professor Middlebrook teaches The Literature of England. She mounts the little platform, sits, places the heavy textbook on the desk, reads from it, comments and looks at the class only to ask an occasional question. She starts with Beowulf and ends with John Milton who, she says, is sublime, somewhat in disfavor in our time but his day will come, his day will come. Students read newspapers, work at crossword puzzles, pass notes to each other, study for other courses. After my all-night shifts at various jobs it's hard to stay awake and when she asks me a question Brian McPhillips jabs me with his elbow, whispers the question and the answer and I stammer it back to her. Sometimes she mutters into the textbook and I know I'm in trouble and that trouble takes the form of a C at the end of the term.

With all my latenesses and absences and falling asleep in class I know I deserve a C and I'd like to tell the professor how guilty I feel and if she failed me completely I wouldn't blame her. I'd like to explain that even if I'm not a model student she should see the way I am with the Literature of England textbook, all excited reading it in the NYU library, on subway trains, even on piers and warehouse platforms during lunch hour. She should know I'm probably the only student in the world who ever got into trouble with men on warehouse platforms over a literature book. The men taunt me, Hey, look at the college boy. Too good to talk to us, eh? and when I tell them about the strangeness of the Anglo-Saxon language they tell me I am full of shit, that isn't English at all and who the fuck do you think you're kiddin', kid? Maybe they never went to college, they said, but they aren't gonna have the wool pulled over their eyes by a half-ass shithead just off the boat from Ireland telling them this is the English language when you could see there wasn't an English word on the whole goddam page.

After that they won't talk to me and the platform boss shifts me inside to run the elevator so that the men won't be pulling tricks on me, dropping loads to jerk the arms out of my sockets or pretending to run me down with forklift trucks.

I'd like to tell the professor how I look at the authors and poets in the textbook and ask myself which of them I'd like to have a pint with in a Greenwich Village pub and the one that stands out is Chaucer. I'd buy him a pint anytime and listen to his stories about the Canterbury pilgrims. I'd like to tell the professor how much I love the sermons of John Donne and how I'd like to buy him a pint except that he was a Protestant priest and not known for sitting in taverns knocking back the pint.

I can't talk about this because it's dangerous to raise your hand in any class to say how much you love anything. The professor will look at you with a pitying little smile and the class will see that and the pitying little smile will travel around the room till you feel so foolish the face turns red and you promise you'll never love anything in college again or if you do keep it to yourself. I can say this to Brian McPhillips sitting next to me but someone in the seat before me turns and says, Aren't we being a little paranoid?

Paranoid. That's another word I have to look up with the way everyone at NYU uses it. From the way this student looks at me with his superior left eyebrow nearly up to his hairline I can only guess he's accusing me of being demented and there's no use trying to answer him till I find out what that word means. I'm sure Brian McPhillips knows what that word means but he's busy talking to Joyce Timpanelli on his left. They're always looking at each other and smiling. That means there's something going on and I can't bother them with the word paranoid. I should carry a dictionary and when anyone throws a strange word at me I could look it up on the spot and shoot back with a smart answer that would collapse the superior eyebrow.

Or I could practise the silence I learned in the army and go my own way which is the best thing of all because people who torment other people with strange words don't like it when you go your own way.

Andy Peters sits next to me in Introduction to Philosophy and tells me about a job in a bank, Manufacturer's Trust Company down on

Broad Street. They're looking for people to work with personal loan applications and I could choose a four to midnight shift or a midnight to eight a.m. He says the best thing about this job is once you finish the work you can leave, that no one works a full eight hours.

There's a typing test and I have no trouble with that because of the way the army dragged me away from my dog and made me a company clerk typist. The bank says, OK, I can work the four to midnight shift so that I can take my classes in the morning and sleep at night. Wednesdays and Fridays I have no classes and I can shape up at the warehouses and piers and make extra money against the day my brother, Michael, is out of the air force and the allotment to my mother ends. I can put the Wednesday-Friday money in a separate account and when the time comes she won't have to be running to the St Vincent de Paul Society for food or shoes.

There are seven women and four men on the shift at the bank and all we have to do is take piles of applications for personal loans and send notices to the applicants that they've been accepted or rejected. Andy Peters tells me during a coffee break that if I ever see an application from a friend that's been rejected I can change it to acceptance. There's a little code the daytime loan officers use and he'll show me how to alter it.

Night after night we see hundreds of applications for loans. People want them for new babies, vacations, cars, furniture, consolidation of debts, hospital expenses, funerals, decorating apartments. Sometimes there are letters attached and if there's a good one we all stop typing and read them back and forth. There are letters that make the women cry and the men want to cry. Babies die and there are expenses and would the bank help. A husband runs away and the applicant doesn't know what to do, where to turn. She never had a job in her life, how could she with raising three kids, and she needs three hundred dollars to tide her over till she finds work and a cheap baby-sitter.

One man promises that if the bank loans him five hundred dollars they can take a pint of his blood every month for the rest of his life and it's a good deal, he says, because he has a rare blood type which he's not ready to divulge at this moment but if the bank helps him out they're getting blood that's as good as gold, the best collateral in the world.

The blood man is rejected and Andy lets it pass but he changes the code for the desperate woman with the three kids who was rejected for having no collateral. Andy says, I don't understand how they can give loans to people who want to spend two weeks lying on the sand at the goddam Jersey shore and then turn down a woman with three kids hanging on by her fingernails. This, my friend, is where the revolution starts.

He changes a few applications every night to prove how stupid a bank can be. He says he knows what happens during the day when asshole loan people go through the applications. Harlem address? Negro? Points off. Puerto Rican? Mucho points off. He tells me there are dozens of Puerto Ricans around New York who think they were accepted for their good credit but it was Andy Peters all the time feeling sorry for them. He says it's a big thing in PR neighborhoods to get out there on the weekend and polish the car. They might never go anywhere but it's the polishing that matters, old guys on the stoop watching the polishing and drinking the old cerveza from bodegas in quart bottles, the radio blasting away with Tito Puente, the old guys checking out the girls shaking their asses along the sidewalks, man, that's living, man, that's living and what more do you want?

Andy talks about Puerto Ricans all the time. He says they're the only people who know how to live in this goddam tight-ass city, that it's a tragedy the Spaniards didn't sail up the Hudson instead of the goddam Dutch and the goddam limeys. We'd have siestas, man, we'd have color. We wouldn't have the Man in the Gray Flannel Suit. If he had his way he'd give a loan to every Puerto Rican applying for a car loan so that all over the city you'd have them polishing their new cars, drinking their beer out of brown paper bags, digging Tito, and flirting with the girls shaking their asses along the sidewalks, girls with those see-through peasant blouses and Jesus medallions nestling in their cleavage, and wouldn't that be a city to live in?

The women in the office laugh at the way Andy talks but they tell him be quiet because they want to finish the work and get outa here. They have kids at home and husbands waiting.

When we finish early we go for a beer and he tells me why he's a thirty-one-year-old student studying philosophy at New York University. He was in the war, not Korea, the big one in Europe, but he has to work nights in this goddam bank because of his dishonorable discharge in the spring of 1945, just before the war ended and isn't that a bitch.

Taking a shit, that's what he was, a nice quiet shit in a French ditch, all wiped and ready to button up when who comes along but a goddam lieutenant and a sergeant and the lieutenant has nothing else to do but march up to Andy and accuse him of an unnatural act with that sheep standing there a few feet away. Andy admits that in a way the lieutenant had a right to jump to the wrong conclusion since just before pulling up his pants Andy had a hard-on which made it difficult to pull up the aforesaid pants and even though he hated anything in the shape of an officer he felt an explanation would help.

Well, Lieutenant, I may have fucked that sheep or I may not have fucked that sheep but what's interesting here is your peculiar concern with me and my relationship with that sheep. There's a war on, Lieutenant. I come out here to take a shit in a French ditch and there's a sheep at eye level and I'm nineteen years old and I haven't been laid since my high school prom and a sheep, especially a French sheep, looks very tempting and if I looked like I was ready to jump on that sheep you're right, Lieutenant, I was, but I didn't. You and the sergeant interrupted a beautiful relationship. I thought the lieutenant would laugh, instead he said I was a goddam liar, that I had sheep written all over me. I wanted sheep all over me. I dreamed of it but it hadn't happened and what he said was so unfair I pushed him, didn't hit him, just pushed, and the next thing, Jesus, they had all kinds of artillery sticking in my face, pistols, carbines, M1 rifles, and before you know it there was a court martial where I had a drunken captain defending me who told me in private that I was a disgusting sheep fucker and he was sorry he couldn't be at the other end prosecuting me because his father was a Basque from Montana where they respected their sheep, and I still don't know if I was sent to the stockade for six months for assaulting an officer or screwing a sheep. What I got out of it was a dishonorable discharge and when that happens you might as well study philosophy at NYU.

30

Because of Mr Calitri I scribble memories of Limerick in notebooks. I make lists of streets, schoolmasters, priests, neighbors, friends, shops.

After "The Bed" essay I'm sure people in Mr Calitri's class are looking at me in a different way. The girls are probably telling each other they'd never go out with someone who spent his life in a bed a man might have died in. Then Mike Small tells me she heard about the essay and how it moved so many people in the class, boys and girls. I didn't want her to know what I came from but now she wants to read the essay and afterwards her eyes fill up and she says, Oh, I never knew. Oh, it must have been awful. It reminds her of Dickens though I don't know how that can be because everything in Dickens always ends well.

Of course I won't say this to Mike Small for fear she might think I'm arguing with her. She might turn on her heel and march back to Bob the football player.

Now Mr Calitri wants us to write a family essay where there's adversity, a dark moment, a setback, and even though I don't want to go into the past there's something that happened to my mother that demands to be written.

THE PLOT

When the war started and food was rationed in Ireland the government offered poor families plots of land in fields outside Limerick. Each family could have a sixteenth of an acre, clear it, and grow whatever vegetables they liked.

My father applied for a plot out the road in Rosbrien and the government lent him a spade and a fork for the work. He took my brother Malachy and me to help him. When my brother Michael saw the spade he cried and wanted to go too but he was only four and he would have been in the way. My father told him, Whisht, that when we came back from Rosbrien we'd bring him berries.

I asked my father if I could carry the spade and I was soon sorry because Rosbrien was miles outside Limerick. Malachy had started out carrying the fork but my father took it away from him because of the way he was swinging it and nearly knocking people's eyes out. Malachy cried till my father said he'd let him carry the spade all the way home. My brother soon forgot the fork when he saw a dog who was willing to chase a stick for miles till he frothed white stuff with the weariness and lay down on the road looking up with the stick between his paws and we had to leave him.

When my father saw the plot he shook his head. Rocks, he said, rocks and stones. And all we did that day was to make a pile by the low wall along the road. My father used the spade to keep digging up rocks and even though I was only nine I noticed two men in the next plots talking and looking at him and laughing in a quiet way. I asked my father why and he gave a small laugh himself and said, The Limerickman gets the dark earth and the man from the North gets the rocky plot.

We worked till the darkness came and we were so weak with hunger we couldn't pick up another rock. We didn't mind one bit if he carried the fork and spade and wished he could carry us, too. He said we were big boys, good workers, our mother would be proud of us, there would be tea and fried bread, and he marched ahead with his long strides till halfway home he stopped suddenly. Your brother Michael, he said. We promised him berries. We'll have to go back out the road to the bushes.

Malachy and I complained so much that we were tired and could hardly walk another step that my father told us go home, he'd get the berries himself. I asked why couldn't he get the berries tomorrow and he said he had promised Michael berries for tonight, not tomorrow, and away he went with the spade and fork on his shoulder.

When Michael saw us he started to cry, Berries, berries. He stopped when we told him, Dad is out the road in Rosbrien getting your berries so will you quit the crying and let us have our fried bread and tea.

We could have eaten a whole loaf between us but my mother said, Leave some for your father. She shook her head. He's such a fool going all the way back there for the berries. Then she looked at Michael the way he was standing at the door looking up the lane for a sign of my father and she shook her head in a smaller way.

Soon Michael spotted my father and he was gone up the lane calling out, Dad, Dad, did you get the berries? We could hear Dad, In a minute, Michael, in a minute.

He stood the spade and fork in a corner and emptied his coat pockets on to the table. Berries he brought, the great black juicy berries you find at the tops and backs of bushes beyond the reach of children, berries he plucked in the dark of Rosbrien. My mouth watered and I asked my mother if I could have a berry and she said, Ask Michael, they're his.

I didn't have to ask him. He handed me the biggest of the berries, the juiciest, and he handed one to Malachy. He offered berries to my mother and father but they said no thanks, they were his berries. He offered Malachy and me another berry each and we took them. I thought if I had berries like that I'd keep them all for myself but Michael was different and maybe he didn't know any better because he was four.

After that we went to the plot every day but Sunday and cleared it of rocks and stones till we reached the earth and helped my father with the planting of potatoes, carrots and cabbage. There were times we left him and roamed the road, hunting for berries and eating so many it gave us the runs.

My father said in no time we'd be digging up our crop but he wouldn't be here to do it. There was no work in Limerick and the English were looking for people to work in their war factories. It was hard for him to think of working for the English after what they did to us but the money was tempting and as long as the Americans had entered the war it was surely a just cause.

He went off to England with hundreds of men and women. Most sent money home but he spent his in the pubs of Coventry and forgot he had a family. My mother had to borrow from her own mother and ask for credit from Kathleen O'Connell's grocery shop. She had to beg for food from the St Vincent de Paul Society or wherever she could get it. She said it would be a great relief to us and we'd be saved when the time came to dig up our spuds, our carrots, our lovely heads of cabbage. Oh, we'd have a right feed then and if God was good He might send us a nice piece of ham and that wasn't asking too much when you lived in Limerick, the ham capital of all Ireland.

The day came and she put the new baby, Alphie, in the pram. She borrowed a coal sack from Mr Hannon next door. We'll fill it, she said. I carried the fork and Malachy the spade so that he wouldn't be knocking people's eyes out with the prongs. My mother said, Don't be swinging those tools or I'll give ye a good clitther on the gob.

A smack in the mouth.

When we arrived at Rosbrien there were other women digging in the plots. If there was a man in the field he was old and not able for the work in England. My mother said hello across the low wall to this woman and that woman and when they didn't answer back she said, They must be all gone deaf with the bending over.

She left Alphie in the pram outside the plot wall and told Michael mind the baby and don't be hunting for berries. Malachy and I jumped over the wall but she had to sit on it, swing her legs over, and get down on the other side. She sat a minute and said, There's nothing in the world like a new potato with salt and butter. I'd give me two eyes for it.

We lifted the spade and fork and went to the plot but for all we got there we might as well have stayed at home. The earth was still fresh from being dug and turned over and white worms crawled in the holes where the potatoes and carrots and heads of cabbage used to be.

My mother said to me, Is this the right plot?

'Tis.

She walked the length of it and back. The other women were busy bending over and picking things out of the ground. I could see she wanted to say something to them but I could see also she knew it was no use. I went to pick up the spade and fork and she barked at me, Leave them. They're no use to us now with everything gone. I wanted to say something but her face was so white I was afraid she'd hit me and I backed away, over the wall.

She came over the wall herself, sitting, swinging her legs, sitting again till Michael said, Mam, can I go hunting berries?

You can, she said. You might as well.

If Mr Calitri likes this story he might make me read it to the class and they'll roll their eyes and say, More misery. The girls might have felt sorry for me over the bed but that's enough, surely. If I go on writing about my miserable childhood they'll say, Stop, stop, life is hard enough, we have our own troubles. So, from now on, I'll write stories about my family moving to the suburbs of Limerick where everyone is well fed and clean from taking a bath at least once a week.

31

P addy Arthur McGovern warns me that if I keep on listening to that noisy jazz music I'll wind up like the Lennon brothers so American I'll forget I'm Irish altogether and what will I be then. It's no use telling him how the Lennons could be so excited about James Joyce. He'd say, Oh, James Joyce, me arse. I grew up in the County Cavan and no one there ever heard of him and if you don't watch your step you'll be running to Harlem and jitterbuggin' with Negro girls.

He's going to an Irish dance on Saturday night and if I have any sense I'll go with him. He wants to dance only with Irish girls because if you dance with Americans you never know what you're getting.

At the Jaeger House on Lexington Avenue Mickey Carton is up there with his band and Ruthie Morrissey singing "A Mother's Love is a Blessing". A great crystal ball revolves on the ceiling, flecking the ballroom with floating silver spots. Paddy Arthur is no sooner in the door than he's waltzing around with the first girl he asks to dance. He has no trouble getting girls to dance and why should he with his six feet one, his black curly hair, his rich black eyebrows, his blue eyes, the dimple on his chin, the cool way he has of offering his hand that says, Come up, girl, so that the girl would never dream of saying no to this vision of a man and when they move out on the floor, no matter what class of a dance it is, waltz, foxtrot, lindy, two-step, he steers her around with hardly a glance at her and when he leads her back to her seat she's the envy of every giggling girl on the seats along the wall.

He comes to the bar where I'm having a beer for the courage that might be in it. He wants to know why I'm not up dancing. Sure what's the use of coming here if you don't dance with them grand girls along the wall?

He's right. The grand girls sitting along the wall are like the girls in Cruise's Hotel in Limerick except they're wearing dresses the likes of which you'd never see in Ireland, silk and taffeta and materials strange to me, pink, puce, light blue, ornamented here and there with lacy bows, dresses with no shoulders so stiff at the front that when the girl turns to the right the dress stays where it is. Their hair is trapped with pins and combs for fear it might tumble rich to the shoulders. They sit with their hands in their laps holding fancy purses and they smile only when they talk to each other. Some sit dance after dance, ignored by the men, till they're forced to dance with the girls beside them. They clump across the floor and when the dance ends move to the bar for lemonade or orange squash, the drink of girl couples.

I can't tell Paddy I'd rather stay where I am, safe at the bar. I can't tell him that going to any kind of a dance gives me a sick empty feeling, that even if a girl got up to dance with me I wouldn't know what to say to her. I could manage a waltz, oompah oompah, but I could never be like the men on the floor who whisper and make girls laugh so hard they can hardly dance for a whole minute. Buck used to say in Germany that if you can make a girl laugh you're halfway up her leg.

Paddy dances again and comes to the bar with a girl named Maura and tells me she has a friend, Dolores, who's shy because she's Irish-American and would I dance with her since I was born here and we'd make a good match with her ignorance of Irish dancing and my listening to that jazz music all the time.

Maura looks up at Paddy and smiles. He smiles down at her and winks at me. She says, Excuse me. I want to make sure Dolores is OK, and when she's gone Paddy whispers she's the one he's going home with. She's a head waitress in Schrafft's Restaurant with her own apartment, saving money to go back to Ireland and this will be Paddy's lucky night. He says I should be nice to Dolores, you never know, and he winks again. I think I'll be gettin' me hole tonight, he says.

Me hole. Of course that's what I'd like myself but that's not the way I'd say it. I prefer Mikey Molloy's way of saying it in Limerick when he called it the excitement. If you're like Paddy with Irish women jumping into your arms you probably don't remember one from another and they all become one hole until you meet the girl you like and she makes you realize she wasn't put into the world to fall on her back for your pleasure. I could never think about Mike Small like that or even Dolores who's standing there blushing and shy, the way I feel myself. Paddy nudges me and talks out of the side of his mouth. Ask her to dance, for Christ's sake.

All that comes out of me is a mumble and I'm lucky Mickey Carton is playing a waltz with Ruthie singing "There's One Fair County in Ireland", the only dance where I might not make a fool of myself. Dolores smiles at me and blushes and I blush back and there go the two of us blushing around the floor with the little silver spots floating across our faces. If I stumble she steps along with me in such a way that the stumble becomes a dance step and after a while I think I'm Fred Astaire and she's Ginger Rogers and I whirl her around sure the girls along the wall are admiring me and dying for a dance with me.

The waltz stops and even though I'm ready to leave the floor for fear Mickey might start a lindy or a jitterbug Dolores pauses as if to say, Why don't we dance this? And she's so easy on her feet and so light with her touch I look at the other couples, how cool they are, and it's no trouble at all to do it with Dolores, whatever it is, and I push her and pull and twirl her like a top till I'm sure all the girls are eyeing me and envying Dolores till I'm so full of myself I don't notice there's a girl sitting near the door with a crutch sticking out where it shouldn't be and when my foot catches in it I go flying into the laps of the grand girls along the wall who push me off in a rough unfriendly way remarking that some people shouldn't be allowed on the dance floor if they can't hold their drink.

Paddy is at the door with his arm around Maura. He's laughing but she's not. She looks at Dolores as if to sympathize with her but Dolores helps me to my feet, asking me if I'm all right. Maura comes over and whispers to her and turns to me. Will you take care of Dolores?

I will.

She and Paddy leave and Dolores says she'd like to leave, too. She lives in Queens and she says I really don't have to see her all the way home, the E train is safe enough. I can't tell her I'd like to take her home in the hope she might ask me in and there might be some excitement. She surely has her own apartment and she might feel so sorry about the way I tripped over the crutch she wouldn't have the heart to turn me away and we'd be in her bed in no time, warm, naked, mad for each other, missing Mass, breaking the Sixth Commandment over and over and not giving a fiddler's fart.

When the E train rocks or stops quickly we're thrown together and I can smell her perfume and feel her thigh against mine. It's a good sign when she doesn't pull away from me and when she lets me hold her hand I'm in heaven till she starts talking about Nick, her boyfriend in the navy, and I put her hand back in her lap.

I can't understand the women in this world, Mike Small who drinks beer with me in Rocky's and then runs to Bob, now this one who lures me on to the E train all the way to the last stop at 179th Street. Paddy Arthur would never have put up with this. Back at the dance hall he would have made certain there was no Nick in the navy and no one at home to interfere with his all-night plans. If there was any doubt he'd have jumped off the train at the next stop, so why don't I? I was soldier of the week in Fort Dix, I trained dogs, I go to college, I read books, and look at me now sneaking through the streets around NYU to avoid Bob the football player and taking a girl home who's planning to marry someone else. It seems everyone in the world has someone, Dolores her Nick, Mike Small her Bob, and Paddy Arthur is well into his night of excitement with Maura in Manhattan and what kind of a bloody fool am I traveling to the end of the line?

I'm ready to jump off at the next stop and leave Dolores entirely when she takes my hand and tells me how nice I am, that I'm a good dancer, too bad about the crutch, we could have danced all night, that she likes the way I talk, the cute brogue, it's easy to see I was well brought up, it's so nice that I go to college, and she doesn't understand why I'm hanging around with Paddy Arthur who, it was easy to see, had no good on his mind with respect to Maura. She squeezes my hand and tells me I'm so nice to travel all the way home with her and she'll never forget me and I feel her thigh against mine all the way to the last stop and when we stand to leave the train I have to bend to hide the excitement that's throbbing in my trousers. I'm ready to walk her home but she stands by a bus stop and tells me she lives farther out, in Queen's Village, and really, I don't have to go all the way, she'll be all right on the bus. She squeezes my hand again and I wonder if there's any hope that this might be my lucky night and I'll wind up wild in bed like Paddy Arthur.

While we wait for the bus she holds my hand again and tells me all about Nick in the navy, how her father doesn't like him because he's Italian and calls him all kinds of insulting names behind his back, how her mother really likes Nick but would never admit it in case her father might come home in a drunken rage and smash the furniture which wouldn't be the first time. The worst nights are when her brother, Kevin, visits and stands up to her father and you wouldn't believe the swearing and the rolling on the floor. Kevin is a linebacker at Fordham and a good match for her father.

What's a linebacker?

You don't know what a linebacker is?

I don't.

You're the first boy I ever met who didn't know what a linebacker is.

Boy. I'm twenty-four years old and she's calling me a boy and I'm wondering do you have to be forty to be a man in America?

All along I'm hoping that things are so terrible with her father she might have her own place but, no, she lives at home and there go my dreams for a night of excitement. You'd think a girl her age would have her own place so that she could invite in the likes of me who see her to the end of the line. I don't care if she squeezes my hand a thousand times. What's the use of having your hand squeezed on a bus in the middle of the night in Queens if there's no promise of a bit of excitement at the end of the journey?

She lives in a house with a statue of the Virgin Mary and a pink bird on the little front lawn. We stand at the small iron gate and I'm wondering if I should kiss her and get her into such a state we might go behind a tree for the excitement but there's a roar from inside, Goddamit it, Dolores, get your ass in here, hell of a nerve you have coming home at this goddam hour and tell that goddam shithead run for his life, and she says, Oh, and runs inside.

By the time I get back to Mary O'Brien's everyone is up and

having bacon and eggs followed by rum and slices of pineapple in heavy syrup. Mary puffs on her cigarette and gives me the knowing smile.

You look like you had a good time last night.

32

When the day workers at the bank leave their offices Bridey Stokes comes in with her mop and bucket to clean three floors. She pulls a large canvas bag behind her, fills it with trash from the waste paper baskets and drags it to the freight elevator to empty it somewhere in the basement. Andy Peters tells her she should have extra canvas bags so that she won't have to travel up and down so much and she says the bank won't supply even one more canvas bag they're that cheap. She could buy them herself but she's working nights to keep her son, Patrick, at Fordham University and not to be supplying the Manufacturer's Trust Company with canvas bags. Every night on each floor she fills the bag twice and that means six trips to the basement. Andy tries to explain to her that if she had six canvas bags she could fill the elevator once and that would save so much time and energy she could finish earlier and go home to Patrick and her husband.

Husband? He drank himself to death ten years ago.

I'm sorry to hear that, says Andy.

I'm not a bit sorry. He was too handy with his fists and I bear the marks to this day. Patrick, too. He'd think nothing of knocking little Patrick around the house till the little fella couldn't even cry anymore and it was so bad one night I took him from the house and begged the man in the subway booth to let us in and I asked a cop where was Catholic Charities and they took care of us and got me this job and I'm grateful even if there's only one canvas bag.

Andy tells her she doesn't have to be a slave.

I'm not a slave. I'm up in the world since I got away from that lunatic. God forgive me but I didn't even go to his funeral.

She lets out a sigh and leans on the handle of the mop which comes up to her chin she's that small. She has large brown eyes and no lips and when she tries to smile there's nothing to smile with. She's so thin that when Andy and I go out to the coffee shop we bring her a cheeseburger with french fries and a milkshake to see if we could put some fat on her bones till we realize she's not touching the food but taking it home to Patrick who's studying accounting at Fordham.

Then one night we find her crying and stuffing the freight elevator with six bulging canvas bags. There's room for us with the bags and we ride down with her wondering if the bank suddenly turned generous and lavished canvas bags on her.

No. 'Tis my Patrick. One more year and he'd be graduated from Fordham but he left me a note to say he's in love with a girl from Pittsburgh and they're gone off to start a new life in California and I said to myself if that's the way I'm going to be treated I'm not going to kill myself with the one canvas bag anymore and I went up and down the streets of Manhattan till I found a place on Canal Street that sells them, a Chinese place. You'd think in a city like this you wouldn't have trouble finding canvas bags and I don't know what I'd do without the Chinese.

She cries harder and pulls the sleeve of her sweater across her eyes. Andy says, All right, Mrs Stokes.

Bridey, she says. I'm Bridey now.

All right, Bridey. We'll go across the street and you can eat something for your strength.

Ah, no. I have no appetite.

Take off the apron, Bridey. We're going across the street.

She tells us in the coffee shop she doesn't even want to be Bridey anymore. She's Brigid. Bridey is a name for skivvies and Brigid has the bit of dignity. No, she could never manage a cheeseburger but she eats it and all the french fries slathered with ketchup and tells us her heart is broken while she sucks her milkshake through a straw. Andy wants her to explain why she suddenly decided to get the canvas bags. She doesn't know. There was something about Patrick leaving like that and the memories of the way her husband beat her that opened a little door in her head and that's all she can say about it. The days of the one bag are over. Andy says there's no rhyme nor reason to it. She agrees but she doesn't care anymore. She got off the *Queen Mary* over twenty years ago, a healthy girl excited over America, and look at her now, a scarecrow. Well, her scarecrow days are over, too, and she'd love a piece of apple pie if they have it. Andy says he studies rhetoric, logic, philosophy but this is beyond him and she says they're very slow with the apple pie.

There are books to be read, term papers written, but I'm so obsessed with Mike Small I sit at the library window and watch her movements along Washington Square between the main university building and the Newman Club where she goes between classes even though she's not a Catholic. When she's with Bob the football player my heart sinks and that song runs through my head, "I Wonder Who's Kissing Her Now?" though I know very well who's kissing her now, Mr Football Player himself, two hundred pounds of him bending to plant his lips on her and even though I know I'd like him if there were no Mike Small in the world, he's that decent and good-humored, I still want to find the back of a comic book where Charles Atlas promises to help me build muscles that will let me kick sand in Bob's face the first time I meet him at a beach.

When summer comes he puts on his ROTC uniform and travels to North Carolina for training and Mike Small and I are free to meet and roam Greenwich Village, eating at Monte's on MacDougal Street, drinking beer at the White Horse or the San Remo. We ride the Staten Island Ferry and it's lovely to stand on deck, hand in hand, to watch the Manhattan skyline recede and loom even though I can't stop thinking again of the ones who were sent back with the bad eyes and the bad lungs and wondering what it was like for them in towns and villages all over Europe once they had a glimpse of New York, the tall towers over the water and the way the lights twinkle at dusk with tugboats hooting and ships blaring in the Narrows. Did they see and hear all this through the windows at Ellis Island? Did the memory bring pain and did they ever again try to slip into this country through a place where there weren't men in uniform rolling back their eyelids and tapping at their chests?

When Mike Small says, What are you thinking about? I don't know what to say for fear she might think I'm peculiar the way I wonder about the ones who were sent back. If my mother or father had been sent back I wouldn't be on this deck with the lights of Manhattan a sparkling dream before me.

Besides, it's only Americans who ask questions like that, What are you thinking about? or What do you do? In all my years in Ireland no one ever asked me such questions and if I weren't madly in love with Mike Small I'd tell her mind her own business about what I'm thinking or what I do for a living.

I don't want to tell Mike Small too much about my life because of the shame and I don't think she'd understand especially when she grew up in a small American town where everyone had everything. But when she starts talking about her days in Rhode Island with her grandmother there are clouds. She talks about swimming in the summer, ice skating in the winter, hay rides, trips to Boston, dates, proms, editing her high school yearbook, and her life sounds like a Hollywood movie till she goes back to the time her father and mother separated and left her with his mother in Tiverton. She talks about how much she missed her mother and how she cried herself to sleep for months and now she cries again. This makes me wonder if ever I had been sent to live in comfort with a relation would I have missed my family? It's hard to think I would have missed the same tea and bread every day, the collapsed bed swarming with fleas, a lavatory shared by all the families in the lane. No, I wouldn't have missed that but I would have missed the way it was with my mother and brothers, the talk around the table and the nights around the fire when we saw worlds in the flames, little caves and volcanoes and all kinds of shapes and images. I would have missed that even if I lived with a rich grandmother and I felt sorry for Mike Small who had no brothers and sisters and no fire to sit at.

She tells me how excited she was the day she graduated from elementary school, how her father was to travel all the way up from New York for the party but called at the last minute to say he had to go to a picnic for tugboat men and the memory of that brings the tears again. That day on the phone her grandmother blasted her father, told him he was a no-good skirt-chasing bastard and not to set foot in Tiverton again. At least her grandmother was there. She was there for everything, always. She wasn't much for the kissing and hugging and tucking in but she kept the house clean, the clothes laundered, the lunch box well stuffed every day for school.

Mike wipes her tears and says you can't have everything and even if I say nothing I wonder why you can't have everything or at least give everything. Why can't you clean the house, launder the clothes, stuff the lunch box and still kiss, hug, and tuck in? I can't say this to Mike because she admires her grandmother for being tough and I'd prefer to hear that grandma might have hugged, kissed, and tucked in.

With Bob away at ROTC camp Mike invites me to visit her family. She lives on Riverside Drive near Columbia University with her father, Allen, and her new stepmother, Stella. Her father is a tugboat captain for the Dalzell Towing Company in New York harbor. Her stepmother is pregnant. Her grandmother, Zoe, is here from Rhode Island for a while till Mike settles in and gets used to New York.

Mike tells me her father likes to be called Captain and when I say, Hello, Captain, he growls till the phlegm rattles in his throat and squeezes my hand till the knuckles crack so that I'll know how manly he is. Stella says, Hi, honey, and kisses my cheek. She tells me she's Irish, too, and it's nice to see Alberta going out with Irish boys. Even she says boys and she's Irish. Grandmother lies on the living room couch with her hands joined under her head and when Mike introduces me Zoe's hairline twitches forward and she says, Howya doin'?

It slips out of my mouth, Nice easy life you have there on the couch.

She glares at me and I know I've said the wrong thing and it's awkward when Mike and Stella go to another room to look at a dress and I'm left standing in the middle of the living room with the Captain smoking a cigarette and reading the *Daily News*. No one speaks to me and I'm wondering how Mike Small can go off and leave me standing here with the father and the grandmother ignoring me. I never know what to say to people at times like this. Should I say, How's the tugboat business? or should I tell the grandmother she did a wonderful job raising Mike.

My mother in Limerick would never leave anyone standing in the middle of the room like this. She'd say, Sit down there and we'll have a nice cup of tea, because in the lanes of Limerick it's a bad thing to ignore anyone and even worse to forget the cup of tea.

It's strange that a man with a good job like the Captain and his mother on the couch wouldn't bother to ask me if I had a mouth in my head or if I'd like to sit down. I don't know how Mike can leave me standing like this though I know if this ever happened to her she'd simply sit down and make everyone feel cheerful the way my brother Malachy does.

What would happen if I sat down? Would they say, Oh, you're feeling pretty relaxed sitting down without being asked? Or would they say nothing and wait till I leave to talk behind my back?

They'll talk behind my back anyway and tell each other Bob is a much nicer boy and looks handsome in his ROTC uniform though they might have said as much if they'd seen me in my summer khakis with my corporal's stripes. I doubt it. They probably prefer him with his high school diploma and his clear healthy eyes and his bright future and his cheerful nature all done up in his officer's uniform.

And I know from the history books the Irish were never liked up there in New England, that there were signs everywhere saying, No Irish Need Apply.

Well, I don't want to beg anyone for anything and I'm ready to turn on my heel and walk out when Mike bounces down the hall all blonde and smiling and ready for a walk and dinner in the Village. I'd like to tell her I don't want to have anything to do with people who leave you standing in the middle of the floor and hang out signs rejecting the Irish but she's so bright and blue-eyed and cheerful, so clean and American, I think if she told me stand there forever I'd be like a dog and wag my tail and do it.

Then on the way down in the elevator she tells me I said the wrong thing to grandma, that grandma is sixty-five and works very hard cooking and keeping the house clean and doesn't like people's smartass remarks about taking a few minutes on the couch.

What I want to say is this, Oh, fuck your grandma and her cooking and cleaning. She has plenty of food and drink and clothes and furniture and hot and cold running water and no shortage of money and what the bloody hell is she complaining about? There are women all over the world raising large families and not whining and there's your grandmother lying on her arse complaining she has to take care of an apartment and a few people. Fuck your grandma again.

That is what I want to say except that I have to swallow my words in case Mike Small might be offended and never see me again and

207

it's very hard going through life not saying what comes to your tongue. It's hard being with a beautiful girl like her because she'd never have any trouble getting someone else and I'd probably have to find a girl not as good-looking who didn't mind my bad eyes and my lack of a high school diploma though a girl not as good-looking might offer me a chair and a cup of tea and I wouldn't have to swallow my words all the time. Andy Peters is always telling me life is easier with plain-looking girls, especially ones with small tits or no tits, because they're always grateful for the least bit of attention and one might even love me for myself, as they say in the movies. I can't even think of Mike Small having tits the way she's reserving the whole body for the wedding night and the honeymoon and it gives me a pain to picture Bob the football player having the excitement with her on the wedding night.

The platform boss from the Baker and Williams Warehouse sees me on the subway train and tells me I can get work during the summer with men going on vacation. He lets me work eight to noon and when I'm finished on the second day I walk over to Port Warehouses to see if I can have a sandwich with Horace. I often think he's the father I'd like to have even if he's black and I'm white. If ever I said that to anyone at the warehouse I'd be laughed off the platform. He must know himself the way they talk about black people and he surely hears the word nigger floating through the air. When I worked on the platform with him I wondered how he could keep his fists to himself. Instead he'd put his head down and have a little smile and I thought he might be a bit deaf or simple in his mind but I knew he wasn't deaf and the way he talked about his son getting an education in Canada showed that if he'd had a chance he would have been in a university himself.

He's coming out of a diner on Laight Street and when he sees me he smiles, Oh, mon. I must have known you were coming. I got a hero sandwich a mile long and beer. We eat on the pier, okay?

I'm ready to walk back down Laight Street to the pier but he steers me away. He doesn't want the men at the warehouse to see us. They'd ride him all day. They'd laugh and ask Horace when he knew my mother. That makes me want to defy them and walk Laight Street even more. No, mon, he says. Save your emotions for bigger things.

This is a big thing, Horace.

It's nothing, mon. It's ignorance.

We should fight back.

No, son.

God, he's calling me son.

No, son. I don't have time for fighting back. I won't step on their ground. I pick my own fights. I have a son in college. I have a wife who is ailing and still cleaning offices at night on Broad Street. Eat your sandwich, mon.

It's ham and cheese slathered with mustard and we wash it down with a quart of Rheingold passing the bottle back and forth, and I have a sudden thought and a feeling that I'll never forget this hour on the pier with Horace with seagulls circling for what might come and ships strung along the Hudson waiting for tugboats to dock them or push them out to the Narrows, traffic rushing behind us and over our heads on the West Side Highway, a radio in a pier office with Vaughn Monroe singing "Buttons and Bows", Horace offering me another chunk of sandwich telling me I could use a few pounds on my bones and his surprised look when I nearly drop the sandwich, nearly drop it because of the weakness in my heart and the way tears are dropping on the sandwich and I don't know why, can't explain it to Horace or myself with the power of this sadness that tells me this won't come again, this sandwich, this beer on the pier with Horace that makes me feel so happy all I can do is weep with the sadness in it and I feel so foolish I'd like to rest my head on his shoulder and he knows that because he moves closer, puts his arm around me as if I were his own son, the two of us black or white or nothing, and it doesn't matter because there's nothing to do but put down the sand-wich where a seagull swoops in and gobbles it and we laugh, Horace and I, and he puts in my hand the whitest handkerchief I've ever seen and when I offer it back he shakes his head, keep it, and I tell myself I'll keep that handkerchief till my last breath.

I tell him what my mother used to say when we cried, Oh, your bladder must be near your eye, and he laughs. He doesn't seem to mind if we go back up Laight Street, and the men on the platform say nothing about him and my mother because it's hard to hurt people already laughing and beyond you.

33

Sometimes she's invited to cocktail parties. She takes me along and I'm confused with the way people stand nose to nose chatting and eating little things on bits of stale bread and crackers, no one singing or telling a story the way they did in Limerick, till they start looking at their watches and saying, Are you hungry? Wanna go eat something? and out they drift and that's what they call a party.

That's the uptown New York and I don't like it one bit especially when a man in a suit talks to Mike, tells her he's a lawyer, nods towards me, asks her why in heaven's name she's going out with someone like me and invites her to go to dinner as if she should walk away and leave me with the empty glass, everything stale, and nobody singing. Of course she says, No, thanks, though you can see she's flattered and I often wonder if she'd like to go with Mr Lawyer in the Suit rather than stay with me, a man from a slum who never went to high school and gawks at the world with two eyes like pissholes in the snow. Surely she'd like to marry someone with clear blue eyes and spotless white teeth who would take her to cocktail parties and move to Westchester where they'd join the country club, play golf and drink martinis, and frolic in the night in the grip of the gin.

I know already what I prefer myself, the downtown New York where men with beards and women with long hair and beads are reading poetry in coffee houses and bars. Their names are in the papers and magazines, Kerouac, Ginsberg, Brigid Murnaghan. When they're not living in lofts and tenements they roam the country. They drink wine from great jugs, they smoke marijuana, they lie on floors and dig the jazz. Dig. That's the way they talk and they click their fingers, cool, man, cool. They're like my Uncle Pa in Limerick, they don't give a fiddler's fart about anything. If they had to go to a cocktail party or wear a tie they'd die.

A tie was the cause of our first disagreement and the first time I saw Mike Small's temper. We were to go to a cocktail party and when I met her outside her apartment building on Riverside Drive she said, Where's your tie?

It's at home.

But this is a cocktail party.

I don't like wearing ties. They don't wear them down in the Village.

I don't care what they wear in the Village. This is a cocktail party and all the men will be wearing ties. You're in America now. Let's go up to a men's store on Broadway and get you a tie.

Why should I buy a tie when I have one at home?

Because I'm not going to that party with you in that condition.

She walked away from me, up 116th Street to Broadway, stuck her hand out, jumped into a taxi without giving me a second look to see if I was coming.

I took the Seventh Avenue train to Washington Heights in a blind agony, cursing myself for my stubbornness and worrying she might give me up completely for a Mr Lawyer in a Suit, that she might spend the rest of the summer going to cocktail parties with him till Bob the football player returned from ROTC. She might even give up Bob for the lawyer, finish college and move to Westchester or Long Island where all the men wear ties, where some have ties for every day of the week and social functions on top of it. She might be happy going to the country club all dressed up and remembering what her father said, A lady is not properly dressed till she has white gloves up to her elbows.

Paddy Arthur was coming down the stairs, all dressed up, no tie, on his way to an Irish dance and why didn't I go with him, I might meet Dolores again, ha ha.

I turned and went back downstairs telling him I didn't care if I never saw Dolores again in this life or the next after what she did luring me on to the E train and all the way to Queens Village letting me think there might be a bit of excitement at the end of the night. Before getting on the downtown train Paddy and I stopped for a beer at a Broadway bar and Paddy said, Jesus, what's up with you? Is it some kind of a bee you have up your arse?

When I told him about Mike Small and the tie he wasn't a bit sympathetic. He said that's what I get for running around with them fookin' Protestants and what would my poor mother say back in Limerick.

I don't care what my mother would say. I'm mad about Mike Small.

He asked for a whiskey and told me I should have one, too, loosen me up, calm me down, clear my head, and once I had two whiskeys in my system I told him how I'd like to lie on a Greenwich Village floor smoking marijuana, sharing a jug of wine with a long-haired girl, Charlie Parker on the phonograph floating us to heaven and easing us down again on a long low sweet wail.

Paddy gave me the fierce look. Arrah, for Jasus' sake, is it coddin' me you are? Do you know the trouble with you? Protestants and Negroes. Next thing it'll be Jews and then you're doomed altogether.

There was an old man smoking a pipe on the stool beside Paddy and he said, That's right, son, that's right. Tell your friend there that you have to stick with your own. All me life I stuck with me own, dug holes for the phone company, all Irish, never a bit of trouble because, by Jesus, I stuck with me own and I seen young fellas comin' over marryin' all kinds an' losin' their faith an' the next thing they're goin' to baseball games an' that's the end of them.

The old man said he knew a man from his own town who worked twenty-five years in a pub in Czechoslovakia and came home to settle down without a word of Czechoslovakian in his head and all because he stuck to his own kind, the few Irishmen he could find there, all sticking together, thank God an' His Blessed Mother. The old man said he'd like to buy us a drink to honor the men and women of Ireland who stick with their own so that when a child is born they know who the father is and that, by Christ, God forgive the language, is the most important thing of all, knowing who the father is.

We raised the glasses and toasted all who stick with their own and know who the father is. Paddy leaned towards the old man and they talked about home, which is Ireland, though the old man hadn't seen it for forty years and hoped to be buried in the lovely town of Gort beside his poor old Irish mother and his father who did his bit in the long struggle against the perfidious Saxon tyrant, and he raised his glass to sing,

> God save Ireland, sez the heroes,
> God save Ireland, sez 'em all,
> Whether on the scaffold high
> Or the battlefield we die,
> Oh, what matter when for Erin's sake we fall.

They sank deeper and deeper into their whiskey and I stared into the bar mirror wondering who's kissing Mike Small now, wishing I could be parading the streets with her so that heads would turn and I'd be the envy of one and all. Paddy and the old man talked to me only to remind me that thousands of men and women died for Ireland who'd hardly be happy with my behavior the way I run around with Episcopalians betraying the cause. Paddy gave me his back again and I was left to gawk at what I could see of myself in the mirror and wonder at the world I found myself in. From time to time the old man leaned around Paddy to tell me, Stick to your own, stick to your own. I'm in New York, land of the free and home of the brave but I'm supposed to behave as if I were still in Limerick, Irish at all times. I'm expected to go out only with Irish girls who frighten me with the way they're always in a state of grace saying no to everything and everyone unless it's a Paddy Muck who wants to settle on a farm of land in Roscommon and bring up seven children, three cows, five sheep and a pig. I don't know why I returned to America if I have to listen to the sad stories of Ireland's sufferings and dance with country girls, Mullingar heifers, beef to the heels.

There's nothing in my head but Mike Small, blonde, blue-eyed, delicious, sailing through life in her easy Episcopalian way, the all-American girl, with sweet memories of Tiverton in her head, the small town in Rhode Island, the house where her grandmother reared her, the bedroom with little curtains moving gently at the windows that looked out on the Narragansett River, the bed dressed with sheets, blankets, pillows galore, blonde head on pillow filled with dreams of outings, hayrides, trips to Boston, boys boys boys, and grandma in the morning setting out the nourishing all-American breakfast so that her little girl can move through the day charming the arse off every boy, girl, teacher and anyone she meets including me and mostly me as I sit stricken on the bar stool.

There was a darkness in my head from the whiskey and I was ready to tell Paddy and the old man, I'm weary of Ireland's sufferings and I can't live in two countries at the same time. Instead I left them, the two of them colloguin' on their bar stools, and walked from 179th Street down Broadway to 116th Street hoping that if I waited long enough I'd have one glimpse of Mike Small being brought home by Mr Lawyer in a Suit, a glimpse I want and don't want, till a cop in a patrol car calls to me and tells me, Move on, buddy, all the Barnard girls are gone to bed.

Move on, says the cop, and I did because there was no use trying to tell him I know who's kissing her now, that she's surely at a movie with the lawyer's arm around her, the tips of his fingers dangling at the border of her breast which is reserved for the honeymoon, that there might be a kiss or a squeeze between popcorn munches, and I'm here on Broadway looking at the gates of Columbia University across the street and I don't know which way to turn, wishing I could find a girl from California or Oklahoma, all blonde and blue-eyed like Mike Small, all cheerful with teeth that never knew an ache or cavity, all cheerful because her life is laid out so that she'll graduate from college and marry a nice boy, boy she calls him, and settle down in peace, ease and comfort, as my mother used to say.

The cop came at me again and told me keep moving, pal, and I tried to cross 116th Street with a bit of dignity so that he wouldn't be able to point the finger and tell his partner, There goes another whiskey-head Mick from the Old Country. They didn't know and wouldn't care that all this was happening because Mike Small wanted me to wear a tie and I refused.

The West End Bar was packed with Columbia students and I thought if I had a beer I might merge in and be mistaken for one of them, higher on the scale than NYU students. A blonde might take a fancy to me and get my mind off Mike Small though I didn't think I could shrug her off even if Brigitte Bardot herself slipped between my sheets.

I might as well be in the NYU cafeteria the way these Columbia students argued at the top of their voices about the emptiness of life, how absurd everything is and how all that matters is grace under pressure, man. When that bull's horn comes at you and grazes your hip you know that's the moment of truth, man. Read your Hemingway, man, read your J. Paul Sartre, man. They know the score.

If I didn't have to work in banks, docks, warehouses, I'd have time to be a proper college student and moan over the emptiness. I wish my father and mother had lived respectable lives and sent me to college so that I could spend my time in bars and cafeterias telling everyone how I admired Camus for his daily invitation to suicide and Hemingway for risking the bull's horn in the side. I know if I had money and time I'd be superior to every student in New York in the despair department though I could never mention any of this to my mother because she'd say, Arrah, for God's sake, don't you have your health and shoes and a fine head o' hair and what more do you want?

I drank my beer and wondered what kind of a country is this where cops keep telling you move on, where people put pigeonshit in your ham sandwich, where a girl who's engaged to be engaged to a football player walks away from me because I'm not wearing a tie, where a nun will baptize Michael what's left of him though he suffered in a concentration camp and deserves to be left in his Jewish condition bothering no one, where college students eat and drink to their hearts' content and moan about existentialism and the emptiness of everything, and cops tell you once again, Move on.

I walked back up Broadway past Columbia into Washington Heights and over to the George Washington Bridge where I could look up and down the Hudson River. My head was filled with dark clouds and noises and a coming and going of Limerick and Dachau and Ed Klein where Michael what's left of him, a piece of offal, was saved by GIs, and my mother moved in and out of my head with Emer from Mayo and Mike Small from Rhode Island, and Paddy Arthur laughed and said you'll never dance with Irish girls with them two eyes like pissholes in the snow, and I looked up and down the river and felt sorry for myself till the sky brightened beyond and the sun coming up traveled from tower to tower turning Manhattan into pillars of gold.

34

A few days later she calls me in tears. She's out on the street and would I come and get her at 116th and Broadway. There was trouble with her father, she has no money and doesn't know what to do. She's waiting on the corner and on the train she tells me how she got dressed with every intention of calling me and meeting me even though I had strong feelings about ties but her father said no, she wasn't going out and she said yes, she was going out and he punched her on the mouth which, as I can see, is swelling. She ran from her father's house and there's no going back. Mary O'Brien says she's in luck. One of the boarders is gone back to Ireland to marry the girl down the road and his room is available.

In a way I'm glad her father punched her because she came to me instead of Bob and that surely means she prefers me. Of course Bob is unhappy and in a few days there he is at the door calling me a sneaky little bogtrotter and telling me he's going to break my head but I move my head to one side and his fist crashes into the wall and he has to go to the hospital for a cast. On the way out he threatens he'll see me again and I'd better make my peace with my Maker though when I run into him a few days later at NYU he offers his good hand in friendship and I never see him again. He may be calling Mike Small behind my back but it's too late and she shouldn't even be talking to him since she already allowed me into her room and into her bed forgetting how she was reserving the body for the wedding night and the honeymoon. The night of our first excitement she tells me I've taken her virginity and if I should feel guilty or sad I can't especially when I know I'm the first, the one that stays forever in any girl's memory, as they used to say in the army.

We can't stay at Mary O'Brien's because we can't resist the temptation to be in the same bed and there are knowing looks. Paddy Arthur stops talking to me altogether and I'm not sure if he's being pious or patriotic, angry that I'm with someone neither Catholic nor Irish.

The Captain sends word he's ready to give Mike a certain amount of money every month and that means she can rent a small apartment in Brooklyn. I'd like to live with her but the Captain and the grandmother would think that disgraceful, so I rent my own cold water flat at 46 Downing Street in Greenwich Village. They call it a cold water flat and I don't know why. It has hot water but no heat except for a large kerosene heater which turns so red I'm afraid it might blow up. The only thing I can do to keep warm is to buy an electric blanket at Macy's and plug it into a long cord that lets me wander around. There's a bath tub in the kitchen, and a lavatory in the hallway I must share with an old Italian couple across the hall. The old Italian man knocks on my door to tell me I'm to put my own toilet paper on the holder in the lavatory and I'm to keep my hands off his. He and his wife mark their toilet paper and they'll know if I try to use it so watch out. His English is poor and when he starts to tell me of the troubles he had with the previous tenants in my flat he becomes so frustrated he shakes his fist in my face and warns me I could be in big trouble if I touch his toilet paper, big trouble, yet gives me a roll to start me off, to make sure I don't touch his. He says his wife is a nice woman and giving me the roll is her idea, that she's a sick woman who wants a quiet life and no trouble. Capice?

Mike finds a small apartment on Henry Street in Brooklyn Heights. She has her own bathroom and no one torments her over toilet paper. She says my apartment is a disgrace and she doesn't know how I can live like that, no heat, no place to cook, Italians yelling over toilet paper. She feels sorry for me and lets me stay over. She makes delicious dinners even though she didn't even know how to make coffee when her father punched her out of the house.

When classes end she goes back to Rhode Island to have her dentist examine the abscess caused by her father's fist. I'm taking summer session courses at NYU, reading, studying, writing term papers. I'm working at the bank, the midnight to eight shift, and operating the forklift at the Baker and Williams warehouse two days a week, dreaming of Mike Small nice and cozy with her grandmother in Rhode Island.

She calls to tell me her grandmother isn't that angry with me anymore over what I said about her easy life. Grandma even said something nice about me.

What was that?

She said you have a nice head of black curly hair and she feels so sorry about the thing with my father she doesn't mind if you come here for a day or two.

After what happened to me in the bank I could go to Rhode Island for a week. A man sat next to me in a coffee shop on Broad Street near where I worked, told me he had heard me talk the night before and figured I was Irish, right?

I am.

Yeah, well, I'm Irish, too, Irish as Paddy's pig, father from Carlow, mom from Sligo. I hope you don't mind but I got your name from someone and found you're a member of the Teamsters and the ILA.

My ILA card expired.

That's okay. I'm an organizer and we're trying to break into these fucking banks, excuse the language. Are you on for that?

Oh, sure.

I mean you're the only one we could get on your shift with any kind of union history and what we'd like you to do is just drop little hints. You know and they know the banks pay shit wages. So, just a little hint here and there, not too many, not too soon, and I'll see you in a few weeks. Here, I'll take care of the bill.

Next night is Thursday, pay night, and when we receive our checks the supervisor says, You've got the rest of the night off, McCourt.

He makes sure everyone on the shift hears him. You're off tonight, McCourt, and all the other nights and you can tell that to your union friends. This is a bank and we don't need any goddam unions.

They say nothing, the typists, the clerks. They nod. Andy Peters would say something but he's still on the four to twelve shift.

I take my check and as I wait for the elevator an executive comes out of his office. McCourt, right?

I nod.

So, you're finishing college, right?

I am.

Ever think of joining us here? You could come aboard and we'd have you up to a nice five-figure salary in three years. I mean you're one of our own, right? Irish?

I am.

Me, too. Father from Wicklow, mom from Dublin, and when you work at a bank like this doors open, you know, AOH, Knights of Columbus, all that there. We take care of our own. If we don't, who will?

I was just fired.

Fired? What the hell you talking about? Fired for what?

For letting a union organizer talk to me in a coffee shop.

You did that? Let a union organizer talk to you?

I did.

That was a stupid damn thing to do. Look, pal, we're outa the coal mines, we're outa the kitchens and the ditches. We don't need unions. Will the Irish ever get sense? Asking you a question. Talkin' a yeh.

I say nothing here and on the elevator going down. I say nothing because I've been fired from this bank and there's nothing to say anyway. I don't want to talk about the Irish getting sense and I don't know why everyone I meet has to tell me where his father and mother came from in Ireland.

The man wants to argue with me but I won't give him the satisfaction. It's better to walk away and leave him to the height he grew, as my mother used to say. He calls after me to tell me I'm an asshole, that I'll wind up digging ditches, delivering beer barrels, pouring whiskey for boozy micks in a Blarney Stone bar. He says, Jesus, is there anything wrong with looking after your own kind? and the strange thing is there's something in his voice that's sad as if I were a son that disappointed him.

Mike Small meets my train in Providence, Rhode Island, and takes me by bus to Tiverton. On the way we stop at a liquor store for a bottle of Pilgrim's rum, grandma's favorite. Zoe, the grandmother, says hi but doesn't offer hand or cheek. It's dinner time and there's corned beef and cabbage and boiled potatoes because that's what the Irish like to eat, according to Zoe. She says I must be tired from the trip and surely I'd like a drink. Mike looks at me and smiles and we know it's Zoe who wants a drink, rum and Coke.

How about you, grandma? Would you like a drink?

Well, I dunno, but all right. Are you making the drinks, Alberta?

Yes.

Well, go easy with the Coke. It kills my stomach.

We sit in a living room dark from layers of blinds, curtains, drapes. There are no books, magazines, newspapers and the only pictures are of the Captain in his army lieutenant's uniform and one of Mike, a blonde angel of a child.

We sip our drinks and there's a silence because Mike is in the hallway answering the phone and Zoe and I have nothing to say to each other. I wish I could say, This is a nice house, but I can't because I don't like the darkness of this room when the sun is beaming outside. Then Zoe calls out, Alberta, you gonna stay on that goddam phone all night? You have a guest. She says to me, That's Charlie Moran she's talking to. They was great friends all through school but goddam he likes to talk.

Charlie Moran, is it? Mike leaves me here in this gloomy room with grandma while she chatters away with her old boyfriend. All these weeks in Rhode Island she's been having a grand time of it with Charlie while I'm slaving away in banks and warehouses.

Zoe says, Make yourself another drink, Frank. That means she wants one, too, and when she tells me go easy on the Coke, it kills her stomach, I double her rum dosage hoping it will knock her out so that I can have my way with her granddaughter.

But no, the drink makes her livelier and after a few swallows she says, Let's eat, goddamit. Irishmen like to eat, and while we're eating, she says, Do you like that, Frank?

I do.

Well, then, eat it. You know what I always say. A meal ain't a meal without a potato and I'm not even Irish. No, goddamit, not a drop of Irish though there's a bit of Scotch. MacDonald was my mother's name. That's Scotch, isn't it?

'Tis.

Not Irish?

No.

After dinner we watch television and she falls asleep in her armchair after telling me that Louis Armstrong there on the screen is ugly as sin and can't sing worth a damn. Mike shakes her and tells her go to bed.

Don't tell me go to bed, goddamit. You might be a college student but I'm still your grandmother, isn't that right, Bob?

I'm not Bob.

You're not? Well, who are you?

I'm Frank.

Oh, the Irishman. Well, Bob's a nice fellow. He's gonna be an officer. What are you gonna be?

A teacher.

A teacher? Oh, well, you won't be drivin' no Cadillac, and she pulls herself up the stairs to bed.

Now, surely, with Zoe snoring away in her room Mike will visit my bed but, no, she's too nervous. What if Zoe woke suddenly and discovered us? I'd be out on the road hailing the bus to Providence. It's a torment when Mike comes to kiss goodnight and even in the dark I know she's in her pink baby doll pajamas. She won't stay, oh, no, grandma might hear and I tell her I wouldn't care if God Himself were in the next room. No, no, she says, and leaves, and I wonder what kind of world is this where people will walk away from a chance of a wild fling in the bed.

At dawn Zoe runs the vacuum cleaner upstairs and downstairs and complains, This goddam house looks like Hogan's Alley. The house is spotless because she has nothing else to do but clean it and she barks about Hogan's Alley to put me in my place because she knows I know it was a dangerous Irish slum in New York. She complains the vacuum cleaner doesn't pick up the way it used to though it's easy to see there's nothing to pick up. She complains that Alberta sleeps too late and is she supposed to make three separate breakfasts, her own, mine, Alberta's?

Her neighbor, Abbie, drops in and they drink coffee and complain about kids, dirt, television, that goddam ugly Louis Armstrong who can't sing, dirt, the price of food and clothes, kids, the goddam Portuguese taking over everything in Fall River and surrounding towns, bad enough when the Irish ran everything, at least they could speak English long as they were sober. They complain about hairdressers who charge a fortune and can't tell a decent hairdo from a donkey's ass.

Oh, Zoe, says Abbie, your language.

Well, I mean it, goddamit.

If my mother were here she'd be puzzled. She'd wonder why these women complain. Lord above, she'd say, they have everything. They're warm and clean and well fed and they complain about everything. My mother and the women in the slums of Limerick had nothing and rarely complained. They said it was the will of God.

Zoe has everything but complains with the music of the vacuum cleaner and that may be her way of prayer, goddamit.

In Tiverton Mike is Alberta. Zoe complains she doesn't know why a girl would want to use a goddam name like Mike when she has her own name, Agnes Alberta.

We walk around Tiverton and I imagine again what it would be like to be a teacher here, married to Alberta. We'd have a sparkling kitchen where every morning I'd have my coffee and an egg and read the *Providence Journal*. We'd have a big bathroom with plenty of hot water and thick towels with powerful naps and I might loll there in the tub and gaze on the Narragansett River through little curtains billowing gently in the morning sun. We'd have a car for trips to Horseneck Beach and Block Island, and we'd visit Alberta's mother's relations in Nantucket. As the years passed my hair would recede, my belly protrude. Friday nights we'd attend local high school basketball games and I'd meet someone who might sponsor me for the country club. If they admitted me I'd have to take up golf and that would surely be the end of me, the first step towards the grave. A visit to Tiverton is enough to drive me back to New York.

35

In the summer of 1957 I complete my degree courses at NYU and in the autumn pass the Board of Education exams for teaching high school English.

An afternoon newspaper, *The World-Telegram and Sun*, has a School Page where teachers can find jobs. Most of the vacancies are for vocational high schools and friends have already warned me, Don't go near those vocational high schools. The kids are killers. They'll chew you up and spit you out. Look at that movie, *The Blackboard Jungle*, where a teacher says vocational schools are the garbage cans of the school system and the teachers are there to sit on the lids. See that movie and you'll run in the other direction.

There is a vacancy for an English teacher at Samuel Gompers Vocational High School in the Bronx but the chairman of the Academic Department tells me I look too young and the kids would give me a hard time. He says his father was from Donegal, his mother from Kilkenny, and he'd like to help me. We should take care of our own but his hands are tied and the way he shrugs and extends his open palms contradicts what he said entirely. Still, he heaves himself from his chair and walks me to the front door with his arm across my shoulders, tells me I should try Samuel Gompers again, maybe in a year or two I'd fill out and lose that innocent look, and he'd keep me in mind though I needn't bother to come back if I grew a beard. He can't stand beards and he wants no goddam beatniks in his department. Meanwhile, he says, I might try the Catholic high schools where the pay wasn't that good but I'd be with my own kind of people and a nice Irish kid should stick with his own.

The Academic Chairman at Grady Vocational High School in Brooklyn says, Yeah, he'd like to help me out but, you know, with that brogue you'd have trouble with the kids, they might think you talk funny and teaching is hard enough when you speak properly and doubly hard with a brogue. He wants to know how I passed the speech part of the teachers' license examination and when I tell him I was issued a substitute license on condition I take remedial speech he says, Yeah, maybe you could come back when you don't sound like Paddy-off-the-boat, ha ha ha. He tells me in the meantime I should stick with my own people, he's Irish himself, well, three-quarters Irish and you never know with other people.

When I meet Andy Peters for a beer I tell him I can't get a teaching job till I fill out and look older and talk like an American and he says, Shit. Forget the teaching. Go into business. Specialize in something. Hubcaps. Corner the market. Get a job in a garage and learn all you can about hubcaps. People come into the garage and hubcaps are mentioned and everyone turns to you. A hubcap crisis, you know? where a hubcap falls off, flies through the air and decapitates a model housewife and all the TV stations call you for your expert opinion. Then you go out on your own. McCourt's Hubcap Emporium. Foreign and Domestic Hubcaps New and Old. Antique Hubcaps for the Discerning Collector.

Is he serious?

Maybe not about hubcaps. He says, Look at what they do in the academic world. You corner a half-acre of human knowledge, Chaucer's phallic imagery in *The Wife of Bath*, or Swift's devotion to shit, and you build a fence around it. Decorate the fence with footnotes and bibliographies. Post a sign, Keep off, Trespassers Will Lose Their Tenure. I'm engaged, myself, in a noble search for a Mongolian philosopher. I thought of cornering the market on an Irish philosopher but all I could find was Berkeley and they've got their claws into him already. One Irish philosopher, for Christ's sakes. One. Don't you people ever ponder? So I'm stuck with the Mongolians or the Chinese and I'll probably have to learn Mongolian or Chinese or whatever the hell they speak there and when I find him he'll be my very own.

When was the last time you heard a Mongolian philosopher mentioned at those East Side cocktail parties you like so much? I'll get my PhD, write a few articles on my Mongolian in obscure scholarly journals. I'll deliver learned lectures to drunken Orientalists at MLA conventions and wait for the job offers to pour in from the Ivy League and its cousins. I'll get a tweed jacket, a pipe, and a pompous manner, and faculty wives will be throwing themselves at me, begging me to recite, in English, erotic Mongolian verses smuggled into the country up the ass of a yak or a panda at the Bronx Zoo. And I'll tell you another thing, piece of advice in case you go to graduate school. When you take a course always find out what the professor wrote his doctoral dissertation on and give it back to him. If the guy specializes in Tennyson's water images then pour it all over him. If the guy specializes in George Berkeley give him the sound of one hand clapping while a tree falls in the forest. How do you think I got through these fucking philosophy courses at NYU? If the guy's a Catholic I give him Aquinas. Jewish? I give him Maimonides. Agnostic? You never know what to tell an agnostic. You never know where you stand with them though you can always try old Nietzsche. You can bend that old fucker any way you like.

Andy tells me Bird was the greatest American who ever lived, right up there with Abraham Lincoln and Max Kiss, the guy who invented Ex-Lax. Bird should be given the Nobel Prize and a seat in the House of Lords.

Who's Bird?

For Christ's sakes, McCourt. I worry about you. You tell me you love jazz and you don't know Bird. Charlie Parker, man. Mozart. You listenin' to me? You dig? Mozart, for Christ's sakes. That's Charlie Parker.

What does Charlie Parker have to do with teaching jobs or hubcaps or Maimonides or anything else?

You see, McCourt, that's your problem, always looking for relevance, a sucker for logic. That's why the Irish don't have philosophers. Lotta goddam barroom theologians and shithouse lawyers. Loosen up, man. Thursday night I finish early and we'll take a trip to Fifty-Second Street for a little music. Okay?

We go from club to club till we come to one place where a black woman in a white dress croaks into a microphone and holds on to it as if she were on a swaying ship. Andy whispers, That's Billie and it's a disgrace they're letting her make an ass of herself up there.

He marches to the stage and tries to take her hand to help her down but she curses him and swings at him till she stumbles and falls off the stage. Another man leaves his barstool and leads her out the door and I know from the clear sounds between her croaks that was Billie Holiday, the voice I heard on the Armed Forces Network when I was a boy in Limerick, a pure voice telling me, "I Can't Give You Anything But Love, Baby."

Andy says, That's what happens.

What do you mean, that's what happens?

I mean that's what happens, that's all. Jesus, do I have to write a book?

How is it you know Billie Holiday?

I have loved Billie Holiday since I was a child. I come to Fifty-Second Street to catch glimpses of her. I would hold her coat. I would scour her toilet bowl. I would run her bath water. I would kiss the ground she walks on. I told her I got a dishonorable discharge for not fucking a French sheep and she thought it should be made into a song. I don't know what God intends to do with me in the next life but I'm not going unless I can sit between Billie and Bird for eternity.

In the middle of March, 1958, there's another notice in the paper, Vacancy for English teacher at McKee Vocational and Technical High School, Staten Island. The assistant principal, Miss Seested, examines my license and takes me to see the principal, Moses Sorola, who doesn't move from his chair behind the desk where he squints at me through a cloud of smoke drifting from his nose and from the cigarette in his hand. He says this is an emergency situation. The teacher I'd be replacing, Miss Mudd, has made an abrupt decision to retire in the middle of the term. He says teachers like that are inconsiderate and make life hard for a principal. He doesn't have a full English program for me, that I'd have to teach three classes in Social Studies every day, two in English.

But I don't know anything about Social Studies.

He puffs and squints and says, Don't worry about it, and takes me to the office of the Academic Chairman, Acting, who says I'd be teaching three classes of Economic Citizenship and here's the text-book, *Your World and You*. Mr Sorola smiles through the smoke and says, *Your World and You*. That should cover just about everything.

I tell him I know nothing about economics or citizenship and he says, Just stay a few pages ahead of the kids. Everything you tell them will be news. Tell them this is 1958, tell them their names, tell them they live on Staten Island, and they'll be surprised and grateful for the information. By the end of the year even your name will be news to them. Forget your college literature courses. This is not high IQ plateau.

He takes me to see Miss Mudd, the teacher I'm replacing. When he opens the classroom door boys and girls are leaning out the windows calling to others across the schoolyard. Miss Mudd sits at her desk, reading travel brochures, ignoring the paper airplane that zooms over her head.

Miss Mudd has retired.

Mr Sorola leaves the room and she says, That's right, young man. I can't wait to get outa here. What's this? Wednesday? Friday's my last day and you're welcome to this looney bin. Thirty-two years I've been at this and who cares? The kids? Parents? Who, young man, gives a shit, forgive my French? We teach their brats and they pay us like dishwashers. What was the year? Nineteen and twenty-six. Calvin Coolidge was in. I came in. I worked right through him and the Depression man, Hoover, and Roosevelt and Truman and Eisenhower. Look out that window. You got a good view of New York Harbor from here and Monday morning if these kids aren't driving you crazy you'll see a big ship sailing by and that'll be me on the deck waving, son, waving and smiling, because there's two things I never want to see again in my life, with God's help, Staten Island and kids. Monsters, monsters. Look at 'em. You'd be better off working with chimpanzees in the Bronx Zoo. What's this? Nineteen and fifty-eight. How did I ever last? You'd need to be Joe Louis. So, good luck, son. You're gonna need it.

36

Before I leave Mr Sorola says I should return next day to observe Miss Mudd with her five classes. I'd learn something about procedure. He says half of teaching is procedure and I don't know what he's talking about. I don't know what to make of the smile through the cigarette smoke and I wonder if he's joking. He pushes my typed program across the desk, three classes of EC, Economic Citizenship, two classes of E4, sophomore English in the fourth term. The top of the program card says, Official Class, PRA, and at the bottom, Building Assignment, School Cafeteria, fifth period. I don't ask Mr Sorola what these mean for fear he might think I'm ignorant and change his mind about hiring me.

As I make my way down the hill to the ferry a boy's voice calls, Mr McCourt, Mr McCourt, are you Mr McCourt?

I am.

Mr Sorola would like to see you again.

I follow the student up the hill and I know why Mr Sorola wants to see me again. He has changed his mind. He's found someone with experience, someone with a grasp of procedure, someone who knows what an official class is. If I don't get this job I'll have to start my search again.

Mr Sorola waits at the front door of the school. He lets his cigarette dangle from his mouth and puts his hand on my shoulder. He says, I have good news for you. The job is opening sooner than we expected. Miss Mudd must have been impressed by you because she decided to leave today. In fact she's gone, out the back door, and it's barely noon. So we're wondering if you can take over tomorrow and then you won't have to wait till Monday.

But I . . .

Yeah, I know. You're not ready. That's okay. We'll give you some stuff to keep the kids busy till you get the hang of it and I'll look in from time to time to keep them in line.

He tells me this is my golden opportunity to jump right in and start my teaching career, I'm young, I'll like the kids, they'll like me, McKee High School has a hell of a faculty all ready to help and support.

Of course I say yes, I'll be in tomorrow. It isn't the teaching job of my dreams but it will have to do since I can't get anything else. I sit on the Staten Island ferry thinking of teacher recruiters from suburban high schools at NYU, how they told me I seemed intelligent and enthusiastic but really my accent would be a problem. Oh, they had to admit it was charming, reminded them of that nice Barry Fitzgerald in *Going My Way* but but but. They said they had high standards of speech in their schools and it wouldn't be possible to make an exception in my case since the brogue was infectious and what would parents say if their kids came home sounding like Barry Fitzgerald or Maureen O'Hara?

I wanted to work in one of their suburban schools, Long Island, Westchester, where the boys and girls were bright, cheerful, smiling, attentive, their pens poised as I discoursed on *Beowulf, The Canterbury Tales*, the Cavalier Poets, the Metaphysicals. I'd be admired and once the boys and girls had passed my classes their parents would surely invite me to dinner at the finest houses. Young mothers would come to see me about their children and who could tell what might happen when husbands were absent, the men in grey flannel suits, and I trolled the suburbs for lonely wives.

I'll have to forget the suburbs. I have here on my lap the book that will help me through my first day of teaching, *Your World and You*, and I flip the pages through a short history of the United States from an economic point of view, chapters on American government, the banking system, how to read the stock market pages, how to open a savings account, how to keep household accounts, how to get loans and mortgages.

At the end of each chapter there are questions of fact and questions for discussion. What caused the stock market crash of 1929? How can this be avoided in future? If you wanted to save money and gain interest would you a) keep it in a glass jar b) invest in the Japanese stock market c) keep it under your mattress d) put it in a savings bank account.

There are suggested activities, with insertions penciled in by a former student. Call a family meeting and discuss your family finances with Dad and Mom. Show them from your study of this book how they might improve their bookkeeping. (Insertion, Don't be surprised if they beat you up.) Take a tour of the New York Stock Exchange with your class. (They'll be glad to get out of school for a day.) Think of a product your community might need and start a small company to supply it. (Try Spanish fly.) Write to the Federal Reserve Board and tell them what you think of them. (Tell them leave a little for the rest of us.) Interview a number of people who remember the crash of 1929 and write a one-thousand-word report. (Ask them why they didn't commit suicide.) Write a story in which you explain the gold standard to a ten-year-old child. (It'll help him sleep.) Write a report on what it cost to build the Brooklyn Bridge and what it might cost now. Be specific. (Or else.)

The ferry sails by Ellis Island and the Statue of Liberty and I'm so worried about Economic Citizenship I don't even think of the millions who landed here and the ones who were sent back with the bad eyes and the weak chests. I don't know how I'll be able to stand before these American teenagers and talk to them about the branches of government and preach the virtues of saving when I owe money everywhere myself. And with the ferry sliding into its slip and the day that's facing me tomorrow why shouldn't I treat myself to a few beers at the Bean Pot bar and after those few beers why shouldn't I take a train to the White Horse Tavern in Greenwich Village to chat with Paddy and Tom Clancy and listen to them sing in the back room? When I call Mike to tell her the good news about the new job she wants to know where I am and gives me a lecture on the stupidity of staying out drinking beer the night before the most important day of my life and I'd better get my ass home if I know what's good for me.

Sometimes she talks like her grandmother who always tells you what to do with your ass. Get your ass in here. Get your ass out of that bed.

Mike is right but she graduated from high school and she'll know what to say to her classes when she starts teaching and even though I have a college degree I don't know what I'm going to say to Miss Mudd's classes. Should I be Robert Donat in *Goodbye, Mr Chips* or Glenn Ford in *The Blackboard Jungle*? Should I swagger into the classroom like James Cagney or march in like an Irish schoolmaster with a stick, a strap and a roar? If a student sends a paper airplane zooming at me should I shove my face into his and tell him try that one more time, kid, and you're in trouble? What am I to do with the ones looking out the window calling to their friends across the yard? If they're like some of the students in *The Blackboard Jungle* they'll be tough and they'll ignore me and the rest of the class will despise me.

Paddy Clancy leaves his singing in the back room of the White Horse and tells me he wouldn't be in my shoes for anything. Everyone knows what the high schools in this country are like, that's right, blackboard jungles. With my college degree why didn't I become a lawyer or a businessman or something where I could make some money? He knows a few teachers around the Village and they're getting out of it the first opportunity.

He's right, too. Everybody is right and I'm too muddled with all the beer in my body to worry anymore. I go to my apartment and fall into bed with all my clothes on and even though I'm worn out with the long day and the beer I can't sleep. I keep getting up to read chapters of *Your World and You*, testing myself with questions of fact, imagining what I'm going to say about the stock market, the differences between stocks and bonds, the three branches of government, the recession of this year, the depression of that year, and I might as well get up, go out, and fill myself with coffee to keep me going the rest of the day.

At dawn I sit in a coffee shop on Hudson Street with longshoremen, truck drivers, warehousemen, checkers. Why shouldn't I live like them? They work their eight hours a day, read the *Daily News*, follow baseball, have a few beers, go home to their wives, raise their kids. They're paid better than teachers and they don't have to worry about *Your World and You* and sex-crazed teenagers who don't want to be in your class. In twenty years workingmen can retire and sit in the Florida sun, waiting for lunch and dinner. I could call McKee Vocational and

Technical High School and tell them, Forget it, I want an easier life. I could tell Mr Sorola they're looking for a checker at the Baker and Williams Warehouse, a job I could easily get with my college degree, and all I'd have to do the rest of my life is stand on the platform with manifests on a clipboard checking what comes and what goes.

Then I think of what Mike Small would say if I told her, No, I didn't go to McKee High School today. I took a job as checker with Baker and Williams. She'd have a tantrum. She'd say, All that work in college to be a goddam checker down at the docks? She might throw me out of the house and return to the arms of Bob the football player and I'd be alone in the world, forced to go to Irish dances and take home girls reserving their bodies for the wedding night.

I'm ashamed of myself that I'm going to my first day of teaching in this condition, hung over from the White Horse Tavern, jumping out of my skin from seven cups of coffee this morning, my eyes like two pissholes in the snow, two days of black hair sprouting on my face, my tongue furry from lack of a toothbrush, my heart banging in my chest from fatigue and fear of dozens of American adolescents. I'm sorry I ever left Limerick. I could be back there with a pensionable job in the post office, postman respected by one and all, married to a nice girl named Maura, raising two children, confessing my sins every Saturday, in a state of grace every Sunday, a pillar of the community, a credit to my mother, dying in the bosom of Mother Church, mourned by a large circle of friends and relations.

There's a longshoreman at a table in the diner telling his friend how his son is graduating from St John's University in June, how he worked his ass off all these years to send the kid to college and he's the luckiest man in the world because his son appreciates what he's doing for him. Graduation Day he'll give himself a pat on the back for surviving a war and sending a son to college, a son who wants to be a teacher. His mother is so proud of him because she always wanted to be a teacher herself but never had the chance and this is the next best thing. Graduation Day they'll be the proudest parents in the world and that's what it's all about, right?

If this longshoreman and Horace down at Port Warehouses knew what I was thinking they'd have no patience with me. They'd tell me how lucky I am to have a college degree and a chance to teach.

★　　★　　★

The school secretary tells me see Miss Seested who tells me see Mr Sorola who tells me see the chairman of the Academic Department who says I have to check in with the school secretary to get my time card and why were they sending me to him in the first place?

The school secretary says, Oh, back already? and shows me how to dip my time card into the time clock, how to place it in my slot on the In Side and how to move it to the Out side. She says that if I have to leave the building for any reason whatsoever, even during my lunch period, I'm to sign out and back in with her because you never know when you might be needed, never know when there might be an emergency and you can't have teachers wandering in and out, back and forth at will. She tells me see Miss Seested who looks surprised. Oh, you're back, she says, and gives me a red Delaney book, the attendance book for my classes. She says, Of course you know how to use this, and I pretend I do for fear of being thought stupid. She sends me back to the school secretary for my home room attendance book and I have to lie to the secretary too and tell her I know how to use it. She says if I have any problems ask the kids. They know more than the teachers.

I'm trembling from the hangover and the coffee and the fear of what lies ahead of me, five classes, a home room, a Building Assignment, and I wish I were on the ferry to Manhattan where I could sit at a desk in a bank and make decisions about loans.

Students jostle me in the hallway. They push and scuffle and laugh. Don't they know I'm a teacher? Can't they see under my arm two attendance books and *Your World and You*? The schoolmasters in Limerick would never tolerate this carryon. They'd march up and down the halls with sticks and if you didn't walk properly you'd get that stick across the backs of your legs so you would.

And what am I supposed to do with this class, the first in my whole teaching career, students of Economic Citizenship, pelting each other with chalk, erasers, bologna sandwiches? When I walk in and place my books on the teacher's desk they'll surely stop throwing things. But they don't. They ignore me and I don't know what to do till the words come out of my mouth, the first words I ever utter as a teacher, Stop throwing sandwiches. They look at me as if to say, Who's this guy?

The bell signals the start of the class and the students slide into

233

their seats. They whisper to each other, they look at me, laugh, whisper again and I'm sorry I ever set foot on Staten Island. They turn to look at the blackboard along the side of the room where someone has printed in a large scrawl, Miss Mudd Is Gone. The Old Bag Reetired, and when they see me looking at it they whisper and laugh again. I open my copy of *Your World and You* as if to start a lesson till a girl raises her hand.

Yes?

Teacher, ain'tcha gonna take the attendance?

Oh, yes, I am.

That's my job, teacher.

When she sways up the aisle to my desk the boys make woo woo sounds and, Whaddya doin' the rest of my life, Daniela? She comes behind my desk, faces the class, and when she leans over to open the Delaney book it's easy to see her blouse is too small and that starts the woo woo all over again.

She smiles because she knows what the psychology books told us at NYU, that a fifteen-year-old girl is years ahead of a boy that age and if they want to shower her with woo woos it means nothing. She whispers to me she's already going out with a senior, a football player up at Curtis High School, where all the kids are smart, not a bunch of automechanic grease monkeys like the ones in this class. The boys know this, too, and that's why they pretend to clutch their hearts and faint when she calls out their names from the Delaney cards. She takes her time with the attendance book and I'm a fool standing off to the side, waiting. I know she's teasing the boys and I wonder if she's toying with me, too, showing her control of the class with a well-filled blouse and keeping me from whatever I might want to do with Economic Citizenship. When she calls the name of someone who was absent yesterday she demands a parent's note and if the absentee doesn't have it she reprimands him and writes N on the card. She reminds the class that five Ns could get you an F on your report card and turns to me, Isn't that right, teacher?

I don't know what to say. I nod. I blush.

Another girl calls out, Hey, teach, you cute, and I blush harder than ever. The boys roar and slap the desks with their open palms and the girls smile at each other. They say, You crazy, Yvonne, to the one who called me cute, and she tells them, But he is, he's really cute, and I wonder if the redness will ever leave my face, if I'll ever be able to stand here and talk about Economic Citizenship, if I'll be forever at the mercy of Daniela and Yvonne.

Daniela says she's finished with the attendance and now she needs the pass to go to the bathroom. She takes a piece of wood from a drawer and wiggles her way out the door to another woo woo chorus and one boy calling to another, Joey, stand up, Joey, let's see how much you love her, let's see you stand, Joey, and Joey blushes so hard there's a wave of laughter and giggling across the room.

We're halfway through the period and I haven't said a word about Economic Citizenship. I try to be a teacher, a schoolmaster. I pick up *Your World and You* and tell them, OK, open your book to chapter, ah, what chapter were you up to?

We weren't up to no chapter.

You mean you weren't up to any chapter? Any chapter.

No, I mean we weren't up to no chapter. Miss Mudd didn't teach us nothing.

Miss Mudd didn't teach you anything. Anything.

Hey, teacher, why you repeating everything I'm sayin'? Nothing, anything. Miss Mudd never bothered us like that. Miss Mudd was nice.

They nod and murmur, Yeah, Miss Mudd was nice, and I feel I have to compete with her even if they drove her into retirement.

A hand is up.

Yes?

Teacher, you Scotch or somethin'?

No. Irish.

Oh, yeah? Irish like to drink, eh? All that whiskey, eh? You gonna be here Paddy's Day?

I'll be here on St Patrick's Day.

You not gonna be drunk an' throwin' up at the parade like all the Irish?

I said I'll be here. All right, open your books.

A hand.

What books, teacher?

This book, *Your World and You*.

We ain't got that book, teacher.

We don't have that book.

There you go again repeatin' everything we say.

We have to speak proper English.

Teacher, this ain't no English class. This is Ecanawmic Cizzenship. We supposed to be learnin' about money an' all an' you ain't teachin' us about money.

Daniela returns just as another hand is raised. Teacher, what's your name? Daniela returns the pass to the desk and tells the class. His name is McCoy. I just found out in the bathroom an' he ain't married.

I print my name on the blackboard, Mr McCourt.

A girl in the back of the room calls out, Mister, you got a girl-friend?

They laugh again. I blush again. They nudge each other. The girls say, Isn't he cute? and I take refuge in *Your World and You*.

Open your books. Chapter One. We'll start at the beginning. "A Brief History of the United States of America."

Mr McCoy.

McCourt. McCourt.

OK, yeah, we know all that about Columbus an' everything. We get that in history class with Mr Bogard. He'll be mad if you teach history an' he's gettin' paid to teach it an' that's not your job.

I have to teach what's in the book.

Miss Mudd didn't teach what's in the book. She didn't give a shit, excuse me, Mr McCoy.

McCourt.

Yeah.

And when the bell rings and they rush from the room Daniela comes to my desk and tells me not to worry, don't lissena to these kids, they're all so stoopid, she's taking the commercial course to be a legal secretary, and who knows she might be a lawyer herself some day, she'll take care of the attendance and everything. She tells me, Don't take no shit from nobody, Mr McCoy, excuse the language.

There are thirty-five girls in the next class, all dressed in white with buttons down the front from neck to hem. Most have the same hairstyle, the beehive. They ignore me. They set up little boxes on their desks and peer into mirrors. They pluck their eyebrows, they dab at their cheeks with powder puffs, they apply lipstick and pull their lips back between their teeth, they file their nails and blow at the nail dust. I open the Delaney book to call their names and they look surprised. Oh, you the substitute? Where's Miss Mudd?

She has retired.

Oh, you gonna be our regular teacher?

Yes.

I ask them what shop they're in, what they're studying.

Cosmetology.

What's that?

Beauty Culture. And what's your name, teacher?

I point to my name on the board. Mr McCourt.

Oh, yeah. Yvonne said you was cute.

I let this pass. If I attempt to correct every grammatical error in these classes I'll never get to Economic Citizenship and, worse, if I'm asked to explain the rules of grammar I'm bound to show my ignorance. I will put up with no distractions. I will begin with Chapter One from *Your World and You*, "A Brief History of the United States". I flip the pages from Columbus to the Pilgrims to the War of Independence, the War of 1812, the Civil War, and there's a hand and a voice in the back of the room.

Yes?

Mr McCourt, why you telling us this stuff?

I'm telling you this because you can't understand Economic Citizenship unless you have a grasp of the history of your country.

Mr McCourt, this is an English class. I mean you're the teacher an' you don't even know what class you're teaching.

They pluck their eyebrows, they file their nails, they shake their beehives, they pity me. They tell me my hair is a mess and it's easy to see I never had a manicure in my life.

Why don'tcha come up to Beauty Culture Shop an' we'll do you?

They smile and nudge each other and my face is on fire again and they say that's cute, too. Aw, gee, lookit him. He's shy.

I have to take control. I have to be the teacher. After all, I was once a corporal in the United States Army. I told men what to do and if they didn't do it I'd have their ass because they were in direct defiance of military regulations and subject to court martial. I will simply tell these girls what to do.

Put everything away and open your books.

What books?

Whatever books you have for English.

All we got is this *Giants in the Earth* and that's the most boring book in the world. And the whole class chants, Uh, huh, boring, boring, boring.

They tell me it's about some family from Europe out there on the prairie and everyone is depressed and talking about suicide and no one in the class can finish this book because it makes you want to commit suicide yourself. Why can't they read a nice romance where you don't have all these Europe people all gloomy on the prairie? Or why couldn't they watch movies? They could watch James Dean, oh, gawd, James Dean, can't believe he's dead, they could watch him and talk about him. Oh, they could watch James Dean forever.

When the Beauty Culture girls leave there is homeroom, an eight-minute period when I have to take care of the clerical work for thirty-three students from printing shop. They swarm in, all boys, and they're helpful. They tell me what has to be done and not to worry. I am to take attendance, send a list of absentees to Miss Seested, collect absentee excuse notes supposedly written by parents and doctors, distribute transportation passes for bus, train, ferry. One boy brings the contents of Miss Mudd's mail box in the office. There are notes and letters from various officials in and out of the school, notes summoning wayward students for counseling, requests and demands for lists and forms and second and third reminders for everything. Miss Mudd seems to have ignored everything in her mail box for weeks and my head feels heavy with the thought of the work she's left me.

The boys tells me I don't have to take attendance every day but once I start I can't stop. Most are Italian and taking the attendance is light opera: Adinolfi, Buscaglia, Cacciamani, DiFazio, Esposito, Gagliardo, Miceli.

I'm supposed to lead the class in reciting the Pledge of Allegiance and singing "The Star Spangled Banner". I barely know them but that doesn't matter. The boys stand, place their hands on their hearts and recite their own version of the Pledge, I pledge allegiance to the flag of Staten Island, and to one night stands, one girl under me, invisible to all, with love and kisses for me only me.

When they sing "The Star Spangled Banner" some hum along with "You ain't nothin' but a hounddog".

There's a note from the Academic chairman requesting I go to his office next period, the third, my prep period when I'm supposed to plan my lessons. He tells me I should have a lesson plan for every class and there is a standard form for lesson plans, I should insist all students keep notebooks that are clean and neat, I should make sure their textbooks are covered, points off if they don't, I should check to see that windows are open six inches from the top, I should send a student around the room at the end of every period to collect litter, I should stand at the door to greet classes entering and again leaving, I should print clearly on the blackboard the title and aim of every lesson, I should never ask a question requiring a yes or no answer, I shouldn't allow unnecessary noise in the room, I should require all students to stay in their seats unless they raise their hands for the bathroom pass, I should insist on boys removing their hats, I should make it clear that no student is allowed to speak without first raising his hand. I should make sure all students stay till the end of the period, that they're not to be allowed out of the room at the warning bell which, for my information, rings five minutes before the end of the period. If my students are caught in the hallways before the end of the period I'll have to answer to the principal himself. Any questions?

The chairman says there will be mid-term exams in two weeks and my teaching should focus on the areas that will be covered in the exams. Students in English should have mastered spelling and vocabulary lists, one hundred of each which they are supposed to have in their notebooks and if they don't, points off, and be prepared to write essays on two novels. Economic Citizenship students should be more than halfway through *Your World and You*.

The bell rings for the fifth period, my Building Assignment, the school cafeteria. The chairman tells me that's an easy assignment. I'll be up there with Jake Homer, the teacher the kids fear most.

I climb the stairs to the cafeteria, my head throbbing, my mouth dry and I wish I could sail away with Miss Mudd. Instead I'm pushed and jostled by students on the staircase and stopped by a teacher who demands to see my pass. He's short and broad and his bald head sits, neckless, on his shoulders. He glares at me through thick glasses and his chin is a challenging jut. I tell him I'm a teacher and he won't believe me. He wants to see my program card. Oh, he says, I'm sorry. You're McCourt. I'm Jake Homer. We'll be in the cafeteria together. I follow him upstairs and along the hallway to the students' cafeteria. There are two lines waiting to be served in the kitchen, a boys and a girls. Jake tells me that's one of the big problems, keeping the boys and girls separated. He says they're animals at this age, especially the boys, and it's not their fault. It's nature. If he had his way he'd have the girls in a separate cafeteria altogether. The boys are always strutting and showing off and if two like the same girl there's bound to be a fight. He tells me if there is a fight don't interfere right away. Let the little bastards go at it and get it out of their systems. It's worse in the warm weather, May, June, when the girls take off their sweaters and the boys go tit crazy. The girls know what they're doing and the boys are like lap dogs, panting. Our job is to keep them separated and if a boy wants to visit the girls' section he has to come over here for permission. Otherwise you'll have two hundred kids going at it in broad daylight. We also have to patrol the cafeteria and make sure the kids take their trays and garbage back to the kitchen, make sure they clean the area around their tables.

Jake asks if I'd ever been in the army and when I tell him yes he says, Bet you didn't know you'd be pulling this kind of shit detail when you decided to become a teacher. Bet you didn't know you'd be a cafeteria guard, a garbage supervisor, a psychologist, a babysitter, eh? Tells you what they think of teachers in this country that you have to spend hours of your life looking at these kids eating like pigs and telling them clean up afterwards. Doctors and lawyers don't run around telling people clean up. You won't find teachers in Europe stuck with this kind of crap. Over there a high school teacher is treated like a professor.

A boy carrying his tray to the kitchen doesn't notice that an ice cream wrapper has fallen from his tray. On the way back to his table Jake calls him over.

Kid, pick up that ice cream wrapper.

The boy is defiant. I didn't drop that.

Kid, I didn't ask you that. I said pick it up.

I don't have to pick it up. I know my rights.

Come here, kid. I'll tell you your rights.

It is suddenly quiet in the cafeteria. With everyone looking on Jake grabs the skin over the boy's left shoulder blade and twists it clockwise. Kid, he says, you have five rights. Number one, you shut up. Number two, you do what you're told, and the other three don't count.

As Jake twists the skin the boy tries not to grimace, tries to look good, till Jake twists so hard the boy's knees buckle and he cries, All right, all right, Mr Homer, all right. I'll pick up the paper.

Jake releases him. Okay, kid. I can see you're a reasonable kid.

The boy slouches back to his seat. He's ashamed and I know he needn't be. When a master in Leamy's National School in Limerick tormented a boy like that we were always against the master and I can feel that's how it is here the way students, boys and girls, glare at Jake and me. It makes me wonder if I'll ever be as hard as an Irish schoolmaster or as tough as Jake Homer. The psychology teachers at NYU never told us what we should do in such cases and that's because university professors never have to supervise students in high school cafeterias. And what will happen if Jake is ever absent and I'm the only teacher here trying to keep two hundred students under control? Surely if I tell a girl pick up a piece of paper and she refuses I can't twist the skin of her shoulder blade till her knees tremble. No, I'll have to wait till I'm old and tough like Jake, though even he surely wouldn't twist the skin of a girl's shoulder blade. He's more polite with the girls, calls them dear, and would they mind helping keep this place clean. They say, Yes, Mr Homer, and he waddles away smiling.

He stands by me near the kitchen and tells me, You gotta come down on the little bastards like a ton of bricks. Then he says to a boy standing before us, Yes, son?

Mr Homer, I gotta give you back the dollar I owe you.

What was that, son?

Day I didn't have lunch money last month. You gave me a lend of a buck.

Forget it, son. Get yourself an ice cream.

But, Mr Homer.

Go on, son. Get yourself a treat.

Thanks, Mr Homer.

Okay, kid.

He tells me, That's a nice kid. You wouldn't believe what a hard time he has, still comes to school. His father tortured, nearly killed by a Mussolini gang in Italy. Jesus, you wouldn't believe the hard times they have, these kids' families, and this is the richest country in the world. Count your blessings, McCourt. Mind if I call you Frank?

Not at all, Mr Homer.

Call me Jake.

Okay, Jake.

It's my lunch hour and he directs me to the teachers' cafeteria on the top floor. Mr Sorola sees me and introduces me to teachers at different tables, Mr Rowantree, Printing, Mr Kriegsman, Health Ed., Mr Gordon, Machine Shop, Miss Gilfinane, Art, Mr Garber, Speech, Mr Bogard, Social Studies, Mr Maratea, Social Studies.

I take my tray with sandwich and coffee and sit at an empty table but Mr Bogard comes over, tells me his name is Bob, and invites me to sit with him and the other teachers. I'd like to stay by myself because I don't know what to say to anyone and as soon as I open my mouth they'll say, Oh, you're Irish, and I'll have to explain how that happened. It's not as bad as being black. You can always change your accent but you can never change the color of your skin and it must be a nuisance when you're black and people think they have to talk about black matters just because you're there with that skin. You can change your accent and people will stop telling you where their parents came from in Ireland but there's no escape when you're black.

But I can't say no to Mr Bogard after he went to all the trouble of coming to my table and, when I'm settled with my coffee and sandwich, the teachers introduce themselves again with first names. Jack Kriegsman says, Your first day, eh? You sure you want to do this?

Some teachers laugh and shake their heads as if to say they're sorry they ever got into this. Bob Bogard doesn't laugh. He leans across the table and says, If there's any profession more important than teaching I'd like to know what it is. No one seems to know what to say after that till Stanley Garber asks me what subject I teach.

English. Well, not exactly. They have me teaching three classes of Economic Citizenship, and Miss Gilfinane says, Oh, you're Irish. It's so nice to hear the brogue here.

She tells me her ancestry and wants to know where I came from, when I came, will I ever go back, and why are the Catholics and Protestants always fighting in the Old Country. Jack Kriegsman says they're worse than the Jews and the Arabs and Stanley Garber disagrees. Stanley says at least the Irish on both sides have one thing in common, Christianity, and the Jews and the Arabs are as different as day and night. Jack says, Bullshit, and Stanley comes back with a sarcastic, That's an intelligent comment.

When the bell rings Bob Bogard and Stanley Garber walk me downstairs and Bob tells me he knows the situation in Miss Mudd's classes, that the kids are wild after weeks where there was no teaching, and if I need help to let him know. I tell him I do need help. I'd like to know what the hell I'm supposed to do with Economic Citizenship classes facing mid-term exams in two weeks who haven't even looked at the book. How am I supposed to give grades on report cards based on nothing?

Stanley says, Don't worry. A lot of the report card grades in this school are based on nothing anyway. There are kids here reading on a third grade level and it's not your fault. They should be in elementary school but they can't be kept there because they're six feet tall, too big for the furniture and trouble for the teachers. You'll see.

He and Bob Bogard look at my program and shake their heads. Three classes at the end of the day That's the worst possible program you can get, an impossible one for a new teacher. The kids have had their lunch and they're all charged up with protein and sugar and they want to be outside horsing around. Sex. That's all it is, says Stanley. Sex, sex, sex. But that's what happens when you arrive in the middle of the term and take over for the Miss Mudds of the world.

Good luck, says Stanley.

Let me know if I can help, says Bob.

I grapple with the protein and the sugar and the sex sex sex in periods six, seven, and eight but I'm silenced by a hail of questions and objections. Where's Miss Mudd? She dead? She eloped? Ha ha ha. You our new teacher? You gonna be with us forever and ever? You gotta girlfriend, teacher? No, we don't have no *World and You*. Dumb book. Why can't we talk about movies? I had a teacher in fifth grade talked about movies all the time and they fired her. She was a great teacher. Teacher, don't forget to take the attendance. Miss Mudd always took the attendance.

Miss Mudd didn't have to take the attendance because in every class there is a monitor to do it. The monitor is usually a shy girl with a neat notebook and good handwriting. For taking the attendance she gets service credits and that impresses employers when she goes looking for a job in Manhattan.

The sophomore English students break into cheers at the news that Miss Mudd is gone forever. She was mean. She tried to make them read that boring book, *Giants in the Earth*, and she said when they were finished with that they'd have to read *Silas Marner* and Louis by the window who reads lots of books told everyone it's a book about a dirty old man in England and a little girl and that's the kind of book we shouldn't be reading in America.

Miss Mudd said they'd have to read, *Silas Marner* because there was a mid-term exam coming up and they'd have to write an essay comparing it with *Giants in the Earth* and the students in eighth-period sophomore English would like to know where does she get off thinking you can compare a book about gloomy people on the prairie with a book about a dirty old man in England?

They cheer again. They tell me, We don't want to read no dumb books.

You mean you don't want to read any dumb books.

What?

Oh, nothing. The warning bell rings and they gather up their coats and bags to pile out the door. I have to shout, Sit down. That's the warning bell.

They look surprised. What's up, teacher?

You're not supposed to leave at the warning bell.

Miss Mudd let us leave.

I'm not Miss Mudd.

Miss Mudd was nice. She let us leave. Why you so mean?

They're out the door and I can't stop them. Mr Sorola is in the hallway to tell me my students are not supposed to leave at the warning bell.

I know, Mr Sorola. I couldn't stop them.

Well, Mr McCourt, a little more discipline tomorrow, eh?

Yes, Mr Sorola.

Is this man serious or is he pulling my leg?

37

Old Italian men patrol the Staten Island Ferry for shoeshine customers. I've had a hard night and a harder day and is there any reason why I shouldn't spend a dollar plus a quarter tip on a shoeshine even if this old Italian shakes his head and tells me in his broken English I should buy a new pair of shoes from his brother who sells them on Delancey Street and would give me a good price if I mention Alfonso on the ferry.

When he finishes he shakes his head and says he'll charge me only fifty cents because these are the worst shoes he's seen in years, a bum's shoes, shoes you wouldn't put on a dead man, and I should go to Delancey Street and don't forget to tell his brother who sent me. I tell him how I don't have the money for a new pair, I just started a new job, and he says, Alla right, alla right, gimme a dolla. He says, You teacha, right? and I say, How do you know? Teachas always have the lousy shoes.

I give him the dollar and the tip and he walks away shaking his head and calling Shine, shine.

It's a bright March day and pleasant to sit on the deck outside to watch tourists excited with their cameras over the Statue of Liberty, the long finger of the Hudson River ahead and the Manhattan skyline drifting toward us. The water is alive with little choppy white waves and there's a warm spring touch in the breeze blowing up the Narrows.

Oh, it's good and I'd like to stand up there on the bridge steering this old ferry back and forth back and forth through the tugs and scows and freighters and liners that heave the harbor into swells that plash against the ferry car deck.

That would be a pleasant life, easier than facing dozens of high school kids every day with their secret little nudges, winks and laughs, their complaints and objections, or the way they have of ignoring me as if I were a piece of furniture. A memory floats into my head from a morning at NYU, a face saying, Aren't we being a little paranoid?

Paranoid. I looked it up. If I'm standing before a class and one kid whispers something to another and they laugh will I think they're laughing at me? Will they sit in the cafeteria imitating my accent and joking about my red eyes? I know they will because we did the same thing in Leamy's National School and if I'm going to worry about it I might as well spend my life in the loan department of the Manufacturer's Trust Company.

Is this what I'll do the rest of my life, take the subway then the ferry to Staten Island, climb the hill to McKee Vocational and Technical High School, punch in at the time clock, extract a bulge of paper from my mail box, tell my students class after class day after day, Sit down, please, open your notebooks, take out your pens, you don't have paper? here's paper, you don't have a pen? borrow one, copy the notes on the board, you can't see from there? Joey would you change seats with Brian? come on, Joey, don't be such a, no, Joey, I didn't call you a jerk, I just asked you to change seats with Brian who needs glasses, you don't need glasses, Brian? well, why do you have to move, never mind, Joey, just move, will you? Freddie, put that sandwich away, this isn't the lunchroom, I don't care if you're hungry, no, you can't go to the bathroom to eat your sandwich, you're not supposed to be eating sandwiches in the toilet, what is it, Maria? you're sick, you have to see the nurse? OK, here's a pass, Diane, would you take Maria to the nurse's office and let me know what the nurse says, no, I know they won't tell you what's wrong with her, I just want to know if she'll be coming back to class, what is it, Albert, you're sick, too? no, you're not, Albert, you just sit there and do your work, you gotta see the nurse, Albert? you're really sick? you have diarrhea? well, here, here's the pass to the boys' room and don't stay there all period, the rest of you finish copying the notes on the board, there will be a test, you know that, don't you? there will be a test, what's that, Sebastian, your pen ran out of ink? well, why didn't you say something? yes, you're saying it now but you could have said it ten minutes ago, oh, you didn't want to interrupt all these sick people? that's nice of you, Sebastian, does anyone have a pen to loan Sebastian? oh, come on, what's that, Joey? Sebastian is a what? a what? you shouldn't say things like that, Joey, Sebastian sit down, no fighting in the classroom, what's that, Ann? you gotta go? go where, Ann? oh, you got your period? you're right, Joey, she doesn't have to tell the whole world, yes, Daniela? you want to take Ann to the bathroom? why? oh, she don't ah doesn't speak good English, so what does that have to do with her having her? what's that, Joey? you don't think girls should talk like that, easy, Daniela, easy, you don't have to be insulting, what's that, Joey? you're religious and people shouldn't talk like that, okay, easy, Daniela, I know you're defending Ann who needs to go to the toilet, the bathroom, so go, take her there, and the rest of you copy the notes on the board, oh, you can't see, either? you want to move up? ok, move up, here's an empty seat but where's your notebook? you left it on the bus, all right, you need paper, here's paper, you need a pen? here's a pen? you need to go to the bathroom? well, go go go to the bathroom, eat a sandwich, hang out with your friends, Jesus.

Mr McCoy.

McCourt.

You shun't swear like dat. You shun't say God's name like dat.

They say, Oh, Mr McCourt, you should take off tomorrow, Paddy's Day. Gee, you're Irish. You should go to the parade.

If I took off and stayed in bed all day they'd be just as pleased. Substitutes for absent teachers rarely bother with attendance and students simply cut class. Aw, come on, Mr McCourt, you need a holiday with your Irish friends. I mean you wouldn't come to school if you was in Ireland, would you?

They groan when I appear on the day. Aw, shit, man, excuse the language, what kinda Irishman are you? Hey, teacher, maybe you'll go out tonight with all the Irish an' maybe you won't be in tomorrow?

I'll be here tomorrow.

They bring me green things, a potato sprayed, a green bagel, a bottle of Heineken because it's green, a head of cabbage with holes for eyes, nose, mouth, wearing a little green leprechaun cap made in the art room. The cabbage is Kevin and has a girl friend, an eggplant named Maureen. There is a greeting card two feet by two wishing me Happy St Paddy's Day with a collage of green paper things, shamrocks, shillelaghs, whiskey bottles, a drawing of a green corned beef, St Patrick holding a glass of green beer instead of a crozier and saying, Faith an' Begorrah, it's a great day for the Irish, a drawing of me with a balloon saying, Kiss Me I'm Irish. The card is signed by dozens of students from my five classes and decorated with happy faces shaped like shamrocks.

The classes are noisy. Hey, Mr McCourt, how come you ain't wearin' green? Because he don't have to, stoopid, he's Irish. Mr McCourt, whyn't you goin' to the parade? Because he just started this job. Chrissakes, he's here only a week.

Mr Sorola opens the door. Is everything all right, Mr McCourt?

Oh, yes.

He comes to my desk, looks at the card, smiles. They must like you, eh? And you've been here how long? A week?

Almost.

Well, this is very nice but see if you can get them back to work. He goes towards the door and he's followed by, Happy Paddy's Day, Mr Sorola, but he leaves without turning around. When someone at the back of the room says, Mr Sorola is a miserable guinea, there is a scuffle that ends only when I threaten them with a test on *Your World and You*. Then someone says, Sorola ain't no Italian. He's Finnish.

Finnish? What's Finnish?

Finland, stoopid, where it's dark all the time.

He don't look Finnish.

So, shithead, what does Finnish look like?

I dunno but he don't look it. He could be Sicilian.

He's not Sicilian. He's Finnish and I'm layin' a dollar bet. Anyone wanna bet?

No one wants to challenge the bet and I tell them, All right, open your notebooks.

They're indignant. Open our notebooks? Paddy's Day an' you're tellin' us open our notebooks after we got you the card an' everything.

I know. Thank you for the card but this is a regular schoolday, there will be tests and we have to cover *Your World and You*.

There is a groaning around the room and the green is gone out of the day. Oh, Mr McCourt, if you only knew how we hate that book.

Oh, Mr McCourt, can't you tell us about Ireland or something?

Mr McCourt, tell us about your girlfriend. You must have a nice girlfriend. You're real cute. My mother is divorced. She'd like to meet you.

Mr McCourt, I got a sister your age. She got a big job in a bank. She likes all that old music, Bing Crosby an' all.

Mr McCourt, I seen this Irish movie, *The Quiet Man*, on TV an' John Wayne was beatin' up his wife, what's her name, and is that what they do in Ireland, beat up their wives?

They would do anything to avoid *Your World and You*. Mr McCourt, did you keep pigs in your kitchen?

We didn't have a kitchen.

Yeah, but if you didn't have a kitchen how could you cook?

We had a fireplace where we boiled water for tea and we ate bread.

They couldn't believe we had no electricity and wanted to know how we kept food refrigerated. The one who asked about pigs in the kitchen said everyone has a refrigerator till another boy told him he was wrong, that his mother grew up in Sicily and didn't have a refrigerator and if the pigs-in-the-kitchen boy didn't believe him they'd meet in a dark alley after school and only one of them would come out. Some girls in the class told them cool it and one said she felt so sorry for me growing up like that if she could go back in time she'd take me home and let me take a nice bath as long as I liked and then I could eat everything in the refrigerator, everything. The girls nodded and the boys were quiet and I was glad the bell rang so that I could escape to the teachers' toilet with my strange emotions.

I am learning the art of the high school students' delaying tactics, how they seize on any occasion to avoid the work of the day. They flatter and cajole and hold their hands over their hearts declaring they are desperate to hear all about Ireland and the Irish, they would have asked days ago but they delayed till St Patrick's Day knowing I'd want to celebrate my heritage and religion and everything and would I tell them about Irish music and is it true Ireland is green all the time and the girls have those cute little upturned noses and the men drink drink drink, is it true, Mr McCourt?

There are muttered threats and promises around the room. I ain't stayin' in school today. I'm goin' to the parade in the city. All the Catlic schools have the day off. I'm Catlic. Why shun't I have the day off? Fuck this. End of this period you'll see my ass on the ferry. You comin,' Joey?

Nah. My mother would kill me. I'm not Irish.

So what? I'm not Irish neither.

Irish only want Irish in that parade.

Bullshit. They got Negroes in the parade an' if they got Negroes why should I be sittin' here an' I'm Italian Catlic?

They won't like it.

I don't care. Irish wouldn't even be here 'cept Columbus discovered this country an' he was Italian.

My uncle said he was Jewish.

Oh, kiss my ass, Joey.

There's a ripple of excitement in the room and calls for, Fight, fight, hit him, Joey, hit him, because a fight is another way of passing the time and keeping the teacher from the lesson.

It is time for teacher intervention, All right, all right, open your notebooks, and there are cries of pain, Notebooks, notebooks, Mr McCourt, why you doin' this to us? An' we don't want no *Your World an' You* on Paddy's Day. My mother's mother was Irish an' we should have respect. Why can't you tell us about school in Ireland, why?

All right.

I'm a new teacher and I've lost the first battle and it's all the fault of St Patrick. I tell this class and all my classes the rest of the day about school in Ireland, about the masters with their sticks, straps, canes, how we had to memorize everything and recite, how the masters would kill us if we ever tried to fight in their classrooms, how we were not allowed to ask questions nor have discussions, how we left school at fourteen and became messenger boys or unemployed.

I tell them about Ireland because I have no choice. My students have seized the day and there's nothing I can do about it. I could threaten them with *Your World and You* and *Silas Marner* and satisfy myself that I was in control, that I was teaching, but I know there would be a flurry of requests for passes for the toilets, the nurse, the guidance counselor, and, Can I have the pass to call my aunt who's dying of cancer in Manhattan? If I insisted on hewing to the curriculum today I'd be talking to myself and my instincts tell me one group of experienced students in an American classroom can break one inexperienced teacher.

How about high school, Mr McCourt?

I didn't go.

Sebastian says, Yeah, it shows. And I promise myself, I'll get you later, you little bastard.

They tell him, Shut up, Sebastian.

Mr McCourt, didn't they have no high school in Ireland?

They had dozens of high schools but kids from my school weren't encouraged to go.

Man, I'd like to live in a country where you didn't have to go to high school.

In the teachers' cafeteria there are two schools of thought. The old timers tell me, You're young, you're new but don't let these damn kids ride all over you. Let 'em know who's boss in the classroom and remember, you are the boss. Control is the big thing in teaching. No control and you can't teach. You have the power to pass and fail and they know goddam well if they fail there's no place for them in this society. They'll be sweeping the streets and washing the dishes and it'll be their own fault, the little bastards. Just don't take shit. You're the boss, the man with the red pen.

Most of the old-timers survived the Second World War. They won't talk about it except to hint at bad times at Monte Cassino, the Battle of the Bulge, Japanese prisoner of war camps, riding a tank into a German town and searching for your mother's family. You see all this and you're not gonna take shit from these kids. You fought so they could sit on their asses in school every day and get the school lunch they whine about all the time and that's more than your own father and mother ever had.

Younger teachers are not so sure. They've taken courses in Educational Psychology and The Philosophy of Education, they've read John Dewey, and they tell me these children are human beings and we have to meet their felt needs.

I don't know what a felt need is and I don't ask for fear of exposing my ignorance. The younger teachers shake their heads over the older ones. They tell me the war is over, these children are not the enemy. They are our children, for God's sakes.

An older teacher says, Felt needs, my ass. Jump from a plane into a field full of krauts and you'll know what a felt need is. And John Dewey can kiss my ass, too. Just like the rest of these goddam college professors bullshittin' about teaching in high schools and they wouldn't know a high school kid if he walked up and pissed on their leg.

Stanley Garber says, That's right. Every day we put on our armor and go into battle. Everyone laughs because Stanley has the easiest job in the school, speech teacher, no paper work, no books, and what the hell would he know about going into battle? He sits behind his desk and asks his small classes what they'd like to talk about today and all he has to do is correct their pronunciation. He tells me it's really too late to help them by the time they get to high school. This is not *My Fair Lady* and he's not Professor Henry Higgins. On days when he's not in the mood or they don't want to talk he tells them get lost and he comes to the cafeteria to discuss the terrible state of American education.

Mr Sorola smiles at Stanley through his cigarette smoke. So, Mr Garber, he says, how does it feel to be retired?

Stanley smiles back. You should know, Mr Sorola. You've been retired for years.

We'd all like to laugh but you never know with principals.

When I tell my students bring their books to class they claim, Miss Mudd never gave us no books. Economic Citizenship classes say, We don't know nothin' about *Your World and You,* and English classes say they never saw *Giants in the Earth* or *Silas Marner.* The chairman of the Academic Department says, Of course they got books and when they got them they had to fill out book receipts. Look in Miss Mudd's desk, excuse me, your desk, and you'll find them.

There are no book receipts in the desk. There are travel brochures, crossword puzzle books, an assortment of forms, directives, letters Miss Mudd wrote and never sent, a few letters to her from former students, a life of Bach in German, a life of Balzac in French, and there are innocent looks around the room when I say, Didn't Miss Mudd hand out books and didn't you fill in book receipts? They look at one another and shake their heads. Did you get a book? I don't remember getting a book? Miss Mudd, she never did nothin'.

I know they're lying because in each class there are two or three with books and I know they got the books in the normal way. Teacher distributes them. Teacher gets books receipts. I don't want to embarrass the students who have the books by asking them how they came by them. I can't ask them to make liars of their classmates.

The chairman stops me in the hallway. Well, how about those books? and when I tell him how I can't embarrass the students who have the books he says, Bullshit, and storms into my class next period. All right, the ones who have books, raise your hands.

There is one hand.

All right, where did you get that book?

Ah, I got it, ah, from Miss Mudd.

And you signed a receipt?

Ah, yeah.

What's your name?

Julio.

And when you got that book didn't the rest of the class get books, too?

I feel my heart beating hard and I'm angry that even if I'm a new teacher this is my class and no one should barge in here and embarrass one of my students and, Christ, I have to say something. I have to come between this boy and this chairman. I tell the chairman, I already asked Julio about that. He was absent and got the book from Miss Mudd at the end of the day.

Oh, yeah. Is that right, Julio?

Yeah.

And the rest of you. When did you get your books?

There is silence. They know I lied and Julio knows I lied and the chairman surely suspects me of lying but he doesn't know what to do. He says, We'll get to the bottom of this, and leaves.

The word goes from class to class and next day there is a book on every desk, *Your World and You* and *Silas Marner*, and when the chairman returns with Mr Sorola he doesn't know what to say. Mr Sorola gives his little smile. So, Mr McCourt, we're back in business, eh?

There may be books on every desk this one day when students and teacher present a united front to the outsiders, the chairman, the principal, but once they leave the honeymoon ends and there is a chorus of complaints about these books, how boring they are, how heavy, and why do they have to bring them to school every day? The

English students say, Oh, *Silas Marner*'s a small book, but if they have to carry *Giants in the Earth* you need a big breakfast, it's such a big book and it's so boring. Will they have to carry it every day? Why can't they leave it in the classroom closet?

If you leave it in the closet how are you going to read it?

Why can't we read it in class? All the other teachers tell their classes, Okay, Henry, you read page nineteen, okay, Nancy, you read page twenty, an' that's how they finish the book and when they're reading we can put our heads down an' take a nap ha ha ha, just kidding, Mr McCourt.

38

In Manhattan my brother, Malachy, is running a bar called Malachy's with two partners. He acts with the Irish Players, appears on radio and television and gets his name into the newspapers. That brings me fame at McKee Vocational and Technical High School. Now my students know my name and I'm not Mr McCoy anymore.

Hey, Mr McCourt, I seen your brother on TV. He's a crazy guy.

Mr McCourt, my mother seen your brother on TV.

Mr McCourt, how come you're not on TV? How come you're just a teacher?

Mr McCourt, you got an Irish accent. Why can't you be funny like your brother?

Mr McCourt, you could be on TV. You could be in a love story with Miss Mudd, holding her hands on a ship and kissing her old wrinkly face.

Teachers who venture into the City, Manhattan, tell me they see Malachy in plays.

Oh, he's funny, your brother. We said hello to him after the play and told him we teach with you and he was very nice but, boy, does he like to drink.

★　　★　　★

My brother, Michael, is out of the air force and working behind the bar with Malachy. If people want to buy my brothers a drink who are they to say no. It's cheers, bottoms, up, *slainte* and *skoal*. When the bar closes they don't have to go home. There are after-hours joints where they can drink and trade stories with police inspectors and gracious madams from the finest brothels on the Upper East Side. They can breakfast at Rubin's on Central Park South where there are always celebrities to keep your neck swiveling.

Malachy was famous for his, Come in, girls, and to hell with the old farts up and down Third Avenue. The old bar owners looked with suspicion on a woman alone. She was up to no good and there was no place at the bar for her. Put her over there in a dark corner and give her no more than two drinks and if there's a hint of a man going near her out she goes on the sidewalk and that's that.

When Malachy's Bar opened the word spread that girls from the Barbizon Women's Residence were actually sitting up on his barstools and soon the men flocked in from P. J. Clarke's, Toots Shor's, El Morocco, to be trailed by a snoop of gossip columnists eager to report celebrity sightings and Malachy's latest wild doings. There were playboys and their ladies, pioneers of the jet set. There were heirs to fortunes so old and deep their tendrils curled in the dark depths of South African diamond mines. Malachy and Michael were invited to parties in Manhattan apartments so vast that guests emerged days later from forgotten rooms. There were skinny-dipping parties in the Hamptons and parties in Connecticut where rich men rode the rich women who rode the thoroughbred horses.

President Eisenhower takes time out from his golf to sign an occasional bill and to warn us of the industrial-military complex and Richard Nixon watches and waits while Malachy and Michael pour the drinks and keep everyone laughing and demanding more, more drinks, Malachy, more stories, Michael, you two are a riot.

Meanwhile my mother Angela McCourt, drinks tea in her comfortable kitchen in Limerick, hears stories from visitors about the great times in New York, sees newspaper clippings about Malachy on *The Jack Paar Show*, and she has nothing else to do but drink that tea, keep the house and herself nice and warm, look after Alphie now that he's out of school and ready for a job whatever that may be, and wouldn't it be lovely if she and Alphie could take a little trip to New

York because she hasn't been there in ages and her sons, Frank, Michael, Malachy are there and doing so well.

My cold water flat on Downing Street is uncomfortable and there's nothing I can do about it because of my small teacher's salary and the few dollars I send my mother till my brother Alphie gets a job. When I moved in I bought kerosene for my cast-iron stove from the little Italian hunchback on Bleecker Street. He said, You ony need a leetle in the stove, but I must have put in too much because the stove turned into a great red living thing in my kitchen and since I didn't know how to turn it down or off I fled the flat and went to the White Horse Tavern where I sat all afternoon in a terrible state of nerves waiting for the boom of the explosion and the wailing and honking of fire engines. I would have to decide then if I should go back to the smoking remains of 46 Downing Street with charred bodies being brought out and face fire inspectors and police or if I should call Alberta in Brooklyn, tell her my building was in ashes, my belongings all gone, and could she see her way to putting me up for a few days till I could find another cold water flat.

There was no explosion, no fire, and I felt so relieved I thought I deserved a bath, time in the tub, a little peace, ease and comfort, as my mother would say.

It's all right to loll in a tub in a cold water flat but there's a problem with the head. The flat is so cold that if you stay in the tub long enough your head begins to freeze and you don't know what to do with it. If you slip under the water, head and all, you suffer when you emerge and the hot water on your head freezes and then you're shivering and sneezing from the chin up.

And you can't read in comfort in a tub in a cold water flat. The body submerged in the hot water might grow pink and wrinkled from the heat but the hands holding the book turn purple from the cold. If it's a small book you can alternate the hands, holding the book with one hand while the other is in warm water. This could be a solution to the reading problem except that the hand that was in the water is now wet and threatening to make the book soggy and you can't reach for the towel every few minutes because you want that towel to be warm and dry at the end of your time in the tub.

I thought I could solve the head problem by wearing a knitted skier's cap and the hand problem with a pair of cheap gloves but then I worried that if I ever died of a heart attack the ambulance people would wonder what I was doing wearing cap and gloves in the tub and of course they'd slip this discovery to the *Daily News* and I'd be the laughing stock of McKee Vocational and Technical High School and the patrons of various bars.

I bought the cap and gloves anyway and on the day of no explosion I filled the tub with hot water. I decided to be good to myself, forget the reading and slide under the water as often as I liked to keep the head from freezing. I turned on the radio to music suitable for a man who had survived a nerve-racking afternoon with a dangerous stove, plugged in my electric blanket and draped it across a chair beside the tub so that I could step out, dry myself quickly with the pink towel Alberta had given me, wrap myself in the electric blanket, put on my cap and gloves and lay on the bed cozy and warm. I watched the snow beat against my window, thanked God the stove had cooled by itself and read myself to sleep with *Anna Karenina*.

The tenant under me is Bradford Rush who moved into the flat when I told him about it on the midnight shift at the Manu-facturer's Trust Company. If anyone at the bank called him Brad he snapped at them, Bradford, Bradford, my name is Bradford, so mean that no one ever wanted to talk to him and when we went out for breakfast or lunch or whatever we called it at three a.m. he was never invited to join us. Then one of the women who was leaving to get married invited him to have a drink with us and he told us, after three drinks, he was from Colorado, a graduate of Yale and living in New York to get over the suicide of his mother who screamed for six months with bone cancer. The woman leaving to get married burst into tears over this story and we wondered why the hell Bradford had to hang such a cloud over our small party. That's what I asked him on the train to Downing Street that night but all I got was a little smile and I wondered if he was right in the head. I wondered why he did clerical work in a bank when he had an Ivy League degree and could have been on Wall Street with his own kind.

Later I wondered why he didn't just say no to me in my time of crisis, the bitter February day my electricity was turned off for nonpayment. I came home to give myself the peace, ease and comfort of a hot bath in the kitchen tub. I draped the electric blanket over the chair, I turned on the radio. There was no sound. There was no warmth in the blanket, no light from the lamp.

The water was steaming into the tub and I was naked. Now I had to put on cap, gloves and socks, wrap myself in an electric blanket with no heat and curse the company that turned off my electricity. It was still daylight but I knew I couldn't stay in that condition.

Bradford. Surely he wouldn't mind doing me a little favor.

I knocked on his door and he opened it with his usual grimness. Yes?

Bradford, I have a bit of a crisis upstairs.

Why are you wrapped up in that electric blanket?

That's what I came to talk to you about. They cut off my electricity and I have no heat but this blanket and I wondered if I dropped a long extension cord out my window you might take it and plug it in and I'd have electricity till I can pay my bill which I promise you will be very soon.

I could tell he didn't want to do it but he gave a little nod and pulled in my extension cord when I dropped it. I knocked on the floor three times hoping he'd understand that I was saying thank you but there was no response and whenever I saw him on the stairs he barely acknowledged me and I knew he was brooding on the extension cord. The Electrical Shop teacher at McKee told me an arrangement like this would cost a few measly pennies a day and couldn't understand why anyone would resent it. He said I could offer the cheap bastard a few dollars for the great inconvenience of having a cord plugged into an outlet but people like that were so miserable anyway it wasn't the money. It was the way they had of not being able to say no so that that no turned into acid in their guts and destroyed their lives.

I thought the Electrical Shop teacher was exaggerating till I noticed Bradford was becoming more and more hostile. He used to smile a little or nod or grunt something. Now he passes me without a word and I'm worried because I still don't have the money for the bills and I don't know how long our arrangement will last. It makes me so nervous I always turn on the radio to make sure I can take a bath and have the blanket warming up.

My cord stayed in his outlet for two months and then on a bitter night at the end of April there was an act of treachery. I turned on the radio, laid my electric blanket on a chair to warm up, put towel, cap and gloves on the blanket so that they'd be warm too, filled the tub, soaped myself and lay back listening to the *Symphonie fantastique* of Hector Berlioz and in the middle of the second movement when I'm ready to float out of the tub with the excitement everything stops, the radio is off, the light is out and I know the blanket will grow cold on the back of the chair.

And I knew what he did, this Bradford, pulled the cord on a man in a tub of hot water in a cold water flat. I knew I could never have done that to him or anyone else. I might do it to someone with central heating but never to a fellow cold water flat tenant, never.

I leaned over the side of the tub and knocked on the floor hoping he might have made a mistake, that he'd have the decency to plug me back in, but no, not a sound from him and no radio, no light. The water was still warm so I could lie there awhile thinking about the villainy of the human race, how a man with a degree from Yale could deliberately take hold of an electric cord and yank it from the outlet leaving me to freeze to death upstairs. One act of treachery like that is enough to make you give up hope and think of revenge.

No, it wasn't revenge I wanted. It was electricity and I'd have to find another way to bring Bradford to his senses. There was a spoon and there was a long piece of string and if I tied string to spoon I could open the window and dangle spoon so that it tapped against Bradford's window and he might understand that I was up there at the other end of the string, tapping, tapping for the gift of electricity. He might be annoyed and ignore my spoon but I remembered how he once told me that a dripping faucet was enough to keep him awake all night and if necessary I'd tap on his window with my spoon till he could stand it no longer. He could have climbed the stairs and banged on my door and told me to stop but I knew he could never be that direct and I knew I had him cornered. I felt sorry for him and the way his mother screamed for six months with bone cancer and I'd try to make all this up to him some day but this was a crisis and I needed my radio, my light, my electric blanket or I'd have to call Alberta for a night's lodgings and if she asked me why I could never tell her about Bradford plugging me in all these weeks. She'd get into a state of righteous indignation, the New England kind, and tell me I should be paying my bills and not tapping on people's windows with spoons on bitter nights, especially the windows of people whose mothers had died screaming of bone cancer. Then I'd tell her there was no connection between my spoon and Bradford's dead mother and that would lead to more disagreement and a fight and I'd have to storm out, back to my flat in the cold and the dark.

It was a Friday night, his night off from the bank, and I knew he couldn't escape by going to work. I imagined him downstairs with the cord in his hand trying to decide what to do with the spoon at his window. He could have gone out but where would he go? Who would want to have a beer with him in a bar and listen to how his mother died screaming? On top of that he'd probably tell the world someone upstairs was tormenting him with a spoon and anyone in a bar with a beer would move away from him.

I tapped on and off for a few hours and and suddenly there was light and music from the radio. *Symphonie fantastique* was long over and that irritated me but I turned the dial up on the electric blanket, put on cap and gloves and got back into bed with *Anna Karenina* which I couldn't read because of the darkness in my head over Bradford and his poor mother in Colorado. If my mother were dying of bone cancer in Limerick and someone upstairs tormented me with a spoon at my window I'd go up and kill him. I felt so guilty now I thought of knocking on Bradford's door and telling him, I'm sorry over the spoon and your poor mother and you can pull the plug, but I was so warm and cozy in the bed I fell asleep.

The following week I met him loading his things into a van. I asked if I could help and all he said was, Prick. He moved out but he left me plugged in and I had weeks of electricity till I blew the cord with an electric heater and had to go to Beneficial Finance Company for a loan to pay my electricity bills so that I wouldn't freeze to death.

39

The old-timers in the teachers' cafeteria say the classroom is a battleground, that teachers are warriors bringing the light to these damn kids who don't want to learn, who just want to sit on their asses and talk about movies and cars and sex and what they're gonna do Saturday night. That's the way it is in this country. We've got free education and no one wants it. Not like Europe where there's respect for teachers. Parents of kids in this school don't care because they never went to high school themselves. They were too busy struggling with the Depression and fighting wars, World War Two and Korea. Then you have all these bureaucrats who never liked teaching in the first place, all these goddam principals and assistant principals and chairmen who got out of the classroom as fast as their little legs could carry them and now spend their lives harassing the classroom teacher.

Bob Bogard is at the time clock. Ah, Mr McCourt, would you like to go for some soup?

Soup?

He has a little smile and I know he means something else. Yes, Mr McCourt. Soup.

We walk down the street and turn into the Meurot Bar.

Soup, Mr McCourt. Would you like a beer?

We settle on our bar stools and drink beer after beer. It's Friday and other teachers drift in and the talk is kids, kids, kids and the school, and I learn that in every school there are two worlds, the world of the classroom teacher and the world of the administrator and supervisor, that these worlds are forever at sword's point, that when anything goes wrong the teacher is the scapegoat.

Bob Bogard tells me don't worry about *Your World and You* and the mid-term test. Go through the motions. Distribute the test, watch the kids scribble what they don't know, retrieve the tests, give the kids passing grades, it isn't their fault Miss Mudd neglected them, the parents will be satisfied, and the chairman and principal will stay off my back.

I should be leaving the Meurot and taking the ferry to Manhattan where I'm having dinner with Alberta but the beers keep coming and it's hard to say no to such generosity and when I leave my barstool to call Alberta she screams at me that I'm a common Irish drunk and that's the last time she'll ever wait for me because she's finished with me forever and there are plenty of men who'd like to go out with her, goodbye.

All the beer in the world won't relieve my misery. I struggle with five classes a day, I live in a flat Alberta calls a hovel, and now I'm in danger of losing her because of my hours at the Meurot. I tell Bob I have to go, it's nearly midnight, we've been on the barstools for nine hours and I have dark clouds fluttering in my head. He says, One more and then we'll eat. You can't go on that ferry without eating. He says it's important to eat the kind of food that will ward off any unpleasant feeling in the morning, and the food he orders at the St George Diner is fish with eggs sunny-side up, hash brown potatoes, toast and coffee. He says the combination of fish and eggs after a day and night of beer is miraculous.

I'm on the ferry again where the old Italian patroling for shoeshine customers tells me my shoes look worse than ever and there's no use telling him I can't afford his offer of a shine, half price, if I'll buy shoes from his brother up on Delancey Street.

No, I don't have money for shoes. I don't have money for a shine.

Ah, *professore, professore*, I give you free shine. Make you feel good, the shine. You go see my brother for the shoes.

He sits on his box, pulls my foot to his lap and looks up at me.

I smella beer, *professore*. Teacher come home late, eh? Terrible shoes, terrible shoes, but I shine. He dabs on the polish, draws the brush around the shoe, snaps the polishing cloth across the toe, taps my knee to say it's done, replaces his things in the box and stands. He waits for the question and I don't ask because he knows it, What about my other shoe?

He shrugs. You go see my brother and I do your other shoe.

If I buy new shoes from your brother I won't need a shine for this.

He shrugs again. You are the *professore*. You smart, eh, with the brains? You teach and think about the shine and the no shine.

And he waddles away humming and calling shine shine to sleeping passengers.

I'm a teacher with a college degree and this old Italian, with little English, toys with me and sends me ashore with one shoe shined, the other streaked with marks of rain, snow, mud. If I grabbed him and demanded a shine for the dirty shoe he might yell and bring crew members to his aid and how would I explain the offer of a free shine, the shining of one shoe and then the trick? I'm sober enough by now to know you can't force an old Italian to shine your dirty shoe, that I was foolish to let him at my foot in the first place. If I protested to the crew members he might tell them he smelled beer and they'd laugh and walk away.

He waddles up and down the aisles. He keeps saying shine to the other passengers and I have a great urge to grab him and his box and heave him over the side. Instead, when I'm leaving the ferry, I tell him, I'll never buy shoes from your brother on Delancey Street.

He shrugs. I don't have a no brother on Delancey. Shine, shine.

When I told the shoeshine man I had no money I wasn't lying. I don't have fifteen cents for the subway fare. Whatever I had went for beer and when we went to the St George Diner I asked Bob Bogard to pay for my fish and eggs and I'll pay him back next week and it won't do me any harm to walk home, up Broadway, past Trinity Church and St Paul's Church where Robert Emmet's brother, Thomas, is buried, past City Hall, up to Houston Street and over to my cold water flat on Downing Street.

It is two o'clock in the morning, few people, an occasional car. Broad Street, where I worked at the Manufacturer's Trust Company, is over to my right and I wonder what became of Andy Peters and

Brigid formerly Bridey. I walk and look back over the eight and a half years since I arrived in New York, days at the Biltmore Hotel, the army, NYU, jobs in warehouses, on the docks, in banks. I think of Emer and Tom Clifford and wonder what became of Rappaport and the men I knew in the army. I never dreamed I'd be able to get a college degree and become a teacher and now I'm wondering if I can survive a vocational high school. The office buildings I pass are dark now but I know that during the day people sit at desks, study the stock market and make millions. They wear suits and ties, they carry briefcases, they go to lunch and talk about money money money. They live in Connecticut with their long-legged Episcopalian wives, who probably lolled in the lounge of the Biltmore Hotel when I cleaned up for them, and they drink martinis before dinner. They play golf at the country club and they have affairs and no one cares.

I could do that. I could spend time with Stanley Garber to get rid of my accent though he told me already I'd be an ass to lose it. He said the Irish accent is charming, opens doors, reminds people of Barry Fitzgerald. I told him I didn't want to remind people of Barry Fitzgerald and he said, Would you prefer to have a Jewish accent and remind people of Molly Goldberg? I asked him who Molly Goldberg was and he said if you don't know who Molly Goldberg is there's no use talking to you.

Why can't I have a bright carefree life like my brothers Malachy and Michael, uptown in the bar serving drinks to beautiful women and bantering with Ivy League graduates? I'd make more money than this forty-five-hundred dollars a year for regular substitute teachers. There would be large tips, all the food I could eat, and nights in the beds of Episcopalian heiresses frolicking and dazzling them with bits of poetry and scraps of wit. I'd sleep late, have lunch at a romantic restaurant, walk the streets of Manhattan, there would be no forms to fill out, no papers to correct, the books I'd read would be for my own pleasure and I'd never have to worry about sullen high school teenagers.

And what would I say if I ever met Horace again? Would I be able to tell him I went to college and became a teacher for a few weeks and it was so hard I became a bartender so that I could meet a better class of people on the Upper East Side? I know he'd shake his head and probably thank God I wasn't his son.

I think of the longshoreman in the coffee shop working for years so that his son can go to St John's University to become a teacher. What would I say to him?

If I told Alberta I was planning to leave teaching for the exciting world of the bars she'd surely run off and marry a lawyer or a football player.

So I won't give up teaching, not because of Horace or the long-shoreman or Alberta, but because of what I might say to myself at the end of a night of serving drinks and amusing the customers. I'd accuse myself of taking the easy way and all because I was defeated by boys and girls resisting *Your World and You* and *Giants in the Earth*.

They don't want to read and they don't want to write. They say, Aw, Mr McCourt, all these English teachers want us to write about dumb things like our summer vacation or the story of our life. Boring. Every year since our first grade we write the story of our life and teachers just give us a check mark and they say, Very Nice.

In the English classes they're cowed by the mid-term test with its multiple choice questions on spelling, vocabulary, grammar and reading comprehension. When I hand out the tests in Economic Citizenship there is muttering. There are hard words against Miss Mudd and how her ship should hit a rock and she should become fish food. I tell them, Do your best, and I'll be reasonable with report card grades, but there is a coldness and resentment in the room as if I had betrayed them by forcing this test on them.

Miss Mudd saves me. While my classes are taking the mid-term test I explore the closets at the back of the room and find them stuffed with old grammar books, newspapers, Regents exams and hundreds of pages of uncorrected student compositions going back to 1942. I'm about to dump everything into the trash till I start reading the old compositions. The boys back then yearned to fight, to avenge the deaths of brothers, friends, neighbors. One wrote, I'm gonna kill five Japs for every one they killed from my neighborhood. Another wrote, I don't want to go in the army if they tell me kill Italians because I'm Italian. I could be killing my own cousins and I won't fight unless they let me kill Germans or Japs. I'd prefer to kill Germans because I don't want to go to the Pacific where there's all kinds of jungles with bugs and snakes and crap like that.

The girls would wait. When Joey comes home me and him gonna

get married and move to Jersey and get away from his crazy mother.

I pile the crumbling papers on my desk and begin reading to my classes. They sit up. There are familiar names. Hey, that was my father. He was wounded in Africa. Hey, that was my Uncle Sal that was killed in Guam.

While I read the essays aloud there are tears. Boys run from the room to the toilets and return red-eyed. Girls weep openly and console one another.

Dozens of Staten Island and Brooklyn families are named in these papers so brittle we worry they'll fall apart. We want to save them and the only way is to copy them by hand, the hundreds still stacked in the closets.

No one objects. We are saving the immediate past of immediate families. Everyone has a pen and all through the rest of the term, April till the end of June, they decipher and write. Tears continue and there are outbursts. This is my father when he was fifteen. This is my aunt and she died when she was having a baby.

They are suddenly interested in compositions with the title, My Life, and I want to say, See what you can learn about your fathers and uncles and aunts? Don't you want to write about your lives for the next generation?

But I let it pass. I don't want to interfere with a room so quiet Mr Sorola has to investigate. He walks around the room, looks at what the class is doing and says nothing. I think he's grateful for the silence.

In June I give everyone a passing grade, thankful I've survived my first months of teaching in a vocational high school, though I wonder what I would have done without the crumbling compositions.

I might have had to teach.

40

Since I long ago lost the key the door of my flat is always open and it doesn't matter because there's nothing to steal. Strangers begin to appear, Walter Anderson, an aging public relations man, Gordon Patterson, aspiring actor, Bill Galetly, man in search of the truth. They are homeless bar patrons sent by Malachy in the largeness of his heart.

Walter begins to steal from me. Goodbye, Walter.

Gordon smokes in bed and causes a fire but worse than that his girlfriend complains to me at Malachy's bar about Gordon's discomfort and my hostility. He, too, goes.

School is over and I have to work again, day by day, on piers and warehouse platforms. Every morning I shape up to replace men on vacation, men out sick, or when there's a sudden rush of business and they need more help. When there's no work I roam the docks and the streets of Greenwich Village. I can make my way to Fourth Avenue to browse in one bookshop after another and dream of the day I'll come here and buy all the books I like. All I can afford now is cheap paperbacks and I'm content on my way home with my package of F. Scott Fitzgerald's *This Side of Paradise*, D. H. Lawrence's *Sons and Lovers*, Ernest Hemingway's *The Sun Also Rises*, Herman Hesse's *Siddhartha*, a weekend of reading. I'll heat up a can of beans on my electric ring and boil water for tea and read in the light that comes from the flat below. I'll start with Hemingway because I saw the film with Errol Flynn and Tyrone Power, everyone having a fine time of it in Paris and Pamplona, everyone drinking, going to bullfights, falling in love even if there was a sadness between Jake Barnes and Brett Ashley over his condition. It's the way I'd like to live, roaming the world without a care, though I wouldn't want to be Jake.

I take my books home and there is Bill Galetly. After Walter and Gordon I want no more interlopers but Bill is harder to dislodge and after a while I don't mind if he stays. He has already installed himself by the time Malachy calls to say his friend, Bill, who has renounced the world, left his job as an executive in an advertising agency, divorced his wife, sold his clothes books records, needs shelter for a short time and surely I won't mind.

Bill stands naked on a bathroom scale before a long mirror propped against the wall. On the floor are two flickering candles. He looks from the mirror to the scale and back again and again. He shakes his head and turns to me. Too much, he says. This too, too solid flesh. He points to his body, a collection of bones topped with a head of lank black hair and a bushy black beard flecked with grey. His eyes are blue wide staring. You're Frank, eh? Hi. He steps from the scale, stands with his back to the mirror, twists to look at himself over his shoulder and tells himself, Thou art fat and pursy, Bill.

He asks me if I've ever read *Hamlet* and tells me he's read it thirty times.

And I've read *Finnegans Wake,* that's if anyone can read *Finnegans Wake.* I've spent seven years with the damn book and that's why I'm here. Yeah, you're wondering. Read *Hamlet* thirty times and you start talking to yourself. Read *Finnegans Wake* for seven years and you want to put your head under water. The thing to do with *Finnegans Wake* is to chant it. It might take you seven years but it's something you'll be able to tell your grandchildren. They'll look up to you. What's that you have there, beans?

Would you like some? I'm heating them on the ring there.

No, thanks. No beans for me. You have your beans and I'll give you the message while you're eating. I'm trying to reduce the body to bare necessity. The world is too much with me. Know what I mean? Too much flesh.

I don't see it.

There you are. Through prayer, fasting and meditation I will drop below one hundred pounds, the despicable three digits. I want to be ninety-nine or nothing. Want. Did I say want? I shouldn't say want. I shouldn't say shouldn't. You're confused? Oh, have your beans. I'm trying to eliminate my ego but that action is ego itself. All action is ego. Are you following me? I'm not here with my mirror and scale for the good of my health.

From the next room he brings two books and tells me all my questions will be answered in Plato and the Gospel According to St John. Excuse me, he says, I gotta take a leak.

He takes the key and goes naked to the hall toilet. He returns to stand on the scale to see how much he lost with the leak. Quarter pound, he says, and lets out a sigh of relief. He squats on the floor, faces the mirror again flanked by the candles, with Plato on his left, St John on his right. He studies himself in the mirror and talks to me. Go ahead. Eat your beans. Books. That's what you have there, eh?

I eat my beans and when I tell him the book titles he shakes his head. Oh, no, oh, no. Hesse, maybe. Forget the rest. All Western ego. All Western crap. I wouldn't wipe my ass with Hemingway. But I shouldn't say that. Arrogant. Ego stuff. I take it back. No, wait. I said it. I'll leave it out there. It's gone. I read *Hamlet*. I read *Finnegans Wake* and here I am sitting on a floor in Greenwich Village with Plato, John and a man eating beans. What do you make of those ingredients?

I don't know.

I despair sometimes and you know why?

Why?

I despair I might push too far with Plato and John and find them wanting. I might come to a nowhere. You know?

No.

You ever read Plato?

I did.

St John?

They read the gospels all the time at Mass.

Not the same. You have to sit down and read St John, hold him in your hands. No other way. John is an encyclopedia. He changed my life. Promise me you'll read John and not that goddam stuff you brought home in the bag. Sorry, there's that ego popping up again.

He cackles into the mirror, pats himself where his belly should be, and rocks from book to book reading verses from John and paragraphs from Plato, squeaks with pleasure, Eek, eek, oh the Greek and the Jew, the Greek and the Jew.

He talks to me again. I take it back, he says. There's no nowhere with these guys. No nowhere. The form, the cave, the shadow, the cross. Jesus, I need a banana. He takes half a banana from behind the mirror and after mumbling something over it eats it. He crosses his legs under him, rests the backs of his hands on his knees, lotus position. When I cross behind him to drop my bean can into the garbage I can see he's staring at the tip of his nose. When I tell him goodnight he doesn't respond and I know I'm not in his world anymore, that I might as well go to bed and read. I'll read Hesse to keep the mood.

41

Alberta talks about marriage. She'd like to settle down, have a husband, go to antique shops on weekends, make dinner, get a decent apartment some day, be a mother.

But I'm not ready yet. I see Malachy and Michael having their grand times uptown. I see the Clancy Brothers singing in the back room of the White Horse Tavern, acting in plays at the Cherry Lane Theatre, recording their songs, being discovered and moving on to glamorous clubs where beautiful women invite them to parties. I see the Beats in cafes all over the Village reading their work with jazz musicians in the background. They're all free and I'm not.

They drink. They smoke pot. The women are easy.

Alberta follows her grandmother's Rhode Island routines. Every Saturday you make coffee, smoke a cigarette, put your hair up in pink curlers, go to the supermarket, get a big order, stock the refrigerator, take soiled things to the laundromat and wait till they're cleaned and ready to be folded, go to the dry cleaner with garments which look clean to me and when I object she simply says, What would you know about dry cleaning? clean the house whether it needs it or not, have a drink, make a big dinner, go to a movie.

Sunday morning you sleep late, have a big lunch, read the paper, look at antiques on Atlantic Avenue, come home, prepare lessons for the week, correct papers, make a big dinner, have a drink, correct more papers, have tea, smoke a cigarette, go to bed.

She works harder at teaching than I do, prepares her lessons carefully, corrects papers conscientiously. Her students are more academic than mine and she can encourage them to talk about literature. If I mention books, poetry, plays my students groan and whine for the lavatory pass.

The supermarket depresses me because I don't want a big dinner every night. It exhausts me. I want to roam the city, drink coffee in cafés and beer in bars. I don't want to face the Zoe routine every weekend the rest of my life.

Alberta tells me things have to be taken care of, that I have to grow up and settle down or I'll be like my father, a mad wanderer drinking myself to death.

This leads to an argument where I tell her I know my father drank too much and abandoned us but he's my father, not hers, and she'll never understand how it was when he didn't drink, mornings I had with him by the fire, listening to his talk about Ireland's noble past and Ireland's great sufferings. She never had mornings like that with her father who left her with Zoe when she was seven and I wonder how she could ever get over that. How could she ever forgive her mother and father for dumping her on the grandmother?

The argument is so bad I walk out and live in my Village flat, ready for the wild bohemian life. Then I hear she has found someone else and suddenly I want her, I'm desperate, I'm mad for her. I can think only of her virtues, her beauty and energy and the sweetness of her weekend routines. If she takes me back I'll be the perfect husband. I'll take coupons to the supermarket, wash the dishes, vacuum the whole apartment every day of the week, chop vegetables for the big dinners every night. I'll wear a tie, polish my shoes, turn Protestant.

Anything.

I don't care anymore about the wild life of Malachy and Michael uptown, the scruffy Beats in the Village with their useless lives. I want Alberta, crisp and bright and womanly, all warm and secure. We'll be married, oh we will, and we'll grow old together.

She agrees to meet me in Louis' Bar near Sheridan Square and when she walks in the door she's more beautiful than ever. The bartenders stop pouring to look at her. Necks are craned. She's wearing the rich blue coat with a light grey fur collar her father bought her as a peace offering after he punched her in the mouth years ago. There's a silken lavender scarf over the collar and I know I'll never look at that color again without thinking of this moment, that scarf. I know she's going to sit on the stool beside me and tell me it was all a mistake, that we were made for each other and I should come with her now to her apartment, she'll make dinner and we'll live happily ever after.

Yes, she'll have a martini and no she won't go with me to my apartment and no I won't go with her to her apartment because it's over. She's had enough of me and my brothers, the uptown scene and the Village scene, and she wants to get on with her life. It's hard enough teaching every day without the strain of putting up with me and my whining about how I want to do this that and the other thing, how I want to be everything but responsible. Too much complaining, she says. Time to grow up. She tells me I'm twenty-eight years old but I act like a kid and if I want to waste my life in bars like my brothers it's my business but she'll have no part of it.

The more she talks the angrier she grows. She won't let me hold her hand or even kiss her on the cheek and, no, she won't have another martini.

How can she talk to me like this with my heart breaking there on the barstool? She doesn't care that I was the first man in her life, the first ever in the bed, the one a woman never forgets. All that doesn't matter because she's found someone who is mature, who loves her, who will do anything for her.

I'll do anything for you.

She says it's too late. You had your chance.

My heart is banging away, and there's a great pain in my chest and all the dark clouds in the world are gathered in my head. I want to cry into my beer there in Louis' Bar but there would be talk, oh, yeah, another lovers' quarrel and we'd be asked to leave or at least I would. I'm sure they'd like Alberta to stay to adorn the place. I don't want to be out on the street with all those happy couples strolling to dinners and movies and a little snack later before they climb into the bed all naked and, Jesus, is this her plan for tonight when I'm alone in my cold water flat and no one in the world to talk to but Bill Galetly?

I appeal to her. I invoke my miserable childhood, brutal school-masters, the tyranny of the Church, my father who chose the bottle over the babies, my defeated mother moaning by the fire, my eyes blazing red, my teeth crumbling in my head, the squalor of my flat, Bill Galetly tormenting me with people in Platonic caves and the Gospel According to St John, my hard days at McKee Vocational and Technical High School, older teachers telling me whip the little bastards into shape, the younger ones declaring our students are real people and it's up to us to motivate them.

I plead with her to have another martini. It might soften her so much she'll come to my apartment where I'll tell Bill, Take a walk, Bill, we need privacy. We want to sit in the candlelight and plan a future of Saturday shopping, vacuuming, cleaning, Sunday antique hunting, lesson planning and hours romping in the bed.

No, no, she won't have another martini. She's meeting her new man and she has to go.

Oh, God, no. It's a knife in my heart.

Stop the whining. I've heard enough about you and your miserable childhood. You're not the only one. I was dumped on my grandmother when I was seven. Do I complain? I just get on with it.

But you had hot and cold running water, thick towels, soap, sheets on the bed, two clear blue eyes and fine teeth and your grandmother packed your little lunch box to capacity every day.

She climbs from the bar stool, lets me help her with her coat, drapes the lavender scarf around her neck. She has to go.

Oh, Christ. I could easily whimper like a kicked dog. My belly is cold and there's nothing in the world but dark clouds with Alberta in the middle all blonde, blue-eyed, lavender-scarved, ready to leave me forever for her new man and it's worse than having doors shut in my face, worse than dying itself.

Then she kisses my cheek. Goodnight, she says. She doesn't say goodbye. Does that mean she's leaving a door open? Surely if she's finished with me forever she should be saying goodbye.

It doesn't matter. She's gone. Out the door. Up the steps with every man in the bar looking at her. It's the end of the world. I might as well be dead. I might as well jump into the Hudson River and let it carry my corpse past Ellis Island and the Statue of Liberty across the Atlantic and up the River Shannon where at least I'd be among my own people and not rejected by Rhode Island Protestants.

The bartender is about fifty and I'd like to ask him if he's ever suffered the way I'm suffering now and what did he do about it?

Is there a cure? He might even be able to tell me what it means when a woman who's leaving you forever says goodnight instead of goodbye.

But this man has a great bald head and massive black eyebrows and I have a feeling he has his own troubles and there's nothing for it but to get off the barstool and leave. I could go uptown and join Malachy and Michael in their exciting lives but I walk home to Downing Street instead hoping happy passing couples won't hear the escaping whimpers of a man whose life is over.

Bill Galetly is there with his candles, his Plato, his Gospel According to St John and I wish I could have my own place to myself for a night of whimpering into my pillow but he's sitting on the floor staring at himself in the mirror and pinching whatever flesh he can find on his belly. He looks up and tells me I look heavy-laden.

What do you mean?

The burden of the ego. You're sagging. Remember, the Kingdom of God is within you.

I don't want God or His Kingdom. I want Alberta. She gave me up. I'm going to bed.

Bad time to go to bed. To lie down is to lie down.

It irritates me to have to listen to the obvious and I tell him, Of course it is. What are you talking about?

To lie down is to succumb to gravity at a time when you could spiral to the perfect form.

I don't care. I'm lying down.

Okay. Okay.

I'm in the bed a few minutes when he sits on the edge and tells me of the madness and emptiness of the advertising business. Plenty of money and everyone wretched with stomach ulcers. All ego. No purity. He tells me I'm a teacher and I could save many lives if I studied Plato and St John but first I have to save my own life.

I'm not in the mood.

Not in the mood to save your own life?

No, I don't care.

Yeah, yeah, that's what happens when you're rejected. You take it personally.

Of course I take it personally. How else would I take it?

Look at her side of the story. She's not rejecting you, she's accepting herself.

He's going around in circles and the Alberta pain is so great I have to get away. I tell him I'm going out.

Oh, you don't have to go out. Sit on the floor with the candle behind. Look at the wall. Shadows. Are you hungry?

No.

Wait, and he brings a banana from the kitchen. Have this. The banana is good for you.

I don't want a banana.

It makes you peaceful. All that potassium.

I don't want a banana.

You only think you don't want a banana. Listen to your body.

He follows me into the hallway preaching bananas. He's naked but he follows me down the stairs, three flights, along the hallway that leads to the front door. He keeps talking about bananas, the ego and Socrates happy under a tree in Athens and when we reach the front door he stands on the top step waving the banana while children playing hopscotch on the sidewalk whoop and scream and point and women with bosoms and elbows resting on windowsill pillows scream at him in Italian.

Malachy isn't at his bar. He's at home and happy with his wife, Linda, planning the life of the baby to come. Michael is off for the night. There are women at the bar and the tables but they're with men. The bartender says, Oh, you're Malachy's brother, and won't let me pay for my drinks. He introduces me to couples at the bar, This is Malachy's brother.

Really? We didn't know he had another brother. Oh, yeah, we know your brother Michael. And your name is?

Frank.

And what do you do?

I'm a teacher.

Really? You're not in the bar business?

They laugh. And when do you think you'll go into the bar business?

When my brothers become teachers.

That's what I say but what flows through my head is different. I want to tell them they're condescending twits, that I knew their likes in the lobby of the Biltmore Hotel, that they probably flicked their cigarette ash on the floor for me to clean up and looked through me the way you look through people who clean up. I'd like to tell them to kiss my arse and if I had a few more drinks I would but I know that inside I'm still plucking at my forelock and shuffling my feet in the presence of superior people, that they'd laugh at anything I said to them because they know what I am inside and if they don't know they don't care. If I fell dead off the barstool they'd move to a table to avoid the unpleasantness and tell the world later how they ran into a drunken Irish schoolteacher.

None of this matters anyway. Alberta is surely in a romantic little Italian restaurant with her new man, the two of them smiling at each other across the glow of the light from the candle stuck in a Chianti bottle. He's telling her what's good on the menu and after they order their dinner they talk about what they'll do tomorrow, maybe tonight, and if I think about that my bladder will move near my eye.

Malachy's Bar is at Sixty-Third Street and Third Avenue, five blocks from my first furnished room at Sixty-Eighth Street. Instead of going home straightway I can sit on Mrs Austin's steps and look back over the contents of my ten years in New York, the trouble I had trying to see *Hamlet* at the Sixty-Eighth Street Playhouse with my lemon meringue pie and my bottle of ginger ale.

Mrs Austin's house is gone. There's a large new building, the New York Foundling Hospital, and it brings me to tears the way they're tearing down my early days in the city. At least the cinema is here and it must be the night of beer because I have to press my whole body against the cinema wall with arms stretched out till a head calls from a police car, Hey, buddy, what's going on?

What if I told him about *Hamlet* and the pie and Mrs Austin and the night of glug and how her house is gone and my furnished room with it and how the woman in my life is with another man and is it against the law, Officer, to kiss a cinema of sad and happy memories when it's the only comfort you have left, is it, Officer?

Of course I'm not going to say this to a New York cop or anyone else. I just tell him, It's all right, Officer, and he tells me move on, the favorite words of the police department.

I move on and all along Third Avenue music pours through the doors of Irish pubs with the smells of beer and whiskey and snatches of talk and laughter.

Good man yourself, Sean.

Arrah, Jasus, we might as well be drunk as the way we are.

God above, I can't wait to get back to Cavan for the decent pint that's in it.

Do you think you'll ever go back, Kevin?

I will when they build a bridge.

They laugh and Mickey Carton on the jukebox pumps his accordion with Ruthie Morrissey's voice sailing over all the noise of the night, It's my old Irish home, far across the foam, and I'm tempted to turn in, sit up on a stool and tell the bartender, Give us an oul' drop of the craythur there, Brian, or make it two because bird never flew on one wing, good lad yourself. And wouldn't that be better than sitting on Mrs Austin's steps or kissing the walls of the Sixty-Eighth Street Playhouse and wouldn't I be among my own, wouldn't I?

My own. The Irish.

I could drink Irish, eat Irish, dance Irish, read Irish. My mother often warned us, Marry your own, and now old-timers tell me, Stick with your own. If I listened to them I wouldn't be rejected by a Rhode Island Episcopalian who once said, What would you do with yourself if you weren't Irish? And when she said that I would have walked out except that we were halfway through the dinner she'd cooked, stuffed chicken with a bowl of pink new potatoes tossed in salt butter and parsley and a bottle of Bordeaux that gave me such shivers of pleasure I could have tolerated any number of barbs at myself and the Irish in general.

I'd like to be Irish when it's time for a song or a poem. I'd like to be American when I teach. I'd like to be Irish-American or American-Irish though I know I can't be two things even if Scott Fitzgerald said the sign of intelligence is the ability to carry opposed thoughts at the same time.

I don't know what I'd like to be and what does it matter with Alberta over in Brooklyn with her new man?

Then in a shop window I catch a glimpse of my sad face and I laugh when I remember what my mother would have called it, the gloomy puss.

At Fifty-Seventh Street I walk west towards Fifth Avenue for a taste of America and the richness that's in it, the world of the people who sit in the Palm Court of the Biltmore Hotel, people who don't have to go through life carrying ethnic hyphens. You could wake them in the middle of the night, ask them what they are and they'd say, Tired.

I turn the gloomy puss south on Fifth Avenue and there's the dream I had all those years in Ireland, the avenue nearly deserted at this hour of the morning except for double-decker buses, one going north, the other south, jewelry shops, bookshops, women's shops with mannequins all dressed up for Easter, rabbits and eggs everywhere in windows and not a sign of the risen Jesus, and far down the avenue the Empire State Building, and I have my health, don't I? a little weak in the eye and teeth department, a college degree and a teaching job and isn't this the country where all things are possible, where you can do anything you like as long as you stop complaining and get off your ass because life, pal, is not a free lunch.

If only Alberta came to her senses and back to me.

Fifth Avenue tells me how ignorant I am. There are the window mannequins in their Easter garb and if one of them came to life and asked me what kind of fabric she was wearing I wouldn't have a notion. If they wore canvas I'd spot it straightway because of the coal bags I delivered in Limerick and used for cover when they were empty and the weather was desperate. I might be able to recognize tweed because of the coats people wore winter and summer though I'd have to admit to the mannequin I don't know the difference between silk and cotton. I could never point to a dress and say that's satin or wool and I'd be lost entirely if challenged to identify damask or crinoline. I know novelists like to hint at the wealth of their characters by dwelling on damask drapes though I don't know if anyone wears such material unless the characters fall on hard times and take the scissors to the damask. I know you can hardly pick up a novel set in the South where there isn't a white plantation family lolling on the verandah sipping bourbon or lemonade listening to the darkies singing "Swing Low, Sweet Chariot", the verandah women fanning themselves against the crinoline heat.

Down in Greenwich Village I buy shirts and socks in shops called haberdasheries and I don't know what material they're made of even though there are people telling me you have to be careful what you put on your body nowadays, you might have allergies and break out in a rash. I never worried about such things in Limerick but here danger lurks even in the buying of socks and shirts.

Things in shop windows have names I don't know and I don't know how I traveled this far in life in such a state of ignorance. There are florist shops along the avenue and all I can name beyond these windows is geraniums. Respectable people in Limerick were mad for the geraniums and when I delivered telegrams there were often notes on the front door, Please slide the window up and leave messages under the geranium pot. It's strange to stand at a florist's shop on Fifth Avenue remembering how delivering telegrams helped me become an expert on geraniums and now I don't even like them. They never excited me like other flowers in people's gardens with all that color and fragrance and the sadness of their dying in the autumn. Geraniums have no fragrance, they live forever and the taste makes you sick though I'm sure there are people over there on Park Avenue who would take me aside and spend an hour persuading me of the glories of the geranium and I suppose I'd have to agree with them because everywhere I go people know more about everything than I do and it's not likely you'd be rich and living on Park Avenue unless you had a profound knowledge of geraniums and growing things in general.

All along the avenue there are shops with gourmet foods and if I ever enter such a place I'll have to bring someone who grew up respectable and knows the difference between pâté de foie gras and mashed potatoes. All these shops are obsessed with French and I don't know what they're thinking of. Why can't they say spuds instead of pommes or is it that you pay more for something printed in French?

There's no sense at all looking in the windows of antique furniture shops. They'll never let you know the price of something till you ask and they'll never plant a sign on a chair to tell you what it is or where it came from. Most of the chairs you wouldn't want to sit in anyway. They're so upright and stiff they'd give you such a pain in your back you'd wind up in the hospital. Then there are little tables with curved legs so delicate they'd collapse under the weight of a pint and destroy a priceless carpet from Persia or wherever people sweat for the pleasure of rich Americans. There are delicate mirrors, too, and you wonder what it's like in the morning to see your face in a frame agog with little Cupids and maidens frolicking and where would you look in such confusion? Would I look at the stuff oozing from my eyes or would I be enchanted with a maiden succumbing to a Cupid arrow?

With the dawn glimmering far down in Greenwich Village Fifth Avenue is nearly deserted except for people making their way to St Patrick's Cathedral to save their souls, mostly old women who seem to have greater fear than the old men mumbling along beside them or it may be that old women live longer and there are more of them. When the priest dispenses Communion the pews empty and I envy the people coming back down the aisles with the wafers in their mouths and the holy look that tells you they're in a state of grace. They can go home now and have the big breakfast and if they fall dead while eating sausages and eggs they go straight to heaven. I'd like to make my peace with God but my sins are so terrible any priest would drive me from the confessional and I know once again my only hope for salvation is that I'll have an accident where I'll linger for a few minutes so that I can make an Act of Perfect Contrition that will open the gates of heaven.

Still, it's comforting to sit in the cathedral in the hush of a dawn Mass especially when I can look around and put names on what I see, pews, the Stations of the Cross, the pulpit, the tabernacle with the monstrance holding the Eucharist inside, the chalice, the ciborium, the cruets for wine and water at the altar's right side, the paten. I know nothing about jewelry and the flowers in the shop but I can recite the priestly vestments, the amice, the alb, the girdle, the maniple, the stole, the chasuble, and I know the priest up there wearing the purple chasuble of Lent will change to white on Easter Sunday when Christ is risen and Americans give their children chocolate rabbits and yellow eggs.

After all the Sunday mornings in Limerick I can skip as easily as an altar boy from the Introit of the Mass to the Ite, missa est, Go, you are dismissed, the signal for the thirsty men of Ireland to rise from their knees and flock to the pubs for the Sunday pint, cure for the woes of the night before.

I can name the parts of the Mass and the priestly vestments and the parts of a rifle like Henry Reed in his poem but what use is all this if I rise in the world and sit in a stiff chair at a table where they're serving fancy food and I can't tell the difference between mutton and duck?

It's full daylight on Fifth Avenue and there's no one but myself sitting on the steps between the two great lions of the Forty-Second Street Public Library where Tim Costello told me to go nearly ten years ago to read *The Lives of the Poets*. There are little birds of different sizes and colors flitting from tree to tree telling me spring will soon be here and I don't know their names either. I can tell the difference between a pigeon and a sparrow and there it ends except for the seagull.

If my students at McKee High School could look into my head they'd wonder how I ever became a teacher at all. They know already I never went to high school and they'd say, That's it. Here's a teacher who stands up there giving us vocabulary lessons and he doesn't even know the names of the birds in the trees.

The library will be open in a few hours and I could sit in the Main Reading Room with big picture books that tell me the names of things but it's still early morning and it's a long way to Downing Street, Bill Galetly cross-legged and squinting at himself in the mirror, Plato and the Gospel According to St John.

He's flat on his back on the floor, naked and snoring, a candle guttering by his head, banana peels everywhere. It's cold in the flat but when I place a blanket over him he sits up and pushes it away. Sorry about the bananas, Frank, but I had a little celebration this morning. Big breakthrough. Here it is.

He points to a passage in St John. Read it, he says. Go ahead, read it.

And I read, It is the spirit that quickeneth, the flesh profiteth nothing, the words that I speak unto you, they are the spirit, and they are the life.

Bill stares at me. So?

What?

You get it? You dig?

I don't know. I'd have to read it a few times and it's nearly nine o'clock in the morning. I've been up all night.

I fasted for three days to get inside that. You have to get inside things. Like sex. But I'm not finished. I'm looking for the parallel world in Plato. Guess I'll have to go to Mexico.

Why Mexico?

283

Great shit there.

Shit?

You know. Variety of chemicals to help the seeker.

Oh, yes. I'm going to bed for a while.

Wish I could offer you a banana but I had the celebration.

I sleep a few hours this Sunday morning and when I awake he's gone leaving behind nothing but banana skins.

42

Alberta is back. She calls me and asks me to meet her over at Rocky's for the sake of old times. She's wearing a light spring coat with the lavender scarf she wore when she said good-night instead of good-bye and this meeting must have been what she had in mind all the time.

All the men in Rocky's stare at her and their women glare at them to stop looking at someone else and look back at them.

She slips off her coat and sits with the lavender scarf on her shoulders and my heart is beating so hard I can hardly talk. She'll have a martini straight up with a twist and I'll have a beer. She tells me it was all a mistake going off with someone else but he was mature and ready to settle down and I acted all the time like a single man with the hovel in the Village. She realized in no time it was me she loved and even though we have our differences we can work them out especially if we settle down and get married.

When she mentions marriage there's a different sharp pain in my chest from the fear I'll never have that free life I see everywhere in New York, the kind of life they had in Paris where everyone sat in cafés drinking wine, writing novels, sleeping with other men's wives and beautiful rich American women eager for the passion.

If I say anything like this to Alberta she'll say, Oh, grow up. You're twenty-eight going on twenty-nine not a goddam beatnik.

Of course neither one of us is going to talk like this in the middle of our reconciliation especially since I have a nagging feeling she's right and I might be just a drifter like my father. Even though I've been a teacher for a year I still envy people who can sit in coffee shops and pubs and go to parties where there are artists and models and a jazz combo in the corner blowing cool and lowdown.

No use telling her anything of my freedom dreams. She'd say, You're a teacher. You never dreamed when you got off the boat you'd come this far. Get on with it.

Once in Rhode Island we argued over something and Zoe the grandmother said, You're nice people, but not together.

She won't come to my cold water flat, the hovel, and she won't let me come to hers with her father there for a short time because of a rift with his wife, Stella. She puts her hand on mine and we look at each other so hard she has tears and I'm ashamed of the redness she must be seeing and the oozing.

On the way to the subway she tells me that when the school term ends in a few weeks she's going to Rhode Island to be with her grandmother for a while and sort out her life. She knows there's a question in the air, Will I be invited? and the answer is no, I'm not in favor with the grandmother at this moment. She kisses me goodnight, tells me she'll talk to me on the phone soon, and after she disappears into the subway I walk across Washington Square Park torn between my yearning for her and my dreams of the free life. If I don't fit in with the way she wants to live, clean, organized, respectable, I'll lose her and I'll never find anyone like her. I never had women throwing themselves at me in Ireland, Germany or the USA. I could never tell the world about the weekends in Munich where I consorted with the lowest whores in Germany or the time when I was fourteen and a half frolicking with a dying girl on a green sofa in Limerick. All I have is dark secrets and shame and it's a wonder Alberta has anything to do with me at all. If I had any belief left in anything I could go to confession but where is the priest who could hear my sins without throwing his hands up in disgust and sending me to the bishop or some part of the Vatican reserved for the doomed?

The man at the Beneficial Finance Company says, Do I detect a brogue? He tells me where his mother and father came from in Ireland

and how he plans to visit himself though that'd be hard with six kids, ha ha. His mother comes from a family of nineteen. Can you believe that? he says. Nineteen kids. Of course seven died but what the hell. That's how it was in the old days in the Old Country. They had kids like rabbits.

So, back to the application. You want to borrow three hundred and fifty dollars to visit the Old Country, eh? You haven't seen your mother in what, six years? The man congratulates me on wanting to see my mother. Too many people nowadays forget their mothers. But not the Irish. No, not us. We never forget our mothers. The Irishman that forgets his mother is no Irishman and should be drummed out, goddamit, excuse the language, Mr McCourt. I see you're a teacher and I admire you for that. It must be rough, big classes, low pay. Yeah, all I have to do is look at your application to see the low pay. Don't know how you can live on it and that, I'm sorry to tell you, is the problem. That's what causes the hitch in this application, the low pay and absence of any collateral if you know what I mean. They're gonna shake their heads at the head office over this application but I'm gonna push it because you got two things in your favor, you're an Irishman that wants to see his mother in the Old Country and you're a teacher killing himself in a vocational high school and, as I say, I'm going to bat for you.

I tell him I'll be shaping up at the warehouses in July to replace men going on vacation but that means nothing to the Beneficial Finance Company unless there's proof of steady employment. The man advises me to say nothing about sending money to my mother. They'd shake their heads at the main office if there was anything that might threaten my monthly payments on the loan.

The man wishes me good luck. He says, it's such a pleasure to do business with one of my own.

The platform boss at Baker and Williams looks surprised. Jesus, you back again. I thought you became a teacher or some goddam thing.

I did.

So what the hell you doin' here?

I need the money. The teacher's pay is not princely.

You shoulda stood in the warehouses or drove a truck or somethin'

287

an' you'd be makin' money an' not strugglin' with them goddam kids that don't care.

Then he asks, Didn't you used to hang around with that guy, Paddy McGovern?

Paddy Arthur?

Yeah. Paddy Arthur. So many Paddy McGoverns they have to get another name. You know what happened to him?

I don't.

Dumb bastard is on the A train platform at 125th Street. Harlem, you know. What the hell was he doin' in Harlem? Lookin' for a little of that black stuff. So he gets bored standing on the platform like everybody else and decides to wait for the train down on the tracks. On the goddam tracks, avoiding the third rail. You could get killed with the third rail. Lights a cigarette and stands there with that stupid smile on his face till the A train comes in and ends his troubles. That's what I heard. What was it with that dumb bastard?

He must have been drinking.

Course he was drinking. Goddam Irish are always drinking but I never heard of no Irishman waiting for the train on the tracks before. But your friend there, Paddy, always said he was going back. He'd save enough money and live in the Old Country. What happened? Know what I think? You wanna know what I think?

What do you think?

Some people should stay where they are. This country could drive you crazy. It drives people crazy that was born here. How come you're not crazy? Or maybe you are, eh?

I don't know.

Lissena me, kid. I'm Italian an' Greek an' we have our problems but my advice to a young Irishman is this, Stay away from the booze an' you won't have to wait for the train on the tracks. You got me?

I do.

At lunch I see a figure from the past washing dishes in the diner kitchen, Andy Peters. He sees me and tells me hold on, try the meatloaf and the mashed potatoes and he'll be out in a minute. He sits beside me on a counter stool and asks how I like the gravy.

Fine.

Yeah, well I made it. It's my practice gravy. I'm really the dishwasher

288

here but the cook is a drunk and he lets me do gravy and salads though there isn't much call for salads around here. Guys from docks and warehouses think salads are for cows. I came here to wash dishes so I can think, finished with that fucking NYU. I need to clear my head. What I'd really like to do is get a job vacuuming. I've gone from hotel to hotel offering to vacuum but there's always the form, always the shitass investigation into my past which reveals my dishonorable discharge for not having congress with a sheep and that puts the kibosh on vacuuming. You take a shit in a French ditch and your life is ruined till you hit on the brilliant solution of re-entering American life on the lowest level, dishwashing, and watch my speed, man. I'll be the dishwasher supremo. They'll blink in amazement and before you know it I'll be salad man. How? Learning, watching in an uptown kitchen, promoted to salad man, assistant assistant chef and before you know it I'll be on sauces. Sauces, for Christ's sakes, because the sauce is the great bullshit ingredient in French cooking and Americans are suckers for it. So watch my style, Frankie boy, watch for my name in the papers, André Pierre, pronounced in the proper French way with your eyebrows up to your hairline, sauce man supreme, wizard with pot pan and wire whisk, yacking away on all the talk shows on TV with no one giving a damn if I diddled every sheep in France and adjoining monarchies. People in fancy restaurants will ooh and ah, compliments to the chef, me, and I'll be invited to visit their tables so they can patronize me in my white hat and apron and of course I'll let the word slip out I was this close to a PhD at NYU and the Park Avenue wives will have me up for sauce consultations and the meaning of it all while the husbands are in Saudi Arabia buying oil and I'm with their wives drilling for gold.

He takes a moment to ask me what I'm doing with my life.

Teaching.

I was afraid of that. I thought you wanted to be a writer.

I do.

So?

I have to earn a living.

You're falling into the trap. I beg you, don't fall into the trap. I nearly fell into it myself.

I have to earn a living.

You'll never write while you're teaching. Teaching is a bitch. Remember Voltaire? Cultivate your garden.

I remember.

And Carlyle? Make money and forget the universe.

I'm earning a living.

You're dying.

A week later he is gone from the diner and no one knows where.

With the money from the Beneficial Finance Company and the wages from the warehouses I'm able to spend a few weeks in Limerick and it's the same old feeling when the plane descends and follows the Shannon Estuary to the airport. The river gleams silver and the fields rolling away are somber shades of green except where the sun shines and emeralds the land. It's a good time to be sitting near a window in case there are tears.

She's at the airport with Alphie and a hired car and the morning is fresh and dewy on the road to Limerick. She tells me about Malachy's visit with his wife, Linda, and what a wild party they had with Malachy going out to a field and riding home on a horse which he wanted to bring into the house till everyone persuaded him a house was no place for a horse. There was plenty of drink that night and more than drink, poteen, which someone got from a man out in the country and 'twas the luck o' God the guards never came near the house for the possession of poteen is a serious offense that could land you in the Limerick Jail. Malachy said she and Alphie might be able to come to New York for a visit at Christmas and wouldn't that be grand, we'd all be together.

They meet me on the streets and tell me I look grand, that I look more like a Yank all the time. Alice Egan argues, Frankie McCourt hasn't changed one hour, not one hour. Isn't that right, Frankie?

I don't know, Alice.

You don't have the slightest bit of an American accent.

Whatever friends I had in Limerick are gone, dead or emigrated, and I don't know what to do with myself. I could read all day in my mother's house but why did I come all the way from New York to sit on my arse and read? I could sit in pubs all night and drink but I could have done that in New York, too.

I walk from one end of the city to the other and out into the country where my father walked endlessly. People are polite but they're working and they have families and I'm a visitor, a returned Yank.

Is that yourself, Frankie McCourt?

'Tis.

When did you come?

Last week.

And when are you going back?

Next week.

That's grand. I'm sure your poor mother is glad to have you at home and I hope the weather keeps fine for you.

They say, I suppose you notice all kinds of changes in Limerick?

Oh, yes. More cars, fewer snotty noses and scabby knees. No barefoot children. No women in shawls.

Jesus, Frankie McCourt, them's peculiar things to be noticing.

They'll watch to see if I put on airs and they'll cut me down but I have none to put on. When I tell them I'm a teacher they seem disappointed.

Only a teacher. Lord above, Frankie McCourt, we thought you'd be a millionaire by now. Sure wasn't your brother Malachy here with his glamorous model of a wife and isn't he an actor and everything.

The plane lifts into a western sun which touches the Shannon with gold and even though I'm happy to be returning to New York I hardly know where I belong anymore.

43

Malachy's bar is so successful he provides passage for my mother and my brother, Alphie, on the SS *Sylvania* which arrives in New York on December 21st, 1959.

When they emerge from the customs shed there's a piece of broken leather flapping from Mam's right shoe so that you can see the small toe of a foot that was always swollen. Does it ever end? Is this the family of the broken shoe? We embrace and Alphie smiles with broken blackened teeth.

The family of broken shoes and teeth destroyed. Will this be our coat of arms?

Mam looks past me to the street beyond. Where's Malachy?

I don't know. He should be here in a minute.

She tells me I look fine, that it didn't do me any harm to put on a bit of weight though I should do something about my eyes they're that red. That irritates me because I know that if I even think of my eyes or anyone mentions them I can feel them flush red and of course she notices.

See, she says. You're a bit old to be having bad eyes.

I want to snap at her that I'm twenty-nine and I don't know the proper age for not having bad eyes and is this what she wants to talk about the minute she arrives in New York? but Malachy arrives in a taxi with his wife, Linda. More smiles and embraces. Malachy keeps the taxi while we retrieve the suitcases.

Alphie says, Will we put these in the boot?

Linda smiles. Oh, no, we put them in the trunk.

Trunk? We didn't bring a trunk.

No, no, she says, we put your bags in the trunk of the taxi.

Isn't there a boot in the taxi?

No, that's the trunk.

Alphie scratches his head and smiles again, a young man understanding lesson number one in American English.

In the taxi Mam says, Lord above, look at all those motor cars. The roads are packed. I tell her it's not so bad now. An hour earlier it was the height of the rush hour and traffic was even worse. She says she doesn't see how it could ever be worse. I tell her it's always worse earlier and she says, I don't see how it could be worse than this the way the motor cars are crawling along this minute.

I am trying to be patient and I speak slowly. I am telling you, Mam, this is how the traffic is in New York. I live here.

Malachy says, Oh, it doesn't matter. It's a lovely morning, and she says, I lived here, too, in case you've forgotten.

You did, I tell her. Twenty-five years ago and you lived in Brooklyn, not Manhattan.

Well, it's still New York.

She won't give up and I won't though I'm looking at the pettiness of the two of us and wondering why I'm arguing instead of celebrating the arrival of my mother and my youngest brother in the city all of us dreamed of all our lives. Why does she pick on my eyes and why do I have to contradict her over the traffic?

Linda tries to ease the moment. Well, as Malachy says, it is a beautiful day.

Mam gives a little begrudging nod. 'Tis.

And how was the weather when you left Ireland, Mam?

A begrudging word, Raining.

Oh, it's always raining in Ireland, isn't it, Mam?

No, it's not, and she folds her arms and stares straight ahead at the traffic that was much busier an hour earlier.

At the apartment Linda makes breakfast while Mam dandles the new baby, Siobhan, and croons to her the way she crooned to seven of us. Linda says, Mam, would you like tea or coffee?

Tea, please.

When the breakfast is ready Mam puts the baby down, comes to the table and wants to know what is that thing floating around in her cup. Linda tells her it's a tea bag and Mam puts her nose in the air. Oh, I wouldnt drink that. Sure, that's not proper tea at all.

Malachy's face tightens and he tells her through his teeth, That's the tea we have. That's the way we make it. We don't have a pound of Lyons' tea and a teapot for you.

Well, then, I won't have anything. I'll just eat my egg. I don't know what kind of country this is where you can't get a decent cup of tea.

Malachy is ready to say something but the baby cries and he goes to lift her from her crib while Linda flutters around Mam, smiling, trying to please. We could get a teapot, Mam, and we could get loose tea, couldn't we, Malachy?

But he's parading the living room with the baby whimpering on his shoulder and you can see that in the matter of tea bags he won't yield, not this morning anyway. Like anyone who has ever had a decent cup of tea in Ireland he despises tea bags but he has an American wife who knows nothing but tea bags, he has a baby and things on his mind and little patience with this mother with her nose in the air over tea bags her first day in the United States of America and he doesn't know why, after all his expense and trouble, he has to tolerate her picky ways for the next three weeks in this small apartment.

Mam pushes away from the table. Lavatory? she asks Linda. Where's the lavatory?

What?

Lavatory. W C.

Linda looks at Malachy. The toilet, he says. The bathroom.

Oh, says Linda. In there.

While Mam is in the bathroom Alphie tells Linda the teabag wasn't that bad after all. If you didn't see it floating in the cup you'd think it was all right, and Linda smiles again. She tells him that's why the Chinese don't serve great chunks of meat. They don't like looking at the animal they're eating. If they cook chicken they chop it into little pieces and mix it with other things so you barely know it's chicken. That's why you never see a chicken leg or breast in a Chinese restaurant.

Is that right? Alphie says.

The baby is still whimpering on Malachy's shoulder but all is sweet at the table with Alphie and Linda discussing teabags and the delicacy of Chinese cooking. Then Mam comes from the bathroom and tells Malachy, That child is full of wind, so she is. I'll take her.

Malachy hands over Siobhan and sits at the table with his tea. Mam walks the floor with the piece of leather flapping from her broken shoe and I know I'll have to take her down Third Avenue to a shoe shop. She pats the baby and there's a powerful burp that makes us all laugh. She puts the baby back in the crib and leans over her. There, there, leanv, there, there, and the baby gurgles. She returns to the table, rests her hands in her lap and tells us, I'd give me two eyes for a decent cup of tea, and Linda tells her she'll go out today and get a teapot and loose tea, right, Malachy?

He says, Right, because he knows in his heart there's nothing like tea made in a pot which you rinse with water boiling madly, where there's a heaping spoon for each cup, where you pour in the madly boiling water, keeping the pot warm with a tea cozy while the tea brews for six minutes exactly.

Malachy knows that's how Mam will make tea and he softens his stand on teabags. He knows also that in the matter of baby burping she has finer instincts and superior ways and it's a fair exchange, a decent cup of tea for her and comfort for the baby Siobhan.

For the first time in ten years we're all together, Mam and her four sons. Malachy has his wife, Linda, and his baby, Siobhan, the first of a new generation. Michael has a girlfriend, Jan, and Alphie will soon find one, too. I'm reconciled with Alberta and living with her in Brooklyn.

Malachy is the life of the party in New York and no party can start without him. If he doesn't appear there's restlessness and whimpering, Where's Malachy? Where's your brother? and when he roars in they're happy. He sings and drinks and passes his glass for more drink and sings again till he rushes off to the next party.

Mam loves the life, the excitement of it. She loves having a highball at Malachy's Bar and being introduced as Malachy's mother. Her eyes twinkle and her cheeks glow and she dazzles the world with a flash of false teeth. She follows Malachy to the parties, the oul' hooleys, she calls them, basks in the mother spotlight and tries to join in

Malachy's songs till she runs out of breath with the first signs of emphysema. After all the years sitting by the fire in Limerick wondering where the next loaf of bread was coming from she's having a lovely time and isn't this a grand country altogether? Ah, maybe she'll stay a little longer. Sure, what's the use of going back to Limerick in the middle of the winter with nothing to do but sit there by the fire warming her poor shins? She'll go back when the weather warms up, Easter maybe, and Alphie can get a job here to keep them going.

Malachy has to tell her if she wants to stay in New York even for a short time she can't stay with him in his small apartment with Linda and the baby, four months old.

She calls me at Alberta's and tells me, I'm hurted, so I am. Four sons in New York and no place for me to lay my head.

But we all have small apartments, Mam. No room.

Well, one would wonder what ye're all doing with the money ye're making. Ye should have told me this before ye dragged me from my own comfortable fireplace.

No one dragged you. Didn't you say over and over you wanted to come for Christmas and didn't Malachy pay your fare?

I came because I wanted to see my first grandchild and, don't worry, I'll pay Malachy back if I have to get down on my two knees and scrub floors. If I knew the way I was going to be treated here I would have stayed in Limerick and had a nice goose for myself and a roof over my head.

Alberta whispers I should invite Mam and Alphie for dinner on Saturday night. There's a silence at the other end and then a sniffle.

Well, I don't know what I'll be doing on Saturday night. Malachy said there might be a party.

All right. We invited you to dinner but if you want to go to another party with Malachy, go.

You don't have to sound so huffy. It's an awful long distance to Brooklyn. I know because I used to live there.

It's less than half an hour.

She whispers something to Alphie and he takes the phone. Francis? We'll come.

When I open the door she brings her own chill along with the January chill. She acknowledges Alberta's existence with a nod and asks if I have a match for her cigarette. Alberta offers her a cigarette but she says, no, she has her own and these American cigarettes barely have any taste anyway. Alberta offers her a drink and she'll have a highball. Alphie says he'll have a beer and Mam says, Oh, you're starting, are you?

I tell her it's only a beer.

Well, that's how it starts. One beer and the next thing ye're roaring and singing and waking the child.

There's no child here.

There is in Malachy's house and the roaring and singing, too.

Alberta calls us into dinner, tuna casserole with green salad. Mam takes her time coming to the table. She has to finish her cigarette and what's the hurry anyway.

Alberta says it's nice to eat casserole when it's good and hot.

Mam says she hates hot food that burns the roof of your mouth.

I tell her, For Christ's sake, finish your cigarette and come to the table.

She comes with her offended look. She pulls her chair in and pushes the salad away. She doesn't like the lettuce in this country. I try to control myself. I ask her what the hell is the difference between the lettuce in this country and the lettuce in Ireland. She says there's a big difference, that the lettuce in this country is tasteless.

Alberta says, Oh, never mind. Not everyone likes lettuce anyway.

Mam stares at her casserole and forks noodles and tuna aside while she hunts for peas. She says she loves peas though these are not as good as the ones in Limerick. Alberta asks if she'd like more peas.

No, thank you.

After which she probes the noodles for bits of tuna.

I ask her, Don't you like the noodles?

What?

The noodles. Don't you like them?

I don't know what they are but I'm not fond of 'em.

I want to lean into her face and tell her she's acting like a savage, that Alberta went to great lengths thinking of something that might please her and all she can do now is to sit with her nose in the air as if someone had done something to her and if she doesn't like it she can put on her damn coat and go back to Manhattan to the party she's missing and I'll never bother her again with an invitation to dinner.

I want to say all this but Alberta makes peace. Oh, that's all right. Maybe Mam is tired with the excitement of coming to New York and if we have a nice cup of tea and a piece of cake we'll all relax.

Mam says, No, thank you to the cake, she couldn't eat another morsel but she would like a cup of tea till, again, she sees the tea bag in her cup and tells us this isn't a proper cup of tea at all.

I tell her that's what we have and that's what she's getting though what I don't tell her is that I'd like to throw the tea bag between her eyes.

She said no to the cake but here she is pushing it into her mouth and swallowing with hardly a chew and then picking up and eating the crumbs from around her plate, the woman who didn't want the cake.

She glances at the tea cup. Well, if that's the only tea ye have I suppose I'll have to drink it. She lifts the tea bag on her spoon and squeezes it till the water turns brown and wants to know why there's a lemon on her saucer.

Alberta says some people like lemon with their tea.

Mam says she never heard the likes of that, it's disgusting.

Alberta removes the lemon and Mam says she'd like milk and sugar, if you don't mind. She asks for a match for her cigarette and smokes while she drinks only half the tea to show she doesn't care for it.

Alberta asks if she and Alphie would like to see a movie in the neighborhood but Mam says, no, they have to be getting back to Manhattan and it's too late.

Alberta says it isn't that late and Mam says it's late enough.

I walk with my mother and Alphie up Henry Street and over to the subway at Borough Hall. It's a bright January night and all along the street there are still Christmas lights glowing and flickering in the windows. Alphie talks about the elegance of the houses and says thanks for the dinner. Mam says she doesn't know why people can't put the dinner in a bowl and give it to you without a plate under it. She thinks that kind of thing is putting on airs.

When the train comes in I shake hands with Alphie. I bend over to kiss my mother and hand her a twenty-dollar bill but she pulls her face away and sits in the train with her back to me and I walk away with the money back in my pocket.

44

For eight years I traveled on the Staten Island Ferry. I would take the RR train from Brooklyn to Whitehall Street in Manhattan, walk to the terminal, slip a nickel into a turnstile slot, buy coffee and a doughnut, plain no sugar, and wait on a bench with a newspaper filled with yesterday's disasters.

Mr Jones taught music at McKee High School though when you saw him on the ferry you might have thought he was a university professor or head of a law firm. You might have thought that even though he was a Negro who would become a black and, in later years, an African-American. Every day he wore a different three-piece suit and a hat to match. He wore shirts with collars or held in place with gold stick pins. His watch and rings were gold, too, and delicate. The old Italian shoeshine men loved him for the daily trade and generous tips and they left his shoes dazzling. Every morning he read the *Times* and held it with fingers protruding from little leather gloves that covered the area below the wrist to beyond the knuckles. He smiled when he told me of concerts and operas he'd attended the night before or of summer trips to Europe especially to Milan and Salzburg. He put his hand on my arm and told me I must not die before I sit in La Scala. Another teacher joked one morning that the kids at McKee must be impressed with his clothes, all that elegance, you know, and Mr Jones said, I dress for what I am. The teacher shook his head and Mr Jones went back to his *Times*. On the ferry back that day the other teacher told me Mr Jones didn't see himself as a Negro at all, that he'd call to the black kids to stop bopping down the hall. The black kids didn't know what to make of Mr Jones with all that elegance. They knew that whatever music they liked Mr Jones would be up there talking about Mozart, playing his music on the phonograph or illustrating passages on the piano, and when it was time for the Christmas assembly he'd have his boys and girls up on the stage caroling like angels.

Every morning on the ferry I passed the Statue of Liberty and Ellis Island and thought of my mother and father coming to this country. When they sailed in were they excited as I was that first sunny October morning? Teachers going to McKee and other schools on Staten Island sat on the ferry and looked towards the Statue and the island. They must have thought of their parents and grandparents coming into this place and they might have thought of all the hundreds who were sent back. It must have saddened them the way it saddened me to see Ellis Island neglected and crumbling and that ferry docked by the side low in the water, the ferry that took the immigrants from Ellis Island to the island of Manhattan and if they looked hard enough they saw ghosts hungry for the landing.

Mam had moved with Alphie to an apartment on the West Side. Then Alphie left to be his own man in the Bronx and Mam moved to Flatbush Avenue near Grand Army Plaza in Brooklyn. Her building was shabby but she felt comfortable having a place of her own where she'd be under obligation to nobody. She could walk to any number of bingo games and she was content, thank you.

In my early years at McKee High School I enrolled at Brooklyn College for classes leading to a master's degree in English. I started with summer courses and continued with afternoon and evening classes into the academic year. I would take the ferry from Staten Island to Manhattan and walk to a subway train at Bowling Green that took me to the end of the Flatbush line near Brooklyn College. On ferry and train I could read for my classes or correct the work of my students at McKee.

I told my students I wanted neat, clean, legible work but they handed in whatever they had scribbled quickly on buses and trains, in shop classes when the teacher wasn't looking, or in the cafeteria. The papers were dotted with the stains of coffee, Coke, ice cream, ketchup, sneezes, and a lusciousness where girls had blotted their lips. A set of such papers would so irritate me I'd fling them over the side of the ferry and watch with satisfaction while they sank below the water to create a Sargasso of illiteracy.

When they asked for their papers I told them they were so bad that if I had returned them each paper would have been given a zero and would they prefer that to nothing at all?

They weren't sure and when I thought of it I wasn't sure myself. Zero or nothing at all? We discussed it for a whole period and decided that nothing at all was better than zero on your report card because you can't divide nothing at all by anything and you can divide zero if you use algebra or something like that because a zero is something and nothing at all is nothing at all and nobody could argue with that. Also, if your parents see a zero on your report card they're upset, the ones who care, but if they see nothing they don't know what to think and it's better to have a father and mother who don't know what to think than a father and mother looking at a zero and giving you a punch upside your head.

After my classes at Brooklyn College I would sometimes leave the train at Bergen Street to visit my mother. If she knew I was coming she'd make soda bread so warm and delicious it melted in the mouth as fast as the butter she slathered on it. She made tea in a teapot and couldn't help sniffing at the idea of tea bags. I told her tea bags were just a convenience for people with busy lives and she said no one is so busy they can't take time to make a decent cup of tea and if you are that busy you don't deserve a decent cup of tea for what is it all about anyway? Are we put into this world to be busy or to chat over a nice cup of tea?

My brother Michael married Donna from California in Malachy's apartment on West Ninety-Third Street. Mam bought a new dress for the occasion but you could see she didn't approve of the proceedings. There was her lovely son Michael getting married and no sign of a priest, nothing but a Protestant minister in the living room who could pass for a grocer or an off-duty policeman in his collar and tie. Malachy had rented two dozen folded chairs and when we took our places I noticed Mam's absence. She was in the kitchen smoking a cigarette. I told her the wedding was about to begin and she told me she had to finish her cigarette. Mam, for Christ's sake, your son is getting married. She said that was his problem, she had to finish her fag and when I told her she was keeping everyone waiting her face tightened, the nose went up in the air; she stubbed out her butt in the ashtray and took her time going to the living room. On the way in she whispered she had to go to the bathroom and I hissed at her that she'd bloody well have to wait. She sat in her chair and stared over the head of the Protestant minister. No matter what was said, no matter what softness or sweetness surged here, she wouldn't be part of it, wouldn't yield, and when bride and groom were kissed and hugged Mam sat with her purse in her lap staring straight ahead so that the world would know she was seeing nothing, especially the sight of her lovely son Michael falling into the clutches of Protestants and their ministers.

When I visited Mam on Flatbush Avenue and we had the tea she said wasn't it a peculiar thing she was back in this part of the world after all these years, a place where she had five children, though three would die, the little girl here in Brooklyn, and twin boys in Ireland. It might have been too much for her to think about that little girl, dead at twenty-one days, a short distance from here. She knew that if you walked down Flatbush Avenue to where it crossed Atlantic Avenue you'd still see the bars my father went wild in, spending his wages, forgetting his children. No, she wouldn't talk about that, either. When I asked her about her days in Brooklyn she doled out scraps and then went silent. What was the use? The past is the past and it's dangerous to go back.

She must have had nightmares alone in that apartment.

45

Stanley spends more time in the teachers' cafeteria than anyone. When he sees me he sits with me, drinks coffee, smokes cigarettes and delivers monologues on everything.

Like most teachers he has five classes but his speech therapy students are often absent because of the shame of stammering and trying to make themselves understood with cleft palates. Stanley gives them inspirational speeches and even though he tells them they're as good as anyone else they don't believe him. Some are in my regular English classes and they write compositions saying it's all right for Mr Garber to talk, he's a nice guy and all, but he doesn't know what it's like to walk up to a girl and ask her to dance when you can't get the first word out of your mouth. Oh, yeah, it's all right for Mr Garber to help their stammer with singing in his class but what good is that when you go to the dance?

In the summer of 1961 Alberta wanted to be married at Grace Episcopal Church in Brooklyn Heights. I refused. I told her I'd rather be married in City Hall than in some pale imitation of the One, Holy, Roman, Catholic and Apostolic Church. Episcopalians irritated me. Why couldn't they stop the damned nonsense? They're up there with their statues and crosses and holy water and even confession, so why don't they call Rome and tell them they want to return?

Alberta said, All right, all right, and we went to the Municipal Building in Manhattan. It wasn't required but we had Brian McPhillips as best man and his wife, Joyce, as bridesmaid. Our ceremony was delayed because of a quarrel between the couple ahead of us. She said to him, You goin' be married to me with that green umbrella on you arm? He said that was his umbrella and he wasn't going to leave it out in this office to be stolen. She nodded towards us and told him, These people ain't gonna steal you goddam green umbrella, excuse the language on my wedding day. He said he wasn't accusin' nobody of nothin' but goddam he paid a lot for that umbrella on Chambers Street from a guy that steals them and he wasn't givin' it up for nobody. She told him, Well, then, marry you damn umbrella, and she picked up her bag and walked out. He told her if she walked out now that was the end and she turned to the four of us and the woman behind the desk and the official coming out of the small wedding chapel and said, The end? What you talkin' about, man? We be livin' together three years an' you tell me this is the end? You don't tell me this is the end. I tell you and I'm tellin' you that umbrella ain't goin' to my weddin' an' if you insist there's a certain party in South Carolina, a certain ex-wife, that would like to know where you at an' I be glad to tell her if you know what I mean, certain party lookin' for alimony an' child support. So take you choice, Byron, me in that little room with the man an' no umbrella or you back in South Carolina with you umbrella standin' before a judge tellin' you, Pay up, Byron, support you wife an' child.

The official at the door of the wedding chapel asked if they were ready. Byron asked me if I was the one getting married today and would I mind holding his umbrella because he could see that I was like him, going nowhere but into that little room. End of the road, man, end of the road. I wished him good luck but he shook his head and said, Damn, why we all whupped like this?

In a few minutes they were back to sign papers, the bride smiling, Byron grim. We all wished them good luck again and followed the official into the room. He smiled and said, Are we all atthembled?

Brian looked at me, raised his eyebrows.

The official said, Do you promith to love, honor, cherith? and I struggled to keep myself from laughing. How could I survive this wedding conducted by a man with such a powerful lisp? I'd have to think of some way of controlling myself. That's it. The umbrella on my arm. Oh, God, I'll fall apart. I'm caught between the lisp and the umbrella and I can't laugh. Alberta would kill me for laughing at our own wedding. You're allowed to weep with joy but you must never laugh and here I am made helpless by this man with the lisp, promithing thith and that, first man ever in New York to be married with a green umbrella on his arm, solemn thought that kept me from laughing, and the ceremony was over, the ring on Alberta's finger, groom and bride kissing and being congratulated by Brian and Joyce till the door opened and there was Byron. Man, you got my umbrella? You did that for me? Kep' it right here? Wanna have a drink? Celebrate?

Alberta signaled no to me with a little shake of her head.

I told Byron I was sorry. We were meeting friends who were giving us a party.

You lucky, man, you have friends. Me an' Selma goin' out to have a sangwidge an' go to a movie. I don't mind. Movie keeps her quiet, ha ha ha. Thanks for watchin' my umbrella.

Byron and Selma left and I fell against the wall, laughing. Alberta tried to keep a bit of dignity in the occasion but she gave way when she saw Brian and Joyce laughing, too. I tried to tell them how the thought of the green umbrella saved me from laughing over the lisp but the more I tried to talk the more helpless I became till we were clutching each other going down in the elevator and wiping our eyes outside in the August sun.

It was a short walk to Diamond Dan O'Rourke's Saloon for drinks and sandwiches with friends, Frank Schwake and his wife, Jean, and Jim Collins and his new wife, Sheila Malone. After that there was to be a party out in Queens given by Brian and Joyce who would drive Alberta and me in their Volkswagen.

Schwake bought me a drink. So did Collins and Brian. The bartender bought us a round and I bought him a drink and left him a big tip. He laughed and said I should get married every day. I bought drinks for Schwake and Collins and Brian and they all wanted to buy me one again. Joyce whispered to Brian and I knew she was worried about the drinking. Alberta told me to slow down. She understood it was my wedding day but it was early and I should have respect for her and the guests at the reception later. I told her we were married barely five minutes and she was already telling me what to do. Of course I had respect for her and the guests. That's all I ever had was respect and I was weary of having respect. I told her back off and there was such a state of tension Collins and Brian intervened. Brian said it was his job, that's what best men are for. Collins said he knew me longer than Brian but Brian said, No, you don't. I went to college with him. Collins said he didn't know that. McCourt, how come you never told me you went to college with McPhillips? I told him I never saw a need to tell the world who I went to college with and for some reason that made us all laugh. The bartender said it was nice to see people happy on their wedding day and we laughed even harder thinking of lisps and green umbrellas and Alberta telling me have respect for her and the guests. Of course I had respect for her on our wedding day till I went to the toilet and started thinking of how she rejected me for another man and I was ready to go out and confront her till I slipped on the slimy floor of the toilet in Diamond Dan O'Rourke's and banged my head so hard against the big urinal I had a headache that made me forget the rejection. Alberta wanted to know why the back of my jacket was damp and when I told her there was a leak in the men's room she didn't believe me. You fell, didn't you? No, I didn't fall. There was a leak. She wouldn't believe me, told me I was drinking too much and that so irritated me I was ready to walk out and live with a ballerina in a loft in Greenwich Village till Brian said, Oh, come on, don't be an ass, it's Alberta's wedding day, too.

Before going out to Queens we had to pick up a wedding cake at Schrafft's on West Fifty-Seventh Street. Joyce said she'd drive because Brian and I had been too enthusiastic with the celebrations at Diamond Dan's while she and Alberta were saving themselves for the party that night. She stopped opposite Schrafft's and said no when Brian offered to get the cake but he insisted and dodged the traffic. Joyce shook her head and said he was going to get killed. Alberta told me go help him but Joyce shook her head again and said that would only make things worse. Brian came out of Schrafft's holding a big cake box against his chest and once more dodged cars till a taxi sideswiped him slightly at the street's dividing line and the box fell to the ground. Joyce put her forehead against the steering wheel. Oh, God, she said, and I said I was going to help my best man, Brian. No, no, Alberta said, I'll go. I told her this was man's work, that I wouldn't risk her life with these mad taxis on Fifty-Seventh Street and I went to help Brian who was on his hands protecting the wrecked cake from the traffic zooming by him right and left. I knelt with him, tore a cardboard flap from the box, and we shoveled the cake back in with bits hanging here and there. The little bride and groom figures looked sad but we wiped them off and stuck them back on the cake, not the top, because we didn't know where the top was anymore, but somewhere in the cake where we could push them in for the security. Joyce and Alberta called to us from the car that we'd better get off the street before the police came or we were killed and they were tired of waiting anyway, hurry up. When we got into the car Joyce told Brian pass the cake back to Alberta for safekeeping but he turned stubborn and said no, after all his troubles he'd hold on to it till we were at the apartment, and he did even if he had bits of cream and little green and yellow decorations all over his lap and his suit in general.

The wives treated us coolly the rest of the way in the car, talking only to each other and making comments on the Irish and how you can't trust them with a simple task like crossing a street with a wedding cake, how these Irish couldn't have one or two drinks and be content till the reception, oh, no, they had to talk and treat each other to rounds till they're in such a condition you couldn't send them to the grocery for a quart of milk.

Look at him, Joyce said, and when I saw Brian dozing away with his chin on his chest I nodded off while the wives went on with their lamentation about the Irish in general and this day in particular, Alberta saying, Everyone warned me that the Irish are great to go out with but never marry them. I would have defended my race and told her how her Yankee ancestors had nothing to be proud of the way they treated the Irish with those signs everywhere that said, No Irish Need Apply, except that I was weary from the strain of being married by a man with a lisp while I carried Byron's green umbrella and my heavy responsibility as groom and host at Diamond Dan O'Rourke's. If I hadn't slumped with the weariness I would have reminded her how her ancestors hanged women right and left for being witches, how they were a dirty-minded lot, rolling their eyes in shock and horror at the mention of sex, but having a grand time between their thighs listening in court to hysterical Puritan maidens claiming the devil appeared in various forms and frolicked with them in the woods and how they became so devoted to him all decency went out the window.

I would have told Alberta how the Irish never carried on like that. In the whole history of Ireland only one witch was hanged and she was probably English and deserved it. And, just to clinch it, I would have told her the first witch to be hanged in New England was Irish and they did it to her because she said her prayers in Latin and wouldn't stop.

Instead of saying all this I fell asleep till Alberta shook me and told me we were there. Joyce insisted on taking the cake from Brian. She didn't want him to fall forward on the stairs and crush the cake entirely and she still had hopes of reconstructing it so that we'd have some resemblance of a cake and people could sing, The bride cuts the cake.

People arrived and there was eating, drinking, dancing and mis-understandings between all the couples, married and unmarried. Frank Schwake wouldn't talk to his wife, Jean. Jim Collins quarrelled in a corner with his wife, Sheila. There was still a coolness between Alberta and me and between Brian and Joyce. Other couples were affected and there were islands of tension all over the apartment. The night would have been ruined except for the way we all united against an outside danger.

One of Alberta's friends, a German named Dietrich, drove off in his Volkswagen to replenish the beer supply and when he returned there was trouble with the owner of a Buick he had backed into. Someone told me about the trouble outside and since I was the bride-groom it was my duty to make peace. The Buick man was a giant and poking his fist into the face of Alberta's friend. When I stepped between them he let loose with his big punch. His arm swung around the back of my head, into Dietrich's eye and we all fell to the ground. We wrestled a bit, one with another, no one a bit particular, till Schwake, Collins and McPhillips separated us with the Buick man threatening to tear Dietrich's head from his shoulders. When we dragged the German inside I discovered my trouser knee was ripped, the kneecap bleeding. The knuckles of my right hand bled, too, from being scraped along the ground.

Upstairs Alberta started to cry, telling me I was ruining the whole night. My blood boiled a bit and I told her I was only trying to be a peacemaker and it wasn't my fault if I was knocked down by that baboon next door. Besides, I was helping her German friend and she should be grateful.

The argument would have continued if Joyce hadn't stepped in to call everyone to the table for the cutting of the cake. When she slipped off the covering cloth Brian laughed and kissed her for being such a genius of an artist you'd never know this cake was scooped off the street a short time ago. The little bride and groom were secure though his head wobbled and fell and I told Joyce, Uneasy lies the groom that wears a head. Everyone sang, The bride cuts the cake, the groom cuts the cake, and Alberta looked mollified even though we couldn't cut proper slices and the cake had to be dished out in chunks.

Joyce said she was making coffee and Alberta said that would be nice but Brian said we should have one more drink to toast the newlyweds and I agreed and Alberta got so angry she ripped the wedding ring from her finger and threw it out the window though she remembered suddenly that was her grandmother's wedding ring from early in the century and now it was out the window, God knows where in Queens and what was she going to do, it was all my fault, and her great mistake for marrying me. Brian said we'd have to find that ring. We didn't have a flashlight but we were able to light up the night with matches and cigarette lighters as we crawled across the lawn below Brian's window till Dietrich shouted he had the ring and everyone forgave him for stirring up trouble with the big Buick man. Alberta refused to replace the ring on her finger. She'd keep it in her purse till she was sure of this marriage. She and I took a taxi with Jim Collins and Sheila. They would drop us at our apartment in Brooklyn and continue in to Manhattan. Sheila wasn't talking to Jim and Alberta wasn't talking to me but as we swung into State Street I grabbed her and told her, I'm going to consummate this marriage tonight.

She said, Oh, consummate my ass, and I said, That'll do.

The taxi stopped and I climbed from the back seat I had shared with Sheila and Alberta. Jim got out of the seat by the driver and came to where I stood on the sidewalk. He intended to say goodnight and get back in with Sheila but Alberta pulled the door shut and the taxi drove away.

Christ Almighty, said Collins, this is your goddam wedding night, McCourt. Where is your bride? Where is mine?

We climbed the stairs to my apartment, found a six-pack of Schlitz in the refrigerator, sat on the couch, the two of us, and watched television Indians drop from the bullets of John Wayne.

46

In the summer of 1963 Mam called to say she had a letter from my father. He claimed he was a new man, that he hadn't had a drink in three years and worked now as a chef in a monastery.

I told her if my father was a monastery chef the monks must have been on a permanent fast.

She didn't laugh and that said she was troubled. She read from the letter where he said he was coming with a three-week return ticket on the *Queen Mary* and how he looked forward to the day when we could all be together again, he and she sharing a bed and a grave for he knew and she knew that whatever God hath joined let no man put asunder.

She sounded uncertain. What should she do? Malachy had already told her, Why not? She wanted to know what I thought. I put it back to her. What do you think? After all, this was the man who put her through hell in New York and Limerick and now he wants to sail to her side, a safe harbor in Brooklyn.

I don't know what to do, she said.

She didn't know what to do because she was lonely in that dingy place on Flatbush Avenue and she was now illustrating that Irish saying, Contention is better than loneliness. She could take back this man or, at fifty-five, face the years alone. I told her I'd meet her for coffee at Junior's Restaurant.

She was there before me, puffing and gasping on a strong American cigarette. No, she wouldn't have tea. The Americans can send a man into space but they can't make a decent cup of tea, so she'd have coffee and some of that nice cheesecake. She drew on the cigarette, sipped the coffee and told me she didn't know under God what to do. She said the whole family was falling apart with Malachy separated from his wife, Linda, and the two small children, Michael off to California with his wife, Donna, and their child, Alphie disappeared into the Bronx. She said she could have a nice life for herself in Brooklyn with the bingo and the odd meeting of the Limerick Ladies' Association in Manhattan and why should she let the man from Belfast upset that life.

I drank my coffee and ate my strudel knowing she'd never admit she was lonely though she might have been thinking, Ah, sure if it wasn't for the drink he wouldn't be bad to live with at all, at all.

I told her what I was thinking. Well, she said, he'd be company for me if he's not drinking, if he's a new man. We could take walks in Prospect Park and he could meet me after the bingo.

All right. Tell him to come for the three weeks and we'll see if he's a new man.

On the way back to her apartment she stopped often to press her hand against her chest. 'Tis my heart, she said, going a mile a minute so 'tis.

It must be the cigarettes.

Oh, I don't know.

Then it must be nervousness over that letter.

Oh, I don't know. I just don't know.

At her door I kissed her cold cheek and watched her gasping her way upstairs. My father had put years on her.

When Mam and Malachy went to meet the new man at the pier he arrived so drunk he had to be helped off the ship. The purser told them he had gone wild with the drink and had to be kept in restraint.

I was away that day and when I returned I took the subway to see him at Mam's apartment but he had gone with Malachy to a meeting of Alcoholics Anonymous. We drank tea and waited. She said again she didn't know under God what to do. He was the same lunatic with the drink and all that talk about being a new man was a lie and she was glad he had a three-week return ticket. Still, there was a darkness in her eyes that told me she must have had hopes of a normal family, her man by her side with sons and grandchildren coming to her from all over New York.

They returned from the meeting, Malachy big, red-bearded and sober because of his troubles, my father older and smaller. Malachy had tea. My father said, Och, no, and lay on the couch with his hands joined under his head. Malachy left his tea to stand over him and lecture him. You have to admit you're an alcoholic. That's the first step.

Dad shook his head.

Why are you shaking your head? You are an alcoholic and you have to admit it.

Och, no. I'm not an alcoholic like those poor people at the meeting. I don't drink kerosene.

Malachy threw up his hands and returned to his tea at the table. We didn't know what to say to each other in the presence of this man on the couch, husband, father. I had my memories of him, mornings by the fire in Limerick, his stories and songs, his cleanliness, neatness and sense of order, the way he helped us with our schoolwork, his insistence on obedience and attention to our religious duties, all destroyed by his payday madness when he threw his money around the pubs buying pints for every hanger-on while my mother despaired by the fire knowing the next day she'd have to stick her hand out for charity.

I knew in the days that followed that if blood called to blood I'd drift to my father's side of the family. My mother's people had often said in Limerick I had the odd manner of my father and a strong streak of the North in my character. They may have been right because whenever I went to Belfast I felt at home.

The night before he left he asked if we'd like to go for a walk. Mam and Malachy said no, they were tired. They had spent more time with him than I and must have been weary of his shenanigans. I said yes because this was my father and I was a nine-year-old thirty-three-year-old.

He put on his cap and we walked down Flatbush Avenue. Och, he said, it's a very warm kind of a night.

'Tis.

Very warm, he said. You'd be in danger of drying up on a night like this.

Ahead of us was the Long Island Railroad Station ringed with bars for the thirsty commuters. I asked if he remembered the bars.

Och, he said, why should I remember such places?

Because you drank in them and we searched for you.

Och, well, I might have worked in one or two when times were hard for the bread and meat they gave me to take home to you childer.

He remarked again on the heat of the night and surely it wouldn't do us any harm to cool ourselves in one of these places.

I thought you didn't drink.

That's right. Gave it up.

Well, what about the ship? You had to be carried off.

Och, that was the sea sickness. We'll have something here for the coolness.

While we drank our beer he told me my mother was a fine woman and I should be good to her, that Malachy was a fine big lad though you'd hardly know him with that red beard and where did it come from, that he was sorry to hear I had married a Protestant though it wasn't too late for her to convert nice girl that she was and he was happy to hear I was a teacher like all his sisters in the North and would there be any harm in having another beer?

No, there wouldn't be any harm and there wasn't any harm in the beers we had up and down Flatbush Avenue and when we arrived back at my mother's apartment I left him at the door because I didn't want to see the looks on the faces of Mam and Malachy that would accuse me of leading my father astray or vice versa. He wanted to continue the drinking up towards Grand Army Plaza but my guilt told me to say no. He was supposed to leave next day on the *Queen Mary* though he hoped my mother would say, Ah, stay. Sure we'll find some way of getting along.

I said that would be lovely and he said we'd all be together again and things would be better because he was a new man. We shook hands and I left.

Next morning Mam called and said, He went pure mad, so he did.

What did he do?

You brought him home drunk as a lord.

He wasn't drunk. He had a few beers.

He had more than that and I was here by myself with Malachy gone into Manhattan. A bottle of whiskey he had, your father, that he brought from the ship and I had to call the cops and he's gone now, bag and baggage, and sailed away today on the *Queen Mary* because I called Cunard and they told me, oh, yes, they had him on board and they'd be watching closely for any signs of the lunacy he came with.

What did he do?

She wouldn't tell me and she didn't have to because it was easy to guess. He probably tried to get into bed with her and that was not part of her dream. She hinted and suggested that if I hadn't spent hours with him in saloons he would have behaved himself and wouldn't be on the *Queen Mary* now heading out into the Atlantic. I told her his drinking wasn't my fault but she was sharp with me. Last night was the last straw, she said, and you were part of it.

47

For teachers Fridays are bright. You leave the school with a bag filled with papers to read and correct, books to read. This weekend you will surely catch up with all those uncorrected, unmarked papers. You don't want to let them pile up in the closets like Miss Mudd so that decades hence a young teacher will pounce on them to keep his classes busy. You will take the papers home, pour a glass of wine, stack Duke Ellington, Sonny Rollins and Hector Berlioz on the phonograph and try to read a hundred and fifty student compositions. You know that some don't care what you do with their work as long as you give them a decent grade so that they can pass and get on with real life in their shops. Others fancy themselves as writers and want their papers back corrected and graded high. The class Romeos would like you to comment on their papers and read them aloud so that they can bask in the admiring glances of the girls. The ones who don't care are sometimes interested in the same girls and verbal threats are passed from desk to desk because the ones who don't care are weak in written expression. If a boy is a good writer you have to be careful about praising him too much because of the danger of accidents on the stairs. The ones who don't care hate goody-goodies.

You intend to go straight home with your bag but you then discover Friday afternoon is the time for beer and teacher enlightenment. An occasional teacher might say he has to go home to his wife till he finds Bob Bogard standing by the time clock to remind us of first things first, that the Meurot Bar is a few steps away, next door in fact, and what harm would there be in one beer, one? Bob is not married and may not understand the dangers for a man who might go beyond the one beer, a man who might have to face the wrath of a wife who has cooked a fine Friday fish and now sits in the kitchen watching the grease congeal.

We stand at the Meurot Bar and order our beers. There is teacher small talk. When there's a mention of good-looking women on our staff or even nubile students we roll our eyes. What we wouldn't do if we were high school kids nowadays. We talk tough at the mention of troublesome boys. One more word out of that goddam kid and he's gonna beg for a transfer. We unite in our hostility to authority, all the people who emerge from their offices to supervise and observe us and tell us what to do and how to do it, people who spent as little time as possible in the classroom themselves and don't know their ass from their elbow about teaching.

A young teacher might drop in, just graduated from college, newly licensed. The drone of university professors and the chatter from college cafeterias is still in his ears and if he wants to discuss Camus and Sartre and how existence precedes essence or vice versa he'll be talking to himself in the mirror of the Meurot Bar.

None of us had followed the Great American Path, elementary school, high school, college, and into teaching at twenty-two. Bob Bogard fought in the war in Germany and was probably wounded. He won't tell you. Claude Campbell served in the navy, graduated from college in Tennessee, published a novel when he was twenty-seven, teaches English, has six children with his second wife, took a master's degree at Brooklyn College with a thesis, *Ideational Trends in the American Novel*, fixes everything in his house, wiring, plumbing, carpentry. I look at him and think of Goldsmith's lines on the village schoolmaster, "And all around the wonder grew/That one small head could carry all he knew." And Claude hasn't even reached the age of Christ at his crucifixion, thirty-three.

When Stanley Garber drops in for a Coke he tells us he often feels he made a mistake by not going into college teaching where you amble through life thinking you shit cream puffs and suffering if you have to teach more than three hours a week. He says he could have written a bullshit PhD dissertation on the bilabial fricative in the middle period of Thomas Chatterton who died when he was seventeen because that's the kind of crap that goes on in colleges while the rest of us hold the front lines with kids who won't get their heads out from between their thighs and supervisors content to keep their heads up their asses.

There will be trouble tonight in Brooklyn. I'm supposed to have dinner with Alberta at an Arabic restaurant, the Near East, bring your own wine, but it's six going on seven and if I call now she'll complain she's been waiting for hours, that I'm just an Irish drunk like my father and she doesn't care if I stay on Staten Island the rest of my life, goodbye.

So I won't call. Better not to. No use having two rows, one on the phone now, another when I get home. It's easier to sit at the bar where's there's a glow and important matters are discussed.

We agree that teachers are sniped at from three fronts, parents, kids, supervisors, and you either have to be diplomatic or tell them all kiss your ass. Teachers are the only professionals who have to respond to bells every forty-five minutes and come out fighting. All right, class, sit down. Yes, you, sit down. Open your notebooks, that's right, your notebooks, am I speaking a foreign language, kid? Don't call you kid? Okay, I won't call you kid. Just sit down. Report card grades are just around the corner and I can put you on the welfare rolls. All right, bring in your father, bring in your mother, bring in your whole damn tribe. You don't have a pen, Pete? Okay, here's a pen. Goodbye, pen. No, Phyllis, you can't have the pass. I don't care if you're having a hundred periods, Phyllis, because what you really want to do is meet Eddie and disappear into the basement where your future could be determined by one smooth panty drop and one swift upward stroke from Eddie's impatient member, the start of a little nine-month adventure that will end with you squawking Eddie better marry you, the shotgun aimed at his lower frontal region and his dreams dead. So I'm saving you, Phyllis, you and Eddie and no, you don't have to thank me.

This is talk along the bar that will never be heard in the classroom unless a teacher loses his wits entirely. You know you can never deny the lavatory pass to a menstrual Phyllis for fear of being dragged before the highest court in the land where the black robes, all men, will excoriate you for insulting Phyllis and the future mothers of America.

There is talk along the bar about certain efficient teachers and we agree we don't like them and the way their classes are so organized they hum from bell to bell. In these classes there are monitors for every activity, every part of the lesson. There is the monitor who goes immediately to the board to write the number and title of the day's lesson, Lesson #32, Strategies in Dealing with the Dangling Participle. Efficient teachers are known for their strategies, the darling new word at the Board of Education.

The efficient teacher has rules for taking notes and the organization of the notebook and there are notebook monitors who roam the classroom to check for proper form, top of page filled with student's name, homeroom class, title of course and date with the month written out, not numbers, it must be written out so that the student will have practice in writing out because there are too many people in this world that we live in, business people and others, who are too lazy to write out the months. There are to be prescribed margins and no scribbling. If the notebook doesn't adhere to the rules the monitor will enter demerits on the student's card and when report card time rolls around there will be suffering and no mercy.

Homework monitors collect and return assignments, attendance monitors preside over the little cards in the attendance book and collect excuses for absences and latenesses. Failure to submit written excuses leads to further suffering and no mercy.

Some students are known for their skill in writing excuse notes from parents and doctors and they'll do it in return for favors in the cafeteria or the far reaches of the basement.

Monitors who take blackboard erasers to the basement to knock out the chalk must first promise they're not taking this important job to sneak a smoke or make out with the boy or girl of their choice. The principal is already complaining there is too much activity in the basement and he'd like to know what's going on there.

There are monitors to distribute books and collect receipts, monitors to handle the lavatory pass and the sign-in sign-out sheet, monitors to put everything in the room in alphabetical order, monitors to carry the trash can along the aisles in the war against litter, monitors who decorate the room to make it so bright and cheerful the principal brings in visitors from Japan and Liechtenstein.

The efficient teacher is monitor of monitors though he may lighten his monitor load by appointing monitors who monitor the other monitors or he may have dispute monitors who settle arguments between monitors accusing other monitors of interfering with their jobs. The dispute monitor has the most dangerous job of all because of what might happen on the stairs or the street.

A student caught trying to bribe a monitor is immediately reported to the principal who will enter a remark on his permanent record that will blacken his reputation. This is a warning to others that such a blot could be an impediment to a career in sheet metal, plumbing, automechanics, anything.

Stanley Garber snorts that with all this efficient activity there is little time for instruction but what the hell, the students are in their seats, completely monitored and behaving themselves, and that pleases the teacher, the chairman, the principal and his assistants, the superintendent, the Board of Education, the Mayor, the Governor, the President, and God Himself.

So says Stanley.

If a university professor discusses *Vanity Fair* or anything else his classes listen with notebooks open and pens poised. If they dislike the novel they won't dare complain for fear of lowered grades.

When I distributed *Vanity Fair* to my junior class at McKee Vocational and Technical High School there was moaning in the room. Why do we have to read this dumb book? I told them it was about two young women, Becky and Amelia, and their adventures with men, but my students said it was written in that old English and who can read that? Four girls read it and said it was beautiful and should be made into a movie. The boys pretended to yawn and told me English teachers were all the same. They just wanted to make you read that old stuff and how was that gonna help you if you was fixin' a car or a busted air conditioner, ah?

I could threaten them with failure. If they refused to read this book they'd fail the course and they wouldn't graduate and everyone knew girls didn't want to go out with anyone who wasn't a high school graduate.

For three weeks we toiled through *Vanity Fair*. Every day I tried to motivate and encourage them, to draw them into a discussion of what it's like to make your way through the world when you're a young nineteenth-century woman, but they didn't care. One wrote on the board, Becky Sharp Drop Dead.

Then, as decreed by the school syllabus, it was on to *The Scarlet Letter*. This would be easier. I'd talk about the New England witch hunts, the accusations, the hysteria, the hangings. I'd talk about Germany in the 1930s and how a whole nation was brainwashed.

Not my students. They'd never be brainwashed. No, sir, they'd never be able to get away with that here. They'd never fool us like that.

I chanted to them, Winston tastes good like . . . and they finished the sentence.

I sang, My beer is Rheingold the dry beer . . . and they finished the jingle.

I chanted again, You wonder where the yellow went when . . . and they finished the line.

I asked if they knew any more and there was an eruption of jingles from radio and television, proof of the power of advertising. When I told them they were brainwashed they were indignant, Oh, no, they weren't brainwashed. They could think for themselves and nobody could tell them what to do. They denied they'd been told what cigarette to smoke, what beer to drink, what toothpaste to use though they'd admit that when you're in a supermarket you'll buy the brand in your head. No, you'd never buy a cigarette called Turnip.

Yeah, they heard about Senator McCarthy and all that but they were too young and their fathers and mothers said he was a great man for getting rid of the Communists.

From day to day I struggled to make connections between Hitler and McCarthy and the New England witch hunts, trying to soften them up for *The Scarlet Letter*. From parents there were indignant calls. What is this guy telling our kids about Senator McCarthy? Tell him back off. Senator McCarthy was a good man, fought for his country. Tailgunner Joe. Got rid of the Communists.

Mr Sorola said he didn't want to interfere but would I please tell him was I teaching English or was I teaching history. I told him about my troubles trying to get the kids to read anything. He said I shouldn't listen to them. Just tell them, You're going to read *The Scarlet Letter* whether you like it or not because this is high school and that's what we do here and that's that and if you don't like it, kid, you fail.

They complained when I distributed the book. Here we go again with the old stuff. We thought you was a nice guy, Mr McCourt. We thought you was different.

I told them this book was about a young woman in Boston who got into trouble over having a baby with a man who wasn't her husband though I couldn't tell them who the man was in case it might ruin the story. They said they didn't care who the father was. One boy said you never know who your father is anyway because he had a friend who discovered his father wasn't his father at all, that his real father was killed in Korea, but the pretend father was the one he grew up with, a good guy, so who gives a shit about this woman in Boston.

Most of the class agreed though they wouldn't want to wake up in the morning to find their fathers weren't their real fathers. Some wished they had other fathers, their own fathers were so mean they made them come to school and read dumb books.

But that's not the story of *The Scarlet Letter*, I said.

Aw, Mr McCourt, do we have to talk about that old stuff? This guy Hawthorne don't even know how to write so's we can understand and you're always saying write simple, write simple. Why can't we read the *Daily News*? They have good writers. They write simple.

Then I remembered I was broke and that's what led to *Catcher in the Rye* and *Five Great Plays of Shakespeare* and a change in my teaching career. I had forty-eight cents to get me home on the ferry and the subway, no money for lunch, not even for a cup of coffee on the ferry and I blurted to the class that if they wanted to read a good book that didn't have big words and long sentences and was all about a boy their age who was mad at the world I'd get it for them but they'd have to buy it, a dollar twenty-five each which they could pay in instalments starting now, so if you have a nickel or a dime or more you can pass it up and I'll write your name and amount on a sheet of paper and order the books today from the Coleman Book Company in Yonkers, and they'd never know, my students, I'd have a pocketful of change for lunch and maybe a beer at the Meurot next door, though I didn't tell them that, they'd be shocked.

Small change was passed up and when I called the book company I saved a dime by using the assistant principal's phone because it's illegal to have students buy books when bookrooms are spilling over with copies of *Silas Marner* and *Giants in the Earth*.

Catcher in the Rye arrived in two days and I passed them out, paid for or not. Some students never offered a penny, others less than their share, but the money collected kept me going till pay day when I'd satisfy the book company.

When I handed out the books someone discovered the word crap on the first page and that brought silence to the room. That's a word you'd never find in any book in the English bookroom. Girls covered their mouths and giggled and boys tittered over shocking pages. When the bell rang there was no stampede to the door. I had to ask them to leave, another class was coming in.

The class coming in were curious about the class going out and why was everyone looking at this book and if it was that good why couldn't they read it. I reminded them they were seniors and the class going out were juniors. Yeah, but why couldn't they read that small book instead of *Great Expectations*? I told them they could but they'd have to buy it and they said they'd pay anything not to read *Great Expectations*, anything.

Next day Mr Sorola came into the room with his assistant, Miss Seested. They went from desk to desk snatching copies of *Catcher in the Rye* and dropping them into two shopping bags. If the books weren't on the desks they demanded the students take them from their bags. They counted the books in the shopping bags and compared them with the class attendance and threatened the four students who hadn't turned in their books with big trouble. Raise your hands, the four people who still have the book. No hands were raised and on the way out Mr Sorola told me I was to see him in his office right after this class, not a minute later.

Mr McCourt, you in trouble?

Mr McCourt, that's the only book I ever read and now that man took it.

They complained about the loss of their books and told me if anything happened to me they'd go on strike and that would teach the school a lesson. They nudged and winked over the strike and they knew I knew it would simply be another excuse for avoiding school and not any great concern for me.

Mr Sorola sat behind his desk reading *Catcher in the Rye*, puffing on his cigarette and letting me wait while he turned the page, shook his head and put the book down.

Mr McCourt, this book is not on the syllabus.

I know, Mr Sorola.

You know I've had calls from seventeen parents and you know why?

They didn't like the book?

That's right, Mr McCourt. There's a scene in this book where the kid is in a hotel room with a prostitute.

Yes, but nothing happens.

That's not what the parents think. You telling me that kid was in that room to sing? The parents don't want their kids reading this kind of trash.

He warned me to be careful, that I was endangering my satisfactory rating on the yearly performance report and we wouldn't want that, would we? He would have to place a note in my file as a record of our meeting. If there were no further incidents in the near future the note would be removed.

Mr McCourt, what are we gonna read next?

The Scarlet Letter. We have tons of them in the bookroom.

Their faces fell. Aw, Gawd, no. All the kids in the other classes told us it's that old stuff again.

All right, I said, jokingly. We'll read Shakespeare.

Their faces fell even farther and the room was filled with moans and hisses. Mr McCourt, my sister went to college for a year and dropped out because she couldn't read Shakespeare and she can speak Italian and everything.

I said it again, Shakespeare. There was fear in the room and I felt myself drawn to the edge of a cliff with something in my head demanding, How can you move from Salinger to Shakespeare?

I told the class, It's Shakespeare or *The Scarlet Letter*, kings and lovers or a woman having a baby in Boston. If we read Shakespeare we'll act out the plays. If we read *The Scarlet Letter* we'll sit here and discuss the deeper meaning and I'll give you the big exam they keep in the department office.

Oh, no, not the deeper meaning. English teachers always be going on about the deeper meaning.

All right. It's Shakespeare, no deeper meaning and no exams except what you decide. So, write your name on this paper and the amount you're paying and we'll get the book.

They passed up their nickels and dimes. They groaned when they thumbed the book, *Five Great Plays of Shakespeare*. Man, I can't read this old English.

I wished I could have dominated my classes like other teachers, imposed on them classic English and American literature. I failed. I caved in and took the easy way with *Catcher in the Rye* and when that was taken dodged and danced my way to Shakespeare. We'd read the plays and enjoy ourselves and why not? Wasn't he the best?

Still my students complained till someone called out, Shit, man, excuse the language, Mr McCourt, but here's this guy saying Friends, Romans, countrymen, lend me your ears.

Where? Where? The class wanted to know the page number and all around the room boys declaimed Mark Antony's speech, flung out their arms and laughed.

Another discovered Hamlet's To be or not to be soliloquy and soon the room was filled with ranting Hamlets.

The girls raised their hands. Mr McCourt, the boys have all these great speeches and there's nothing for us.

Oh, girls, girls, there's Juliet, Lady Macbeth, Ophelia, Gertrude.

We spent two days plucking morsels from the five plays, *Romeo and Juliet*, *Julius Caesar*, *Macbeth*, *Hamlet*, *Henry IV*, Part One.

My students led and I followed because there was nothing else to do. Remarks had been passed in the hallways, in the students' cafeteria.

Hey, wass dat?

It's a book, man.

Oh, yeah? What book?

Shakespeare. We're reading Shakespeare.

Shakespeare? Shit, man, you not reading Shakespeare.

When the girls wanted to act out *Romeo and Juliet* the boys yawned and obliged. This would be sissy romantic stuff till the fight scene where Mercutio dies in style, telling the world about his wound.

> *Tis not so deep as a well, nor so wide as a church door,*
> *But 'tis enough, 'twill serve.*

* * *

324

To be or not to be was the passage everyone memorized but when they recited it they had to be reminded this was a meditation on suicide and not an incitement to arms.

Oh, yeah?

Yeah.

The girls wanted to know why everyone picked on Ophelia especially Laertes, Polonius, Hamlet. Why didn't she fight back? They had sisters like that who were married to bastard sons o' bitches, excuse the language, and you wouldn't believe what they put up with.

A hand went up. Why didn't Ophelia run away to America?

Another hand. Because there was no America in the old days. It had to be discovered.

Whadda you talkin' about? There was always an America. Where do you think the Indians lived?

I told them they'd have to look it up and the opposing hands agreed to go to the library and report next day.

One hand, There was an America in Shakespeare's time and she coulda went.

The other hand. There was an America in Shakespeare's time but no America in Ophelia's time and she cuddena went. If she went in Shakespeare's time there was nothing but Indians and Ophelia woulda been uncomfortable in a tepee which is what they called their houses.

We moved on to *Henry IV*, Part One, and all the boys wanted to be Hal, Hotspur, Falstaff. The girls complained again there was nothing for them except for Juliet, Ophelia, Lady Macbeth and Queen Gertrude and look what happened to them. Didn't Shakespeare like women? Did he have to kill everyone who wore a skirt?

The boys said that's the way it is and the girls snapped back they were sorry we didn't read *The Scarlet Letter* because one of them had read it and told the rest how Hester Prynne had her beautiful baby, Pearl, and the father was a jerk who died miserable and Hester got her revenge on the whole town of Boston and wasn't that much better than poor Ophelia floating down a stream, out of her mind, talking to herself and throwin' flowers around, wasn't it?

Mr Sorola came to observe me with the new head of the Academic Department, Mrs Popp. They smiled and didn't complain about this Shakespeare book not being on the syllabus though the next term Mrs Popp took this class away from me. I lodged a grievance and had a hearing before the superintendent. I said that was my class, I had started them reading Shakespeare and I wanted to continue in the next term. The superintendent ruled against me on the grounds that my attendance record was spotty and erratic.

My Shakespeare students were probably lucky in having the head of the department as their teacher. She was surely more organized than I and more likely to discover deeper meanings.

48

Paddy Clancy lived around the corner from me in Brooklyn Heights. He called to see if I'd like to go to the opening of a new bar in the Village, the Lion's Head.

Of course I'd like to go and I stayed till the bar closed at four a.m. and missed work the next day. The bartender, Al Koblin, thought for a while I was one of the singing Clancy Brothers and charged me nothing for the drinks till he discovered I was only Frank McCourt, a teacher. Now even though I had to pay for my drinks I didn't mind because the Lion's Head became my home away from home, a place where I could feel comfortable the way I never did in uptown bars.

Reporters from the first office of the *Village Voice* drifted in from next door and they attracted journalists from everywhere. The wall opposite the bar was soon adorned with the framed book jackets of writers who were regular customers.

That was the wall I coveted, the wall that haunted me and had me dreaming that some day I'd look up at a framed book jacket of my own. Up and down the bar writers, poets, journalists, playwrights talked about their work, their lives, their assignments, their travels. Men and women would have a drink while waiting for cars to planes that would take them to Vietnam, Belfast, Nicaragua. New books came out, Pete Hamill, Joe Flaherty, Joel Oppenheimer, Dennis Smith, and went up on the wall, while I hung on the periphery of the accomplished, the ones who knew the magic of print. At the Lion's Head you had to prove yourself in ink or be quiet. There was no place here for teachers and I went on looking at the wall, envious.

Mam moved into a small apartment across the street from Malachy on the Upper West Side of Manhattan. Now she could see Malachy, his new wife, Diana, their sons, Conor and Cormac, my brother, Alphie, his wife, Lynn, and their daughter, Allison.

She could have visited all of us as often as she liked and when I asked her why she didn't she barked at me, I don't want to be beholden to anyone. It irritated me always when I called and asked her what she was doing and she said, Nothing. If I suggested that she get out of the house and visit a community center or a senior citizens' center she'd say, Arrah, for the love o' Jesus, will you leave me alone. Whenever Alberta invited her to dinner she always made a point of being late, complaining of the long journey from her Manhattan apartment to our house in Brooklyn. I wanted to tell her she didn't have to come at all if it was such a bother to her and the last thing she needed anyway was a dinner she was getting that fat, but I curbed my tongue so that there wouldn't be tension at the table. Unlike the first time she came to dinner and pushed the noodles aside she now devoured everything before her though if you offered her a second helping she'd look prim and say no thanks as if she had the appetite of a butterfly and then pick at the crumbs on the table. If I told her she didn't have to pick at crumbs, there was more food in the kitchen, she'd tell me leave her alone, that I was getting to be a right bloody torment. If I told her she'd be better off if she'd stayed in Ireland she'd bristle, What do you mean I'd be better off?

Well, you wouldn't be lying in bed half the day with the radio stuck to your ear listening to every half-witted show they have.

I listen to Malachy on the radio and what's wrong with that?

You listen to everything. You do nothing.

Her face would grow pale, her nose pointed, she'd pick at crumbs no longer there and there might be a hint of watery eyes. Then I'd be pricked with guilt and invite her to stay for the night so that she wouldn't have to take that long subway ride to Manhattan.

No, thank you, I'd rather be in my own bed, if you don't mind.

Oh, I suppose you're afraid of the sheets, all those diseases from foreigners in the Laundromat?

And she'd say, I think now 'tis the drink talking. Where's my coat?

Alberta would try to soften the moment with another invitation to stay, that we had new sheets and Mam needn't be nervous.

'Tisn't the sheets at all. I just want to go home, and when she saw me put on my coat she'd say, I don't need anyone to walk me to the subway. I can find my own way.

You're not going to walk these streets by yourself.

I walk the streets by myself all the time.

It was a long silent walk up Court Street to the subway at Borough Hall. I wanted to say something to her. I wanted to get past my irritation and my anger and ask her that simple question, How are you, Mam?

I couldn't.

When we reached the station she said I didn't have to pay a fare to get through the turnstiles. She'd be all right on the platform. There were people there and she'd be safe. She was used to it.

I went in with her thinking we might say something to each other but when the train arrived I let her go without even an attempt at a kiss and watched her stumble towards a seat as the train pulled from the station.

Down near Court Street and Atlantic Avenue I remembered something she had told me months ago while we sat waiting for Thanksgiving dinner. Isn't it remarkable, she said, the way things turn out in people's lives?

What do you mean?

Well, I was sitting in my apartment and I was feeling lonesome so I went up and sat on one of those benches they have in the grassy island in the middle of Broadway and this woman came along, a shopping bag woman, one of the homeless ones, all tattered and greasy, rootin' around in the garbage can till she found a newspaper and sat beside me reading it till she asked me if she could borrow my glasses because she could only read the headlines with the sight she had and when she talked I noticed she had an Irish accent so I asked her where she came from and she told me Donegal a long time ago and wasn't it lovely to be sitting on a bench in the middle of Broadway with people noticing things and asking where you came from. She asked if I could spare a few pennies for soup and I said instead she could come with me to the Associated supermarket and we'd get some groceries and have a proper meal. Oh, she couldn't do that, she said, but I told her that's what I was going to do anyway. She wouldn't come inside the store. She said they wouldn't want the likes of her. I got bread and butter and rashers and eggs and when we got home I told her she could go in and have a nice shower and she was delighted with herself though there wasn't much I could do about her clothes or the bags she carried. We had our dinner and watched television till she started falling asleep on me and I told her lie down there on the bed but she wouldn't. God knows the bed is big enough for four but she laid down on the floor with a shopping bag under her head and when I woke up in the morning she was gone and I missed her.

I know it wasn't the dinner wine that had me against the wall in a fit of remorse. It was the thought of my mother being so lonesome she had to sit on a street bench, so lonesome she missed the company of a homeless shopping bag woman. Even in the bad days in Limerick she always had an open hand and an open door and why couldn't I be like that to her?

49

Teaching nine hours a week at New York Community College in Brooklyn was easier than twenty-five hours a week at McKee Vocational and Technical High School. Classes were smaller, students older, and there were none of the problems a high school teacher has to deal with, the lavatory pass, the moaning over assignments, the mass of paperwork created by bureaucrats who have nothing to do but create new forms. I could supplement my reduced salary by teaching at Washington Irving Evening High School or substituting at Seward Park High School and Stuyvesant High School.

The chairman of the English Department at the Community College asked me if I'd like to teach a class of paraprofessionals. I said yes though I had no notion of what a paraprofessional was.

That first class I found out. Here were thirty-six women, African-American with a sprinkling of Hispanics, ranging in age from early twenties to late fifties, teacher aides in elementary schools and in college now with government help. They'd get two-year associate degrees and, perhaps, continue their education so that some day they might become fully qualified teachers.

That night there was little time for teaching. After I had asked the women to write a short autobiographical essay for the next class they gathered up their books and filed out, apprehensive, still unsure of themselves, of each other, of me. I had the whitest skin in the room.

When we met again the mood was the same except for one woman who sat with her head on the desk, sobbing. I asked what was the matter. She raised her head, tears on her cheeks.

I lost my books.

Oh, well, I said, you'll get another set of books. Just go to the English Department and tell them what happened.

You mean I won't get throwed out of college?

No, you won't be throwed, thrown out of college.

I felt like patting her head but I didn't know how to pat the head of a middle-aged woman who has lost her books. She smiled, we all smiled. Now we could begin. I asked for their compositions and told them I'd read some aloud though I wouldn't use their real names.

The essays were stiff, self-conscious. As I read I wrote some of the more common misspelled words on the chalkboard, suggested changes in structure, pointed out grammatical errors. It was all dry and tedious till I suggested the ladies write simply and clearly. For their next assignment they could write on anything they liked. They look surprised. Anything? But we don't have anything to write about. We don't have no adventures.

They had nothing to write about, nothing but the tensions of their lives, summer riots erupting around them, assassinations, husbands who so often disappeared, children destroyed by drugs, their own daily grind of housework, jobs, school, raising children.

They loved the strange ways of words. During a discussion on juvenile delinquency Mrs Williams sang out, No kid o' mine gonna be no yoot.

Yoot?

Yeah, you know. Yoot. She held up a newspaper where the headline howled, Youth Slays Mom.

Oh, I said, and Mrs Williams went on, These yoots, y'know, runnin' around slayin' people. Killin' 'em, too. Any kid o' mine come home actin' like a yoot an' out he go on his you-know-what.

The youngest woman in the class, Nicole, turned the tables on me. She sat in the back in a corner and never spoke till I asked the class if they'd like to write about their mothers. Then she raised her hand. How about your mother, Mr McCourt?

Questions came like bullets. Is she alive? How many children did she have? Where's your father? Did she have all those children with one man? Where is she living? Who's she living with? She's living alone? Your mother's living alone and she has four sons? How come?

They frowned. They disapproved. Poor lady with four sons shouldn't be living alone. People should take care of their mothers but what do men know? You can never tell a man what it's like to be a mother and if it wasn't for the mothers America would fall apart.

In April Martin Luther King was killed and classes were suspended for a week. When we met again I wanted to beg forgiveness for my race. Instead I asked for the essays I had already assigned. Mrs Williams was indignant. Look, Mr McCourt, when they tryin' to burn your house down you ain't sittin' around writin' no cawm-po-zishuns.

In June Bobby Kennedy was killed. My thirty-six ladies wondered what was happening to the world but they agreed you have to carry on, that education was the only road to sanity. When they talked about their children their faces brightened and I became irrelevant to their talk. I sat on my desk while they told each other that now they were in college themselves they stood over their kids to make sure the homework was done.

On the last night of classes in June there was a final examination. I watched those dark heads bent over papers, the mothers of two hundred and twelve children, and I knew that, no matter what they wrote or didn't write on those papers, no one would fail.

They finished. The last paper had been handed in but no one was leaving. I asked if they had another class here. Mrs Williams stood and coughed. Ah, Mr McCourt, I must say, I mean we must say, it was a wonderful thing to come to college and learn so much about English and everything and we got you this little something hopin' you'll like it an' all.

She sat down, sobbing, and I thought, This class begins and ends in tears.

The gift was passed up, a bottle of shaving lotion in a fancy red and black box. When I sniffed it I was nearly knocked over but I sniffed again with gusto and told the ladies I'd keep the bottle forever in memory of them, this class, their yoots.

Instead of going home after that class I took the subway to West Ninety-Sixth Street in Manhattan and called my mother from a street telephone.

Would you like to have a snack?

I don't know. Where are you?

I'm a few blocks away.

Why?

I just happened to be in the neighborhood.

Visiting Malachy?

No. Visiting you.

Me? Why should you be visiting me?

For Christ's sake, you're my mother and all I wanted to do was invite you out for a snack. What would you like to eat?

She sounded doubtful. Well, I love them jumbo shrimps they have in the Chinese restaurants.

All right. We'll have jumbo shrimps.

But I don't know if I'm able for them this minute. I think I'd prefer to go to the Greeks for a salad.

All right. I'll see you there.

She came into the restaurant gasping for breath and when I kissed her cheek I could taste the salt of her sweat. She said she'd have to sit a minute before she could even think of food, that if she hadn't given up the cigarettes she'd be dead now.

She ordered the feta salad and when I asked her if she liked it she said she loved it, she could live on it.

Do you like that cheese?

What cheese?

The goat cheese.

What goat cheese?

The white stuff. The feta. That's goat cheese.

'Tis not.

'Tis.

Well, if I knew that was goat cheese I'd never touch it because I was attacked by a goat once out the country in Limerick and I'd never eat a thing that attacked me.

It's a good thing you were never attacked by a jumbo shrimp.

50

In 1971 my daughter Maggie was born at Unity Hospital in the Bedford-Stuyvesant area of Brooklyn. There would be no problem taking home the right infant since she seemed to be the only white one in the nursery.

Alberta wanted a natural Lamaze childbirth but the doctors and nurses at Unity Hospital had no patience with middle-class women and their peculiarities. They had no time for this woman and her breathing exercises and jabbed her with an anaesthetic to hasten the birth. Instead, that slowed the rhythm so much the impatient doctor clamped forceps on Maggie's head and yanked her from her mother's womb and I wanted to punch him for the flatness he left on her temples.

The nurse took the child to a corner to clean and wash her and when she finished beckoned that I might now see my daughter with her red astonished face and her black feet.

The soles of her feet were black.

God, what kind of a birthmark have you inflicted on my child? I couldn't say anything to the nurse because she was black and might be offended that I didn't find my daughter's black feet attractive. I had a vision of my child as a young woman lolling on a beach, lovely in a bathing suit, but forced to wear socks to conceal her disfigurement.

The nurse asked if the baby was to be breast-fed. No. Alberta had said she wouldn't have the time when she went back to work and the doctor did something to dry up her milk. They wanted to know the child's name and even though Alberta had toyed with Michaela she was still under anaesthetic and powerless and I told the nurse, Margaret Ann, for my two grandmothers and my sister who had died at twenty-one days in this very borough of Brooklyn.

Alberta was wheeled back to her room and I called Malachy to tell him the good news, that a child had been born but that she was afflicted with black feet. He laughed in my ear and told me I was an ass, that the nurse probably took footprints instead of fingerprints. He said he'd meet me at the Lion's Head where everyone bought me a drink and I got stocious drunk, so drunk Malachy had to hoist me home in a taxi which made me so sick I threw up the length of Broadway with the driver yelling that would cost me twenty-five dollars for the cleaning of the cab, an unreasonable demand that deprived him of a tip and had him threatening to call the cops and, What are you going to tell them? said Malachy, are you going to tell them that you're a zigzag driver going from one side of Broadway to the other and making everyone sick, is that what you're going to tell them? and the driver was so angry he wanted to step out and confront Malachy but changed his mind when my brother, holding me up, stood large and red-bearded on the sidewalk and asked the driver politely if he had any more comments before he went to meet his Maker. The driver uttered obscenities about us and the Irish in general and drove through a red light, his left arm at the window, middle finger rigid in the air.

Malachy brought me aspirins and vitamins and told me I'd be as right as rain in the morning and I wondered what that meant, right as rain, though that question was pushed from my head by the image of Maggie and the forcep flatness of her temples and I was ready to jump from the bed to hunt down that damn doctor who wouldn't let my daughter be born in her own good time but my legs wouldn't oblige me and I fell asleep.

Malachy was right. There was no hangover, only delight that a little child in Brooklyn had my name and I'd have a lifetime watching her grow and when I called Alberta I could hardly talk with the tears in my throat and she laughed and quoted my mother, Your bladder is near your eye.

★   ★   ★

That same year Alberta and I bought the brownstone house where we'd been tenants on the parlor floor. We were able to buy it only because our friends, Bobby and Mary Ann Baron, lent us money and because Virgil Frank had died and left us eight thousand dollars.

When we lived at 30 Clinton Street on Brooklyn Heights Virgil was two floors below us. He was over seventy, had a full head of combed-back white hair, a strong nose, his own teeth and hardly a scrap of flesh on his bones. I visited him regularly because an hour with him was better than movies, television and most books.

His apartment was one narrow room with a kitchenette and a bathroom. His bed was a cot against the wall and beyond that a desk and a window with an air conditioner. Opposite the bed was a book-case filled with volumes on flowers, trees and birds which, he said, he'd get around to some day as soon as he bought a pair of binoculars. You have to be careful about buying binoculars because you go into a store and how are you gonna test them? Salesmen in the store say, Oh, they're okay, they're strong, and how can you tell? They won't let you take them outside to look up and down Fulton Street in case you make a run for it with the binoculars and that's dumb. How the hell you gonna make a run for it when you're seventy? In the meantime he'd like to be able to see birds out his window but all you can see from his apartment is pigeons fornicating on top of his air conditioner and that pisses him off.

He watches them, oh, yeah, he watches them, bangs on the window with a fly swatter, tells them, Get outa here, goddam pigeons. Go fornicate on someone else's air conditioner. He tells me they're just rats with wings, all they do is eat and fornicate and when they're finished with fornicating they drop a load on the air conditioner, one load after another, like that crap the boids, I mean the birds, damn, I'm talkin' Brooklyn again and that ain't good when you're selling water coolers, like that bird crap in South America where the moun-tains are covered with it, what is it? guano, yeah, which is good for growing things but not for air conditioners.

Besides the books on outdoor life he had a three-volume set of the *Summa Theologica of St Thomas Aquinas* and when I opened a volume he said, I didn't know you liked that stuff. Wouldn't you prefer the birds? I told him you can always get bird books but his *Summa* was rare and he said I could have it except I'd have to wait till he died. But don't worry, Frank, I'll put it in my will.

He also promised to leave me his collection of ties which dazzled me whenever he opened his closet door, the loudest, most colorful ties I had ever seen.

You like 'em, eh? Some of these ties go all the way back to the twenties and on down to the thirties and forties. Men knew how to dress then. They didn't go around tippy-toe like the Man in the Gray Flannel Suit afraid of a little color. I always said never stint on the tie and the hat because you have to look good when you're selling water coolers which I did for forty-five years. I'd go into an office and I'd say, What? What? You telling me you still drinking tap water from these old cups and glasses. Don't you know the danger to your health?

And Virgil would stand between bed and bookcase rocking like a preacher and delivering his sales spiel on water coolers.

Yes, sir, I sell water coolers and I wanna tell you there's five things you can do with water. You can clean it, you can pollute it, you can heat it, you can cool it and, ha ha, you can sell it. You know and I don't have to tell you, Mr Office Manager, you can drink it and you can swim in it though there isn't much call for swimming water in the average American office. I wanna tell you my company has made a study of offices that drink our water and offices that don't drink our water and, you're right, you're right, Mr Office Manager, the people who drink our water are healthier and more productive. Our water drives away the flu and improves digestion. We're not saying, no we're not saying, Mr Office Manager, that our water is solely responsible for the great productivity and the prosperity of America but we are saying that our studies show offices without our water are barely hanging on, desperate and wondering why. A copy of our study is available when you sign our yearly contract. At no extra charge we'll survey your staff and give you an estimate of water consumption. I am happy to observe you don't have air conditioning because that means you'll need extra drinking water for your fine staff. And we know, Mr Office Manager, that our water coolers bring people together. Problems are settled over a paper cup of water. Eyes meet. Romances flourish. Everybody happy, everybody eager to come to work every day. Increased productivity. We get no complaints. Sign right here. A copy for you, a copy for me and we're in business.

A knock on the door interrupted him.

Who is it?

A faint old voice. Virgil, it's Harry.

Can't talk to you now, Harry. I got the doctor here and I'm naked getting examined.

All right, Virgil. I'll come back later.

Tomorrow, Harry, tomorrow.

Okay, Virgil.

He told me that was Harry Ball, eighty-five years old, so old you can't hear his voice over a clothesline, who drives Virgil crazy with his parking problems. He's got this big car, a Hudson that they don't make no more, is that right, no more or anymore? You're an English teacher. I dunno. Never went beyond the seventh grade. Ran away from the Sisters of St Joseph Orphanage even if I'm leaving them money in my will. Anyway, Harry's got this car and he goes nowhere with it. Says some day he's gonna drive it to Florida to see his sister but he's going nowhere because that car is so old it wouldn't make it across the Brooklyn Bridge and that goddam Hudson is his life. He moves it from one side of the street to the other, back and forth, back and forth. Sometimes he brings the little aluminum beach chair and sits near his car looking for a parking spot to open for next day. Or he walks around the neighborhood looking for a spot and if he finds one he gets excited and gives himself a heart attack rushing to his car to drive it to the new spot which is now gone and so is the one he was in and there he is driving around with no spot, cursing the government. I was with him once and he nearly ran down a rabbi and two old women and I said, Christ, Harry, lemme out, and he wouldn't, but I jumped out at the first red light and he yelled after me I was the type that flashed lights so the Japs could find Pearl Harbor till I told him he was a dumb bastard that didn't know Pearl Harbor was bombed in broad daylight and he sat there contradicting me with the light turning green and people honking and yelling who gives a shit about Pearl Harbor, buddy, move your goddam Hudson. He could park that car in a garage for eighty-five bucks a month but that's more than he pays for rent and that'll be the day Harry Ball ever wastes a penny. I'm frugal myself, I admit that, but he could make Scrooge look like a spendthrift. Is that the right word, spendthrift? I ran away from the orphanage in seventh grade.

He asked me to go with him to a hardware store on Court Street so that he could get an egg timer for the telephone just installed.

An egg timer?

Yeah, this is a kind of hourglass with sand that runs for three minutes and that's the way I like my egg and when I use the telephone I'll know when the three minutes is up because that's how they charge you at the phone company, the bastards. I'll have the egg timer on my desk and I'll hang up at the last grain of sand.

On Court Street I asked him if he'd like a beer and a sandwich at the Blarney Rose. He never went to bars and was shocked at the prices of beer and whiskey. Ninety cents for a little shot of whiskey. Never.

I went with him to a liquor store where he ordered cases of Irish whiskey and told the salesman his friend Frank liked it, and cases of wine, vodka and bourbon because he liked it himself. He told the man he wouldn't pay the lousy taxes on his purchase. I'm giving you a big order here and you want me to support the goddam government on top of it. No, sir. Pay it yourself.

The man agreed and said he'd deliver the twenty-five cases.

Virgil called me next day. Even though his voice was weak he told me, I got the eggtimer goin' here, so I have to talk fast. Can you come down? I need a little help. The door is open.

He was sitting in his armchair in his bathrobe. I didn't get a wink of sleep last night. Couldn't get into the bed.

He couldn't get into the bed because the liquor store man had piled up the twenty-five cases around his bed so high that Virgil couldn't climb over. He said he had to try some of the Irish whiskey and the wine and that didn't help much when it was time to climb. He said he needed soup, something in his stomach to keep him from being sick. When I opened a can of soup and poured it into a pot with an equal amount of water he asked if I'd read the instructions on the can.

No.

Well, how do you know what to do?

It's common sense, Virgil.

Common sense, my ass.

He was hangover cranky. Listen to me, Frank McCourt. You know why you'll never be a success?

Why?

You never follow the instructions on the package. That's why I have money in the bank and you don't have a pot to piss in. I always followed the instructions on the package.

340

Another knock on the door. What? What? said Virgil.

Voigel, it's me. Pete.

Pete who? Pete who? I can't see through the door.

Pete Buglioso. I got something for you, Voigel.

Don't talk Brooklyn to me, Pete. My name is Virgil, not Voigel. He was a poet, Pete. You should know, you're Italian.

I don't know nothin' about that, Voigel. I got somethin' for you, Voigel.

I don't want nothin', Pete. Call back next year.

But, Voigel, you'll like what I have. Cost you a coupla bucks.

What is it?

Can't tell you through the door, Voigel.

Virgil heaved himself from the armchair and stumbled to the egg timer on his desk. All right, Pete, all right. You can come in for three minutes. I'm setting my egg timer.

He tells me open the door and tells Pete the egg timer is working and even though grains of sand have already dropped Pete still has three minutes, so start talking, Pete, start talking and make it snappy.

All right, Voigel, all right, but how the hell can I talk when you're talking. You talk more than anyone.

You're wasting your time, Pete. You're hanging yourself. Look at the egg timer. Look at that sand. Sands of time, Pete, sands of time.

Whadda you doin' with all them boxes, Voigel. Rob a truck or somethin'?

The egg timer, Pete, the egg timer.

All right, Voigel, what I got here is, will you stop lookin' at the goddam egg timer, Voigel, an' lissena me. What I got here is prescription pads from a doctor's office on Clinton Street.

Prescription pads. You been robbing them doctors again, Pete.

I didn't rob 'em. I know a receptionist. She likes me.

She must be deaf dumb and blind. I don't need no prescription pads.

Come on, Voigel. You never know. You might have a disease or a bad hangover and you'll need something.

Bullshit, Pete. Your time is up. I'm busy.

But, Voigel.

Out, Pete, out. I have no control over that egg timer once it gets goin' and I don't want no prescription pads.

He pushed Pete out the door and yelled after him, You could get

341

me in jail and you're gonna wind up in jail yourself selling stolen prescription pads.

He slumped back into his armchair and said he'd try the soup even though I hadn't followed the instructions on the can. He needed it to settle his stomach but if he didn't like it he'd have a little wine and that would do the job. He tasted the soup and said, yeah, it was okay and he'd have it and the wine, too. When I popped the wine cork he barked that I was not to pour the wine now, I was to let it breathe, didn't I know that and if I didn't how could I teach school. He sipped his wine and remembered he had to call the air conditioning company about his problems with pigeons. I told him stay in his chair and handed him the telephone and the number of the company but he wanted the egg timer, too, so that he could tell them they had three minutes to give him the information he needed.

Hello, you listenin' to me? I got the egg timer goin' and you got three minutes to tell me how I can stop these goddam pigeons, excuse the language, miss, how I can stop these pigeons from making love on the outside part of my air conditioner. They're driving me crazy with the coo coo coo all day and they shit all over the window. You can't tell me that now? You have to look it up? Whaddaya have to look up? Pigeons fornicating on my air conditioner and you have to look it up. Sorry, egg timer ran out and that's the three minutes. Good-bye.

He handed me back the telephone. And I'll tell you something else, he said. It's that goddam Harry Ball that's responsible for all them pigeons shitting on my air conditioner. He sits in his goddam aluminum beach chair when he's looking for a parking spot and feeds them pigeons over at Borough Hall. I told him once cut it out, that they were just rats with wings, and he got so mad he wouldn't talk to me for weeks and that suited me fine. These old guys feed pigeons because they don't have wives no more, anymore? I dunno. I ran away from the orphanage but I don't feed pigeons.

He knocked on our door one night and when I opened it he was in his ragged bathrobe, holding a sheaf of papers, and drunk. It was his will and he wanted to read me part of it. No, he wouldn't have coffee. It killed him, but he'd have a beer.

So, you helped me out and Alberta had me up for dinner and no one ever has old guys up for dinner so I'm leaving you four thousand dollars and Alberta four thousand and I'm leaving you my Thomas

Aquinas and my ties. Here's what it says in the will, To Frank McCourt I leave my collection of ties which he has admired and which are anything but somber.

When we moved to Warren Street we lost touch with Virgil for a while though I wanted him to be godfather at Maggie's christening. Instead there was a call from a lawyer telling me of Virgil Frank's death and the terms of his will as it pertained to us. However, said the lawyer, he changed his mind about the *Summa Theologica* and the ties, so all you get is the money. Do you accept this?

Sure, yes, but why did he change it?

He heard you went to Ireland for a visit and that upset him because you contributed to the gold flow.

What do you mean?

According to Mr Frank's will President Johnson said a few years ago that Americans traveling abroad were draining the country of gold and weakening the economy and that's why you're not getting the ties that are anything but somber and the three volumes of Aquinas. Okay?

Oh, sure.

Now that we had a portion of a down payment we searched the neighborhood for a house. Our landlady, Hortensia Odones, heard we'd been looking and one day she climbed the outside fire escape at the back of the house and startled me when I saw her head at the kitchen window with the great curly wig.

Frankie, Frankie, open the window. It's cold out here. Lemme in.

I reached out to help her in but she yelled, Watch my hair, watch my hair, and I had to do the heavy work of hauling her in the kitchen window while she hung on to her wig.

Whoo, she said, whoo. Frankie, you got any rum?

No, Hortensia, only wine or Irish whiskey.

Gimme a whiskey, Frankie. My ass is frozen.

Here, Hortensia. Tell me, why don't you come up the stairs?

Because it's dark down there, that's why, and I can't afford to keep lights goin' night an' day an' I can see the fire escape day an' night.

Oh.

And what's this I hear? You an' Alberta lookin' for a house? Why don't you buy this one?

How much?

Fifty thousand.

Fifty thousand?

That's right. Is that too much?

Oh, no. That's fine.

The day we signed the agreement we drank rum with her while she told us how sad she was to leave this house after all the years she was there, not with her husband, Odones, but her boyfriend, Louis Weber, who was famous for running the numbers game in the neighborhood and even though he was Puerto Rican he was afraid of nobody, not even the Cosa Nostra who tried to take over till Louis walked into the Don's house down in Carroll Gardens and said, What is this shit? excuse the language, and the Don admired Louis for his balls and told his goombahs back off, don't bother Louis, and you know, Frankie, no one messes with the Italians in Carroll Gardens. You don't see no coloreds or PRs down there, no sir, and if you do they're passing through.

The Mafia might have backed away from Louis but Hortensia said you couldn't trust them and anytime she and Louis went for a drive they rode with two guns between them, his and hers, and he told her if anyone came with trouble and put him out of commission she was to take the steering wheel and yank it towards the sidewalk so that they'd hit a pedestrian instead of traffic and the insurance company would take care of things and if they didn't and gave Hortensia any trouble he'd leave her with a set of phone numbers of a few guys, PRs, the goddam Mafia wasn't the only game in town, and these guys would take care of the insurance companies, the greedy bastards, excuse the language, Alberta, is there any rum left, Frankie?

Poor Louis, she said, the Kefauver Commission was bothering him but he died in his bed and I never go for a ride no more but he left me a gun downstairs, you wanna see my gun, Frankie, no? well, I have it and anyone comes into my apartment without an invitation gets it, Frankie, right between the eyes, bang, boom, he's gone.

Neighbors smiled and nodded and told us we had bought a gold mine, that everyone knew Louis had buried money in the basement of our new house where Hortensia still lived, or over our heads in the false ceiling of the living room. All we had to do was pull down that ceiling and we'd be up to our armpits in hundred-dollar bills.

When Hortensia moved out we dug up the basement to install a new waste line. No buried money. We pulled down false ceilings, exposed bricks and beams. We tapped on walls and someone suggested we consult a psychic.

We found an old doll with tufts of hair, no eyes, no arms, one leg. We kept it for our two-year-old, Maggie, who called it The Beast and loved it over all her other dolls.

Hortensia moved to a small street-level apartment on Court Street and stayed there till she died or moved back to Puerto Rico. I often wished I had spent more time with her and a bottle of rum or that I had introduced her to Virgil Frank so that we could have rum and Irish whiskey and talk about Louis Weber and the gold flow and ways of reducing your telephone bills with an egg timer.

51

It's 1969 and I'm substitute teaching for Joe Curran who is out for a few weeks with the drink. His students ask if I know Greek and seem disappointed that I don't. After all, Mr Curran would sit at his desk and read or recite from memory long passages from *The Odyssey*, yeah, in Greek, and he'd remind his students daily he was a graduate of Boston Latin School and Boston College and tell them anyone who didn't know his Greek or Latin couldn't consider himself educated, could never lay claim to being a gentleman. Yes, yes, this might be Stuyvesant High School, says Mr Curran, and you might be the bright-est kids from here to the foothills of the Rockies, your heads stuffed with science and mathematics, but all you need in this life is your Homer, your Sophocles, your Plato, your Aristotle, your Aristophanes for the lighter moments, your Virgil for the dark places, your Horace to escape the mundane, and your Juvenal when you're completely pissed off with the world. The grandeur, boys, the grandeur that was Greece and the glory that was Rome.

It wasn't the Greeks or the Romans his students loved, it was the forty minutes when Joe droned or declaimed and they could daydream, catch up on homework for other classes, doodle, nibble at sandwiches from home, carve their initials on desks that might have been occupied by James Cagney, Thelonious Monk or certain Nobel Laureates. Or they could dream of the nine girls who had just been admitted for

346

the first time in the school's history. The nine Vestal Virgins, Joe Curran called them, and there were complaints from parents that the suggestiveness of his language was inappropriate.

Oh, inappropriate my ass, said Joe. Why can't they speak simple English? Why can't they use a simple word like wrong?

His students said, Yeah, wasn't it something to see the girls in the hallway, nine girls, nearly three thousand boys and what about the boys in the school, fifty percent for Chrissakes, who didn't want the girls, what about that? They had to be dead from the waist down, didn't they?

Then you'd wonder about Mr Curran himself up there shifting into English to talk about *The Iliad* and the friendship of Achilles and Patroclus, he couldn't stop talking about those two old Greeks, and how Achilles was so furious with Hector for killing Patroclus he killed Hector and dragged his body behind his chariot to show the power of his love for his dead friend, the love that dare not speak its name.

But, boys oh boys, is there a sweeter moment in all of literature than that moment when Hector removed his helmet to calm the fears of his child? Oh, if only all our fathers removed their helmets. And when Joe blubbered into his grey handkerchief and used words like piss you knew he'd left the school at lunch hour for a little tot around the corner at the Gashouse Bar. There were days he returned so excited from thoughts that had come to him on the barstool he wanted to thank God for leading him to teaching so that he could forget the Greeks for a while to sing the praises of the great Alexander Pope and his "Ode on Solitude".

> *Happy the man whose wish and care*
> *A few paternal acres bound*
> *Content to breathe his native air,*
> *In his own ground.*

And remember, boys and girls, is there a girl here? raise your hand if you're a girl, no girls? remember, boys, that Pope was indebted to Horace, and Horace was indebted to Homer and Homer was indebted to God knows who. Will you promise on your mothers' heads to remember that? If you remember Pope's debt to Horace you'll know no one springs full-blown from his father's head. Will you remember?

We will, Mr Curran.

What am I to tell Joe's students who complain that they have to read *The Odyssey* and all this old stuff? Who cares what happened in ancient Greece or Troy with men dying right and left over that stupid Helen? Who cares? Boys in the class say you wouldn't catch them fighting to the death over some girl that didn't want them. Yeah, they could understand *Romeo and Juliet* because a lotta families are dumb about you going out with someone from another religion and they could understand *West Side Story* and the gangs but they could never believe grown men would leave home the way Odysseus left Penelope and Telemachus and go off to fight over this stupid chick who didn't know enough to come inside. They have to admit Odysseus was cool the way he tried to dodge the draft, acting crazy an' all and they like the way Achilles fooled him because Achilles is nowhere near as smart as Odysseus but like they can't believe he'd stay away twenty years fighting and fooling around and expect Penelope to like sit there spinning and weaving and telling the suitors get lost. Girls in the class say they can believe it, they really can, that women can be true forever because that's the way women are, and one girl tells the class what she read in a Byron poem, that man's love is of his life a thing apart, 'tis woman's whole existence. Boys hoot at this but girls applaud and tell them what all the psychology books say, that boys their age are three years behind in mental development though there are some in this class who must be at least six years behind and they should therefore shut up. The boys try to be sarcastic, raising their eyebrows and telling each other, Oh, law de daw, smell me, I'm developed, but the girls look at each other, shrug, toss their hair and ask me in a lofty tone if we could please get back to the lesson.

Lesson? What are they talking about? What lesson? All I can remember is the usual high school whine about why we have to read this and why we have to read that and my irritation, my unspoken response, is that you have to read it, goddamit, because it's part of the curriculum and because I'm telling you read it, I'm the teacher, and if you don't cut the whining and complaining you'll get an English grade on your report card that will make zero look like a gift from the gods because I'm standing here listening to you and looking at you, the privileged, the chosen, the pampered, with nothing to do but go to school, hang out, do a little studying, go to college, get into a moneymaking racket, grow into your fat forties, still whining, still complaining, when there are millions around the world who'd offer fingers and toes to be in your seats, nicely clothed, well-fed, with the world by the balls.

That's what I'd like to say and never will because I might be accused of using inappropriate language and that would give me a Joe Curran fit. No. I can't talk like that because I have to find my way in this place, a far cry from McKee Vocational and Technical High School.

In the spring of 1972 the English Department chairman, Roger Goodman, offers me a permanent position at Stuyvesant High School. I'll have my own five classes and a building assignment where, once more, I'll keep order in the students' cafeteria and make sure no one drops ice cream wrappers or bits of hot dog on the floor though boys and girls are allowed to sit together here and romance kills appetites.

I'll have a small homeroom, the first nine girls, seniors and ready to graduate. The girls are kind. They bring me coffee, bagels, newspapers. They're critical. They say I should do something about my hair, let the sideburns grow, this is 1972 and I should get with it, be cool, and do something about my clothes. They say I dress like an old man, and even though I have a few grey hairs I don't have to look so old. They tell me I look uptight and one of them kneads my neck and shoulders. Relax, she says, relax, we're harmless, and they laugh the way women laugh when they share a secret and you think it's about you.

I'll have five classes a day five days a week where I have to memorize the names of one hundred and seventy-five students along with the names of a full homeroom class next year, another thirty-five, and I'll have to be particularly careful with the Chinese and Korean students with their sarcastic, That's okay if you don't know our names, Mr McCourt, we all look the same. Or they might laugh, Yeah, and all you white people look the same.

I know all this from my days as a substitute teacher but now I watch my students, my very own, stream into my room this first day of February 1972, Feast of St Brigid, and I'm praying to you, Brigid, because these are kids I'll be seeing five days a week for five months and I don't know if I'm up to it. The times they are a-changin' and you can see these Stuyvesant kids are worlds and years away from the ones I first met at McKee. We've had wars and assassinations since then, the two Kennedys, Martin Luther King, Medgar Evers. Boys at McKee wore short hair or pompadours greased back to a duck's ass. Girls had blouses and skirts and their hair was permed to the stiffness of a helmet. Stuyvesant boys wear hair so long people on the streets sneer, You can hardly tell them from the girls, ha ha. They wear tie-dye shirts, jeans and sandals so that no one will ever guess they come from comfortable families all over New York. Stuyvesant girls let hair and breasts hang loose and drive the boys mad with desire and cut their jeans at the knees for that cool poverty effect because like you know they've had it with all that middle-class crap.

Oh, yeah, they're cooler than the McKee kids because they've got it made. In eight months they'll be at colleges and universities all over the country, Yale, Stanford, MIT, Williams, Harvard, lords and ladies of the earth, and here in my classroom they sit where they like, chatting, ignoring me, giving me their backs, one more teacher obstructing their way to graduation and the real world. Some stare as if to say, Who is this guy? They slump and slouch and gaze out the window or over my head. Now I have to get their attention and that's what I say, Excuse me, may I have your attention? A few stop talking and look at me. Others look offended at the interruption and turn away again.

My three senior classes groan with the burden of the textbook they have to carry every day, an anthology of English literature. The juniors complain over the weight of their anthology of American literature. The books are sumptuous, richly illustrated, designed to challenge, motivate, illuminate, entertain, and they're expensive. I tell my students that carrying textbooks strengthens their upper bodies and hope the contents seep up to their minds.

They glare at me. Who is this guy?

There are teaching guides so detailed and comprehensive I need never think for myself. They are packed with enough quizzes, tests, examinations to keep my students in a constant state of nervous tension. There are hundreds of multiple choice questions, true or false questions, fill in the blank spaces, match column A with column B, peremptory questions ordering the student to explain why Hamlet was mean to his mother, what Keats meant by negative capability, what Melville was getting at in his chapter on the whiteness of the whale.

I'm ready, boys and girls, to march through the chapters from

Hawthorne to Hemingway, from *Beowulf* to Virginia Woolf. Tonight you are to read the pages assigned. Tomorrow we'll discuss. There may be a quiz. Then again there may not be a quiz. Just don't gamble on it. Only the teacher knows for sure. On Tuesday there will be a test. Three Tuesdays from now there will be an exam, a big exam, and yes, it will count. Your whole report card grade hinges on this exam. You also have tests on physics and calculus? Sorry for your troubles. This is English, the queen of the curriculum.

And you don't know it, boys and girls, but I am armed with my teaching guides on American and English literature. I have them safe here in my bag, all the questions that will have you scratching your little heads, gnawing your pencils, dreading report card day, and, I suppose, hating me because I'm the one who can thwart your high Ivy League ambitions. I'm the one who skulked around the lobby of the Biltmore Hotel cleaning up for your fathers and mothers.

This is Stuyvesant and isn't this the best high school in the city, some say the best in the country? You asked for it. You could have gone to your neighborhood high schools where you'd be kings and queens, numero uno, top of your class. Here you're just one of the crowd, scrambling for grades to bolster the precious average that will slip you into the Ivy League. It's your great god, isn't it, the average? Down in the Stuyvesant basement they should construct a sanctum with an altar. They should mount on that altar a great red blinking neon 9, blink blink blink, the sacred initial digit you're desperate for on every grade, and you should pray and worship there. Oh, God, send me As and nineties.

Mr McCourt, how come you only gave me a ninety-three on my report card?

I was kind.

But I did all the work, handed in the papers you assigned.

You were late with two papers. Two points off for each one.

But, Mr McCourt, why two points?

That's it. That's your grade.

Aw, Mr McCourt, how come you're so mean?

It's all I have left.

I followed the teacher guides. I launched the prefabricated questions at my classes. I hit them with surprise quizzes and tests and destroyed them with the ponderous detailed examinations concocted by college professors who assemble high school textbooks.

My students resisted and cheated and disliked me and I disliked them for disliking me. I learned their cheating games. Oh, the casual glance at the papers of students around you. Oh, the discreet little morse code cough for your girlfriend and her sweet smile when she catches the multiple choice answer. If she's behind you splay your fingers on the back of your head, three splays of five fingers would be question fifteen, a forefinger scratching the right temple is answer A and other fingers represent other answers. The room is alive with coughs and body movements and when I catch the cheaters I hiss in their ears they'd better cut it out or their papers will be shredded into the waste basket, their lives ruined. I am lord of the classroom, a man who would never cheat, oh, no, not if they flashed the answers in green letters on the bright side of the full moon.

Every day I taught with my guts in a knot, lurking behind my desk at the front of the room playing the teacher game with the chalk, the eraser, the red pen, the teacher guides, the power of the quiz, the test, the exam, I'll call your father, I'll call your mother, I'll report you to the Governor, I'll damage your average so badly, kid, you'll be lucky to get into a community college in Mississippi, weapons of menace and control.

A senior, Jonathan, bangs his forehead on his desk and wails, Why? Why? Why do we have to suffer with this shit? We've been in school since kindergarten, thirteen years, and why do we have to know what color shoes Mrs Dalloway was wearing at her goddam party and what are we supposed to make of Shakespeare troubling deaf heaven with his bootless cries and what the hell is a bootless cry anyway and when did heaven turn deaf?

Around the room rumbles of rebellion and I'm paralyzed. They're saying Yeah, yeah to Jonathan who halts his head banging to ask, Mr McCourt, did you have this stuff in high school? and there's another chorus of yeah yeah and I don't know what to say. Should I tell them the truth, that I never set foot in a high school till I began teaching in one or should I feed them a lie about a rigorous secondary school education with the Christian Brothers in Limerick?

I'm saved, or doomed, by another student who calls out, Mr McCourt, my cousin went to McKee on Staten Island and she said you told them you never went to high school and they said you were an okay teacher anyway because you told stories and talked and never bothered them with all these tests.

Smiles around the room. Teacher unmasked. Teacher never even went to high school and look what he's doing to us, driving us crazy with tests and quizzes. I'm branded forever with the label, teacher who never went to high school.

So, Mr McCourt, I thought you had to get a license to teach in the city.

You do.

Don't you have to get a college degree?

You do.

Don't you have to graduate high school?

You mean graduate from high school, from high school, from from from.

Yeah, yeah. Okay. Don't you have to graduate from high school to get into college?

I suppose you do.

Tyro lawyer grills teacher, carries the day, and word spreads to my other classes. Wow, Mr McCourt, you never went to high school and you're teaching at Stuyvesant? Cool, man.

And into the trash basket I drop my teaching guides, my quizzes, tests, examinations, my teacher-knows-all mask.

I'm naked and starting over and I hardly know where to begin.

In the 1960s and early 70s students wore buttons and headbands demanding equal rights for women, blacks, Native Americans and all oppressed minorities, an end to the war in Vietnam, the salvation of the rain forests and the planet in general. Blacks and curly-haired whites sprouted Afros, and the dashiki and the tie-dye shirt became the garb of the day. College students boycotted class, taught in, rioted everywhere, dodged the draft, fled to Canada or Scandinavia. High school students came to school fresh from images of war on television news, men blown to bits in rice paddies, helicopters hovering, tentative soldiers of the Viet Cong blasted out of their tunnels, their hands behind their heads, lucky for the moment they weren't blasted back in again, images of anger back home, marches, demonstrations, hell no we won't go, sit-ins, teach-ins, students falling before the guns of the National Guard, blacks recoiling from Bull Connor's dogs, burn baby burn, black is beautiful, trust no one over thirty, I have a dream and, at the end of it all, your President is not a crook.

On streets and in subways I'd meet former students from McKee High School who would tell me of the boys who went to Vietnam, heroes when they left and now home in body bags. Bob Bogard called to tell me about the funeral of a boy who had been in both our classes but I didn't go because I knew that on Staten Island there would be pride in this blood sacrifice. The boys from Staten Island would fill more body bags than Stuyvesant could ever imagine. Mechanics and plumbers had to fight while college students shook indignant fists, fornicated in the fields of Woodstock and sat in.

In my classroom I wore no buttons, took no sides. There was enough ranting all around us and, for me, picking my way through five classes was minefield enough.

Mr McCourt, why can't our classes be relevant?

Relevant to what?

Well, you know, look at the state of the world. Look at what's happening.

There's always something happening in the world and we could sit in this classroom for four years clucking over headlines and going out of our minds.

Mr McCourt, don't you care about the babies burned with napalm in Vietnam?

I do, and I care about the babies in Korea and China, in Auschwitz and Armenia, and the babies impaled on the swords of Cromwell's soldiers in Ireland. I told them what I'd learned from my part-time teaching at New York Technical College in Brooklyn, from my class of twenty-three women, most from the Islands, and from my five men. There was a fifty-five-year-old working for a college degree so that he could return to Puerto Rico and spend the rest of his life helping children. There was a young Greek studying English so that he could work towards a PhD in the literature of Renaissance England. There were three young African-American men in the class and when one, Ray, complained he'd been bothered by the police on a subway platform because he was black the women from the Islands had no patience with him. They told him if he stayed home and studied he wouldn't be getting into trouble and no kid of theirs would come home with a story like that. They'd break his head. Ray was quiet. You don't talk back to women from the Islands.

Denise, now in her late twenties, was often late to class and I threatened her with failure till she wrote an autobiographical essay which I asked her to read to the class.

Oh, no, she couldn't do that. She'd be ashamed to let people know she had two children whose father had left her to return to Montserrat and never sends her a penny. No, she wouldn't mind if I read the essay to the class if I didn't tell who wrote it.

She had described a day in her life. She'd wake early to do her Jane Fonda video exercises while thanking Jesus for the gift of another day. She'd take a shower, get her children up, her eight-year-old, her six-year-old, and take them to school and after that she'd rush to her college classes. In the afternoon she'd go straight to her job at a bank in downtown Brooklyn and from there to her mother's house. Her mother had already picked up the children from school and without her Denise didn't know what she'd do especially when her mother had that terrible disease that makes your fingers curl up in knots and Denise didn't know how to spell. After taking the children home, putting them to bed and getting their clothes ready for the next morning Denise would pray by the side of her bed, look up at the cross, thank Jesus once more for another wonderful day and try to fall asleep with his suffering image in her dreams.

The women from the Islands thought that was a wonderful story and looked at each other wondering who wrote it and when Ray said he didn't believe in Jesus they told him shut up, what did he know hanging around subway platforms? They worked, took care of their families, went to school and this was a wonderful country where you could do what you liked even if you were black like the night and if he didn't like it he could go back to Africa if he could ever find it without getting hassled by the police.

I told the women they were heroes. I told the Puerto Rican man he was a hero and I told Ray if he ever grew up he could be a hero, too. They looked at me, puzzled. They didn't believe me and you could guess what was running through their minds, that they were doing only what they were supposed to do, getting an education, and why was this teacher calling them heroes?

My Stuyvesant students were not satisfied. Why was I telling them stories of women from the Islands and Puerto Ricans and Greeks when the world was going to hell?

Because the women from the Islands believe in education. You can demonstrate and shake your fists, burn your draft cards and block the traffic with your bodies, but what do you know in the end? For the ladies from the Islands there is one relevance, education. That is all they know. That is all I know. That is all I need to know.

Still there was a confusion and a darkness in my head and I had to understand what I was doing in this classroom or get out. If I had to stand before those five classes I couldn't let days dribble by in the routine of high school grammar, spelling, vocabulary, digging for the deeper meaning in poetry, bits of literature doled out for the multiple choice tests that would follow so that universities can be supplied with the best and the brightest. I had to begin enjoying the act of teaching and the only way I could do that was to start over, teach what I loved and to hell with the curriculum.

The year Maggie was born I told Alberta something my mother used to say, that a child gains her vision at six weeks and if that was true we should take her to Ireland so that her first image would be of moody Irish skies, a passing shower with the sun shining through.

Paddy and Mary Clancy invited us to stay on their farm in Carrick-on-Suir but newspapers were saying Belfast was in flames, a nightmare city, and I was anxious to see my father. I traveled north with Paddy Clancy and Kevin Sullivan and the night we arrived we walked the streets of Catholic Belfast. The women were out banging on the pavements with the lids of garbage cans, warning their men of approaching army patrols. They were suspicious of us till they recognized Paddy of the famous Clancy Brothers and we passed on without trouble.

Next day Paddy and Kevin stayed in the hotel while I went to my Uncle Gerard's house so that he could take me to my father in Andersonstown. When my father opened his door he nodded at Uncle Gerard and looked through me. Uncle said, This is your son.

My father said, Is it little Malachy?

No. I'm your son Frank.

Uncle Gerard said, It's a sad thing when your own father doesn't know you.

My own father said, Come in. Sit down. Will you have a cup of tea?

He offered the tea but showed no signs of making it in his little kitchen till a woman came from next door and did it. Uncle Gerard whispered, See that. He never lifts a finger. He doesn't have to with the way the ladies of Andersonstown wait on him hand and foot. They tempt him daily with soup and dainty things.

My father smoked his pipe but never touched his mug of tea. He was busy asking about my mother and three brothers. Och, your brother, Alphie, came to see me. Quiet lad your brother Alphie. Och, aye. Quiet lad. And you're all well in America? Attending to your religious duties? Och, you have to be good to your mother and attend to your religious duties.

I wanted to laugh. Jesus, is this man preaching? I wanted to say, Dad, have you no memory?

No, what's the use. I'd be better off leaving my father to his demons though you could see from the peaceful way he had with his pipe and his mug of tea that the demons wouldn't cross his threshold. Uncle Gerard said we ought to leave before darkness fell on Belfast and I wondered how I should say goodbye to my father. Shake his hand? Embrace him?

I shook his hand because that's all we ever did except for one time when I was in hospital with typhoid and he kissed my forehead. Now he drops my hand, reminds me once more to be a good boy, to obey my mother and remember the power of the daily rosary.

When we returned to his house I told my uncle I'd like to walk through the Protestant area, the Shankill Road. He shook his head. Quiet man. I said, Why not?

Because they'll know.

What will they know?

They'll know you're a Catholic.

How will they know?

Och, they'll know.

His wife agreed. She said, They have ways.

Do you mean to say you could spot a Protestant if he walked down this street?

We could.

How?

And my uncle smiled. Och, years of practice.

While we had another cup of tea there was shooting down Leeson Street. A woman screamed and when I went to the window Uncle

Gerard said, Och, get your head away from the window. One little movement and the soldiers are so nervous they'll spray it.

The woman screamed again and I had to open the door. She had a child in her arms and another one clinging to her skirt and she was being forced back by a soldier pushing his slanted rifle. She begged him to let her cross Leeson Street to her other children. I thought I'd help by carrying the child clinging to her but when I went to pick her up the woman dashed around the soldier and across the street. The soldier swung on me and put his rifle barrel against my forehead. Get inside, Paddy, or I'll blow your fawking head off.

My uncle and his wife, Lottie, told me that was a foolish thing I did and it helped no one. They said that whether you were Catholic or Protestant there was a way of handling things in Belfast that outsiders would never understand.

Still, on my way back to the hotel in a Catholic taxi, I dreamed I could easily roam Belfast with an avenging flamethrower. I'd aim it at that bastard in his red beret and reduce him to cinders. I'd pay back the Brits for the eight hundred years of tyranny. Oh, by Jesus, I'd do my bit with a fifty-caliber machine gun. I would, indeed, and I was ready to sing "Roddy McCorley goes to die on the bridge of Toome today", till I remembered that that was my father's song and decided instead I'd have a nice quiet pint with Paddy and Kevin in the bar of our Belfast hotel and before I went to sleep that night I'd call Alberta so that she could hold the phone to Maggie and I'd carry my daughter's gurgle into my dreams.

Mam flew over and stayed with us awhile at our rented flat in Dublin. Alberta went shopping on Grafton Street and Mam strolled with me to St Stephen's Green with Maggie in her pram. We sat by the water and threw crumbs to ducks and sparrows. Mam said it was lovely to be in this place in Dublin in the latter end of August the way you could feel autumn coming in with the odd leaf drifting before you and the light changing on the lake. We looked at children wrestling in the grass and Mam said it would be lovely to stay here a few years and see Maggie grow up with an Irish accent, not that she had anything against the American accent, but wasn't it a pure pleasure to listen to these children and she could see Maggie growing and playing on this very grass.

When I said it would be lovely a shiver went through me and she said someone was walking on my grave. We watched the children play and looked at the light on the water and she said, You don't want to go back, do you?

Back where?

New York.

How do you know that?

I don't have to lift the lid to know what's in the pot.

The porter at the Shelbourne Hotel said it would be no bother at all to keep an eye on Maggie's pram against the railings outside while we sat in the lounge, a sherry for Mam, a pint for me, a bottle of milk for Maggie on Mam's lap. Two women at the next table said Maggie was a dote, a right dote she was, oh gorgeous, and wasn't she the spittin' image of Mam herself. Ah, no, said Mam, I'm only the grandmother.

The women were drinking sherry like my mother but the three men were lowering pints and you could see from their tweed caps, red faces and great red hands they were farmers. One, with a dark green cap, called to my mother, The little child might be a lovely child, missus, but you're not so bad yourself.

Mam laughed and called back to him, Ah, sure, you're not so bad either.

Begod, missus, if you were a little older I'd run away with you.

Well, said Mam, if you were a little younger I'd go.

People all around the lounge were laughing and Mam threw her head back and laughed herself and you could see from the shine in her eyes she was having the time of her life. She laughed till Maggie whimpered and Mam said the child had to be changed and we'd have to go. The man with the dark green cap put on a begging act. Yerra, don't go, missus. Your future is with me. I'm a rich widow man with a farm o' land.

Money isn't everything, said Mam.

But I have a tractor, missus. We could ride together and how would that suit you?

It stirs me, said Mam, but I'm still a married woman and when I put on the widow's weeds you'll be the first to know.

Fair enough, missus. I live in the third house on the left as you enter the south west coast of Ireland, a grand place called Kerry.

I heard of it, said Mam. 'Tis known for sheep.

And powerful rams, missus, powerful.

You're never short of an answer, are you?

Come to Kerry with me, missus, and we'll walk the hills wordless.

Alberta was already at the flat making lamb stew and when Kevin Sullivan dropped in with Ben Kiely, the writer, there was enough for everyone and we drank wine and sang because there isn't a song in the world Ben doesn't know. Mam told the story of our time in the Shelbourne Hotel. Lord above, she said, that man had a way with him and if it wasn't for Maggie needing to be changed and wiped I'd be on my way to Kerry.

In the 1970s Mam was in her sixties. The emphysema that came from years of smoking left her so breathless she dreaded leaving her apartment anymore and the more she stayed at home the heavier she grew. For a while she came to Brooklyn to take care of Maggie on weekends but that stopped when she could no longer climb the subway stairs. I accused her of not wanting to see her granddaughter.

I do want to see her but 'tis hard for me to get around anymore.

Why don't you lose weight?

'Tis hard for an elderly woman to lose weight and anyway why should I?

Don't you want to have some kind of life where you're not sitting in your apartment all day looking out the window?

I had my life, didn't I, and what use was it? I just want to be left alone.

There were attacks which left her gasping and when she visited Michael in San Francisco he had to rush her to the hospital. We told her she was ruining our lives the way she always got sick on holidays, Christmas, New Year's Eve, Easter. She shrugged and laughed and said, Pity about ye now.

No matter how her health was, no matter how breathless, she climbed the hill to the Broadway bingo hall till she fell one night and broke her hip. After the operation she was sent to an upstate convalescent home and then stayed with me at a summer bungalow in Breezy Point at the tip of the Rockaway Peninsula. Every morning she slept late and when she woke sat slumped on the side of her bed, staring out the window at a wall. After a while she'd drag herself into the kitchen for breakfast and when I barked at her for eating too much bread and butter, that she'd be the size of a house, she barked back at me, For the love o' Jesus, leave me alone. The bread and butter is the only comfort I have.

52

When Henry Wozniak taught Creative Writing and English and American Literature he wore a shirt, a tie and a sports jacket every day. He was faculty advisor to the Stuyvesant High School literary magazine, *Caliper*, and to the students' General Organization and he was active in the union, the United Federation of Teachers.

He changed. On the first day of school in September, 1973, he roared up Fifteenth Street on a Harley Davidson motor bike and parked it outside the school. Students said, Hi, Mr Wozniak, though they hardly recognized him with his shaved head, his earring, his black leather jacket, black collarless shirt, worn jeans so tight they didn't need the wide belt with the large buckle, the bunch of keys that dangled from that belt, his black leather boots with the elevated heels.

He said Hi back to the students but he didn't linger and smile the way he used to when he didn't mind if students called him The Woz. Now he was reserved with them and with teachers at the time clock. He told the English Department chairman, Roger Goodman, he wanted regular English classes, that he would even take freshmen and sophomores and drill them in grammar, spelling, vocabulary. He told the principal he was withdrawing from all non-teaching activities.

★   ★   ★

Because of Henry I became the Creative Writing teacher. You can do it, said Roger Goodman, and he bought me a beer and a hamburger at the Gashouse Bar around the corner to fortify me. You can handle it, he said. After all, hadn't I written pieces for the *Village Voice* and other papers and wasn't I planning to write more?

All right, Roger, but what the hell is Creative Writing and how do you teach it?

Ask Henry, said Roger, he did it before you.

I found Henry in the library and asked him how you teach creative writing.

Disneyland, he said.

What?

Take a trip to Disneyland. Every teacher should do it.

Why?

It's an enlarging experience. In the meantime, remember one little nursery rhyme and take it as your mantra.

> *Little BoPeep has lost her sheep*
> *And cannot know where to find them.*
> *Leave them alone. and they'll come home*
> *Wagging their tails behind them.*

That was all I got from Henry and, except for an occasional hallway Hi, we never talked again.

I write my name on the board and think of Mr Sorola's remark that fifty percent of teaching is procedure and if so how should I proceed? This class is an elective and that means they're here because they asked for it and if I ask them to write something there should be no whining.

I have to give myself breathing room. I write on the board, Funeral Pyres, two hundred words, do now.

What? Funeral pyres? What kinda topic is that to write about? What's a funeral pyre anyway?

You know what a funeral is, don't you? You know what a pyre is. You've seen pictures of women in India climbing on their husbands' funeral pyres, haven't you? It's called suttee, a new word for your vocabulary.

A girl calls out, That's disgusting, that's really disgusting.

What?

Women killing themselves just because their husbands are dead. That really sucks.

It's what they believe. Maybe it shows their love.

How could it show their love when the man is dead? Don't these women have any self-respect?

Of course they do and they show it by committing suttee.

Mr Wozniak would never tell us to write stuff like this.

Mr Wozniak isn't here, so write your two hundred words.

They write and hand in their scribbled line and I know I've started off on the wrong foot though I know also that if I ever want a lively class discussion there's always suttee.

On Saturday mornings my daughter Maggie watches television cartoons with her friend Claire Ficarra from down the street. They giggle, scream, clutch each other, jump up and down while I sneer in the kitchen and read the paper. Between their chatter and the television noise I catch snatches of a Saturday morning all-American mythology, names repeated weekly, Road Runner, Woody Woodpecker, Donald Duck, the Partridge Family, Bugs Bunny, the Brady Bunch, Heckel and Jeckel. The idea of mythology loosens my sneer and I take my coffee to join the girls before the television set.

Oh, Dad, are you going to watch with us?

I am.

Wow, Maggie, says Claire, your Dad is cool.

I'm sitting with them because they helped me yoke violently two disparate characters, Bugs Bunny and Odysseus.

Maggie had said, Bugs Bunny, he's so mean to Elmer Fudd, and Claire had said, Yeah, Bugs is nice and funny and clever but why is he so mean to Elmer?

When I returned to my classes on Monday morning I announced my great discovery, the similarities between Bugs Bunny and Odysseus, that they were devious, romantic, wily, charming, that Odysseus was the first draft dodger while Bugs showed no evidence of ever having served his country or of ever having done anything for anyone except to cause mischief, that the major difference between them was that Bugs simply drifted from one mischief to another while Odysseus had a mission, to get home to Penelope and Telemachus.

What prompted me then to ask the simple question that caused the class to explode, When you were a child what did you watch on Saturday mornings?

An eruption of Mickey Mouse, Flotsam and Jetsam, Tom and Jerry, Mighty Mouse, Crusader Rabbit, dogs, cats, mice, monkeys, birds, ants, giants.

Stop. Stop.

I threw out pieces of chalk. Here, you and you and you, go to the board. Write the names of these cartoons and shows. Put them in categories. This is what scholars will be poring over a thousand years hence. This is your mythology. Bugs Bunny. Donald Duck.

The lists covered all the boards and there still wasn't enough room. They could have covered floor and ceiling and continued into the hallway, thirty-five students in each class dredging up the detritus of countless Saturday morning shows. I called above the din, Did these shows have theme songs and music?

Another eruption. Songs, hummings, mood music, reminiscences of favorite scenes and episodes. They could have sung and chanted and acted well past the bell and into the night. From the board they copied lists into their notebooks and they didn't ask why, they didn't complain. They told each other and me they couldn't believe they'd watched so much television in their lives. Hours and hours. Wow. I asked them, How many hours? and they said days, months, maybe years. Wow again. If you were sixteen you probably spent three years of your life before a TV set.

53

Before Maggie was born I dreamed of being a Kodak daddy. I'd wield a camera and assemble an album of milestone pictures, Maggie moments after her birth, Maggie on her first day of kindergarten, Maggie graduating from kindergarten, from elementary school, high school and, above all, college.

The college wouldn't be some sprawling urban affair, NYU, Fordham, Columbia. No, my lovely daughter would spend four years in one of those sweet New England colleges so exquisite they find the Ivy League vulgar. She'd be blond and tanned, strolling the greensward with an Episcopalian lacrosse star, scion of a Boston Brahmin family. His name would be Doug. He'd have bright blue eyes, powerful shoulders, a frank direct look. He'd call me sir and crush my hand in his manly honest way. He and Maggie would be married in the honest stone Episcopalian church on campus, showered with confetti under an arch of lacrosse sticks, the sport of a better class of people.

And I'd be there, proud Kodak dad, awaiting my first grandchild, half Irish Catholic, half Boston Brahmin Episcopalian. There would be a christening and a garden party, and I'd be snapping away with my Kodak, white tents, women in hats, everyone pastelled, Maggie with child, comfort, class, security.

That's what I dreamed when I held her bottle, changed her diapers, bathed her in the kitchen sink, taped her infant gurglings. The first three years I secured her in a little basket and rode my bicycle around Brooklyn Heights. When she toddled I took her to the playground and while she discovered sand and other children I eavesdropped on mothers around me. They talked about kids, husbands, how they couldn't wait to get back to their own careers in the real world. They'd lower their voices and whisper about affairs and I'd wonder if I should make a move. No. They were already suspicious of me. Who was this guy sitting around with mothers on a summer morning when real men were at work?

They didn't know I was born lower-class, using daughter and wife to ease myself into their world. They worried about something that comes before kindergarten, pre-school, and I was learning that kids have to be kept busy. A few wild minutes in the sandbox is okay but play should really be structured and supervised. You just can't have enough structure. If a child is aggressive you have to worry. Quiet? Same worry. It's all anti-social behavior. Kids must learn to adjust, or else.

I wanted to send Maggie to a public elementary school or even the Catholic school down the street but Alberta insisted on an ivy-covered pile that had once been a school for Episcopalian girls and I didn't have the stomach for a fight. It would surely be more respectable and we'd meet a better class of people.

Oh, we did. There were stockbrokers, investment bankers, engineers, heirs to old fortunes, professors, obstetricians. There would be parties where they'd say, And what do you do? and when I said I was a teacher they'd turn away. It didn't matter that we had a mortgage on a Cobble Hill brownstone, that we kept in step with other gentrifying couples, exposing our bricks, our beams, ourselves.

It was too much for me. I didn't know how to be a husband, a father, a house owner with two tenants, a certified member of the middle class. I didn't know how to proceed, how to dress, how to chatter of the stockmarket at parties, how to play squash or golf, how to give a testosteronic handshake and look my man in the eye with a Pleasure to meet you, sir.

Alberta would say she wanted nice things and I never knew what that meant. Or I didn't care. She'd want to go antiquing along Atlantic Avenue and I'd want to chat with Sam Colton in his Montague Street bookshop or have a beer at the Blarney Rose with Yonk Kling. Alberta would talk about Queen Anne tables, Regency sideboards, Victorian ewers and I didn't give a fiddler's fart. Her friends talked about good taste and rounded on me when I said good taste was what pops up when the imagination dies. The air was thick with good taste and I felt suffocated.

The marriage had become a sustained squabble and there was Maggie, trapped in the middle of it. After school every day she had to follow the routine passed down by a Yankee grandmother in Rhode Island. Change your clothes, drink milk, eat cookies, do your homework because you're not getting out of the house till you do. That's what you're supposed to do. That's what your mother did. Then you can play with Claire till it's dinnertime where you have to sit with parents who are civil only because of you.

Mornings redeemed the nights. When Maggie grew from toddler to walker to talker she'd come to the kitchen in her dream state, talking dream talk of a flight over the neighborhood with Claire and a landing in the street outside. In April she'd look at the magnolia tree that bloomed beyond the kitchen window and want to know why we couldn't have that color forever. Why did the green leaves drive away the lovely pink? I told her all the colors must have their day in the world and that seemed to satisfy her.

Mornings with Maggie were as golden or pink or green as the mornings I had with my father in Limerick. Till he went away I had him to myself. Till everything fell apart I had Maggie.

Weekdays I'd walk her to school and then take the train to my classes at Stuyvesant High School. My teenage students wrestled with hormones or struggled with family problems, divorces, custody battles, money, drugs, the death of faith. I felt sorry for them and their parents. I had the perfect little girl and I'd never have their problems.

I did and Maggie did. The marriage crumbled. Slum-reared Irish Catholics have nothing in common with nice girls from New England who had little curtains at their bedroom windows, who wore white gloves right up to their elbows and went to proms with nice boys, who studied etiquette with French nuns and were told, Girls, your virtue is like a dropped vase. You may repair the break but the crack will always be there. Slum-reared Irish Catholics might have recalled what their fathers said, After a full belly all is poetry.

The old Irish had told me, and my mother had warned me, Stick with your own. Marry your own. The devil you know is better than the devil you don't know.

When Maggie was five I walked out and stayed with a friend. It didn't last. I wanted my mornings with my daughter. I wanted to sit on the floor before the fire, tell her stories, listen to *Sergeant Pepper's Lonely Hearts Club Band*. Surely, after all these years, I could work on this marriage, wear a tie, escort Maggie to birthday parties around Brooklyn Heights, charm wives, play squash, pretend an interest in antiques.

I walked Maggie to school. I carried her bookbag, she toted her Barbie lunch box. Around her eighth year she announced, Look, Dad, I want to go to school with my friends. Of course, she was pulling away, going independent, saving herself. She must have known her family was disintegrating, that her father would soon leave forever as his father had long ago and I left for good a week before her eighth birthday.

54

When I look at the framed book jackets on the wall at the Lion's Head I suffer with envy. Will I ever be up there? The writers travel the land, signing books, appearing on television talk shows. There are parties and women and romance everywhere. People listen. No one listens to teachers. They are pitied for their sad salaries.

But there are powerful days in room 205 at Stuyvesant High School, when discussion of a poem opens the door to a blazing white light and everyone understands the poem and understands the understanding and when the light fades we smile at each other like travelers returned.

My students don't know it but that classroom is my refuge, sometimes my strength, the setting for my delayed childhood. We dip into the *Annotated Mother Goose* and the *Annotated Alice in Wonderland*, and when my students bring in the books of their early years there is delight in the room. You read that book, too? Wow.

A wow in any classroom means something is happening.

There is no talk of quizzes or tests and if grades have to be assigned for the bureaucrats well then students are capable of evaluating themselves. We know what's going on in *Little Red Riding Hood*, that if you don't follow the path the way your mother tells you you're gonna meet that big bad wolf and there will be trouble, man, trouble, and like how come everyone complains about violence on television and no one says a word about the viciousness of the father and step-mother in *Hansel and Gretel*, how come?

From the back of the room a boy's angry cry, Fathers are such assholes.

And for a whole class period there's a heated discussion of "Humpty Dumpty."

> *Humpty Dumpty sat on the wall.*
> *Humpty Dumpty had a great fall;*
> *All the king's horses,*
> *And all the king's men*
> *Couldn't put Humpty together again.*

So, I ask, what's going on in this nursery rhyme? The hands are up. Well, like, this egg falls off the wall and if you study biology or physics you know you can never put an egg back together again. I mean, like, it's common sense.

Who says it's an egg? I ask.

Of course it's an egg. Everyone knows that.

Where does it say it's an egg?

They're thinking. They're searching the text for egg, any mention, any hint of egg. They won't give in.

There are more hands, impassioned assertions of egg. All their lives they knew this rhyme and there was never a doubt that Humpty Dumpty was an egg. They're comfortable with the idea of egg and why do teachers have to come along and destroy everything with all this analysis.

I'm not destroying. I just want to know where you got the idea that Humpty is an egg.

Because, Mr McCourt, it's in all the pictures and whoever drew the first picture musta known the guy who wrote the poem or he'd never have made it an egg.

All right. If you're content with the idea of egg we'll let it be but I know the future lawyers in this class will never accept egg where there is no evidence of egg.

As long as there's no threat of grades they're comfortable with the matter of childhood and when I suggest they write their own children's books they don't complain, they don't resist.

Oh, yeah, yeah, what a great idea.

They are to write, illustrate and bind their books, original work, and when they're finished I take them to an elementary school down the street on First Avenue to be read and evaluated by real critics, the ones who would read such books, third and fourth graders.

Oh, yeah, yeah, the little ones, that'd be cute.

On a bitter January day the little ones are brought to Stuyvesant by their teacher. Aw, gee, look at 'em. So c-u-t-e. Look at their little coats and earmuffs and mittens and their little colored boots and their little frozen faces. Aw, cute.

The books are laid out on a long table, books of all sizes, shapes, and the room blazes with color. My students sit and stand, giving up their seats to their little critics who sit on desks, their feet dangling far above the floor. One by one they come to the table to select the books they read and to comment. I've already warned my students these small children are poor liars, all they know for the moment is the truth. They read from sheets their teacher helped them prepare.

The book I read is *Petey and the Space Spider*. This book is okay except for the beginning, the middle and the end.

The author, a tall Stuyvesant junior, smiles weakly and looks at the ceiling. His girlfriend hugs him.

Another critic. The book I read was called *Over There* and I didn't like it because people shouldn't write about war and people shooting each other in the face and going to the bathroom in their pants because they're scared. People shouldn't write about things like that when they can write about nice things like flowers and pancakes.

For the little critic there is wild applause from her classmates, from the Stuyvesant authors a stony silence. The author of *Over There* glares over the head of his critic.

Their teacher had asked her pupils to answer the question, Would you buy this book for yourself or anyone else?

No, I wouldn't buy this book for me or anyone. I already have this book. It was written by Dr Seuss.

The critic's classmates laugh and their teacher tells them shush but they can't stop and the plagiarist, sitting on the window sill, turns red and doesn't know what to do with his eyes. He's a bad boy, did the wrong thing, gave the little ones ammunition for their jeers, but I want to comfort him because I know why he did that bad thing, that he could hardly be in the mood for creating a children's book when his parents separated during the Christmas break, that he's caught in the bitterness of a custody battle, doesn't know what to do when mother and father pull him in opposite directions, that he feels like running to his grandfather in Israel, that with all this he can meet his English assignment only by stapling together a few pages on which he has copied a Dr Seuss story and illustrating it with stick figures, that this is surely the lowest point in his life and how do you handle the humiliation when you're caught in the act by this smartass third-grader who stands there laughing in the spotlight. He looks at me across the room and I shake my head, hoping he understands that I understand. I feel I should go to him, put my arm around his shoulder, comfort him, but I hold back because I don't want third-graders or high school juniors to think I condone plagiarism. For the moment I have to hold the high moral ground and let him suffer.

The little ones get into their winter clothes and leave and my classroom is quiet. A Stuyvesant author who suffered negative criticism says he hopes those damn kids get lost in the snow. Another tall junior, Alex Newman, says he feels okay because his book was praised but what those kids did to a few of the authors was disgraceful. He says some of those kids are assassins and there is agreement around the room.

But they're softened up for the American Literature of the junior year, ready for the rant of *Sinners in the Hands of an Angry God*. We chant Vachel Lindsay and Robert Service and T. S. Eliot who can be recruited for either side of the Atlantic. We tell jokes because every joke is a short story with a fuse and an explosion. We journey back into childhood for games and street rhymes, Miss Lucy and Ring-around-a-rosy, and visiting educators wonder what's going on in this classroom.

And tell me, Mr McCourt, how does that prepare our children for college and the demands of society?

55

On the table by the bed in my mother's apartment there were bottles of pills, tablets, capsules, liquid medicines, take this for that and that for this three times a day when it's not four but not when you're driving or operating heavy machinery, take before during and after meals avoiding alcohol and other stimulants and be sure you don't mix your medications, which Mam did, confusing the emphysema pills with the pills for the pain of her new hip and the pills that put her to sleep or woke her up and the cortisone that bloated her and caused hair to grow on her chin so that she was terrrified to leave the house without her little blue plastic razor in case she might be away a while and in danger of sprouting all kinds of hair and she'd be ashamed of her life, so she would, ashamed of her life.

The city provided a woman to care for her, bathe her, cook, take her for walks if she was able for it. When she wasn't able for it she watched television and the woman watched with her though she reported later that Mam spent much of her time staring at a spot on the wall or looking out the window delighting in the times her grand-son, Conor, called up to her and they chatted while he hung from the iron bars that secured her windows.

The woman from the city lined up the pill bottles and warned Mam to take them in a certain order during the night but Mam would forget and become so confused no one knew what she might have done to herself and the ambulance would have to take her to Lenox Hill Hospital where she was now well known.

The last time she was in the hospital I called her from my school to ask how she was.

Ah, I dunno.

What do you mean you dunno?

I'm fed up, They're sticking things in me and pulling things out of me.

Then she whispered, If you're coming to see me, would you do me a favor?

I would. What is it?

You're not to tell anyone about this.

I won't. What is it?

Will you bring me a blue plastic razor?

A plastic razor? For what?

Never mind. Couldn't you just bring it and stop asking questions?

Her voice broke and there was sobbing.

All right, I'll bring it. Are you there?

She could barely talk with the sobbing. And when you come up give the razor to the nurse and don't come in till she tells you.

I waited while the nurse took in the razor and screened Mam from the world. On her way out, the nurse whispered, She's shaving. It's the cortisone. She's embarrassed.

All right, said Mam, you can come in now and don't be asking me any questions even if you didn't do what I asked you.

What do you mean?

I asked you for a blue plastic razor and you brought me a white one.

What's the difference?

There's a big difference but you wouldn't know. I won't say another word about it.

You look fine.

I'm not fine. I'm fed up, I told you. I just want to die.

Oh, stop. You'll be out by Christmas. You'll be dancing.

I will not be dancing. Look, there's women running around this country getting abortions right and left and I can't even die.

What in God's name is the connection between you and women getting abortions?

Her eyes filled. Here I am in the bed, dying or not dying, and you're tormenting me with theology.

My brother, Michael, came into the room, all the way from San Francisco. He prowled the area around her bed. He kissed her and massaged her shoulders and feet. That'll relax you, he said.

I'm relaxed, she said. If I was any more relaxed I'd be dead and wouldn't that be a relief.

Michael looked at her and at me and around the room and his eyes were watery. Mam told him he should be back in San Francisco with his wife and children.

I'll be going back tomorrow.

Well, it was hardly worth your while, all this traveling, was it?

I had to see you.

She drifted off and we went to a bar on Lexington Avenue for a few drinks with Alphie and Malachy's son, young Malachy. We didn't talk about Mam. We listened to young Malachy who was twenty and didn't know what to do with his life. I told him since his mother was Jewish he could go to Israel and join the army. He said he wasn't Jewish but I insisted he was, that he had the right of return. I told him if he went to the Israeli Consulate and announced he wanted to join the Israeli army it would be a publicity coup for them. Imagine, young Malachy McCourt, a name like that, joining the Israeli army. He'd be on the front page of every paper in New York.

He said no, he didn't want his ass shot off by those crazy Arabs. Michael said he wouldn't be up there on the front lines, he'd be back where he could be used for propaganda purposes and all those exotic Israeli girls would be throwing themselves at him.

He said no again and I told him it was a waste of time buying him drinks when he wouldn't do a simple thing like joining the Israeli army and carving out a career for himself. I told him if I had a Jewish mother I'd be in Jerusalem in a minute.

That night I returned to Mam's room. A man stood at the end of her bed. He was bald, he had a grey beard and a grey three-piece suit. He jingled the change in his trouser pocket and told my mother, You know, Mrs McCourt, you have every right to be angry when you're ill and you do have a right to express it.

He turned to me. I'm her psychiatrist.

I'm not angry, said Mam. I just want to die and ye won't let me.

She turned to me. Will you tell him go away?

Go away, doctor.

Excuse me, I'm her doctor.

Go away.

He left and Mam complained they were tormenting her with priests and psychiatrists and even if she was a sinner she'd done penance a hundred times over, that she was born doing penance. I'm dying for something in my mouth, she said, something tarty like lemonade.

I brought her an artificial lemon filled with concentrated juice and poured it into a glass with a little water. She tasted it. I asked you for lemonade and all you gave me was water.

No, that's lemonade.

She's tearful again. One little thing I ask you, one little thing and you can't do it for me. Would it be too much to ask you to shift my feet, would it? They're in the one place all day.

I want to ask her why she doesn't move her feet herself but that will only lead to tears so I move them.

How's that?

How's what?

Your feet.

What about my feet?

I moved them.

You did? Well, I didn't feel it. You won't give me lemonade. You won't shift my feet. You won't bring me a proper blue plastic razor. Oh, God, what use is it having four sons if you can't get your feet shifted?

All right. Look. I'm moving your feet.

Look? How can I look? 'Tis hard for me to lift my head from the pillow to be looking at my feet. Are you done tormenting me?

Is there anything else?

It's a furnace in here. Would you open the window?

But it's freezing outside.

There are tears. Can't get me lemonade, can't . . .

All right, all right. I open the window to a blast of cold air from Seventy-Seventh Street that freezes the sweat on her face. Her eyes are closed and when I kiss her there is no taste of salt.

Should I stay a while or even all night? The nurses don't seem to mind. I could push this chair back, rest my head against the wall and doze. No. I might as well go home. Maggie will be singing tomorrow with the choir at the Plymouth Church and I don't want her to see me slouching and red-eyed.

All the way back to Brooklyn I feel I should return to the hospital but a friend is having an opening night party for his bar, the Clark Street Station. There is music and merry chatter. I stand outside. I can't go in.

When Malachy calls at three in the morning he doesn't have to say the words. All I can do is make a cup of tea the way Mam did at unusual times and sit up in the bed in a dark darker than darkness knowing by now they've moved her to a colder place, that grey fleshly body that carried seven of us into the world. I sip my hot tea for the comfort because there are feelings I didn't expect. I thought I'd know the grief of the grown man, the fine high mourning, the elegiac sense to suit the occasion. I didn't know I'd feel like a child cheated.

I'm sitting up in the bed with my knees pulled to my chest and there are tears that won't come to my eyes but beat instead like a small sea around my heart.

For once, Mam, my bladder is not near my eye and why isn't it?

Here I am looking at my lovely ten-year-old daughter, Maggie, in her white dress, singing Protestant hymns with the choir at the Plymouth Church of the Brethren when I should be at Mass praying for the repose of the soul of my mother, Angela McCourt, mother of seven, believer, sinner, though when I contemplate her seventy-three years on this earth I can't believe the Lord God Almighty on His throne would even dream of consigning her to the flames. A God like that wouldn't deserve the time of day. Her life was Purgatory enough and surely she's in the better place with her three children, Margaret, Oliver, Eugene.

After the service I tell Maggie her grandmother has died and she wonders why I'm dry-eyed. You know, Dad, it's all right if you cry.

My brother Michael has returned to San Francisco and I'm meeting Malachy and Alphie for breakfast on West Seventy-Second Street near the Walter B. Cooke Funeral Home. When Malachy orders a hearty meal Alphie says, I don't know how you can eat so much with your mother dead, and Malachy tells him, I have to sustain my grief, don't I?

Afterwards, at the funeral home, we meet Diana and Lynn, wives of Malachy and Alphie. We sit in a semi-circle at the desk of the funeral counselor. He wears a gold ring, a gold watch, a gold tie clasp, gold spectacles. He wields a gold pen and flashes a consoling golden smile. He places a large book on the desk and tells us the first casket is a very elegant item and would be somewhat less than ten thousand dollars, very nice indeed. We don't linger. We tell him keep turning the pages till he reaches the last item, a coffin for less than three thousand. Malachy inquires, What is the absolute rock bottom price?

Well, sir, will this be interment or cremation?

Cremation.

Before he answers I try to lighten the moment by telling him and my family of the conversation I had with Mam a week ago.

What do you want us to do with you when you go?

Oh, I'd like to be brought back and buried with my family in Limerick.

Mam, do you know the cost of transporting someone your size?

Well, she said, reduce me.

The funeral counselor is not amused. He says we could do it for eighteen hundred dollars, embalming, viewing, cremation. Malachy asks why we have to pay for a coffin if it's going to be burned anyway and the man says it's the law.

Then, says Malachy, why can't we just put her in a Hefty trash bag and leave her outside for collection?

We all laugh and the man has to leave the room for a while.

Alphie observes, There goes a life of extreme unctuousness, and when the man returns he looks puzzled at our laughter.

It is arranged. My mother's body will be laid out in her coffin for a day so that the children can see and say goodbye to a dead grandmother. The man inquires if we'd like to hire a limousine to attend the cremation but no one except for Alphie is inclined to travel to North Bergen, New Jersey, and even he changes his mind.

In Limerick Mam had a friend, Mary Patterson, who said, Do you know what, Angela?

No, what, Mary?

I often wondered what I'd look like when I died and do you know what I did, Angela?

I don't, Mary.

I got myself all dressed up in my brown habit from the Third Order of St Francis and do you know what I did next, Angela?

I don't, Mary.

I laid down on the bed with a mirror at the end, crossed my hands with the rosary beads around them, and closed my eyes and do you know what I did next, Angela?

I don't, Mary.

I opened one eye and took a little look at myself in the mirror and do you know what, Angela?

I don't, Mary.

I looked very peaceful.

No one can say my mother looks peaceful in her coffin. All the misery of her life is in the face bloated from hospital drugs and there are stray tufts of hair that escaped her plastic razor.

Maggie kneels by me, looking on her grandmother, the first dead body in her ten years. She has no vocabulary for this, no religion, no prayer, and that's another sadness. She can only look at her grandmother and say, Where is she now, Dad?

If there's a heaven, Maggie, she's there and she's queen of it.

Is there a heaven, Dad?

If there isn't, Maggie, I don't understand God's ways.

She doesn't understand my babbling and neither do I because the tears erupt and she tells me again, It's all right to cry, Dad.

When your mother is dead you can't be sitting around looking mournful, recalling her virtues, receiving the condolences of friends and neighbors. You have to stand before the coffin with your brothers Malachy and Alphie and Malachy's sons, Malachy, Conor, Cormac, link arms and sing the songs your mother loved and the songs your mother hated because that's the only way you can be sure she's dead, and we sang

> A mother's love is a blessing
> No matter where you roam,
> Keep her while she's living,
> You'll miss her when she's gone.

and

> Goodbye, Johnny dear, when you're far away,
> Don't forget your dear old mother

Far across the sea.
Write a letter now and then
And send her all you can
And don't forget where'er you roam
That you're an Irishman.

Visitors look at each other and you know what they're thinking. What kind of mourning is this where sons and grandsons sing and dance before the poor woman's casket? Don't they have any respect for their mother?

We kiss her and I place on her breast a shilling I had borrowed from her long ago and when we walk the long corridor to the elevator I look back at her in the coffin, my gray mother in a cheap gray coffin, the color of beggary.

56

In January 1985 my brother Alphie called to say there was sad news from our cousins in Belfast, that our father, Malachy McCourt, had died early that morning at the Royal Victoria Hospital.

I don't know why Alphie used the word sad. It wouldn't describe how I felt myself and I thought of a line from Emily Dickinson, *After great pain a formal feeling comes.*

I had the formal feeling, but no pain.

My father and mother are dead and I'm an orphan.

As a grown man Alphie had visited our father out of curiosity or love or whatever the reasons he had for wanting to see a father who had abandoned us when I was ten and Alphie barely one. Now Alphie was saying he was taking a flight that night for the funeral next day and there was something in his voice that said, Aren't you coming?

That was softer than, Are you coming? less demanding, because Alphie knew the tangled emotions of himself and his brothers, Frank, Malachy, Michael.

Coming? Why should I fly to Belfast to the funeral of a man who went off to work in England and drank every penny of his wages? If my mother were alive would she go to the funeral of one who had left her in beggary?

No, she might not go to the funeral herself but she'd tell me to go. She'd say no matter what he did to us he had the weakness, the curse of the race, and a father dies and is buried only once. She'd say he wasn't the worst in the world and who are we to judge, that's what God is for, and out of her charitable soul she'd light a candle and offer a prayer.

I flew to my father's funeral in Belfast in the hope I might discover why I was flying to my father's funeral in Belfast.

We drove from the airport through the troubled streets of Belfast, armored cars, military patrols, young men stopped, pushed against walls, searched. My cousins said it was quiet now but one bomb anywhere, Protestant or Catholic, and you'd think you were in a world war. No one remembered anymore what it was like to walk the streets in an ordinary way. If you went out for a pound of butter you might come back without a leg or you might not come back. Once they said this it was better not to talk about it anymore. Some day it would end and they'd all saunter out for the pound of butter or even the saunter for its own sake.

My cousin, Francis MacRory, took us to see our father laid out in his coffin at the Royal Victoria Hospital and when we drove up to the death house I realized I was the oldest son, the chief mourner, and all these cousins were watching me, cousins I scarcely remembered, some I had never known, McCourts, MacRorys, Foxes. Three of my father's living sisters were there, Maggie and Eva and Sister Comgall, whose name before she took the veil was Moya. Aunt Vera, the other sister, was too ill to travel from Oxford.

Alphie and I, the youngest and the oldest sons of that man in the coffin, knelt on the prie-dieu. Our aunts and the cousins looked on these two men who had traveled a long way to a mystery and surely they wondered if there was any grief.

How could there be sorrow with my father shrunken there in the coffin, his teeth gone, his face collapsed and his body in a fancy black suit with a little white silken bow tie he would have scorned, all this giving me the sudden impression I was looking at a seagull so that I shook with spasms of silent laughter so hard that all assembled, including Alphie, must have been convinced I was overcome with a grief beyond control.

A cousin touched my shoulder and I wanted to say thank you but I knew if I removed my hands from my face I'd break into such laughter I'd shock everyone and be drummed out of the clan forever. Alphie blessed himself and rose from his knees. I controlled myself, dried my laugh tears, blessed myself and stood to face the sad looks around the little death house.

Outside in the Belfast night there were tears with the embraces of my frail ageing aunts. Oh, Francis, Francis, Alphie, Alphie, he loved you boys, he did, oh, he did, talked about you all the time.

Oh, he did, indeed, Aunt Eva and Aunt Maggie and Aunt Sister Comgall, and he raised many a glass to us in three countries not that we want to whine and whimper at a time like this, after all it's his funeral, and if I could control myself in the presence of my father, that seagull in the coffin, I can surely keep a bit of dignity before my three sweet aunts and cousins galore.

We milled around ready to drive away but I had to return to my father, to satisfy myself, to tell him that if I hadn't laughed to myself over the seagull my heart might have burst with the piling up of the past, images of the day he left us with high hopes of money coming soon from England, remembrances of my mother by the fire waiting for the money that never came and having to beg from the St Vincent de Paul Society, memories of my brothers asking if they could have one more cut of fried bread. All this was your doing, Dad, and even if we came out of it, your sons, you inflicted a life of misfortune on our mother.

I could only kneel by his coffin again and recall mornings in Limerick when the fire glowed and he talked softly for fear of waking my mother and brothers, telling me of Ireland's sufferings and the great deeds of the Irish in America and those mornings are now pearls that turn into three Hail Marys there by the coffin.

We buried him next day on a hill overlooking Belfast. The priest prayed and as he sprinkled the coffin with holy water shots rang out somewhere in the city. They're at it again, someone said.

There was a gathering at the house of our cousin, Theresa Fox, and her husband, Phil. There was talk about the day, a radio report that three IRA men trying to ram through a British Army barricade had been shot by the troops. In the next world my father would have the escort of his dreams, three IRA men, and he'd envy them the manner of their going.

We had tea and sandwiches and Phil brought out a bottle of whiskey to start the stories and the songs for there's nothing else to do the day you bury your dead.

In August of 1985, the year my father died, we brought my mother's ashes to her last resting place, the graveyard at Mungret Abbey outside Limerick City. My brother Malachy was there with his wife, Diana, and their son, Cormac. My fourteen-year-old daughter, Maggie, was there along with neighbors from the old days in Limerick and friends from New York. We took turns dipping our fingers into the tin urn from the New Jersey crematorium and sprinkling Angela's ashes over the graves of the Sheehans and Guilfoyles and Griffins while watching the breeze eddying her white dust around the grayness of their old bone bits and across the dark earth itself.

We said a Hail Mary and it wasn't enough. We had drifted from the church but we knew that for her and for us in that ancient abbey there would have been comfort and dignity in the prayers of a priest, proper requiem for a mother of seven.

We had lunch at a pub along the road to Ballinacurra and you'd never know from the way we ate and drank and laughed that we'd scattered our mother who was once a grand dancer at the Wembley Hall and known to one and all for the way she sang a good song, oh, if she could only catch her breath.

DATE DUE

RAECO